Sepulchral Brass of Robert Hallum, Constance Cathedral.
The inscription reads:
Subiacet hic stratus Robertus Hallum vocitatus
Quondam prelatus Sar' sub honore creatus
Hic decretorum doctor pacisque creator
Nobilis Anglorum regis fuit ambaciator
Festum Cuthberti Septembris mense vigebat
In quo Roberti mortem Constantia flebat
Anno milleno tricent' octuageno
Sex cum ter deno cum Christo vivat ameno

The Canterbury and York Society

GENERAL EDITOR: A. K. McHARDY

M.A., D.Phil.

DIOCESE OF SALISBURY

Canterbury and York Society Vol. LXXII

This volume is published with the help of grants from

THE BRITISH ACADEMY

and

THE LATE MISS ISOBEL THORNLEY'S BEQUEST TO

THE UNIVERSITY OF LONDON

The Register of
Robert Hallum

BISHOP OF SALISBURY

1407–17

EDITED BY

JOYCE M. HORN, M.A., B.Litt.

Institute of Historical Research,

University of London

PRINTED IN GREAT BRITAIN BY
THE DEVONSHIRE PRESS, TORQUAY
MCMLXXXII

CONTENTS

REFERENCES

Works in print and manuscripts which are cited in abbreviated form

Acta Concilii Constanciensis	*Acta Concilii Constanciensis*, ed. H. Finke and others (4 vols., Münster, 1896–1928).
Berks. Place-names	M. Gelling, *The Place-names of Berkshire* (English Place-name Society, xlix–li, 1973–6).
BRUO	*Biographical Register of the University of Oxford to A.D. 1500*, comp., A. B. Emden (3 vols., Oxford, 1957–9).
CCR	*Calendar of the Close Rolls preserved in the Public Record Office, 1396–1422* (8 vols., 1927–38).
CFR	*Calendar of the Fine Rolls preserved in the Public Record Office* (22 vols., 1911–62).
Churchill	I. J. Churchill, *Canterbury Administration* (2 vols., 1933).
Collections of John Aubrey	*Wiltshire . . .Collections of John Aubrey*, ed. J. E. Jackson (Devizes, 1862).
Collinson	J. Collinson, *History of Somerset* (3 vols., Bath, 1791).
Concilia	*Concilia Magnae Britanniae et Hiberniae*, ed. D. Wilkins (4 vols., 1737).
Corpus Iuris Canonici	*Corpus Iuris Canonici*, ed. A. Friedberg (2 vols., Leipzig, 1879–81).
CPL	*Calendar of Entries in the Papal Registers relating to Great Britain and Ireland: Papal Letters* (14 vols. in 15, 1893–1960).
CPR	*Calendar of the Patent Rolls preserved in the Public Record Office*, Edward I, Richard II, Henry IV and Henry V (16 vols., 1893–1911).
Crowder	C. M. D. Crowder, 'Some aspects of the English nation at the council of Constance' (unpublished University of Oxford D.Phil. thesis, 1953).
Decanal Reg. Chandeler	Salisbury, Dean and Chapter Archives, Decanal Register of John Chandeler.
Dignity of a Peer	*Reports from the Lords Committees touching the Dignity of a Peer of the Realm* (5 vols., 1829).
Fasti 1300–1541	*Fasti Ecclesiae Anglicanae, 1300–1541*, comp. H. P. F. King, J. M. Horn and B. Jones (12 vols., 1962–7).
Foedera	*Foedera*, ed. T. Rymer (10 vols., The Hague, 1735–45).

Handbook of British Chronology	*Handbook of British Chronology*, ed. F. M. Powicke and E. B. Fryde (2nd edn., 1961).
Hierarchia Catholica	*Hierarchia Catholica Medii Aevi*, i, ed. C. Eubel (2 edn., Münster, 1913).
Hutchins	J. Hutchins, *History and Antiquities of Dorset* (3rd edn., 4 vols., Westminster, 1861–70).
Lyndwood	W. Lyndwood, *Provinciale* (Oxford, 1679).
Niem	D. von Niem, *De Schismate*, ed. G. Erler (3 vols., Leipzig, 1890).
Proc. Privy Council	*Proceedings and Ordinances of the Privy Council of England*, ed. Sir H. Nicolas (7 vols., Record Commission, 1834–7).
Pountney	Salisbury, Dean and Chapter Archives, Chapter Act Book, Pountney.
Reg. Arundell (Cant.)	Lambeth Palace Library, Register of Thomas Arundell, archbishop of Canterbury.
Reg. Bubwith	*The Register of Nicholas Bubwith, Bishop of Bath and Wells, 1407–24*, ed. T. S. Holmes (Somerset Record Society, xxix, xxx, 1913–14).
Reg. Chandeler	Wiltshire Record Office, Register of John Chandeler, bishop of Salisbury.
Reg. Chichele	*The Register of Henry Chichele, Archbishop of Canterbury, 1414–43*, ed. E. F. Jacob (Canterbury and York Society, xlv, xlii, xlvi, xlvii, 1937–47).
Reg. Medford	Wiltshire Record Office, Register of Richard Medford, bishop of Salisbury.
Reg. Waltham	Wiltshire Record Office, Register of John Waltham, bishop of Salisbury.
VCH	*The Victoria History of the Counties of England*
Vyring	Salisbury, Dean and Chapter Archives, Chapter Act Book, Vyring.
Wilkinson	'An edition of the register of Robert Hallum, bishop of Salisbury, 1408–17' (unpublished University of Oxford B.Litt. thesis, 1960).
Wilts. Place-names	J. E. B. Gover, A. Mawer and F. M. Stenton, *The Place-names of Wiltshire* (English Place-name Society, xvi, 1939).

INTRODUCTION

The register of Robert Hallum, bishop of Salisbury 1407-17, in the Wiltshire Record Office,[1] presents the diocesan aspect of the ecclesiastical statesman and leader of the English delegation at the council of Constance.[2] Distinguished by his learning, oratory and zeal for reform, he was one of the most influential members of the council and his intervention was more than once able to swing the council's decisions.[3] The man who might have been archbishop of York and a cardinal died in Gottlieben castle on 4 September 1417, and was buried in Constance cathedral beneath a magnificent brass, apparently made in England and transported there.[4]

Little is known of Hallum's family. He came from Warrington (Lancs.), and was born before 1370. His will mentions a brother Richard and a Thomas Hallum whose relationship is unspecified,[5] A kinswoman, Alice, lived in the diocese,[6] and another relative, Gilbert, held various prebends of Salisbury cathedral in succession, and is referred to as the bishop's heir.[7] Robert Hallum was educated at Oxford; he was a bachelor of canon or civil law by 1388, bachelor of both laws by 1399 and doctor of laws by 1403.[8]

Before he became bishop of Salisbury, Hallum's career[9] was that of a canon lawyer in the service of the archbishops of Canterbury, Courtenay and Arundel, whom he named in his will as his principal benefactors.[10]

[1] The edition of the register is based on J. M. Wilkinson, 'An edition of the register of Robert Hallum, bishop of Salisbury, 1408–17' (unpublished University of Oxford B.Litt. thesis, 1960).

[2] For Hallum at the councils, see E. F. Jacob, *Essays in the Conciliar Epoch* (2nd edn., Manchester, 1953), pp. 75–84; Crowder, pp. 85–6, 117–21, 185–6, 373–6, 383–5; F. D. Hodgkiss, 'Robert Hallum and the council of Constance' (unpublished University of Manchester M.A. thesis, 1931); R. N. Quirk, 'Bishop Robert Hallum and the council of Constance' in *Friends of Salisbury Cathedral Annual Rept.*, xxii (1952).

[3] For his sermons and speeches at the council of Pisa, see *Sacrorum Conciliorum Nova et Amplissima Collectio*, ed. G. D. Mansi and others (54 vols. in 59, Paris, 1901–27, repr. Graz, 1960–1), xxvi, col. 1139, xxvii, cols. 8, 125; at Constance, see *Acta Concilii Constanciensis*, ii. 393–5, 423–5. For his influence, see Crowder, pp. 185–7; J. Lenfant, *Histoire du Concile de Constance* (Amsterdam, 1714), p. 506. For a contemporary estimate of his greatness, see Richard Fleming's oration at his funeral, *Acta Concilii Constanciensis*, ii. 513.

[4] *Proc. Soc. Antiquaries of London*, 2nd ser., v (1870–3), 375–6; *Archaeologia*, xxx (1844), 431–7.

[5] *Reg. Chichele*, ii. 126–30, given in calendar form in Appendix E; *Ancient Deeds*, v, no. A 10884; cf. Wilkinson, p. viii.

[6] Cf. **992**; she married Thomas Stonor (*CCR 1419–22*, pp. 47, 62, 64; cf. **604**).

[7] Cf. **440**, **616**, **1045–6**; *BRUO*, ii. 854. He is not mentioned in the bishop's will but is called his heir in 1420 (*CCR 1419–22*, pp. 47, 62, 64). It seems likely that he was the son of either Richard or Thomas Hallum.

[8] *BRUO*, ii. 854–5.

[9] There are brief accounts of Hallum's life by R. L. Poole in the *Dictionary of National Biography* and by E. F. Jacob in *Reg. Chichele*, ii. 656; fuller account in F. D. Hodgkiss, 'Robert Hallum and the council of Constance' (unpublished University of Manchester M.A. thesis, 1931).

[10] *Reg. Chichele*, ii. 127.

Only one civil office is known to have been held by him, that of deputy collector of the Irish customs in 1391.[11] He was Courtenay's principal registrar in July 1389 until at least 1394,[12] and one of his executors.[13] Under Arundel, he was appointed archbishop's commissary and auditor of causes of the court of Canterbury in 1399,[14] and in 1400 became his chancellor, an office which he was still holding in June 1406, together with that of archdeacon of Canterbury, to which he was appointed 7 April 1400.[15]

Concurrently, from at least November 1403 to June 1406, he was chancellor of Oxford university, performing some of the routine work in person, and the fact that he held office longer than the customary two years suggests that he was considered worthy of re-election.[16] A great number of benefices are known to have been held by him at various times from 1387, including prebends at Bangor, Chichester, Exeter, Salisbury and York, and other benefices at Halling (Kent); Newington (Oxon.); Biddenham (Kent); West Tarring (Sussex); Northfleet (Kent); and Winwick (Lancs.).[17]

Hallum became bishop of Salisbury almost by chance, as a result of a celebrated series of conflicts between Henry IV and Popes Innocent VII and Gregory XII. In 1404, Archbishop Arundel recommended his archdeacon, Hallum, to Innocent for the vacant bishopric of London, but the king put forward his keeper of the privy seal, Thomas Langley, and Arundel acquiesced.[18] The pope, however, would not accept Langley and provided Roger Walden. The king would not agree to Walden until the execution of Archbishop Scrope of York for treason in June 1405 gave him the opportunity of recommending Langley for that see. The royal assent to Langley's election was given on 8 August,[19] but Innocent again refused to confirm the royal candidate because of the alleged illegality of Scrope's execution. At this point, Arundel brought Hallum forward again as a possible compromise candidate for York. Hallum went to Rome and received papal provision 14 May 1406, Langley being provided the same day to Durham.[20] Henry IV, however, still refused to have any but his own candidate as archbishop

[11] *CPR 1388–92*, p. 467.

[12] Lambeth Palace Library, Reg. Courtenay fo. 273 ; *ibid.*, Reg. Courtenay in Reg. Morton, ii fo. 199 ; Churchill, i. 23 and n., 327; J. H. Dahmus, *The Metropolitan Visitations of Archbishop Courteney* (Urbana, 1950), p. 182.

[13] *CPL 1396–1404*, p. 96.

[14] Reg. Arundell (Cant.), i fo. 93; Churchill, ii. 243.

[15] Reg. Arundell (Cant.), i fos. 93, 267; Bodleian Library, MS. Arch. Selden B 23 fo. 26; *Concilia*, iii. 256, 262; *CPR 1399–1401*, p.364.

[16] *Snappe's Formulary*, ed. H. E. Salter (Oxford Hist. Soc., lxxx, 1924), pp. 37–8, 332; *CPR 1405–8*, p. 496; *Mediaeval Archives of the University of Oxford*, ed. H. E. Salter (Oxford Hist. Soc., lxx, lxxiii, 1917–19), i. 299; Bodleian Library, MS. Arch Selden B 23 fo. 26; J. R. Magrath, *The Queen's College* (2 vols., Oxford, 1921), i. 130; cf. *Rev. d'Hist. Ecclés.*, x (1909), pt. i, 498–9.

[17] Full list in *BRUO*, ii. 854.

[18] *Royal and Historical Letters during the Reign of Henry IV*, ed. F. C. Hingeston and others (2 vols., Rolls Ser., 1860, H.M.S.O., 1964), i. 415.

[19] *CPR 1405–8*, pp. 21, 48; *Foedera*, IV. i. 85.

[20] *CPL 1404–15*, pp. 83–4; *The Episcopal Register of Robert Rede, ordinis predicatorum, Lord Bishop of Chichester, 1397–1415*, ed. C. Deedes (Sussex Record Soc., viii, xi, 1908–10), i. 20 and n.; cf. **872**.

of York, and Hallum's position remained insecure, although the new pope, Gregory XII, is said to have promised not to translate him from York.[21]

A few months later the bishopric of Salisbury became vacant by the death of Richard Medford, and Nicholas Bubwith (who had succeeded Walden at London) was provided by the pope on 22 June 1407 and received the temporalities from the king on 14 August.[22] The deadlock over York continued, but Gregory recognized his need of the king of England's support and on 7 October he translated the new royal candidate, Henry Bowet, from Bath and Wells to York, at the same time translating Bubwith from Salisbury to Bath and Wells, and providing Hallum to Salisbury.[23] Apparently the king had borne Hallum no personal grudge and the temporalities were restored to him on 1 December 1407.[24] However, when Pope John XXIII appointed Hallum a cardinal in 1411 (in company with such distinguished churchmen as Peter d'Ailly, William Filastre and Francis Zabarella), the king again refused to allow him to accept, on the grounds that he could not spare him to go to live permanently in Rome.[25] Thus, despite the high opinions of his ability held by king and popes alike, political considerations kept his status to that of a diocesan bishop.

A famous sermon preached at Constance on the text, 'There will be signs in the sun', delineated Hallum's lofty concept of the bishop's office,[26] and his register reveals him as a conscientious prelate.[27] He was constantly in his diocese, apart from his regular attendance at parliaments and convocations, and he moved from place to place, living principally at his manors of Woodford, Potterne, Ramsbury, Sonning and Sherborne, with brief visits to his palace at Salisbury.[28] In 1409 he was absent for seven months at the council of Pisa and from November 1414 to his death in 1417 he attended the council of Constance. During these periods the diocesan administration was committed to notable men as vicars general, Adam Mottrum and Geoffrey Crukadan, although there are some indications that the administration may have been less efficient in 1414-17 than when the bishop was present.[29] Distinguished men served him as official of Salisbury, presiding over the bishop's consistory court: first Simon Sydenham,[30] then William Lyndwood (subsequently author of the *Provinciale*),[31] and later Geoffrey Crukadan.[32] Below them, the office of principal clerk of the consistory

[21] Bodleian Library, MS, Arch. Selden B 23 fos. 26, 125^{v}; *ibid.*, MS. Bodley 859 fo. 41^{r-v}; Niem, iii. 245.

[22] *CPR 1405–8*, pp. 317, 321; Reg. Arundell (Cant.), i fos. 37, 38^{r-v}.

[23] Reg. Arundell (Cant.), i fos. 40–1; Niem, iii. 245; *Thomae Walsingham . . . Historia Anglicana*, ed. H. T. Riley (2 vols., Rolls Ser., 1863–4), ii. 273, 277.

[24] *CPR 1405–8*, p. 384.

[25] Cf. **1125** and n.

[26] *Acta Concilii Constanciensis*, ii. 432–5.

[27] Details in Wilkinson, pp. xiii–xliv.

[28] See itinerary, Appendix C.

[29] The register was kept less well, and Bishop John Chandeler complained to the archbishop in Jan. 1418 about 'notable defects' left by Hallum in the estates of the bishopric (*Reg. Chichele*, iv. 61–2).

[30] *BRUO*, iii. 1838.

[31] *Ibid.*, ii. 1191–3; *Dictionary of National Biography*; Churchill, i. 439–40.

[32] *BRUO*, i. 524.

court, who also acted as bishop's sequestrator and commissary general, was held in succession by Richard Burgh,[33] John Turry[34] and John Colles.[35] Notable men were licensed to preach in the diocese[36] or acted as the bishop's commissaries in various matters.[37]

Pope Alexander V granted Hallum permission to keep in his service clerks of any kind, even regulars, and those holding benefices in which they were bound by oath to reside.[38] The register gives some information concerning these household clerks, although the picture is far from complete. By June 1410, William Lyndwood, who had earlier served as official of Salisbury, occurs as the bishop's chancellor, the most important officer, who was the bishop's leading expert, with extensive legal and administrative functions.[39] Thomas Teynton had succeeded him by December 1412,[40] having appeared as a witness in the bishop's court of audience on several occasions during the preceding two years.[41] Hallum collated him to a rectory in August 1412 and to a cathedral prebend in April 1413.[42] Others named as bishop's clerks were William Clement and John Newerk.[43] Interesting letters testimonial of May 1411 describe how Newerk had been admitted to Hallum's *familia* while he was at the papal court as archbishop-elect of York. No other clerks are named, though some of those who figure as witnesses may have been members of the household whom it would be natural to employ in this capacity. Of the eighteen witnesses, four occur three times. Two of these are William Lyndwood and Thomas Teynton, and the others are John Luke[44] and John Appulton.[45] Both of these at some time held benefices in Salisbury diocese in the bishop's gift, and John Luke, who also accompanied Hallum to Constance, was collated to two prebends in succession.[46] Two men, Oliver Dyngley and John Bromley, occur twice as witnesses, and these were also beneficed in Salisbury diocese.[47] The remaining twelve occur once only and some are otherwise unknown. Four are known to have held one benefice or more in the diocese, not necessarily in the bishop's gift. Some at least may have been members of the bishop's household. John Fyton, for instance, also appears once as a commissary in an inquiry and was with Hallum at Pisa and

[33] **943–4**.
[34] **813, 840, 849**.
[35] **1022**.
[36] Cf. **832–3, 838–9**.
[37] Cf. **427, 840, 846, 849, 905, 1128–9**.
[38] *CPL 1404–15*, p. 213.
[39] Cf. **166**. He may have been chancellor earlier as he was called the bishop's clerk in Jan. 1410, **129**. For his activities, see **297, 696, 858, 864, 1130**.
[40] **927**.
[41] **858, 971, 1009**.
[42] **350, 405**.
[43] **204, 872**.
[44] **466, 918, 971**.
[45] **858, 927, 971**.
[46] *Reg. Chichele*, ii. 128; **582, 587**.
[47] For Dyngley as witness, see **297, 1009**; as proctor, see **310, 327, 409, 440, 489, 664**; for his benefices, see **288, 451, 564, 649**. For Bromley as witness, see **65, 111**; for his benefices, see **99**.

Constance.[48] He held a succession of prebends but was not a residentiary canon.[49]

More is known of the composition of the household while Hallum was at Constance than at any other time, since many members were left sums in the bishop's will. However it is not safe to assume that all those mentioned served in his household or to generalize from the unusual circumstances of a council. Probably about fifteen of those listed were *familiares*. Five figure in the register, two of them, Thomas Rodeley and William Barbour, in the ordination lists, and Thomas Massy, Simon Membury and Nicholas Sexpenne as being admitted to benefices.[50]

Several of the household clerks would have been employed in secretarial work. At least seven different hands make significant contributions to the register, and others make occasional entries.[51] There is no mention of the names of any of these clerks nor of the registrars who supervised the work of the chancery. In other dioceses, a public notary often acted as registrar, and it is possible, though by no means certain, that Wenceslas Swisiko may have filled this role. Swisiko was a clerk of Brandenburg diocese and notary by both apostolic and imperial authority. He figures regularly in the register from April 1409 to January 1414, as drawing up various instruments and as a witness.[52] Subsequently, the evidence is too scanty to suggest any identification, since none of the public notaries occurs with any frequency.[53]

The register reflects the fact that the chapter of Salisbury cathedral contained some of the most outstanding Englishmen of the time.[54] Of their number, Henry Chichele, John Chandeler, Thomas Polton and Simon Sydenham later became bishops or archbishops. Adam Mottrum, the precentor, had been archbishop's chancellor and archdeacon of Canterbury. William Lyndwood was a member, and Richard Ullerston, the author, at Hallum's instigation, of sixteen 'Petitions for the reformation of the Church militant',[55] was collated by Hallum to a prebend. Many others were involved in the conciliar movement: Robert Brown, John Luke, Roger Basset and John Fyton attended the council of Constance with Hallum, and while the council was in progress, he appointed to prebends Hugh Holbache and William Clynt (a former chancellor of Oxford university[56]), who were also with him at Constance. There had been many violent disputes

[48] **849**, **864**; *Reg. Chichele,* ii. 128; Crowder, pp. 147–8, 508–9.

[49] **204**, **313–14**, **617**.

[50] See Appendix E and notes.

[51] Wilkinson, pp. xliv–xlvi.

[52] **65**, **466**, **858**, **864**, **927**, **1009**.

[53] Wilkinson, pp. xlvii–xlviii.

[54] E. F. Jacob, 'The mediaeval chapter of Salisbury cathedral', *Wilts. Archaeol. and Natural Hist. Mag.*, li (1945–7), 479–92; *idem, Essays in the Conciliar Epoch* (2nd edn., Manchester, 1953), pp. 78–81; *VCH Wilts.*, iii. 176–8; *Fasti 1300–1541*, iii.

[55] J. Lenfant, *Histoire du Concile de Constance* (Amsterdam, 1714), p. 506; H. von der Hardt, *Magnum œcumenicum Constantiense Concilium* (7 vols., Frankfurt and Leipzig, 1700–42), i. 1126–70.

[56] *Snappe's Formulary,* ed. H. E. Salter (Oxford Hist. Soc., lxxx, 1924), p. 333.

between chapter and bishop in the late fourteenth century[57] and the distinguished and energetic men of Hallum's time could be expected to maintain the chapter's rights, but Hallum seems to have linked tact and restraint to his customary firmness, and several disputes which promised to become occasions of major dissension were settled peaceably.[58] Indeed Richard Ullerston, at a meeting of the chapter in May 1416, prayed 'especially for our lord bishop of this diocese, who has borne more labours, and greater, for establishing unity in the Church than any other prelate in all the world, as is fully known'.[59]

Relations with the city of Salisbury appear to have been good also. A list of benefactors to the city issued in 1493 has Hallum's name at its head,[60] and the city corporation on one occasion proposed that a gift of twenty pounds should be made to him.[61]

Only a few evidences are seen in the register of Hallum's international stature.[62] Occasionally one glimpses the rhetorical style which dominated the councils and the love of poetry which prompted him to commission a Latin verse translation of the *Divina Commedia* from John Bartholdi di Serravalle, bishop of Fermo.[63] The introduction to a few letters show something of his faculty of vivid imagery,[64] but the routine business of a bishop's register does not afford many insights into the bishop's character. There are indications of firmness,[65] humanity[66] and concern for spirituality[67] besides care and efficiency in administration, and Hallum seems to have merited Dietrich of Niem's description of him as 'virum valde industrium et etiam virtuosum'.[68]

The register consists of twenty-five quires, with a total of 197 folios, which have been bound together. These quires are made up of from four to sixteen folios of 25.5 cm. to 26.5 cm. × 33.5 cm. to 34 cm., formed by folding in half pieces twice this size to make gatherings. Besides the modern pencil numbering at the bottom of each folio, there are four series of numbering of parts of the register in a fifteenth-century hand, in the top right-hand

[57] K. Edwards. *English Secular Cathedrals in the Middle Ages* (Manchester, 1949), pp. 104, 108–10, 115, 123, 128, 131; *Fasti Ecclesiae Sarisberiensis,* comp. W. H. Jones (1 vol. in 2, Salisbury, 1879–91), pp. 212–13.

[58] Cf. **896**; Vyring, pp. 15, 55, 66, 69, 73; Wilkinson, pp. xxxiv–xxxvii.

[59] A. R. Malden, *The Canonization of St. Osmund* (Salisbury, 1901), p. 238.

[60] Hist. MSS. Comm., *Various Collections,* iv. 211; *The Tropenell Cartulary,* ed. J. S. Davies (2 vols., Devizes, 1908), i. 199–200.

[61] Hist. MSS. Comm., *Various Collections,* iv. 194.

[62] E.g. **872, 1011, 1072, 1125**.

[63] *Joannis Lelandi antiquari de Rebus Britannicis Collectanea,* ed. T. Hearne (6 vols., 1770), iv. 58; W. F. Schirmer, *Der Englische Frühhumanismus* (Leipzig, 1931), pp. 16, 17. A copy of the translation is in British Library, Egerton MS. 2629.

[64] Given in full in Appendix D.

[65] E.g. **856, 1095, 1134, 1145–6**.

[66] E.g. **22, 466, 497, 500, 865**.

[67] Cf. licences to preach, **832–3, 838–9, 965, 970, 981**; mandate concerning Sundays and feast days, **837**, given in full in Appendix D; licence to Augustinian canon to change houses, **842**.

[68] Niem, ii. 245.

corner. There are two successive series of numbering of the quires of institutions, another for the quires of letters and licences, and the fourth for the quires of royal writs. At the beginning of the register is a quire containing the Salisbury portion of the Taxation of Pope Nicholas, while at the end are a few notes and an index of institutions, begun during Hallum's episcopate and completed later. Before the register was bound, the first and last folios of several of the quires became seriously affected by damp, thus making them very difficult to read and in some cases illegible.

The custom of the Salisbury bishops' chanceries was to record different types of business in separate quires, rather than to enter business of all kinds chronologically in a single series of quires. Hence, at the beginning of Hallum's episcopate five quires were started: for institutions (beginning on the present fo. 9), for short licences and letters dimissory (fo. 90B), for royal writs and their execution (fo. 175), for judicial business (fo. 189) and for letters (fo. 152), the second half of which (fos. 158 ff.) was set apart for ordination lists. Generally, when the original quire was filled, another was started to continue the same type of business. Thus, there are seven consecutive quires dealing with institutions, two with royal writs, and two after the original one dealing with ordination lists. However, when Hallum went abroad in 1409, the first quire for institutions was abandoned and a new quire was begun for the vicar general, Adam Mottrum. The first quire was subsequently filled up with wills. In this edition of the register, the wills are given after all the institutions. The *Taxatio* of Pope Nicholas is not given.[69]

The main editorial problem has concerned the quires of letters and licences. In the present bound register there are nine apparent quires dealing with letters, five of which are headed, in a fifteenth-century hand, 'quaternus primus' etc. to 'quaternus quintus'. Despite this, the quires do not follow one another consecutively and their present order is very unlike their original one. In several cases folios have been separated from the quires to which they belonged, foreign folios have been added to the centre of a quire or folios have been folded in reverse order. Even the fifteenth-century headings are misleading, since the quire numbered 'quaternus tertius' was started about two years after both 'quaternus quartus' and 'quaternus quintus'. The confusion seems to have occurred early, before the folios were numbered in a fifteenth-century hand. It is possible to reconstruct the order of compilation in the main,[70] though at some periods two quires were in use concurrently for letters. Sometimes there was a distinction in the type of letters entered in each, but at other times the business seems to have been allocated indiscriminately.

To reproduce the order of the bound register in this edition would have meant a chaotic chronological arrangement with business for the same year occurring at different places. On the other hand, when business was entered

[69] It is substantially as printed in *Taxatio Ecclesiastica Angliae et Walliae auctoritate P. Nicholai IV* (Record Comm., 1802), pp. 177–96. It was transcribed in full in Wilkinson, pp. 1–36.

[70] For details, see *ibid.*, pp. lix–lxiv.

in two quires concurrently it is impossible to reconstruct the order of registration. Therefore the main series of quires is given in order of compilation, and the four other quires or parts of quires[71] are given subsequently. A table of identification with the folios in the bound volume is provided.

During Hallum's absences abroad in 1409 and 1414-17, the register appears to have been less efficiently kept. Appendix A gives some indication (from chapter act books and other contemporary bishops' registers) of appointments to benefices which were not recorded in the register. Appendix B calendars various original documents of Hallum's chancery which were also not entered. An attempt to reconstruct Hallum's movements within England is given in Appendix C. Appendix D contains some examples from the register of Hallum's literary style, transcribed in full. These give some indication of his powers of oratory, otherwise concealed in the calendar of letters. Appendix E has calendars of Hallum's will, inventory of goods and related testamentary matters.

Note on Editorial Method

In this edition, all entries in the register have been assigned numbers and are normally given in calendar form, apart from entries in English and French which are transcribed fully. The foliation of the bound volume is given within square brackets, normally at the head of the first item beginning on that folio. The modern pencil foliation is given first, with the fifteenth-century numbering, where it occurs, in second place. Editorial additions to the text of other kinds are also given in square brackets. Place-names are given in both the original and the modern form,[72] and comment is added if they have changed markedly or disappeared since the fifteenth century. The spelling of Salisbury prebends is based on *Fasti, 1300-1541*. Surnames are given as in the original and variants are brought together in the index. All dates between 1 January and 24 March are given new style. The Old English characters thorn and yogh are rendered by their modern typographical equivalents.

Acknowledgements

I should like to thank Miss Pamela Stewart, archivist of the former Salisbury Diocesan Registry, Dr. Diana E. Greenway, Dr. Jane E. Sayers, Dr. David M. Smith and Miss Janet H. Stevenson for their most generous help and advice. Herr Dirk Veenema of the German Embassy and Herr Oberreigierungsbaurat Mall obtained the frontispiece photograph, and Dr. Moreton Moore kindly prepared the map of Salisbury diocese. The late Professor May McKisack first introduced me to bishops' registers, and Dr. Pierre Chaplais supervised the first version of this edition, and an especial debt is owed to them both.

J.M.H.

[71] Fos. 152–157v, 142–145v and 146–151v.

[72] Based on *Bartholomew's Gazetteer of the British Isles* (9th edn., 1943; repr. 1972).

TABLE OF IDENTIFICATION

Bound register folios		*Printed register numbers*	*Type of Business*
Modern	*15th-century*		
1–2v		**1157–8**	End Pages
3–8		—	*Taxatio* of Pope Nicholas
9–18	1–10	**1–59**	Institutions
18–20	10, 10a, 10b	**695–9**	Wills
20v	10bv	**60**	Institutions
21–22v	10c–10dv	**700–6**	Wills
25–90A	1–69	**60A–694**	Institutions
90B–91v	1–2v	**707–32**	Licences, Letters and Commissions
92–97v	3–8v	**826–56**	,,
98–99v	9–10v	**803–21**	,,
100		**1148**	Not belonging to Hallum's episcopate
101–109v	11–19v	**857–90**	Licences, Letters and Commissions
110r-v	20r-v	**822–5**	,,
111–118v	21–28v	**733–802**	,,
119–133v	29–43v	**891–927**	,,
134–141v	44–51v	**956–1013**	,,
142–145v	52–55v	**950–5**	,,
146–151v	56–61v	**1014–27**	,,
152–157v	62–67v	**928–49**	,,
158–74		**1028–58**	Ordination Lists
175–88	1–14	**1059–1127**	Royal Writs and their Execution
189–92	15–18	**1128–47**	Judicial *Acta*
193v–194		**1150–6**	Not belonging to Hallum's episcopate
194v–196v			Contemporary index to Institutions
197		**1159**	End Pages

ABBREVIATIONS

abp.	archbishop	Inc.C.L.	inceptor in civil law
archd.	archdeacon	ind.	inductor(s)
B.A.	bachelor of arts	lett.dim.	letters dimissory
B.C.L.	bachelor of civil law	Lic.C.L.	licentiate in civil law
B.Cn.L.	bachelor of canon law	M.	master
B.Th.	bachelor of theology	M.A.	master of arts
bp.	bishop	P.R.O.	Public Record Office, London
cath.	cathedral		
conv.	convent	resig.	resignation
D.C.L.	doctor of civil law	vac.	vacant
dioc.	diocese		

THE REGISTER OF ROBERT HALLUM

Institutions

[Fo. 9/1] REGISTRUM REVERENDISSIMI IN CHRISTO PATRIS ET DOMINI DOMINI ROBERTI PERMISSIONE DIVINA ECCLESIE SARESBIRIEN' SERVI HUMILIS ET MINISTRI, DE PRESENTACIONIBUS, INQUISICIONIBUS, ADMISSIONIBUS, COLLACIONIBUS ET PERMUTACIONIBUS BENEFICIORUM, ET DE ANNO DOMINI MILLESIMO QUADRINGENTESIMO OCTAVO, ET ALIIS ACTIS PROUT SEQUITUR

1 Exchange, by authority of Nicholas, bp. of Bath and Wells (*Bathon' et Wellen'*), between Philip Bristowe, rector of Kington (*Kyngton*) Magna; patron, John Typtot, knight—and M. John Hudy, vicar of Queen Camel (*Cammell Regine*), dioc. Bath and Wells. Ind. of Hudy: archd. of Dorset (*Dors'*). Abingdon (*Abyndon*), 7 Apr. 1408.

2 Collation to M. William Pylton, king's secretary, of a canonry and prebend in Salisbury cath., which Thomas Wroghton recently obtained. Cuddesdon (*Codysdon*), 23 Apr. 1408.
[Probably ineffective collation to the prebend of Grimston (*Fasti 1300–1541*, iii. 57).]

3 Exchange, by authority of Thomas, abp. of Canterbury (*Cantuar'*), between Thomas Guldefeld, rector of Hayes (*Hese*), in immediate jurisdiction of the abp. of Canterbury, in person of Walter Clerc *alias* Oke, literate, his proctor; patron, the same abp.—and Robert Burgeys, rector of Wroughton (*Elyngdon*); patron, Henry, bp. of Winchester (*Wynton'*). Ind. of Guldefeld: archd. of Wiltshire (*Wilts'*). Abingdon, 25 Apr. 1408.
[For Wroughton, see *Wilts. Place-names*, p. 278.]

4 [Fo. 9v/1v] Collation to William Reede, priest, of a canonry in Salisbury cath., and the prebend of Maior pars altaris in the same, vac. by resig. of John Parker. Mandate to the dean and chapter of Salisbury for his admission and installation. Abingdon, 24 Apr. 1408.

5 Exchange, by authority of Philip, bp. of Lincoln, between Richard Taunton, rector of Chilton (*Chylton Egge*), in person of John Hurste, literate, his proctor; patrons, abbot and conv. of Abingdon (*Abyndon*)—and John Amy, rector of Hanwell (*Hanewell*), dioc. Lincoln. Ind. of Amy: archd. of Berkshire (*Berks'*). Welford, 27 May 1408.

6 Institution of Henry Lynne, priest, in person of Thomas Alyn, clerk, his proctor, to church of St. Nicholas, Sulham, vac. by resig. of Nicholas Vyrly; patron, Nicholas Carru, esquire, of Surrey (*Surr'*). Ind.: archd. of Berkshire. Welford, 22 May 1408.

7 Institution of John Ruschall, chaplain, to church of Ditchampton (*Dychampton iuxta Wylton*); patron, Humphrey Stafford, esquire. Ind.: archd. of Salisbury. Welford, 6 May 1408.

8 Institution of Stephen Hulle, chaplain, to church [*rectius* vicarage] of Norton Bavant (*Norton Davent*); patrons, prioress and conv. of Dartford (*Derteforde*), dioc. Rochester (*Roffen'*). Ind.: archd. of Wiltshire. Welford, 31 May 1408.

9 [Fo. 10/2] Institution of William Chamberleyn, priest, to church of Pertwood (*Portworth*), vac. by resig. of Nicholas Mason; patron, John Brut of Hindon (*Hynedon*). Ind.: archd. of Salisbury. Culham, 2 June 1408.

10 Exchange, by authority of Nicholas, bp. of Bath and Wells, between Henry Wilcok, rector of Mildenhall (*Mildenhale*); patrons, William Stourton, Thomas Bonham, John Stourton, William Besile, John Flour and Nicholas Palmer— and Richard Slougtre, rector of Norton, dioc. Bath and Wells; patron, the same bp. Ind. of Slougtre: archd. of Wiltshire. Sutton Courtenay (*Sutton*), 9 June 1408.

11 Exchange, by authority of Henry, bp. of Winchester, between Robert Starclife, rector of Worth Matravers (*Worth*) with Swanage (*Swanwyche*) chapel annexed; patron, John Arundell, lord of Mautravers—and William Talbot, rector of Shere (*Shire*), dioc. Winchester. Ind. of Talbot: archd. of Dorset. Culham, 14 June 1408.

12 Exchange, by authority of Philip, bp. of Lincoln, between John Holbroke, rector of Wytham (*Wyghtham*); patron, Richard of Wytham, esquire—and Robert Claypull, rector of Wavendon (*Wavenden*), dioc. Lincoln. Ind. of Claypull: archd. of Berkshire. Culham, 15 June 1408.

13 [Fo. 10v/2v] Institution of William Trenerth, clerk, to church of Pewsey (*Peuesey*); patron, King Henry, custodian of the temporalities of the abbey of Hyde by Winchester during the vacancy of the abbacy. Ind.: archd. of Wiltshire. Culham, 14 June 1408.

[For presentation and subsequent dispute, see *CPR 1405–8*, pp. 375, 443, 444, 448, 477.]

14 Collation to M. Nicholas Rysshton D.Cn. & C.L., auditor of causes at the papal palace, of a canonry in Salisbury cath., and the prebend of Netheravon (*Netherhavene*) in the same, vac. by death of Roger *alias* Reynold Gray. Ind.: dean and chapter of Salisbury. Culham, 4 June 1408.

15 Exchange, by authority of Robert, bp. of Hereford, between Richard Powle, rector of Donnington (*Donyngton*), dioc. Hereford (*Hereforden'*)—and Roger Palmere, vicar of West Ilsley (*Westildesle*); patrons, prior and conv. of Sandleford (*Sandelford*), dioc. Salisbury. Ind. of Powle: archd. of Berkshire. Culham, 20 June 1408.

16 [Fo. 11/3] Exchange, on certificate of M. Richard Bruton, chancellor of Wells, vicar general of Nicholas, bp. of Bath and Wells, then abroad, between Walter Hawkyne, rector of Runnington (*Ronnyngton*), dioc. Bath and Wells—and John Newman, vicar of Fifehead Magdalen (*Fifhide Maugdeleyne*); patrons, abbot and conv. of Bristol, dioc. Worcester (*Wygorn'*). Ind. of Hawkyne: archd. of Dorset. Culham, 28 June 1408.

17 Letter to George Louthorp, priest, collating him to a canonry and the treasurership of Salisbury cath. with the prebend of Calne annexed, vac. by resig. of William Glym. Salisbury, bishop's palace, 11 Dec. 1408.

18 Mandate to the dean and chapter of Salisbury to admit George Louthorp [as in **17**]. Salisbury, bishop's palace, 11 Dec. 1408.
[For dispute between Glym and Louthorp, see *Fasti 1300–1541*, iii. 20.]

19 [Fo. 11v/3v] Exchange, by authority of William, bp. of Carlisle (*Karlen'*), between Ralph Spurner, rector of Cliburn, dioc. Carlisle; patron, the same bp.—and William of Wilton, vicar of Hannington (*Hankyngton*); patron, John Thornebury, rector of Crudwell (*Cruddewelle*). Ind. of Spurner: archd. of Wiltshire. Culham, 5 July 1408.

20 Institution of Nicholas Coventre, priest, to church of Upton Lovell (*Ubeton*), vac. by resig. of Robert Hayward; patron, John Lovell, lord of Lovell and Holand. Ind.: archd. of Salisbury. Culham, 16 July 1408.

21 Institution of Henry Vyller, priest, to vicarage of West Hendred (*Westhenreth*), vac. by resig. of Peter Grete; patrons, Prior Richard and conv. of Holy Trinity, Wallingford (*Walyngford*). Ind.: archd. of Berkshire. An annual pension, to be paid from the income of the vicarage, was granted to Peter Grete. Sonning (*Sonnyng*), 20 July 1408.

22 Letter setting out details of the pension granted by the bp. to Peter Grete, who resigned from the vicarage of West Hendred on account of old age. Ten marks [£6 13*s* 4*d*] annually are to be paid to him by the vicar of West Hendred in equal portions at Christmas, Easter, St. John the Baptist's day [24 June] and Michaelmas [29 Sept.]. The patrons give assent and the vicar, Henry Vyller, gives his oath on the gospels. Sonning manor, 20 July 1408.

23 [Fo. 12/4] Exchange, by authority of Thomas, bp. of Worcester, between John Fytz, vicar of St. Mary, Westport, Malmesbury; patrons, Abbot Thomas and conv. of Malmesbury—and Walter Hatherleye, vicar of Frampton (*Frompton*)-on-Severn, dioc. Worcester. Ind. of Hatherleye: archd. of Wiltshire. London, 27 July 1408.

24 Exchange, by authority of Philip, bp. of Lincoln, between Henry Asshe, rector of Sulhampstead Abbots (*Shilhampstede Abbatis, Silhampstede*

Abbatis); patrons, Abbot Richard and conv. of Reading (*Radyng*)—and Thomas Huchon, rector of the free chapel of Wexham, dioc. Lincoln. Ind. of Huchon: archd. of Berkshire. London, 20 July 1408.

25 [Fo. 12ᵛ/4ᵛ] Exchange by authority of John, bp. of Coventry and Lichfield (*Coventren' et Lichen'*), between Robert Etton, vicar of Sonning (*Sonnyng*) prebendal church; patron, M. John Chaundeler, dean of Salisbury—and Ralph Harewell, rector of Standon (*Staundon*), dioc. Coventry and Lichfield. Ind. of Harewell: dean of Salisbury. London, 31 July 1408.

26 Exchange, by authority of Philip, bp. of Lincoln, between William Ibote, vicar of St. Mary Magdalene, Hullavington (*Huntlavyngton*); patron, King Henry, custodian of the temporalities of the alien priory of Clatford, during the war with France—and John Hore, rector of St. Michael, Northampton, dioc. Lincoln. Ind. of Hore: archd. of Wiltshire. London, 1 Aug. 1408.

27 [Fo. 13/5] Institution of John Lynes of Sloley, priest, to church of Newbury (*Newebury*); patron, Thomas Erpyngham, knight, custodian of the temporalities of the alien priory of Toft Monks (*Toftys*), granted him by the king during the war with France. Ind.: archd. of Berkshire. Culham, 10 Aug. 1408.

28 Exchange, by authority of Robert, bp. of Chichester (*Cicestren'*), between John Coteler, rector of Hazelbury (*Haselbere*); patrons, prior and conv. of St. Mary of Bradenstoke—and John Mayster, rector of Chithurst (*Chydhurste*), dioc. Chichester. Ind. of Mayster: archd. of Wiltshire. Culham, 29 Aug. 1408.

29 Exchange between William Caldewell, warden of the house or chantry of St. Michael, Bridport (*Brydeport*); patron, Thomas Moygne, rector of Bridport—and John Perry or Parry, rector of South Perrott (*Suthperrot*); patron, Philip Mabank, *domicellus*. Ind. of both: archd. of Dorset. Ramsbury (*Remmesbury*) park, 1 Sept. 1408.

30 Institution of M. John Cole B.C.L., in person of John Donnyng, clerk, his proctor, to church of Piddletrenthide (*Pidele Trenthyde*), vac. by death of Reynold Warenner; patrons, abbot and conv. of Hyde by Winchester. Ind.: archd. of Dorset. Ramsbury park, 1 Sept. 1408.

31 [Fo. 13ᵛ/5ᵛ] Institution of William Werkman, chaplain, to free chapel of Athelhampton (*Athelampston*), vac. by resig. of John Cole; patron, Richard Martyn, lord of vill of Athelhampton. Ind.: archd. of Dorset. Salisbury, bishop's palace, 11 Sept. 1408.

32 Exchange between William Stephanus, vicar of Basildon (*Bastelden*); patrons, Warden John de Wevere and the chaplains and fellows of St. John the Baptist's collegiate church, Shottesbrook (*Shottesbrok*)—and Nicholas Welde, vicar of Lacock (*Lacok*); patrons, Abbess Ellen and the conv. of Lacock. Ind. of Stephanus: archd. of Berkshire [*rectius* Wiltshire]. Ind. of Welde: archd. of Berkshire. Salisbury, bishop's palace, 11 Sept. 1408.

33 Exchange, by authority of Richard, bp. of London, between Gilbert Melasyn, vicar of White Waltham; patrons, abbot and conv. of Chertsey (*Certeseye*)—and Richard Bayford, chaplain of the chantry in the church of St. Bride, city of London, for the souls of Thomas Brix and Ellen, his wife, Thomas Banham and all the faithful. Ind. of Bayford: archd. of Berkshire. Woodford (*Wodeford*), 15 Sept. 1408.

34 Institution of John Pert, priest, to church or chapel with cure of souls of Norridge (*Norygg, Noryngg*); patron, Nicholas Leye, *domicellus*. Ind.: archd. of Wiltshire. Potterne (*Poterne*), 20 Sept. 1408.

35 [Fo. 14/6] Institution of Roger Holford, priest, to church of Wittenham (*Whittenam*); patron, Richard de St. Maur, lord of Castle Cary (*Castel Cary*). Ind.: archd. of Salisbury. Holford gave his oath on the gospels to relinquish the benefice if it were found that it was not vac. or that Richard de St. Maur did not have the right of presentation. Potterne, 25 Sept. 1408.

[For Wittenham *alias* Rowley, formerly in Wingfield, see *VCH Wilts.*, vii. 70.]

36 Collation to William Neldere, priest, in person of Gilbert Hallum, literate, his proctor, of the chantry of Laverstock (*Laverkestok*) church, vac. by death of John Douke. Ind.: archd. of Salisbury. Potterne, 8 Oct. 1408.

37 Exchange between William Malle, vicar of Chieveley (*Chevele*); patrons, abbot and conv. of Abingdon (*Abyndon*)—and John White, vicar of Kington St. Michael (*Kyngton Michaelis*); patrons, Prioress Christine and the conv. of Kington. Ind. of White: archd. of Berkshire. Ind. of Malle: archd. of Wiltshire. Ramsbury (*Remmesbury*) park, 9 Oct. 1408.

38 Collation to M. William Clement M.A. of vicarage of Winterbourne Whitchurch (*Hwytchirche*). Ind.: archd. of Dorset. Ramsbury park, 10 Oct. 1408.

39 [Fo. $14^v/6^v$] Exchange, by authority of Robert, bp. of Chichester, between Thomas Skendelby, rector of Hinton Parva (*Stanbrygge*), in person of John Forde, literate, his proctor; patron, Roger Coryngham, dean of the royal free chapel of Wimborne Minster (*Wymbornemynster*), at nomination of Roland Hynton, *domicellus*, lord of the manor of Stanbridge—and John Baron, rector of Treyford (*Trefford*), dioc. Chichester. Ind. of Baron: archd. of Dorset. Sonning (*Sonnyng*), 12 Oct. 1408.

[For Stanbridge, now Hinton Parva, see Hutchins, iii. 137–40.]

40 Collation to William Baker, priest, of vicarage of Littleton Drew (*Litelton Drew*), vac. by resig. of John Crosby. Ind.: archd. of Wiltshire. London, 18 Oct. 1408.

41 Exchange, by authority of Robert, bp. of Hereford, between William Salter, rector of St. Mary the Virgin, Wallingford (*Wallyngford*); patrons, Prior Richard and the conv. of Holy Trinity, Wallingford—and Thomas Myddelton, rector of Tugford (*Togford*), in immediate jurisdiction of the bp. of Hereford; patron, the same bp. Ind. of Myddelton: archd. of Berkshire. London, 24 Oct. 1408.

42 Collation to John Lymbury, priest, of the vicarage of Streatley (*Stretlegh*). Ind.: archd. of Berkshire. London, 2 Nov. 1408.

43 [Fo. 15/7] Letter from the archd. of Wiltshire's official, citing the bishop's commission, dated Abingdon (*Abendon*), 6 Apr. 1408 (under the seal which he formerly used as archd. of Canterbury[1]), to inquire into the vacancy and right of patronage of the church of Castle Combe (*Castelcombe*), to which Stephen Lescrop, knight, had presented Ralph de Derham, priest. The official certified that an inquiry held in Chippenham (*Chyppenham*) church, Malmesbury deanery, established that M. Adam de Uske, rector of Castle Combe, who was also an auditor of causes at the papal curia, had on 13 June 1406 secretly left the Roman curia and joined the anti-pope [Benedict XIII], who within half a year had conferred the bishopric of Llandaff (*Landaven'*) on him.[2] For this he had been excommunicated by the pope [Gregory XII] and deprived of all his benefices since the feast of the Nativity of the B.V.M. last past [8 Sept. 1407]. He had neglected the church of Castle Combe for almost two years, not residing nor appointing anyone to collect the revenues of the church or to administer the sacraments. However, the parishioners on their own authority had paid a chaplain out of the revenues of the church to administer the sacraments and the rest of the revenues remained in the hands of the parishioners.[3] Stephen Lescrop had the right of patronage and had last presented M. Adam de Uske. The church was not burdened with a pension nor subject to any charge on its revenue nor involved in any legal dispute (*non est pensionaria, porcionaria vel litigiosa*). Ralph de Derham was in orders, aged fifty and of good character. Therefore the official had instituted Derham as rector 25 Apr., and inducted him 26 Apr. [*sic*]. The jurors were William Whyte, rector of Wraxhall (*Wroxale*); William Kynton, rector of West Kington (*Westkynton*); Nicholas Sterre, rector of Stanton St. Quintin (*Staunton Quintini*); Richard Pere, vicar of Corsham (*Cosham*); William Bladyndon, vicar of Hullavington (*Huntlavyngton*); John Forde, chaplain of St. Mary's chantry, Wraxhall; William Aldeby of Littleton Drew (*Litelton Drew*); Thomas Pruet of West Kington; Walter Clerk of Wraxhall; John Smyth of Sutton Benger (*Sutton*) and Robert Webbe and Adam Attehulle of Castle Combe. Sealed with the seals of the archdeacon's official and of the jurors. Chippenham, 25 Apr. 1408.

On the day the bp. received this letter, Ralph de Derham swore obedience to him. Culham, 4 July 1408.

[1. Hallum used this seal at least until 20 Apr. 1408. Cf. **707–8** and nn.

2. *Hierarchia Catholica*, i. 292 n. 6 ('Adam Wesk').

3. Webb and Attehulle were ordered to be distrained by the sheriff of Wiltshire in Hilary 9 Hen. IV [1408] to reply concerning tithes owed to Adam de Uske who had forefeited to the king, on account of his desertion to the French anti-pope (P.R.O., L.T.R. Memoranda, E 368/180 fo. 165; cf. *CPR 1408–13*, p. 159).]

44 [Fo. 15v/7v] Letter from M. John Chaundeler, dean of Salisbury, citing the bishop's commission, dated Culham, 1 July 1408, to inquire into the vacancy of the prebendal church of Blewbury (*Blebury*), to which Walter Grendon, prior of hospital of St. John of Jerusalem in England, had presented John Grendon, priest. The dean certified that as the result of an inquiry he had collated John Grendon, 3 July, to the prebendal church and to the canonry and prebend in Salisbury cath., vac. by the death of the last prebendary, in the person of Roger Lowe, his proctor, and had installed him. Sealed with the dean's seal. Salisbury, 4 July 1408.
Letter received by the bp., London, 7 Nov. 1408.

45 [Fo. 16/8] Exchange, by authority of Henry, bp. of Winchester, between Robert atte Mulle, rector of St. Mary, West Street (*Westrete*), Wilton; patrons, abbess and conv. of Wilton—and Thomas atte Ende, rector of Bicton (*Byketon*), dioc. Winchester, in person of Edmund Boure, literate, his proctor. Ind. of Thomas atte Ende: archd. of Salisbury. London, 13 Nov. 1408.

46 [Fo. 16v/8v] Institution of Richard Wodyngton, priest, to chantry in Sparsholt (*Spersholte*) church; patron, Robert de la Mare, *domicellus*. Ind.: archd. of Berkshire. Wodyngton swore and promised that he would relinquish the chantry if it were established that the chantry was not vac. or the alleged patron did not have the right of presentation. London, 16 Nov. 1408.

47 Institution of Walter Kood, clerk, to church of Fovant (*Foffunte*); patrons, abbess and conv. of Wilton. Ind.: archd. of Salisbury. Sonning (*Sonnyng*), 22 Nov. 1408.

48 Exchange between William Welforde, vicar of Ardington (*Ardyngton*); patrons, prior and conv. of Bicester (*Burucestr'*), dioc. Lincoln—and Robert Peek, rector of Draycot Cerne (*Draycote Cerne*); patron, for this turn, Helen Cerne, mother of Edward Cerne, lord of Draycot Cerne, by reason of her dower in the manor of Draycot Cerne. Ind. of Peek: archd. of Berkshire. Ind. of Welforde: archd. of Wiltshire. Ramsbury (*Remmesbury*) park, 27 Nov. 1408.

49 Institution of John Whyte, priest, to vicarage of Hagbourne (*Hakeburne*); patrons, abbot and conv. of Cirencester (*Cirencestr'*), dioc. Worcester. Ind.: archd. of Berkshire. Potterne (*Poterne*), 30 Nov. 1408.

50 Exchange, on certificate of Edmund, bp. of Exeter (*Exonien'*), between William Southam, rector of Fugglestone (*Fogheleston*) with chapel of Bemerton (*Bymerton*); patrons, abbess and conv. of Wilton—and M. John Haget, rector of Kings Nympton (*Nymeton Regis*), dioc. Exeter, in person of Laurence Haukyn, his proctor. Ind. of Haget: archd. of Salisbury. Woodford (*Wodeford*), 7 Dec. 1408.

51 [Fo. 17/9] Exchange, by authority of Edmund, bp. of Exeter, between Nicholas Lovecok, vicar of Buckland Newton (*Bokeland Abbatis*); patron, Ralph Erghum, rector of Buckland Newton—and William Dyber, rector of St. Ives in Cornwall (*Sancti Ivonis in Cornubia*), dioc. Exeter. Ind. of Dyber: archd. of Dorset. Salisbury, 9 Dec. 1408.

52 Institution of William Glym, priest, in person of Roger Curteys, clerk, his proctor, to prebend or prebendal church of Liddington (*Ludyngton*), vac. by resig. of George Louthorp; patrons, abbess and conv. of Shaftesbury (*Shafton*). Ind.: archd. of Wiltshire. Salisbury, 11 Dec. 1408.

53 Letter of M. John Chaundeler, dean of Salisbury, citing the bishop's commission, dated the palace, Salisbury, 11 Dec. 1408, to inquire into the proposed exchange between Thomas Herthevene, vicar of Burbage (*Burbach*) and Alexander Champion, vicar of Chippenham. The dean certified that he had authorized the exchange. Salisbury, 12 Dec. 1408.

54 [Fo. $17^v/9^v$] Institution of William Colman, priest, to chantry at St. Bartholomew's altar in St. Thomas the Martyr's church, Salisbury, vac. by death of William Burgeys, priest; patrons, dean and chapter of Salisbury. Ind.: dean and chapter. Salisbury, 9 Jan. 1409.

55 Institution of Robert Holbroke, priest, to church of Piddlehinton (*Hynepudell* or *Pudelhynton*), vac. by resig. of Thomas Shelford, clerk; patron, Henry, bp. of Winchester. Ind.: archd. of Dorset. London, 29 Jan. 1409.

56 Exchange between Richard Sloughtre, rector of Mildenhall (*Mildenhale*); patrons, William Hankeford, knight, William Stourton, William Poulet, William Besyle and John Prat, rector of Hemington (*Hemyngton*)—and Robert Graffton, rector of Little Somerford (*Somerford Maudut*); patrons, for this turn, John Barton, senior, William Wyat, John Barton, junior, Thomas Goldhopp, clerk, John Stokkyng and William Spelyng. Ind. of both: archd. of Wiltshire. London, 6 Feb. 1409.

57 [Fo. 18/10] Institution of William Britby, clerk, to church of Over Compton (*Compton Hawy*), vac. by death of John Paswar; patron, for this turn, Hugh de Waterton, knight. Ind.: archd. of Dorset. London, 6 Feb. 1409.

58 Exchange between William Stevenes, vicar of Lacock (*Lacok*); patrons, abbess and conv. of Lacock—and Thomas Bertweye, rector of Peasemore (*Pesemer*); patrons, John Hyde, John Isbery and William Broun. Ind. of Bertweye: archd. of Wiltshire. Ind. of Stevenes: archd. of Berkshire. London, 14 Feb. 1409.

59 Exchange between William Malle, vicar of Kington St. Michael (*Kyngton Michaelis*); patrons, prioress and conv. of Kington St. Michael—and John Rasyn, vicar of Letcombe Regis (*Ledecombe*); patrons, prioress and conv. of Amesbury (*Ambresbury*). Ind. of Rasyn: archd. of Wiltshire. Ind. of Malle: archd. of Berkshire. London, 14 Feb. 1409.

[The rest of this quire (fos. 18/10–22v/10dv) contains wills, **695–706**, apart from the commission to the vicars general (**60**, fo. 20v). Fos. 23 and 24 are blank. A new quire was started for the vicar general's register of institutions.]

60 [Fo. 20v/10bv] Commission of Robert, bp. of Salisbury, to M. Adam Mottrum, precentor of Salisbury cath., and M. Geoffrey Crukadan, canon, to act as vicars general during the bishop's absence abroad on matters concerning the English and the universal Church. Together or singly, they have authority to determine all cases and business pertaining to the bishop's diocesan jurisdiction, both instance and *ex-officio*, to hear appeals, to deal with testamentary business, to institute to and deprive of benefices, to carry out exchanges, to grant letters dimissory, to hear confessions, grant absolution and appoint penitenciaries, to absolve excommunicates, to grant licences for non-residence and to collate to benefices in the bishop's gift. Canterbury, 27 Feb. 1409.

[Fo. 25/1] REGISTRUM VENERABILIS IN CHRISTO PATRIS ET DOMINI DOMINI ROBERTI DEI GRACIA SAR' EPISCOPI HABITUM CORAM CIRCUMSPECTO VIRO MAGISTRO ADAM DE MOTTRUM PRECENTORE ECCLESIE SAR' VICARIO IN SPIRITUALIBUS GENERALI, PREDICTO VENERABILI PATRE IN REMOTIS AGENTE, ET DE ANNO DOMINI MILLESIMO CCCC mo OCTAVO

60A Commission of Robert, bp. of Salisbury, to M. Adam de Mottrum Lic.Cn.L., precentor of Salisbury cath., to collate to benefices in the bishop's gift during the bishop's absence. Canterbury, 27 Feb. 1409.

[Apparently an abbreviated version of **60**, omitting mention of Crukadan and giving only the last item in the full commission.]

[All the *acta* in the following section, **61–111**, are by M. Adam de Mottrum, vicar general.]

61 Institution of William Savage, priest, to church of Heddington (*Hedyngton*), vac. by death of Ralph Beurne; patrons, prior and conv. of Monkton Farleigh (*Farlegh*). Ind.: archd. of Wiltshire. Salisbury, 15 March 1409.

62 Institution of William Whyttick, in person of John Shirborn, clerk, B.C.L., his proctor, to church of Symondsbury (*Symondesburgh*); patrons, abbot and conv. of Cerne. Ind.: archd. of Dorset. Salisbury, 15 March 1409.

REGISTRUM HABITUM CORAM PRELIBATO MAGISTRO ADAM VICARIO REVERENDI IN CHRISTO PATRIS ET DOMINI DOMINI ROBERTI DEI GRACIA SAR' EPISCOPI PREDICTI, ET DE ANNO DOMINI MILLESIMO QUADRINGENTESIMO NONO

63 Institution of Thomas Croxton, priest, to vicarage of Seacourt (*Seukeworth*); patrons, prioress and conv. of Studley (*Stodley*), dioc. Lincoln. Ind.: archd. of Berkshire. Salisbury, 26 March 1409.

[For Seacourt, in Wytham, see *VCH Berks.*, iv. 421; *Berks. Place-names*, ii. 465.]

64 Letter to John Cumburworth, canon of St. Mary of Poulton (*Pulton*), order of St. Gilbert, instituting him, in person of John Wodeforde, vicar of Ashton Keynes (*Asscheton*), his proctor, to church of Poulton; patrons, prior and conv. of St. Mary of Poulton. Sealed with precentor's seal, Salisbury, 26 March 1409.

65 [Fo. 25v/1v] Dispensation, pursuant to letters (recited) of Francis, cardinal priest of St. Susanna, dated St. Peter's, Rome, 3 March 14 Boniface IX [1403], to John Stafford, scholar, to proceed to holy orders, notwithstanding that he is of illegitimate birth. Notarial instrument to this effect by Wenceslas Swisiko, clerk (dioc. Brandenburg (*Brandeburgen'*)), notary public. Witnesses: John Bury, priest (dioc. Norwich (*Norwicen'*)) and John Bromley, literate (dioc. Lichfield). Salisbury, 2 Apr. 1409.

[This is the future abp. of Canterbury, 1443–52. His father was probably Sir Humphrey Stafford, of North Bradley (Wilts.).]

66 [Fo. 26/2] Institution of Fulk Stafford, clerk, to church of Ditchampton (*Dychampton*), vac. by resig. of John Russhall; patron, Humphrey Stafford, lord of Ditchampton, as established by an inquiry. Ind.: archd. of Salisbury. Salisbury, 4 Apr. 1409.

67 Letter to John Frank, clerk, instituting him to a canonry in Salisbury cath. and the prebend of Beminster (*Bemynstre*) Prima in the same; patron, King Henry, by reason of the custody by King Richard of the temporalities *sede vacante*. Sealed with precentor's seal, Salisbury, 5 Apr. 1409.

68 Mandate to the dean and chapter of Salisbury to admit John Frank [as in **67**]. Salisbury, 5 Apr. 1409.

69 Institution of John Sheyle, priest, to church of Catmore (*Catmer*); patron, Walter Grendon, prior of hospital of St. John of Jerusalem in England. Ind.: archd. of Berkshire. Salisbury, 24 Apr. 1409.

70 Institution of Thomas Shelford, clerk, in person of George Louthorp, treasurer of Salisbury cath., his proctor, to church of Ashbury (*Asshebury, Aysschebury*); patron, Nicholas, bp. of Bath and Wells. Ind.: archd. of Berkshire. Salisbury, 24 Apr. 1409.

[Cf. *Reg. Bubwith*, i. 52, which adds the information that the church was vac. by death of Thomas Byssebury.]

71 [Fo. 26v/2v] Institution of William Stacy, priest, to church of Hazelbury (*Haselbury*), vac. by death of John Maystur; patrons, prior and conv. of St. Mary of Bradenstoke (*Bradenstok*). Ind.: archd. of Wiltshire. Salisbury, 29 Apr. 1409.

72 Exchange, by authority of Edmund, bp. of Exeter, between Thomas Guldefeld, rector of Wroughton (*Elyngton*), in person of William Kerlele, literate, his proctor; patron, Henry, bp. of Winchester—and M. John Gyles, vicar of Sutton (*Sutton iuxta Plymmouth*), dioc. Exeter, in person of John Blakedon, priest, his proctor. Ind. of Gyles: archd. of Wiltshire. Salisbury, 29 Apr. 1409.

73 Exchange, on certificate of M. John Chaundeler, dean of Salisbury, between John Wynford, prebendary of Tytherington (*Tuderyngton*) and Horningsham (*Hornynggesham*) in Heytesbury (*Heyttedesbury*) collegiate church, in person of William Panter, his proctor; patron, dean of Salisbury—and M. John Symondesburgh, rector of Stoke Abbott (*Abbotestoke*); patrons, abbot and conv. of Sherborne (*Schirborn*). Ind. of Wynford: archd. of Dorset. Salisbury, 23 May 1409.

74 Exchange, by authority of Nicholas, bp. of Bath and Wells, between John Roe, vicar of Twerton (*Tweverton*), dioc. Bath and Wells—and William Launce, vicar of Coombe Keynes (*Combekaynes*), in person of John Knygth, literate, his proctor; patrons, prior and conv. of St. Mary of Merton, dioc. Winchester. Ind. of Roe: archd. of Dorset. Salisbury, 20 May 1409.

75 [Fo. 27/3] Exchange, by authority of Nicholas, bp. of Bath and Wells, between John Gloucestre, rector of Ashley (*Asshelegh*); patrons, William Hankeford, knight, William Stourton, William Powlet, William Besyle and John Prat, rector of Hemington (*Hemmyngton*)—and Nicholas Baker, rector of Farleigh Hungerford (*Hungerfordys Farleigh*), dioc. Bath and Wells, in person of John Prat, priest, his proctor. Ind. of Baker: archd. of Wiltshire. Salisbury, 24 May 1409.

76 Exchange, by authority of Nicholas, bp. of Bath and Wells, between John Whittok, rector of Warmwell (*Warmwelle*); patron, Nicholas Coker, esquire—and Richard Godyngdon, rector of Chilton Cantelo (*Chylton Cauntloo*), dioc. Bath and Wells. Ind. of Godyngdon: archd. of Dorset. Salisbury, 24 May 1409.

77 Institution of John Chaundeler, clerk, to church of Symondsbury (*Symondesburgh*); patrons, abbot and conv. of Cerne. Ind.: archd. of Dorset. Salisbury, 4 June 1409.

78 Institution of John Conche, deacon, to vicarage of Fisherton Delamere (*Fisscherton*); patrons, prior and conv. of Maiden Bradley (*Maydenebradelegh*). Ind.: archd. of Salisbury. Salisbury, 5 June 1409.

79 [Fo. 27v/3v] Exchange, by authority of Philip, bp. of Lincoln, between William Grom, rector of St. Leonard, Wallingford (*Walyngford*); patrons, prior and conv. of St. Frideswide (*Frideswyd*), Oxford—and John Wath, rector of Taplow (*Tappelowe*), dioc. Lincoln, in person of John Chirbry, clerk, his proctor. Ind. of Wath: archd. of Berkshire. Salisbury, 14 June 1409.

80 Institution of Thomas Masy, clerk, to church of Compton Valence; patron, John Kirkeby, esquire, as established by an inquiry. Ind.: archd. of Dorset. Salisbury, 22 June 1409.

81 Exchange, by authority of Thomas, bp. of Worcester, between William Magot, rector of Berwick St. John (*Berewyk*), in person of Thomas Rylee, clerk, his proctor; patrons, abbess and conv. of Wilton—and Thomas Wysebech, rector of Minchinhampton (*Mynchynhampton*), dioc. Worcester. Ind. of Wysebech: archd. of Salisbury. Salisbury, 22 June 1409.

82 Exchange between John Smyth *alias* Mynty, vicar of Purton (*Puryton*); patrons, abbot and conv. of Malmesbury—and John Burnet, rector of Long Critchell (*Langekirchulle*); patron, Willelma, widow of John Roches, knight, as established by an inquiry. Ind. of Smyth: archd. of Dorset. Ind. of Burnet: archd. of Wiltshire. Salisbury, 27 June 1409.

83 [Fo. 28/4] Exchange, by authority of Thomas, bp. of Worcester, between Richard Sloghter, rector of Little Somerford (*Somerford Maudut*); patrons, John Barton, senior, William Wyat, John Barton, junior, Thomas Goldehop, clerk, John Stokkon and William Spelyng—and Thomas Hitteweye, rector of Wichenford (*Wicheford*), dioc. Worcester, in person of John Middilton, literate, his proctor. Ind. of Hitteweye: archd. of Wiltshire. Salisbury, 27 June 1409.

84 Exchange between John Copede, vicar of Buckland (*Bokelande*); patrons, rector and conv. of Edington (*Edyngdon*)—and John Conge, vicar of Fisherton Delamere (*Fisscherton*); patrons, prior and conv. of Maiden Bradley (*Maydenebradelegh*). Ind. of Copede: archd. of Salisbury. Ind. of Conge: archd. of Berkshire. Salisbury, 6 July 1409.

85 Letter to George Louthorp, canon residentiary of Salisbury and warden of the choristers, nominating William Buttys to be presented by Louthorp to the vicarage of Preshute (*Prescchute*), on an exchange with John Bridport, rector of Newton St. Loe (*Newton Seynlo*), dioc. Bath and Wells. Salisbury, 7 July 1409.

86 Letter of George Louthorp, canon residentiary of Salisbury and warden of the choristers, to M. Adam de Mottrum, vicar general, presenting William Buttys to the vicarage of Preshute [as in **85**]. Salisbury, 7 July 1409.

87 [Fo. 28ᵛ/4ᵛ] Exchange, by authority of Nicholas, bp. of Bath and Wells, between William Buttys, rector of Newton St. Loe (*Newton Seynlo*), dioc. Bath and Wells—and John Bridport, vicar of Preshute (*Prescchute*); patron, George Louthorp, canon residentiary of Salisbury and warden of the choristers, on nomination of Robert, bp. of Salisbury. Ind. of Buttys: official of peculiar jurisdiction of Marlborough (*Marleburgh*). Salisbury, 8 July 1409.

88 Institution of Thomas Masonn, priest, to church of Appleton (*Appulton*); patron, William FytzWaryn, *domicellus*, as established by an inquiry. Ind.: archd. of Berkshire. Salisbury, 10 July 1409.

89 Exchange, by authority of Henry, bp. of Winchester, between John Smyth *alias* Mynty, rector of Long Critchell (*Langkyrchull*), in person of John Deneby, clerk, his proctor; patron, John Savage, *domicellus*—and John Knyght, rector of Burghclere, dioc. Winchester, in person of John Beere, literate, his proctor. Ind. of Knyght: archd. of Dorset. Salisbury, 15 July 1409.

90 [Fo. 29A/5] Exchange, by authority of Thomas, bp. of Worcester, between M. Robert Holbrook, rector of Piddlehinton (*Hynepudell* or *Pudelhynton*); patron, Henry, bp. of Winchester—and Richard Lynde, rector Welford-on-Avon (*Welveford*), dioc. Worcester. Ind. of Lynde: archd. of Dorset. Salisbury, 16 July 1409.

91 Exchange, on certificate of Simon Sloley, warden of St. Thomas the Martyr's chantry, Stratford-on-Avon (*Stratford super Avene*), dioc. Worcester, between William Power, vicar of Bishopton (*Bysshopusdon*), dioc. Worcester—and Richard Wythyford, rector of Avington (*Avyngton*); patron, for this turn, William Coventre, as established by an inquiry. Ind. of Power: archd. of Berkshire. Salisbury, 19 July 1409.

92 Exchange, by authority of Philip, bp. of Lincoln, between Thomas Felix, rector of Whaddon; patron, Walter Beauchamp, *domicellus*, lord of manor of Whaddon—and John Sunbury, vicar of Humberstone (*Humburston*), dioc. Lincoln. Ind. of Sunbury: archd. of Salisbury. Salisbury, 21 July 1409.

93 [Fo. 29A^{v}/5^{v}] Exchange, by authority of Thomas, bp. of Worcester, between Thomas Chamburleyn, rector of St. Peter, Marlborough (*Marleburgh*); patron, the bp. of Salisbury—and William Brythlamton, vicar of St. Leonard, Bristol (*Bristoll*), dioc. Worcester. Ind. of Brythlamton: official of peculiar jurisdiction of Marlborough. Salisbury, 26 July 1409.

94 Institution of John Waleys, priest, to church of Winterbourne Abbas (*Wynterborn Abbatis*); patrons, abbot and conv. of Cerne. Ind.: archd. of Dorset. Salisbury, 27 July 1409.

95 Exchange, by authority of Richard, bp. of London, between John Housebonde, rector of Ufton Richard (*Ofton Richer*); patron, Walter Grendon, prior of hospital of St. John of Jerusalem in England—and John Grenelane, rector of Finchley (*Fyncheley*), dioc. London, in person of John Motte, citizen of London, his proctor. Ind. of Grenelane: archd. of Berkshire. Salisbury, 28 July 1409.

[Ufton Richard and Ufton Robert were joined in 1435, and are now called Ufton Nervet (*VCH Berks.*, iii. 443).]

96 Exchange, by authority of John, bp. of Coventry and Lichfield, and Nicholas, bp. of Bath and Wells, between William Glym, canon of Wells and prebendary of Shalford (*Shaldeford*) in the same and prebendary of Liddington (*Ludyngton*) in Shaftesbury (*Shafton*) conventual church, in person of Roger Curteys, clerk, his proctor; patrons of Liddington, abbess and conv. of Shaftesbury—and John Wakeryng, vicar of St. Michael, Coventry, dioc. Coventry and Lichfield, in person of William Sponne, priest, his proctor. Ind. of Wakeryng: archd. of Wiltshire. Salisbury, 29 July 1409.

97 [Fo. 29B/6] Letter to John Wakeryng, priest, collating him to the prebend of Shalford in Wells cath., and instituting him to the prebend of Liddington in Shaftesbury conventual church, on exchange [as in **96**]. Salisbury, 29 July 1409.

98 Exchange, by authority of Richard, bp. of London, between Walter Kod, rector of Fovant (*Foffunte*); patrons, abbess and conv. of Wilton (*Wylton*)—and Nicholas Grave, rector of West Tilbury (*Tillebury*), dioc. London, in person of M. Edward Prentys, his proctor. Ind. of Grave: archd. of Salisbury. Salisbury, 1 Aug. 1409.

99 Exchange, by authority of Philip, bp. of Lincoln, between Richard Taunton, rector of Hanwell (*Hanewell*), dioc. Lincoln—and John Bromley, rector of West Dean (*Westdeon*); patron, Miles de Stapilton, knight. Ind. of Taunton: archd. of Salisbury. Salisbury, 3 Aug. 1409.

100 [Fo. 29B^{v}/6^{v}] Exchange, by authority of Thomas, bp. of Worcester, between John Hore, vicar of Hullavington (*Hunlavyngton*); patron, King Henry, custodian of the temporalities of the alien priory of Clatford, during the war with France—and John Salesbury, vicar of Bledington (*Bladynton*), dioc. Worcester. Ind. of Salesbury: archd. of Wiltshire. Salisbury, 13 Aug. 1409.

101 Exchange, by authority of Thomas, bp. of Worcester, between Richard Poull, vicar of West Ilsley (*Westhildesley*); patrons, prior and conv. of Sandleford (*Sandelford*)—and Richard Sangere, rector of Charfield (*Charfeld*), dioc. Worcester. Ind. of Sangere: archd. of Berkshire. Salisbury, 16 Aug. 1409.

102 Exchange, by authority of Richard, bp. of London, between M. Robert Witton D.Cn.L., rector or warden of free chapel of Stafford Byngham (*Staford Byngham*), in person of William Somerhill, priest, his proctor; patron, Robert Byngham, esquire—and Robert Shiryngton, rector of Woodford (*Wodeford*), dioc. London, in person of M. Simon Sydenham, his proctor. Ind. of Shiryngton: archd. of Dorset. Salisbury, 17 Aug. 1409.

103 Exchange, by authority of Henry, bp. of Winchester, between William Blundell, rector of Woolhampton (*Wulhampton*); patron, Walter Grendon, prior of hospital of St. John of Jerusalem in England—and Robert Rydon, vicar of Wymering (*Wymeryng*), dioc. Winchester. Ind. of Rydon: archd. of Berkshire. Salisbury, 15 Sept. 1409.

104 [Fo. 30A/7] Letter to Robert Grym, priest, collating him to the status of a priest in St. Edmund's collegiate church, Salisbury. Salisbury, 14 Sept. 1409.

105 Collation, in similar form, to Nicholas Swepston, priest, of the status of a priest in St. Edmund's collegiate church, Salisbury. Ind. of Grym and Swepston: Robert Bussch, provost of St. Edmund's. Salisbury, 14 Sept. 1409.

106 Exchange, by authority of Henry, bp. of Winchester, between Nicholas Godewyne, rector of St. Nicholas, Guildford (*Guldeford*), dioc. Winchester—and John Draper, rector of Collingbourne Kingston (*Colyngbourne Abbatis*), in person of John Brok, clerk, his proctor; patrons, abbot and conv. of Hyde (*Hyda*), dioc. Winchester. Ind. of Godewyne: archd. of Wiltshire. Salisbury, 26 Sept. 1409.

107 Institution of Nicholas Mason, priest, to vicarage of West Ilsley (*Westhildesley*); patrons, prior and conv. of Sandleford (*Sandelford*). Ind.: archd. of Berkshire. Salisbury, 27 Sept. 1409.

108 [Fo. 30A^{v}/7^{v}] Institution of Simon Membury, clerk, to church of Long Critchell (*Langekyrchull*), vac. by resig. of John Knycht; patron, for this turn, Willelma, widow of John Roches, knight. Ind.: archd. of Dorset. Salisbury, 29 Sept. 1409.
[MS. margin: *videatur*]

109 Institution of John Partrych, priest, to church of Moreton (*Morton*); patron, John Frampton, lord of Moreton. Ind.: archd. of Dorset. Salisbury, 3 Oct. 1409.

110 Exchange, on certificate of John, prior of Bath cath., between Walter Eymere, rector of St. Michael without the North Gate, Bath, in person of John Baret, clerk, his proctor—and William Savage, rector of Heddington (*Hedyngton*); patrons, subprior and conv. of Monkton Farleigh (*Farley*), order of Cluny, the priorate being vac. by the recent death of William Preston. Ind. of Eymere: archd. of Wiltshire. Salisbury, 11 Oct. 1409.

111 Resig. by Thomas Sendel of the church of Little Langford (*Langeford Parva*). Witnesses: John Bromley, literate, and Thomas Pycot, clerk (dioc. Chichester). Salisbury, 2 Oct. 1409.

[All the *acta*, **112–523**, are by Robert, bp. of Salisbury.]

112 Institution of Robert atte Mulne, chaplain, to church of Padworth, vac. by resig. of John Kyltale; patron, for this turn, King Henry. Ind.: archd. of Berkshire. London inn, 15 Oct. 1409.

113 Institution of John Langthorne, priest, to vicarage of Sturminster Marshall (*Sturmynstre* or *Sturmyntre Marescall*); patron, for this turn, Queen Joan, custodian of the fruits and issues of the said alien church of Sturminster Marshall, granted her by the king. Ind.: archd. of Dorset. London inn, 23 Oct. 1409.
[MS. margin: *Nota*]

114 [Fo. 30B/8] Institution of Roger Langheley, chaplain, to church of St. Peter, Haselbury Bryan (*Haselbere*); patron, Alice, widow of Guy de Bryen, knight. Ind.: archd. of Dorset. London inn, 23 Oct. 1409.

115 Institution of William Ameney, priest, to vicarage of Eisey (*Eysy*), vac. by resig. of Robert Felawe; patrons, abbot and conv. of St. Mary, Cirencester, order of St. Augustine, dioc. Worcester. Ind.: archd. of Wiltshire. London inn, 26 Oct. 1409.

116 Exchange between William Caddo, vicar of Sutton Benger (*Sutton*); patron, the bp.—and Nicholas Mason, vicar of West Ilsley (*Westhildesley*); patrons, prior and conv. of Sandelford (*Sandelford*). Ind. of Mason: archd. of Wiltshire. Ind. of Caddo: archd. of Berkshire. Ramsbury (*Remmesbury*) park, 13 Nov. 1409.

117 Institution of Simon Bradeforde, priest, to church of Ditteridge (*Dycheryche*); patron, for this turn, Thomas Sergeant, lord of Ditteridge, as established by an inquiry. Ind.: archd. of Wiltshire. Ramsbury park, 19 Nov. 1409.

118 Institution of Thomas Godeboye, priest, in person of M. William Holme B.C.L., his proctor, to church of Little Langford (*Langford Parva*), vac. by resig. of Thomas Sendel; patron, William Daungens. Ind.: archd. of Salisbury. Ramsbury park, 19 Nov. 1409.

119 Exchange, by authority of Philip, bp. of Lincoln, between John Sunbury, rector of Whaddon; patron, Walter Beauchamp, *domicellus*—and Thomas atte Vicairs, rector of Oxendon, dioc. Lincoln. Ind. of atte Vicairs: archd. of Salisbury, Salisbury, 30 Nov. 1409.

120 [Fo. 30B[v]/8[v]] Exchange, by authority of Nicholas, bp. of Bath and Wells, between John Grenelane, rector of Ufton Richard (*Ofton Richer*), in person of William Lillymiston, chaplain, his proctor; patron, Walter Grendon, prior of hospital of St. John of Jerusalem in England—and John Blyton, rector of Writhlington (*Wrytelyngton*), dioc. Bath and Wells. Ind. of Blyton: archd. of Berkshire. Salisbury, 1 Dec. 1409.

121 Exchange, by authority of Nicholas, bp. of Bath and Wells, between Roger Holford, rector of Wittenham *alias* Rowley (*Wyttenamroly*); patron, King Henry, custodian of the lands of the heir of the late Richard Seymour, knight, tenant-in-chief—and John Corbyn, vicar of Dunster, dioc. Bath and Wells. Ind. of Corbyn: archd. of Salisbury. Salisbury, 2 Dec. 1409.

122 Exchange, by authority of Philip, bp. of Lincoln, between William Swayn, rector of Huish (*Hywisshe*); patron, John Lovell, lord of Lovell and Holand—and Thomas Milwarde, rector of Stapleford (*Stapulford*), dioc. Lincoln. Ind. of Milwarde: archd. of Wiltshire. Ramsbury park, 7 Dec. 1409.

123 Exchange, by authority of Philip, bp. of Lincoln, between Thomas Hitteway *or* Witteway, rector of Little Somerford (*Somerford Maudut*); patrons, John Barton, senior, William Wyot, John Barton, junior, Thomas Goldehop, clerk, John Stokton and William Spelyng—and Thomas Felix, vicar of Humberstone (*Humberston*), dioc. Lincoln. Ind. of Felix: archd. of Wiltshire. Ramsbury park, 8 Dec. 1409.

124 [Fo. 31/9] Exchange, by authority of Thomas, bp. of Worcester, between John Sheyle, rector of Catmore (*Catmer*); patron, Walter Grendon, prior of hospital of St. John of Jerusalem in England—and William Colet, vicar of Down Ampney (*Donnameney*), dioc. Worcester. Ind. of Colet: archd. of Berkshire. Ramsbury park, 10 Dec. 1409.

125 Exchange, by authority of Philip, bp. of Lincoln, between William Power, rector of Avington (*Avyngton*); patron, William Coventre, *domicellus*—and John Okford, vicar of Ashby-Folville (*Asshelufovell*), dioc. Lincoln. Ind. of Okford: archd. of Berkshire. Ramsbury park, 11 Dec. 1409.

126 Institution of Henry Pyke, chaplain, to vicarage of Purton (*Puryton*); patrons, abbot and conv. of Malmesbury. Inductors: archd. of Wiltshire and William [illegible], chaplain of Purton church. Ramsbury park, 15 Dec. 1409.

127 Exchange, by authority of Philip, bp. of Lincoln, between Richard Bayford, vicar of White Waltham (*Waltham Abbatis*), in person of John Warde, his proctor; patrons, abbot and conv. of St. Peter the Apostle [Chertsey], dioc. Winchester—and Richard Bitham, vicar of Rushden (*Russhenden*), dioc. Lincoln. Ind. of Bitham: archd. of Wiltshire. Ramsbury park, 19 Dec. 1409.

128 [Fo. 31v/90v] Institution of Henry Shelford, chaplain, to church of Cheselbourne (*Cheselborne*); patrons, abbess and conv. of Shaftesbury (*Shafton*). Ind.: archd. of Dorset. Ramsbury park, 28 Dec. 1409.

129 Collation to M. William Lyndewode D.Cn. & C.L., bishop's clerk, of church of Winfrith Newburgh (*Wynford*). Ind.: archd. of Dorset. Ramsbury manor, 14 Jan. 1410.

130 Institution of Robert Cardemakere, chaplain, to church of Upton Lovell (*Ubeton*); patron, Maud Lovell, lady of Lovell and Holand. Ind.: archd. of Salisbury. Ramsbury manor, 19 Jan. 1410.

131 Collation to William Coche, chaplain, of vicarage of Laverstock (*Laverkestok*). Ind.: archd. of Salisbury. Ramsbury manor, 20 Jan. 1410.

132 Institution of Thomas Gereward, chaplain, to church of Sutton Mandeville (*Sutton Maundevyle*), vac. by death of William Holme; patrons, John Halsham, John Kyrkby and John Stanley. Ind.: archd. of Salisbury. Ramsbury manor, 20 Jan. 1410.

133 Institution of Nicholas Coventre, chaplain, to church of Upton Lovell (*Ubeton*); patron, Maud Lovell, [lady of Lovell] and Holand. Ind.: archd. of Salisbury. London inn, 27 Jan. 1410.

134 [Fo. 32/10] Institution of Richard Littilman, chaplain, to church of Ufton Richard (*Ofton Richer*), vac. by resig. of John Bliton; patron, Walter Grendon, prior of hospital of St. John of Jerusalem in England. Ind.: archd. of Berkshire. London inn, 7 Feb. 1410.

135 Institution of John Clerk, chaplain, to church of Manningford Abbots (*Manyngford*), vac. by death of Richard Wortyng; patrons, abbot and conv. of Hyde (*Hyda*), dioc. Winchester. Ind.: archd. of Wiltshire. London inn, 15 Feb. 1410.

136 Exchange, by authority of Nicholas, bp. of Bath and Wells, between Henry Turpyn, rector of Silton (*Sylton*); patron, for this turn, William Stoton, who holds the farm of the manor of Silton, with the advowson of the church, during the minority of William Bydyk, lord of the manor, his ward—and John Hullard, rector of Priston (*Prysshton*), dioc. Bath and Wells. Ind. of Hullard: archd. of Dorset. London, 17 Feb. 1410.

137 Exchange, by authority of Henry, bp. of Winchester, between Stephen Wotton, rector of Chisledon (*Chyselden*); patrons, abbot and conv. of Hyde (*Hyda*), dioc. Winchester—and John Smyth *alias* Mynty, rector of Burghclere, dioc. Winchester. Ind. of Smyth: archd. of Wiltshire. London, 19 Feb. 1410.

138 Collation to Laurence Dangervyle, chaplain, of vicarage of Inglesham (*Inglisham*), vac. by resig. of John Colyns. Ind.: archd. of Wiltshire. London, 20 Feb. 1410.

139 [Fo. 32v/10v] Exchange, on certificate of Roger Coryngham, dean of Wimborne Minster (*Wymburnmynstre*), between John Langthorn, vicar of Sturminster Marshall (*Sturmynstre Marchall*); patron, Queen Joan—and William Marnhull, prebendary of Crantock (*Karentisbern*) in the free chapel of Wimborne Minster. Ind. of Marnhull: archd. of Dorset. London, 28 Feb. 1410.

[For prebend of Crantock in Wimborne Minster, see Hutchins, iii. 190.]

140 Mandate to the archd. of Dorset for the induction of William Marnhull to the vicarage of Sturminster Marshall [as in **139**]. London, 28 Feb. 1410.

141 Exchange, by authority of Henry, bp. of Winchester, between John Overburn, rector of St. Mary, Cricklade (*Creklade*); patron, Richard Draper of Cirencester—and John Grenehull, rector of Eldon (*Elden*), dioc. Winchester, in person of William Oakman [? reading doubtful], his proctor. Ind. of Grenehull: archd. of Wiltshire. [London], 1 March 1410.

142 [Fo. 33/11] Exchange, by authority of Philip, bp. of Lincoln, between Robert Maydekyn *alias* Ludyngton, vicar of Chisledon (*Chesulden*), in person of Richard Gourley, clerk, his proctor; patron, John Mynty, rector of Chisledon—and Richard Brewes, rector of Gunby, dioc. Lincoln. Ind. of Brewes: archd. of Wiltshire. London, 10 March 1410.

143 Exchange, by authority of Nicholas, bp. of Bath and Wells, between Nicholas Sterre, rector of Stanton St. Quintin (*Staunton sancti Quintini*); patron, Henry FitzHugh, knight, lord of Ravensworth (*Ravenswath*) and Stanton—and John Tayllour, vicar of Stanton Drew (*Staunton Drew*), dioc. Bath and Wells. Ind. of Tayllour: archd. of Wiltshire. London, 10 March 1410.

144 Institution of John Schelford, clerk, in person of John Lovelich, clerk, his proctor, to church of Buckland Newton (*Bokelond*), vac. by death of M. Ralph Ergum; patron, Nicholas, bp. of Bath and Wells. Ind.: archd. of Berkshire [*rectius* Dorset]. Salisbury, 19 March 1410.

REGISTRUM REVERENDI IN CHRISTO PATRIS ET DOMINI DOMINI ROBERTI DEI GRACIA SAR' EPISCOPI ANTEDICTI DE PERMUTACIONIBUS INSTITUCIONIBUS ET COLLACIONIBUS BENEFICIORUM ET DE ANNO DOMINI MILLESIMO QUADRINGENTESIMO DECIMO

145 Exchange between Richard Benet, chaplain of the chantry of Langton Long Blandford (*Longblaneford*); patron, Avice Derby, lady of Long Blandford—and Henry Hert, chaplain of the chantry of Wootton Glanville (*Wotton Glamvyle*); patron, Robert More, esquire. Ind. of both: archd. of Berkshire [*rectius* Dorset]. Woodford (*Wodeford*) manor, 29 March 1410.
[For Langton Long Blandford see Hutchins, i. 281–90.]

146 [Fo. 33v/11v] Exchange between Thomas Haynus, rector of Tidmarsh (*Thedemerse, Thidemerse*); patron, John Golofer, esquire—and John Okeford, rector of Avington (*Avyngton*); patron, William Coventre, esquire. Ind. of both: archd. of Berkshire. Woodford manor, 31 March 1410.

147 Institution of Nicholas Brounstele, deacon, in person of Henry Blacborn, clerk, his proctor, to vicarage of Wargrave (*Wergrave*); patrons, abbot and conv. of Reading (*Radyng*). Ind.: archd. of Berkshire. Woodford manor, 31 March 1410.

148 Institution of Thomas Rouland, chaplain, to church of Chalbury (*Chelesbury*); patrons, abbess and conv. of Wilton. Ind.: archd. of Wiltshire [*rectius* Dorset]. Potterne manor, 4 Apr. 1410.

149 Institution of Thomas atte Mulle, chaplain, to chantry in manor of Lackham (*Lakham*), vac. by resig. of William Hunte; patron, Philip Baynard, lord of manor of Lackham. Ind.: archd. of Wiltshire.[1] Potterne, 4 Apr. 1410.
[1. MS. margin: *Nota*]

150 Exchange, on certificate of the prior of Bath cath., between John Churchewarde, rector of St. James, Bath—and John Forde, chaplain of St. Mary's chantry in Wraxhall (*Wroxhale*) church; patron, Edmund Forde, esquire. Ind. of Churchewarde: archd. of Wiltshire. Potterne manor, 11 Apr. 1410.

151 [Fo. 34/12] Mandate of Nicholas, bp. of Bath and Wells, for the induction of Richard Gabriell, recently collated to the prebend of Warminster or Luxville (*Wermynstre alias Luxvile*) in Wells cath., into the *corpus* of the prebend, situated in dioc. Salisbury. London inn, 17 Apr. 1410. Mandate of Robert, bp. of Salisbury, to the archd. of Salisbury for this induction. Potterne manor, 23 Apr. 1410.

152 Letter to John Wotton, canon of St. Mary of Poulton (*Pulton*), order of St. Gilbert, instituting him, in person of Richard Calday, clerk, his proctor, to church of Poulton; patrons, prior and conv. of St. Mary of Poulton, as established by an inquiry. Potterne manor, 25 Apr. 1410.

153 Exchange, by authority of Robert, bp. of Hereford, between Ralph Spurner, vicar of Hannington (*Hankynton*) chapel; patron, John Thornebury, rector of Crudwell (*Cruddewelle*)—and Edward Hunte, rector of Evesbatch (*Esbache*), dioc. Hereford. Ind. of Hunte: archd. of Wiltshire. Potterne manor, 28 Apr. 1410.

154 [Fo. 34ᵛ/12ᵛ] Exchange, by authority of Thomas, bp. of Worcester, between Robert Pyion, rector of Biddesden (*Buddesden*); patrons, prioress and conv. of Amesbury (*Ambresbury*)—and Hugh Brayles, vicar of Guiting (*Guytyng*), dioc. Worcester. Ind. of Brayles: archd. of Salisbury. Potterne manor, 8 May 1410.

[For Biddesden, in Chute, see *Wilts. Place-names*, p. 340; *Collections of John Aubrey*, p. 359. Guiting is probably Guiting Power (Lower Guiting), and Hugh Brayles may be the same as Hugh Swayn who was instituted to that vicarage in 1407 (*Register of Richard Clifford, Bishop of Worcester, 1401–7*, ed. W.E.L. Smith (Toronto, 1976), **344**).]

155 Institution of Adam Raceton, clerk, in person of David Olton, chaplain, his proctor, to church of Knighton (*Knyghton*); patron, Walter Grendon, prior of hospital of St. John of Jerusalem in England, as established by an inquiry. Ind.: archd. of Dorset. Potterne manor, 14 May 1410.

156 Exchange, by authority of Henry, bp. of Winchester, between John Possell, vicar of East Meon (*Estmene*), dioc. Winchester, in person of John Beclys, chaplain, his proctor; patron, the same bp.—and Thomas Smyth, rector of moiety of church of Shillingstone (*Okford Skyllyng*); patrons, prior and conv. of Montacute (*de Monte Acuto*), order of Cluny, dioc. Bath and Wells. Ind. of Possell: archd. of Dorset. Potterne, 8 May 1410.

[For Shillingstone, see Hutchins, iii. 444–5.]

157 [Fo. 35/13] Mandate of Nicholas, bp. of Bath and Wells, for the induction of John Morehay, recently collated to the prebend of Warminster or Luxville (*Wermynstre alias Luxvile*) in Wells cath., on an exchange with Richard Gabriell for the church of Ipplepen (*Ipplepenne*), dioc. Exeter, into the *corpus* of the prebend, situated in dioc. Salisbury. London inn, 10 May 1410. The archd. of Salisbury. is ordered to induct him. Potterne, 16 May 1410.

158 Letter to Henry Crompe, priest, instituting him in person of M. John Turry B.Cn. & C.L., his proctor, to church of St. Nicholas, Abingdon, vac.

by death of John Lyghe; patrons, abbot and conv. of St. Mary, Abingdon. An annual pension is reserved to the bp. Ind.: archd. of Berkshire. Potterne manor, 20 May 1410.

159 Letters of Pope Alexander V, dated Pisa, 18 Sept. 1 Alexander V [1409], revoking the grant of the church of Stalbridge (*Stalbrygg*) made *in commendam* to Benet, bp. of Bangor, by Angelo Carrario, called Pope Gregory XII. These letters, and letters of presentation from the abbot and conv. of Sherborne (*Shirborn*), order of St. Benedict, delivered by M. Richard Betty B.C.L., in the chapel of Sherborne castle, 28 May 1410.

160 [Fo. 35v/13v] Letters of the abbot and conv. of Sherborne, dated 27 May 1410, presenting M. Richard Betty, clerk, B.C.L., to the church of Stalbridge, in their gift, reserving to them an annual pension of 10 marks [£6 13*s* 4*d*]. Betty petitioned the bp. for his admission and institution.

161 Inquiry ordered by the bp. into the vacancy of the church of Stalbridge, to be held in Sherborne prebendal church on the Monday after the feast of St. Vitus and St. Modestus [16 June 1410], M. Benet Nycoll, bp. of Bangor, the present incumbent, being cited to appear.

162 Institution of John Barkere, chaplain, in person of John Wodeford, chaplain, his proctor, to vicarage of Minety (*Mynty*), vac. by death of Gilbert Merssh; patron, John Chytterne, archd. of Wiltshire. Ind.: archd. of Wiltshire. Sherborne, 30 May 1410.

163 [Fo. 36/14] Institution of John Massager, chaplain, to vicarage of Upavon (*Uphavyn*); patron, Queen Joan, custodian of the alien priory of Upavon, granted her by the king, as established by an inquiry. Ind.: archd. of Wiltshire. Sherborne, 3 June 1410.

164 Institution of John Snyput, chaplain, to church of Hardenhuish (*Hardenhuysshe*), vac. by death of John Scot; patron, for this turn, John Raynes, knight, of Clifton Reynes (*Clifton Raynes*), as established by an inquiry. Ind.: archd. of Wiltshire. Sherborne, 7 June 1410.

165 Letters of the dean of Shaftesbury (*Shafton*) deanery, dated Shaftesbury, 11 June 1410, certifying that he has executed the bishop's mandate of 28 May (given in full) to the official of Salisbury, the archd. of Dorset, and the deans and clergy of the archdeaconry, to cite M. Benet Nycoll, bp. of Bangor, present incumbent of Stalbridge (*Stalbrugge*) church, to appear before the bp. in Sherborne prebendal church on 16 June to defend his possession of the church against the claims of M. Richard Betty. Letters received, Sherborne, 16 June 1410.

166 [Fo. 36v/14v] Amoval of M. Benet Nycoll, who failed to appear, from the church of Stalbridge, by M. William Lyndewode D.Cn. & C.L., bishop's chancellor and commissary, at the request of Humphrey Rodeley, clerk, proctor of M. Richard Betty (as seen in a public instrument drawn up by M. John Draper (dioc. Salisbury), notary public). The business was to be completed the following day. Sherborne prebendal church, 16 June 1410.

[The next folio is missing. It contained the conclusion of M. Benet Nycoll's amoval from Stalbridge church, and also, according to the contemporary index of Reg. Hallum, the exchange of Brixton Deverill church, the admission to Kington Magna church, the admission to Stalbridge church, the exchange of Whaddon church and the exchange between Sydling St. Nicholas vicarage and Thruxton church, which is continued on fo. 37. The probable Brixton Deverill exchange is given in Appendix A IV.]

167 [Fo. 37/16] Exchange, by authority of Henry, bp. of Winchester, between William [surname missing], vicar of Sydling St. Nicholas (*Brodesydelyng*); patrons, abbot and conv. of Milton (*Middelton*)—and Richard [surname missing], rector of Thruxton (*Throcleston*), dioc. Winchester. Ind.: archd. of Dorset. Sherborne, —June 1410.

[Information incomplete because this entry began on the missing folio. The exchange is not entered in the Winchester episcopal register (Hampshire Record Office, A1/12), but Richard Salf was instituted to Thruxton 10 Apr. 1408 (*ibid.* fo. 39v; cf. also Hutchins, iv. 509). William may be William Papelon (cf. **636**).]

168 Exchange, by authority of Henry, bp. of Winchester, between William Somerhyll, subdean of Salisbury cath.; patron, the bp. of Salisbury—and John Clere, rector of Bentworth (*Bynteworth*), dioc. Winchester. Clere took the customary oath to reside and to exercise the penitenciary's office in person. Ind. of Clere: dean of Salisbury. Sherborne, 22 June 1410.

169 Exchange, by authority of Henry, bp. of Winchester, between John Wyrsall, rector of Ufton Robert (*Ofton Robert*); patron, Alice Paynell of Ufton Robert—and Richard Shebourne, vicar of West Boarhunt (*Westborhunt*), dioc. Winchester. Ind.: archd. of Berkshire. Sherborne, 26 June 1410.

170 [Fo. 37v/16v] Exchange, by authority of Edmund, bp. of Exeter, between John Fenton, rector of Stoodleigh (*Stodelygh*), dioc. Exeter—and John Corbyn, rector of Wittenham *alias* Rowley (*Wittenam Rouly*); patron, King Henry, custodian of the land and heir of the late Richard Seymour, knight, tenant-in-chief. Ind. of Fenton: archd. of Salisbury. Sherborne,[1] 10 July 1410.

[1. MS.: *loco quo supra,* although the bp. is said to be at Chardstock on 10 July in *acta* of that date, **1085**.]

171 Exchange, on certificate of John Scardevyle, dean of Pagham, in immediate jurisdiction of Canterbury, between John Stoke, chaplain of the chantry of Pagham—and John Ovyng, rector of Charborough (*Cherburgh*); patron, John Morvyle, *domicellus*. Ind. of Stoke: archd. of Dorset. Chardstock (*Cherdestok*), 8 Aug. 1410.

172 Institution of John Grangere, chaplain, to church of Wytham; patron, Richard Wytham, *domicellus*, as established by an inquiry. Ind.: archd. of Berkshire. Chardstock, 10 Aug. 1410.

173 Institution of John Osborn, chaplain, to church of Eaton Hastings (*Eton Hastynge*); patrons, Isabel de Penbrugge, lady of Eaton Hastings, and William Mosse, clerk, after an inquiry by the archd. of Berkshire into the vacancy and patronage. Chardstock, 10 Aug. 1410.

174 [Fo. 38/17] Exchange, on certificate of M. George Louthorp, treasurer of Salisbury cath., between John Wryght, chaplain of St. Mary's chantry in Lambourn (*Lamborne*) church; patron, William Hankford, knight—and Richard Gedesyng, vicar of Figheldean (*Fighelden*); patrons [illegible]. Ind. of Gedesyng: archd. of Berkshire. Chardstock, 17 Aug. 1410.

175 Institution of M. John Stone, clerk, B.C.L., to church of Berwick St. John (*Berewyke sancti Johannis*), vac. by death of Thomas Wysbech; patrons, abbess and conv. of Wilton. Ind.: archd. of Wiltshire. Chardstock, 22 Aug. 1410.

176 Institution of Thomas Shelford, chaplain, to church of Buckland Newton (*Boklond*), vac. by resig. of John Shelford, clerk; patron, Nicholas, bp. of Bath and Wells. Ind.: archd. of Dorset. Chardstock, 28 Aug. 1410.

177 Presentation, by Queen Joan, of Edward Prentys, clerk, to church of Winterbourne Came (*Wynterborne Caam*) received Chardstock, 19 June [*sic*] 1410. Prentys immediately obtained letters of inquiry addressed to the archd. of Dorset. Presentation by Thomas, bp. of Durham (*Dunelmen'*), and Prince John, constable of England and warden of the East March towards Scotland, of William Duresyn, his clerk, to the same church (by virtue of the custody of the alien priory of Frampton, granted them by the king during the war with France) received 4 Aug. Duresyn also obtained letters of inquiry. The archdeacon's reply, received 20 Aug., not being sufficiently clear, the bp. ordered a further inquiry into the right of presentation. The archdeacon's official certified, in letters received 30 Aug., that his inquiry found that Thomas, bp. of Durham, and Prince John were the rightful patrons, and that he had instituted William Duresyn.

178 [Fo. 38v/17v] Exchange, by authority of Thomas, bp. of Worcester, between M. John Tyssibury, rector of Tarrant Hinton (*Tarent Hyneton*); patrons, abbess and conv. of Shaftesbury (*Shafton*)—and Thomas Bubbewyth, rector of Hampton Lucy (*Hampton Episcopi*), dioc. Worcester, in person of Thomas Aileward, his proctor; patron, the bp. of Worcester. Ind. of Bubbewyth: archd. of Dorset. Sherborne (*Shirborn*), 9 Sept. 1410.

179 Exchange, on certificate of Alexander, bp. of Norwich, between John Everdon, junior, rector of Saxmundham (*Saxmondham*), dioc. Norwich—and Robert Draper, rector of Easthampstead (*Yeshampsted*), in person of William Culman, clerk, his proctor; patrons, prior and conv. of Hurley (*Hurlegh*). Ind. of Everdon: archd. of Berkshire. Sherborne, 13 Sept. 1410.

180 Exchange, by authority of Thomas, bp. of Worcester, between Reynold Perry, rector of Upway (*Upwey*), in person of Thomas Pony, clerk, his proctor; patron, the bp. of Salisbury—and Nicholas Tankard, rector of Whitchurch (*Whytchurch*), dioc. Worcester. Ind. of Tankard: archd. of Dorset. Sherborne, 13 Sept. 1410.

181 [Fo. 39/18] Exchange, by authority of M. Richard Bruton, vicar general of Nicholas, bp. of Bath and Wells, between John Lodere, vicar of East Coker (*Estcoker*), dioc. Bath and Wells—and Richard Spycer, vicar of Stockland (*Stokelond*); patrons, abbot and conv. of Milton (*Middelton*). Ind. of Lodere: archd. of Dorset. Sherborne, 12 Sept. 1410.

182 Exchange, by authority of Philip, bp. of Lincoln, between William Colet, rector of Catmore (*Cattemer*); patron, Walter Grendon, prior of hospital of St. John of Jerusalem in England—and Edmund Wodehouse, vicar of Preston Deanery (*Preston*), dioc. Lincoln, in person of Nicholas Fray, literate, his proctor. Ind. of Wodehouse: archd. of Berkshire. Sherborne, 13 Sept. 1410.

[Cf. Lincolnshire Archives Office, Reg. XIV (Repingdon) fos. 246v–247 for identification of Preston Deanery (Northants).]

183 Exchange, by authority of Robert, bp. of Hereford, between Roger Palmer, rector of Donnington (*Donyngton*), dioc. Hereford—and Thomas Kemele, vicar of Seagry (*Segre*); patrons, prior and conv. of Bradenstoke (*Bradenestok*). Ind. of Palmer: archd. of Wiltshire. Sherborne, 18 Sept. 1410.

184 Institution of Thomas Chipet, chaplain, to church of Fifield Bavant (*Fifhide*); patrons, prioress and conv. of St. Mary and St. Margaret of Dartford (*Derteford*). Ind.: archd. of Salisbury. Sherborne, 20 Sept. 1410.

185 [Fo. 39v/18v] Institution of John Pernam, chaplain, to chantry in St. Catherine the Virgin's chapel in the churchyard of St. Edmund's collegiate church, Salisbury; patrons, abbot and conv. of Abbotsbury (*Abbotesbury*). Ind.: provost of St. Edmund's. Sherborne, 20 Sept. 1410.

186 Letters granted to Thomas Chipet, rector of Fifield Bavant (*Fifhide*), for inquiry by archd. of Salisbury into the dilapidations left by M. William Spaddewyk, previous rector. Sherborne, 23 Sept. 1410.

187 Exchange, by authority of Henry, bp. of Winchester, between Robert Rydon, rector of Woolhampton (*Wolhampton*); patron, Walter Grendon, prior of hospital of St. John of Jerusalem in England—and John Grysnale, vicar of Fareham, dioc. Winchester. Ind. of Grysnale: archd. of Salisbury [*rectius* Berkshire]. Sherborne, 23 Sept. 1410.

188 Institution of John Cory *alias* Hochekyn, chaplain, to vicarage of North Bradley (*Northbradlegh*), vac. by resig. of John Yonge; patrons, rector and fellows of conventual church of Edington (*Edyngdon*). Ind.: archd. of Salisbury. Sherborne, 24 Sept. 1410.

189 Institution of Robert Clerk, chaplain, to church of Bradfield (*Bradfeld*), vac. by death of Robert Granereyn; patron, William Langford, knight. Ind.: archd. of Berkshire. Sherborne, 2 Oct. 1410.

190 [Fo. 40/19] Institution of John Tylton, chaplain, to church of Tarrant Monkton (*Tarent Monachorum*); patrons, abbot and conv. of Tewkesbury (*Teukesbury*), order of St. Benedict, dioc. Worcester. Ind.: archd. of Dorset. Sherborne, 6 Oct. 1410.

191 Exchange, by authority of Philip, bp. of Lincoln, between Thomas Drayton, rector of Didcot (*Dudcote*); patron, Edmund Hamdene, esquire—and John Warmyngton, rector of Drayton Beauchamp, dioc. Lincoln, in person of Nicholas Napton, clerk, his proctor. Ind. of Warmyngton: archd. of Berkshire. Ind. of Drayton: archd. of Buckingham (*Buckyngham*). Sherborne, 11 Oct. 1410.

192 Institution of John More, chaplain, to vicarage of Downton (*Dounton*); patrons, warden, fellows, priests and scholars of St. Mary's college, Winchester. Ind.: archd. of Salisbury. Salisbury, 20 Oct. 1410.

193 Institution of Edmund Braye, chaplain, in person of Thomas Bedyll, chaplain, his proctor, to St. Mary's chantry in Englefield (*Englefeld*) church, vac. by death of Philip Wodefold; patrons, for this turn, Edmund Hampden and William Fauwkener. Ind.: archd. of Berkshire. Salisbury, bishop's palace, 22 Oct. 1410.

194 Institution of M. John Perche, priest, in person of Edward Prentys, clerk, his proctor, to prebend or prebendal church of Stanton (*Staunton*) in Wilton conventual church, vac. by resig. of M. Richard Pittes; patrons, abbess and conv. of Wilton. Ind.: archd. of Wiltshire. Salisbury, 23 Oct. 1410.

195 [Fo. 40^{v}/19^{v}] Letter to John Gylmin, chaplain, collating him to the status of a priest in St. Edmund's collegiate church, Salisbury. Ind.: provost of St. Edmund's. Salisbury, bishop's palace, 26 Oct. 1410.

196 Exchange between John Kentyfi, vicar of Bishops Cannings (*Cannynges Episcopi*); patrons, dean and chapter of Salisbury, the church being appropriated to their use, at nomination of M. John Chitterne, *locumtenens et firmarius* in the said church—and Philip Goffe, rector of Melbury Osmond (*Mellebury Osmonde*); patron, Elizabeth Latamer. Ind. of Kentyfi: archd. of Dorset. Ind. of Goffe: archd. of Wiltshire. Salisbury, bishop's palace, 26 Oct. 1410.

197 Exchange, by authority of Henry, bp. of Winchester, between Robert Mere, rector of Little Wittenham (*Wyttenham Abbatis*); patrons, abbot and conv. of Abingdon (*Abyndon*)—and Robert Borugh, rector of Weyhill (*Wee*), dioc. Winchester, in person of Thomas Grysby, literate, his proctor. Ind. of Borugh: archd. of Berkshire. Woodford (*Wodeford*) manor, 28 Oct. 1410.

198 Exchange, by authority of Thomas, abp. of Canterbury, primate of England and papal legate, between William Welleford, rector of Draycot Cerne (*Draycote Cerne*); patron, Edward Cerne, *domicellus*—and John Lavyngton, vicar of Teynham (*Tenham*), dioc. Canterbury. Ind. of Lavyngton: archd. of Wiltshire. Woodford manor, 1 Nov. 1410.

199 [Fo. 41/20] Exchange, by authority of Nicholas, bp. of Bath and Wells, between Thomas Bubbewyth, rector of Tarrant Hinton (*Tarent Henyton, Tarent Hyneton*), in person of Thomas Shelford, clerk, his proctor; patrons, abbess and conv. of Shaftesbury (*Shafton*)—and Henry Morey, rector of Laverton, dioc. Bath and Wells, in person of Richard Huppes, clerk, his proctor. Ind. of Morey: archd. of Dorset. Woodford manor, 1 Nov. 1410.

200 Institution of Thomas Bubbewyth, clerk, to church of Ashbury (*Asschebury* or *Aysshbury*), vac. by resig. of Thomas Shelford, clerk; patron, Nicholas, bp. of Bath and Wells. Ind.: archd. of Berkshire. Woodford manor, 3 Nov. 1410.

201 Exchange, by authority of Henry, bp. of Winchester, between John Tye, rector of Shaw (*Shawe*), in person of John Marschall, chaplain; patrons, Stephen Ansteswell and Nicholas North—and John Wryght, vicar of Wandsworth (*Wandelesworth*), dioc. Winchester. Ind. of Wryght: archd. of Berkshire. Lacock (*Lakock*) monastery, 11 Nov. 1410.

202 Institution of Walter Perkyn, chaplain, to vicarage of Harwell (*Harewell*), vac. by resig. of William Bonnok; patron, dean of St. Nicholas's free chapel in Wallingford (*Walyngford*) castle, with the assent of the other chaplains. Ind.: archd. of Berkshire. Wroughton (*Elyngdon*), 17 Nov. 1410.

203 [Fo. 41v/20v] Institution of John Seymour, chaplain, in person of John Toprest, literate, his proctor, to church of Hinton Waldrist (*Henton*), vac. by resig. of John de Tylton; patron, King Henry, the possessions of the earl of Hereford being in his hands as part of his dukedom of Lancaster, as established by an inquiry. Ind.: archd. of Berkshire. Speen (*Spyne*), 3 Dec. 1410.

[For Hinton Waldrist, see *VCH Berks.*, iv. 464.]

204 Collation to M. William Clement M.A., bishop's clerk, of vicarage of Cumnor (*Comnor*). Inductors: archd. of Berkshire, M. John Fyton, canon of Salisbury, and M. John Turry, commissary general in archdeaconries of Berkshire and Wiltshire. Sonning (*Sonnyng*), 7 Dec. 1410.

205 Exchange, by authority of Philip, bp. of Lincoln, between Nicholas Masonn, vicar of Sutton Benger (*Sutton*); patron, the bp. of Salisbury—and Thomas Exhale, vicar of Segenhoe (*Segenho*), dioc. Lincoln. Ind. of Exhale: archd. of Wiltshire. Sonning, 11 Dec. 1410.

206 Institution of Thomas Beworthy to vicarage of Chisledon (*Chesulden*), vac. by resig. of Richard Brewes; patron, John Mynty, rector of Chisledon. Ind.: archd. of Wiltshire. Sonning, 18 Dec. 1410.

207 Exchange between John Grangere, rector of Wytham; [patron not given]—and Thomas Asselete, vicar of Pusey; patron, the bp. of Salisbury. Ind. of both: archd. of Berkshire. Sonning, 18 Dec. 1410.

208 Institution of Robert Gybon, chaplain, to vicarage of Loders (*Lodres*), vac. by death of John Schepe; patron, prior of Loders. Ind.: archd. of Dorset. Sonning, 5 Jan. 1411.

209 [Fo. 42/21] Institution of William Payn, chaplain, to chantry in Sparsholt (*Spershold*) church, vac. by resig. of Richard Wodyngton; patron, Robert de Lamare, esquire. Ind.: archd. of Berkshire. Sonning, 18 Jan. 1411.

210 Exchange, by authority of Henry, bp. of Winchester, between William Baker, vicar of Littleton Drew (*Lytilton Drew*); patron, the bp. of Salisbury—and Henry Tone, vicar of Carisbrooke (*Caresbrok*), Isle of Wight (*Insula Vecta*), dioc. Winchester, in person of John Speek, literate, his proctor. Ind. of Tone: archd. of Wiltshire. Sonning, 21 Jan. 1411.

211 Exchange between John Pere, rector of Bishopstrow (*Busshoppestre*); patrons, prior and conv. of St. Mary Magdalene of Monkton Farleigh (*Farlegh*), order of Cluny—and Gilbert Capeland, rector of Wraxall (*Wroxhale*); patron, Robert Lovell, *domicellus*. Ind. of Pere: archd. of Dorset. Ind. of Capeland: archd. of Dorset [*rectius* Salisbury]. Sonning, 26 Jan. 1411.

212 Exchange, by authority of Thomas, bp. of Worcester, between M. Fulk Stafford, rector of Ditchampton (*Dichampton*); patron, Humphrey

Stafford, lord of Ditchampton—and John Smythes, rector of Naunton (*Newnton on the Wold*), dioc. Worcester, in person of Peter Wairde, clerk, his proctor; patron, the same bp. of Worcester. Ind. of Smythes: archd. of Salisbury. Sonning, 27 Jan. 1411.

[For Naunton, see *Rudder's New History of Gloucestershire* (Cirencester, 1779), pp. 559–61.]

213 [Fo. 42v/21v] Institution of John Aynolf, chaplain, to church of Sulham (*Sulleham*), vac. by resig. of Henry Lynne; patron, Nicholas de Carru, *domicellus*. Ind.: archd. of Berkshire. Sonning, 5 Feb. 1411.

214 Exchange, by authority of Thomas, bp. of Worcester, between John Enfeld, rector of Porton (*Pourton*), in person of Robert Peion, chaplain, his proctor; patron, Henry Chawsy, *domicellus*—and William Lorymer, vicar of Toddington (*Todyngton*), dioc. Worcester. Ind of Lorymer: archd. of Wiltshire. Sonning, 7 Feb. 1411.

215 Institution of Walter Collee, clerk, in person of Richard Carcy, clerk, his proctor, to church of Woolhampton (*Wolhampton*), vac. by resig. of John Grysnale; patron, Walter Grendon, prior of hospital of St. John of Jerusalem in England. Ind.: archd. of Berkshire. Sonning, 8 Feb. 1411.

216 Exchange, on certificate of M. Richard Brutton, chancellor of Wells cath., vicar general of Nicholas, bp. of Bath and Wells, between Walter Wylmot, vicar of Ford, dioc. Bath and Wells—and John Mascal, rector of Great Chalfield (*Estchaldefeld*); patron, Constance, widow of Henry de la River, knight. Ind. of Wylmot: archd. of Wiltshire. Sonning, 9 Feb. 1411.

[For Great Chalfield, see *VCH Wilts.*, vii. 59–66.]

217 [Fo. 43/22] Exchange, by authority of Thomas, abp. of Canterbury, primate of England and papal legate, between Thomas Smyth, rector of Easton Grey (*Eston Gray*); patrons, abbot and conv. of St. Peter, Gloucester (*Glouc'*)—and William Goldsmyth, vicar of St. Margaret at Cliffe (*Clyve*), dioc. Canterbury. Ind. of Goldsmyth: archd. of Wiltshire. Sonning, 10 Feb. 1411.

218 Institution of Stephen Gyllyngham, chaplain, to church of Holy Trinity, Wilton (*Wylton*); patrons, prior and conv. of St. Denis, by Southampton (*Suthampton*). Ind.: archd. of Salisbury. Sonning, 12 Feb. 1411.

219 Exchange, by authority of Henry, bp. of Winchester, between Thomas Tybold, rector of Stratford Toney (*Stratford Tony*), in person of John Pountenye, clerk, his proctor; patron, King Henry—and Robert Meer, rector of Weyhill (*Wee*), dioc. Winchester, in person of John Gradelee, literate, his proctor. Ind. of Meer: archd. of Salisbury. Sonning, 13 Feb. 1411.

220 Exchange, on certificate of John, bp. of Llandaff, between John Attewater, canon of Llandaff cath. and prebendary of St. Andrew or Fairwater (*Feyrwater*) in the same—and M. John Payn, rector or warden of chapel of St. Catherine of Wanborough (*Wamburgh*); patron, Maud, lady of Lovell and Holand. Ind. of Attewater: archd. of Wiltshire. Sonning, 21 Feb. 1411.

221 [Fo. 43ᵛ/22ᵛ] Institution of John Bod, chaplain, to church of Stanford-in-the-Vale (*Stanforde*), vac. by death of William Barre; patron, for this turn, John Golaffr, as established by an inquiry. Ind.: archd. of Berkshire. Sonning, 28 Feb. 1411.

222 Exchange, on certificate of Thomas More, dean of St. Paul's cath., London, and the same chapter, between Nicholas Fort, vicar of Aldworth (*Aldeworth*); patrons, prioress and conv. of Bromhall (*Bromhale*)—and William Sandiacre, chaplain of one of the two chantries for the soul of Roger Waltham and of a moiety of the third part of a chantry for the soul of Fulk Basset, in St. Paul's. Ind. of Sandiacre: archd. of Berkshire. Sonning, 28 Feb. 1411.

223 Exchange, by authority of Robert, bp. of Chichester, between John Tappere, chaplain of St. Mary's chantry in Handley (*Hanle*) chapel, dependent on Iwerne church; patron, Adam Mottrum, prebendary or rector of Iwerne prebendal church—and William Gyffard, rector of Stopham, dioc. Chichester, in person of John Maldon, his proctor. Ind. of Gyffard: archd. of Dorset. Sonning, 1 March 1411.

224 [Fo. 44/23] Institution of William Ocle, chaplain, to church of Chicklade (*Chykkelade*), vac. by death of Robert Langerygge; patron, Thomas Berkeley, lord of Berkeley. Ind.: archd. of Wiltshire [*rectius* Salisbury].[1] Sonning, 6 March 1411.

[1. MS. margin: *Sar'* and *error*.]

225 Exchange between Stephen Blankcombe, rector of Fonthill Bishop (*Netherfontell*); patron, John Inge, *domicellus*—and John Leante, rector of Beechingstoke (*Bycchyngstok*); patrons, abbess and conv. of Shaftesbury (*Shafton*). Ind. of both: archd. of Salisbury. Sonning, 6 March 1411.

226 Exchange, by authority of Nicholas, bp. of Bath and Wells, between Gilbert Capelond, rector of Bishopstrow (*Bysshopestre*); patrons, prior and conv. of Monkton Farleigh (*Farle Monachorum*)—and M. Thomas Frome, vicar of Burnham, dioc. Bath and Wells. Ind. of Frome: archd. of Salisbury. London inn, 8 March 1411.

227 Institution of William Rodborn, chaplain, in person of Edward Wych, clerk, his proctor, to vicarage of Chaddleworth (*Chadelworth*), vac. by death of John North; patrons, prior and conv. of Poughley (*Poghlee*). Ind.: archd. of Berkshire. London inn, 12 March 1411.

228 Exchange, by authority of Nicholas, bp. of Bath and Wells, between John Craas, rector of Lydlinch (*Lydelynche*); patron, Ives FitzWaryn, knight—and John Muleward, vicar of North Curry (*Northcory*), dioc. Bath and Wells. Muleward protested that if he should happen to be ejected from Lydlinch church for any reason other than his own failing, he would return to his vicarage, notwithstanding his resignation and exchange. Ind. of Muleward: archd. of Dorset. London, 13 March 1411.

229 [Fo. 44^{v}/23^{v}] Exchange, by authority of Henry, bp. of Winchester, between Nicholas Welde, vicar of Basildon (*Basselden, Bastelden*); patrons, warden and priests of St. John the Baptist's collegiate church, Shottesbrook (*Shotesbrok*)—and John Whatecombe, vicar of Whitchurch (*Whytchurche*), dioc. Winchester; patron, the same bp. of Winchester. Ind. of Whatecombe: archd. of Berkshire. London, 14 March 1411.

230 Institution of John Smyth to church of Stour Provost (*Stoureprewes*), vac. by resig. of Henry Blakburn; patron, King Henry. Ind: archd. of Dorset. London inn, 16 March 1411.

231 Institution of Henry Merston to [free] chapel of Sherston Pinkney (*Sherston Pynkeny*), vac. by resig. of John Westhorp; patron, William Esturmy, knight. Ind.: archd. of Wiltshire. London inn, 18 March 1411.

[For Sherston Pinkney, formerly in Sherston, Wilts., see *Collections of John Aubrey*, pp. 109–10 and n.]

232 Mandate of Nicholas, bp. of Bath and Wells, for the induction of John Dyppyll *alias* Brymesgrave, priest, recently collated to the prebend of Warminster or Luxville (*Warmynstre alias Luxvile*) in Wells cath., into the *corpus* of the prebend situated in dioc. Salisbury. London inn, 28 Feb. 1411. The archd. of Salisbury was ordered to induct, and to notify the bp. of Bath and Wells. London inn, 20 March 1411.

[Fo. 45/24] REGISTRUM REVERENDI IN CHRISTO PATRIS ET DOMINI DOMINI ROBERTI DEI GRACIA SAR' EPISCOPI DE PERMUTACIONIBUS INSTITUCIONIBUS ET COLLACIONIBUS BENEFICIORUM DE ANNO DOMINI MILLESIMO QUADRINGENTESIMO UNDECIMO

233 Institution of Richard [surname illegible], chaplain, in person of M. Richard [surname illegible], clerk, his proctor, to vicarage of Ardington (*Ardyngton*); patrons, prior and conv. of Bicester (*Burucestr'*), dioc. Lincoln. Ind.: archd. of Berkshire. Sonning (*Sonnyng*), [date illegible].

[Richard Richevile exchanged this benefice 9 June 1419 (Reg. Chandeler, pt. i fo. 21).]

234 Institution of William Erl, chaplain, in person of William Franhurst, literate, his proctor, to church of Kingston Deverill (*Kyngeston Deverell*), vac. by resig. of John Blounham; patron, Peter Stantor, esquire. Ind.: archd. of Salisbury. Sonning, [date illegible] Apr. 1411.

235 Institution of Nicholas Capron, clerk, to church of Kington Magna (*Kyngton Magna*), vac. by resig. of M. John Forster; patron, John Tiptoft, knight. Ind.: archd. of Dorset. Sonning, 3 Apr. 1411.

236 Exchange, by authority of Thomas, bp. of Worcester, between John Wodeford, vicar of Ashton Keynes (*Asshton*); patrons, abbot and conv. of Tewkesbury (*Teukesbury*)—and William Magot, rector of Minchinhampton (*Munchynhampton*), dioc. Worcester, in person of Simon Smyth, literate, his proctor. Ind. of Magot: archd. of Wiltshire. Sonning, 4 Apr. 1411.

237 Institution of Richard Wyton to vicarage of Winkfield (*Wynkefeld*); patrons, for this turn, dean and chapter of Salisbury, to whom the church is appropriated, united and annexed, there being no *firmarius* nor *locumtenens*. Ind.: archd. of Berkshire. Sonning, 3 Apr. 1411.

[Cf. Vyring, pp. 59, 60, for conflict between bp. and chapter over bishop's alleged refusal to admit Wyton, Aug. 1411.]

238 [Fo. 45v/24v][1] Inquiry into the right of patronage of vicarage of Aldermaston (*Aldermanston*), the decision being given in favour of the king.

[1. This folio is affected by damp and is virtually illegible.]

239 [Fo. 46/25] Exchange, on certificate of Philip, bp. of Lincoln, between John Belyng, vicar of Aldermaston (*Aldermanston*); patron, King Henry—and Joseph Scovyle, rector of South Kelsey (*Southkelsie*), dioc. Lincoln. Ind. of Scovyle: archd. of Berkshire. [No other details legible.]

240 Institution of Martin Osebourne, chaplain, to church of Chilfrome (*Childefrome*); patrons, Humphrey Stafford, knight, and John Fauntleroy. Ind.: archd. of Dorset. Sonning, 9 Apr. 1411.

241 Institution of John Alfred to vicarage of Cranborne (*Craneburn*); patrons, abbot and conv. of Tewkesbury (*Teukesbury*), dioc. Worcester. Ind.: archd. of Dorset. Sonning, 16 Apr. 1411.

242 Institution of Adam Brystowe, chaplain, to church of Studland (*Stondelonde*), vac. by resig. of Thomas Robert; patrons, for this turn, William Alisander and Edith, his wife, Roger Stourton and Alice, his wife, and Elizabeth de la Bere, as established by an inquiry. Ind.: archd. of Dorset. Sonning, 18 Apr. 1411.

243 [Fo. 46v/25v] Institution of Walter Burgh, chaplain, in person of Thomas M. [illegible], clerk, his proctor, to church of Melbury Bubb (*Melburybubbe*), vac. by resig. of Martin Osebourne; [patrons illegible]. Ind.: archd. of Dorset. [Place illegible], 20 Apr. 1411.

244 Exchange, by authority of Henry, bp. of Winchester, between John Coke, vicar of Thatcham (*Thacham*); patrons, abbot and conv. of Reading

(*Radyng*)—and Edmund Barbour, rector of Albury (*Aldebury*), dioc. Winchester. Ind. of Barbour: archd. of Berkshire. Thatcham, 20 Apr. 1411.

245 Institution of Hugh Cotus to church of Manningford Abbots (*Manyngford Abbatis*), vac. by resig. of John Clerk; patrons, abbot and conv. of St. Peter, Winchester. Ind.: archd. of Wiltshire. Ramsbury (*Remmesbury*), 21 Apr. 1411.

246 Exchange between Richard Hamme, rector of Boxford (*Boxore*); patrons, abbot and conv. of Abingdon (*Abyndon*)—and William Broun, chaplain of Holy Trinity chantry in Hungerford church; patron, the bp. of Salisbury. Ind. of Broun: archd. of Berkshire. Ind. of Hamme: vicar of Hungerford. Potterne, 22 Apr. 1411.

247 Institution of Ralph Thomas, in person of Maurice Merton, clerk, his proctor, to church of Clewer (*Clewere*); patron, John Cifrewast, *domicellus*, as established by an inquiry. Ind.: archd. of Berkshire. Potterne, 24 Apr. 1411.

248 [Fo. 47/26] Exchange, by authority of Philip, bp. of Lincoln, between Edmund Wodehous, rector of Catmore (*Catmere*); patron, prior of hospital of St. John of Jerusalem in England—and John Shoveler, rector of St. Andrew, Huntingdon (*Huntyngdon*), dioc. Lincoln, in person of Richard Gourley, clerk, his proctor. Ind. of Shoveler: archd. of Berkshire. Potterne, 30 Apr. 1411.

249 Institution of Peter Freman, chaplain, to wardenship of house or chantry of St. Michael, Bridport (*Brydeport*); patron, Thomas Moyne, rector of Bridport. Ind.: archd. of Dorset. Potterne, 1 May 1411.

250 Institution of John FytzJon, chaplain, to church of Pangbourne (*Pangeborne*), vac. by death of Walter Clynton; patrons, abbot and conv. of Reading (*Radyng*). Ind.: archd. of Berkshire. Potterne, 1 May 1411.

251 Institution of Peter Hynewyk, chaplain, in person of William Alberton, clerk, his proctor, to vicarage of Cholsey (*Cholseye*), vac. by death of Richard Bannebury; patrons, abbot and conv. of Reading. Ind.: archd. of Berkshire. Potterne, 3 May 1411.

252 Exchange, by authority of Richard, bp. of London, between Richard Schypley, rector of Milston (*Myldeston*); patron, Francis de Court, knight, lord of Pembroke (*Pembr'*), guardian of Maurice de Berkeley, a minor, son and heir of Maurice de Berkeley, knight—and M. John Appulton, rector of Lambourne (*Lamborne*), dioc. London. Ind. of Appulton, archd. of Salisbury. Potterne, 4 May 1411.

253 [Fo. 47^{v}/26^{v}] Exchange between John Witham, rector of Teffont Evias (*Teffounte Ewyas*); patron, Joan, widow of Thomas Hungerford, knight, lady of Teffont—and Nicholas Baker *alias* Haydon, rector of Ashley (*Asshelegh*), in person of John Chamberlayne, his proctor; patrons, William Hankford, knight, William Stourton, William Poulet, William Besyles, esquire, and John Prat, rector of Hemington (*Hemyngton*), dioc. Bath and Wells. Ind. of Witham: archd. of Wiltshire. [No ind. given for Baker.] Potterne, 4 May 1411.

254 Institution of Thomas Hervy, chaplain, in person of John Heiceton, his proctor, to vicarage of Latton; patrons, abbot and conv. of St. Mary, Cirencester (*Cirencestr'*), dioc. Worcester. Ind.: archd. of Wiltshire. Potterne, 12 May 1411.

255 Institution of John Plebs, chaplain, to church of Great Chalfield (*Estchalvelde*); patron, Constance, widow of Henry de Larever, knight. Ind.: archd. of Wiltshire. Potterne, 24 May 1411.

256 Institution of John Smyth, chaplain, to church of St. Rowald, Shaftesbury (*Schaftysbury*); patrons, abbess and conv. of Shaftesbury (*Schafton*). Ind.: archd. of Dorset. Potterne, 7 June 1411.

257 Exchange, by authority of Thomas, abp. of Canterbury, primate of England and papal legate, then on a metropolitan visitation of the city and diocese of Lincoln, between Richard Saundre, vicar of Bisham (*Bustelsham, Bustlesham*); patron, Walter Grendon, prior of hospital of St. John of Jerusalem in England—and John Martyn, vicar of Little Marlow (*Parva Merlaw*), dioc. Lincoln. Ind. of Martyn: archd. of Berkshire. Potterne, 7 June 1411.

258 [Fo. 48/27] Exchange, by authority of Robert, bp. of Chichester, between John Petevyne, rector of Hemsworth (*Westhemelesworth, Westhemnelsworth*), in person of John Forde, his proctor; patrons, abbot and conv. of Milton (*Middelton*)—and Thomas Weston, vicar of Didling (*Dudelyng*), dioc. Chichester. Ind. of Weston: archd. of Dorset. Potterne, 7 June 1411.

259 Collation to M. John Slodewell B.C.L. of church [*rectius* vicarage][1] of Winterbourne Whitchurch (*Albi Monasterii*), reserving an annual pension of 20 marks [£13 6*s* 8*d*] to the provost and college of St. Edmund, Salisbury, and one of 20 shillings to the abbot and conv. of Milton (*Middelton*), at the usual terms. Ind.: archd. of Dorset. Potterne, 13 June 1411.

[1. Cf. Hutchins, i. 202.]

260 Exchange, on certificate of M. Richard Bruton, chancellor of Wells cath., vicar general of Nicholas, bp. of Bath and Wells, then abroad, between William Plont, vicar of South Stoke (*Southstok*), dioc. Bath and Wells—and John Nettleton *alias* Knoyle, rector of Tidpit (*Tutpyt*); patrons, abbot and conv. of Glastonbury (*Glaston*). Ind. of Plont: archd. of Salisbury. Potterne, 15 June 1411.

261 Exchange, by authority of Robert, bp. of Chichester, between Richard Scheborn, rector of Ufton Robert (*Ofton Robert*); patron, William Perkyn, *scutifer*, of dioc. Salisbury—and Richard Fygge, vicar of Climping (*Climpyng, Clymping*), dioc. Chichester. Ind. of Fygge: archd. of Berkshire. Potterne, 19[1] June 1411.

[1. This number is written by a different hand, over an erasure.]

262 [Fo. 48^{v}/27^{v}] Exchange between John Mason, rector of Batcombe (*Battecombe*); patron, Humphrey Stafford, knight—and Nicholas Tankard, rector of Upway (*Hupwey, Upwey*); patron, the bp. of Salisbury. Ind. of both: archd. of Dorset. Potterne, 26 June 1411.

263 Exchange, by authority of Henry, bp. of Winchester, between John Moore, vicar of Downton (*Dounton*); patrons, warden, fellows, priests and scholars of St. Mary's college, Winchester—and John Pomeray, rector of St. Faith, Winchester. Ind. of Pomeray: archd. of Salisbury. Sherborne (*Schirborn*), 10 July 1411.

264 Exchange, by authority of Thomas, bp. of Worcester, between William Stacy, rector of Hazelbury (*Haselbur'*); patrons, prior and conv. of Bradenstoke, order of St. Augustine—and Thomas Stub, vicar of Preston, dioc. Worcester. Ind of Stub: archd. of Wiltshire. Sherborne, 11 July 1411.

265 [Fo. 49/28] Exchange between William Percy, vicar of St. James, Shaftesbury (*Schafton*); patrons, abbess and conv. of Shaftesbury—and Walter Tynker, rector of St. Andrew, Winterbourne Houghton (*Wynterborn Houhton, Wynterborn Houhton*); patron, Ives FytzWaryn, knight. Ind. of both: archd. of Dorset. Sherborne, 11 July 1411.

266 Institution of Thomas Dran, chaplain, to church of St. Nicholas, Edmondsham (*Edmundesham*); patron, John Garston, esquire, of the Isle of Wight (*Insulavecta*). Ind.: archd. of Dorset. Sherborne, 13 July 1411.

267 Exchange, by authority of Thomas, abp. of Dublin, between John Umfray, canon of St. Patrick's cath., Dublin, and prebendary of Newcastle by Lyons (*de Novocastro iuxta Lyons*) in the same; patron, the same abp.—and John Warmyngton, rector of Didcot (*Dudcote*); patron, Edmund Hamden. Ind. of Umfray: archd. of Berkshire. Sherborne, 18 July 1411.

268 Institution of Robert Cammel, clerk, M.A., to church of Tidpit (*Tudeput*), vac. by death of William Plonte; patrons, abbot and conv. of Glastonbury (*Glaston*). Ind.: archd. of Salisbury. Sherborne, 20 July 1411.

269 Collation to John Conge, chaplain, of church of Brixton Deverill (*Bryxton Deverell*). Ind.: archd. of Salisbury. Sherborne, 23 July 1411.

[Cf. **700** and Appendix A IV.]

270 Institution of Walter Salesbury, chaplain, to vicarage of Hullavington (*Hunlavyngton*), vac. by resig. of John Salesbury; patron, for this turn, Queen Joan. Ind.: archd. of Wiltshire. Sherborne, 29 July 1411.

271 [Fo. 49v/28v] Exchange, by authority of Robert, bp. of Chichester, between John Okefforde, chaplain of St. Catherine's chantry in Little Critchell (*Parva Kyrchull*)[1] church; patron, John Chidiok, esquire—and Philip Palmere, vicar of Barlavington (*Berlavyngton*), dioc. Chichester. Ind. of Palmere: archd. of Dorset. Sherborne, 28 July 1411.

[1. Given as Critchell More (*Morkirchill*) in *The Episcopal Register of Robert Rede, ordinis predicatorum, Lord Bishop of Chichester, 1397–1415*, ed. C. Deedes (Sussex Record Soc., viii, xi, 1908–10), ii. 314. There was only one church for the two places and it was variously described, though 'Critchell More' was the more usual name (Hutchins, iii. 123, 130).]

272 Exchange between Nicholas Tankard, rector of Batcombe (*Batecombe*); patron, Humphrey Stafford, knight—and Robert Pylard, vicar of Portisham (*Portesham*); patrons, abbot and conv. of Abbotsbury (*Abbotesbury*). Ind. of both: archd. of Dorset. Sherborne, 9 Aug. 1411.

273 Collation to William Marchall, chaplain, of chantry of St. Catherine and St. Margaret in Market Lavington (*Lavyngton Forum*) church. Ind.: archd. of Salisbury. Sherborne, 14 Aug. 1411.

274 Exchange, by authority of Nicholas, bp. of Bath and Wells, between Robert Bochard, vicar of Compton Chamberlayne (*Compton Chamberleyn*); patron, Robert Bussh, provost of St. Edmund's collegiate church, Salisbury—and Edmund Gamage, vicar of Kilmersdon (*Kynmersdon*), dioc. Bath and Wells. Ind. of Gamage: archd. of Salisbury. Sherborne, 21 Aug. 1411.

275 Exchange, by authority of Nicholas, bp. of Bath and Wells, between Thomas Grys, vicar of Norton; patrons, abbot and conv. of Malmesbury—and Robert Stoyt, vicar of Stockland Bristol (*Stoklond Gaunt*), dioc. Bath and Wells. Ind. of Stoyt: archd. of Wiltshire. Chardstock (*Cherdestok*), 4 Sept. 1411.

[For Stockland Bristol, see Collinson, i. 247.]

276 [Fo. 50/29] Institution, on certificate of Thomas, abbot of Reading (*Radyng*), of Roger Langelegh, chaplain, to church of Woolhampton (*Wolhampton*), vac. by resig. of Walter Colle; patron, Walter Grendon, prior of hospital of St. John of Jerusalem in England, as established by an inquiry held by the abbot of Reading. Sonning (*Sonnyng*), 13 Sept. 1411.

277 Exchange, by authority of Philip, bp. of Lincoln, between Henry Tone, vicar of Littleton Drew (*Littelton Drew*); patron, the bp. of Salisbury—and Richard Gode, vicar of South Stoke (*Stoke Abbatis*), dioc. Lincoln, in person of William Maundevyle, literate, his proctor. Ind. of Gode: archd. of Wiltshire. London, 19 Sept. 1411.

278 Institution of William Pacare, chaplain, in person of Richard Willesdon, clerk, his proctor, to church of Caundle Purse (*Caundell Purs*), vac. by death of William Archor; patrons, abbess and conv. of Shaftesbury (*Shafton*). Ind.: archd. of Dorset. London, 21 Sept. 1411.

279 Exchange, by authority of Philip, bp. of Lincoln, between John Langevyle, canon of Salisbury cath. and prebendary of Axford (*Haxford*) in the same; patron, the bp. of Salisbury—and William Werkeman, canon of Lincoln cath. and prebendary of Bedford Major (*Bedeford Maior*) in the same. Inductors of Werkeman: dean and chapter of Salisbury. London, 25 Sept. 1411.

280 Exchange, by authority of Nicholas, bp. of Bath and Wells, between Richard Wete of Brampton, vicar of East Garston (*Estgarston*); patrons, prioress and conv. of Amesbury (*Ambresbury*)—and William of Dalton, rector of Radstock (*Radestoke*), dioc. Bath and Wells. Ind. of William of Dalton: archd. of Berkshire. Sonning (*Sonnyng*), 27 Sept. 1411.

281 [Fo. 50ᵛ/29ᵛ] Institution of John Beke, chaplain, to chantry in Handley (*Henlegh*) chapel, vac. by resig. of William Gyffard; patron, M. Adam Mottrum, canon in conventual church of Shaftesbury (*Shafton*), and prebendary of Iwerne Minster (*Iwerne Mynstr'*). Ind.: archd. of Dorset. Salisbury, 21 Oct. 1411.

282 Institution of Robert Reynhill, deacon, to vicarage of Buckland (*Boklond*); patrons, rector and conv. of Edington (*Edyngdon*). Ind.: archd. of Berkshire. Potterne, 15 Oct. 1411.

283 Institution of John Carter, chaplain, to church of Whelpley (*Welpeley*), vac. by resig. of William Gannok; patron, Margaret Englissh, widow of Philip Dauntesey. Ind.: archd. of Salisbury. Salisbury, 21 Oct. 1411.

284 Institution of Henry Gyles, chaplain, to church of Wylye (*Wyly*), vac. by resig. of M. Richard Puttys; patrons, abbess and conv. of Wilton. Ind.: archd. of Salisbury, Salisbury, 22 Oct. 1411.

285 Institution of Thomas Warr, chaplain, to church of Langton Matravers (*Langeton*), vac. by death of John Aeton; patron, John d'Arundell, knight, lord of Mautravers. Ind.: archd. of Dorset. Salisbury, 23 Oct. 1411.

286 Institution of Edward Crull, chaplain, to chantry in St. Thomas the Martyr's church, Salisbury, vac. by death of William Uphaven *alias* Colman; patrons, dean and chapter of Salisbury. Ind.: dean and chapter of Salisbury. Salisbury, 24 Oct. 1411.

287 Exchange, by authority of Philip, bp. of Lincoln, between John Wattecombe, vicar of Basildon (*Bastylden*); patrons, warden and chaplains of

St. John the Baptist's collegiate church, Shottesbrook (*Shottesbrok*)—and Richard Rayour, rector of Water Stratford (*West Stratford*), dioc. Lincoln. Ind. of Rayour: archd. of Berkshire. Salisbury, 24 Oct. 1411.

288 [Fo. 51/30] Institution of Oliver Dyneley, clerk, to portion of Haxton (*Hakeleston*); patron, Percival Sowdan, knight. Ind.: archd. of Salisbury. Potterne, 2 Nov. 1411.

289 Institution of Clement Stanton, chaplain, to church of Berwick St. Leonard (*Berwyk sancti Leonardi*), vac. by resig. of Henry Gyles; patrons, abbess and conv. of Shaftesbury (*Shafton*). Ind.: archd. of Salisbury. Potterne, 2 Nov. 1411.

290 Institution of Henry Stowt, chaplain, to church of Fyfield (*Fyffyde*), vac. by death of William Bladyngton; patrons, Thomas Chaucer, Robert James and William Holte. Ind.: archd. of Berkshire. Potterne, 2 Nov. 1411.

291 Exchange, on certificate of Dean Thomas More and the chapter of St. Paul's cath., London, between Peter Hynewik, vicar of Cholsey; patrons, abbot and conv. of Reading (*Radyng*)—and John Alby, warden of St. Radegund's free chapel in the crypt of St. Paul's. Ind. of Alby: archd. of Berkshire. Colebrook (*Colbruk*), 7 Nov. 1411.

292 Institution of Thomas Grene, chaplain, to church of Ditchampton (*Dychampton*); patron, Humphrey Stafford, *domicellus*. Ind. of Grene: archd. of Salisbury. London, 11 Nov. 1411.

293 Exchange, by authority of Thomas, bp. of Worcester, between Philip Lye, rector of Little Chalfield (*Chaldefeld*); patron, John Rous de Jumer, esquire—and John Wyseman, warden of Beauvale chantry, dioc. Worcester. Ind. of Wyseman: archd. of Salisbury. London, 12 Nov. 1411.

[For Beauvale chantry in Coberley church, Glos., cf. *Register of Henry Wakefield, Bishop of Worcester, 1375–95*, ed. W.P. Marett (Worcs. Hist. Soc. new ser., vii, 1972), nos. 172, 191, 527, 629.]

294 [Fo. 51^v/20^v] Exchange, by authority of Nicholas, bp. of Bath and Wells, between John Clere *alias* Smyth, subdean of Salisbury cath.; patron, the bp. of Salisbury—and John Hullyng, rector of Limington (*Lymyngton*), dioc. Bath and Wells. London, 14 Nov. 1411.

295 Letter to John Hullyng, chaplain, collating him to the subdeanery of Salisbury cath. [as in **294**].

296 Mandate to the dean and chapter of Salisbury to admit John Hullyng [as in **294**].

297 Oath of John Hullyng as subdean that his archidiaconal jurisdiction in the city and suburb of Salisbury, outside the cath., is independent of the jurisdiction of the dean of Salisbury. Witnesses, M. William Lyndewode D.Cn. & C.L. and Oliver Dyngley, clerk (dioc. Winchester).

298 Exchange, by authority of Edmund, bp. of Exeter, between John Goldeney, rector of North Tidworth (*Northtudeworth Meeles*); patrons, for this turn, Maud, countess of Salisbury, mother of Thomas de Monte Acuto, earl of Salisbury, William Stourton, Richard Hertecombe and John Bailly, attornies and proctors of Earl Thomas, then abroad—and Robert Wantynge, warden of Ottery St. Mary (*Otery St. Mary*) collegiate church, dioc. Exeter, and canon and prebendary in the same church (annexed to the office of warden). Ind. of Wantynge: archd. of Salisbury. London, 23 Nov. 1411.

299 [Fo. 52/31] Exchange, by authority of Thomas, bp. of Worcester, between Richard Lynde, rector of Piddlehinton (*Hynepodyll* or *Podylhynton*); patron, Henry, bp. of Winchester—and Robert Holbrok, rector of Welford-on-Avon (*Welveford*), dioc. Worcester. Ind. of Holbrok: archd. of Dorset. London, 25 Nov. 1411.

300 Exchange, by authority of Nicholas, bp. of Bath and Wells, between William Colbat, rector of Bremilham (*Bremulham*); patron, King Henry, guardian of Walter Dauntesey, a minor, son and heir of the late John Dauntesey, knight, tenant-in-chief—and John atte Water, vicar of Henton (*Henton Monachorum*), dioc. Bath and Wells. Ind. of atte Water: archd. of Wiltshire. London, 27 Nov. 1411.

301 Exchange, by authority of Thomas, bp. of Worcester, between John Begynton, vicar of Fisherton Delamere (*Fischerton*); patrons, prior and conv. of Maiden Bradley (*Maydynbradele*)—and Robert Pyion, vicar of Guiting (*Guytyng*), dioc. Worcester. Ind. of Pyion: archd. of Salisbury. London, 5 Dec. 1411.

302 Institution of M. John Blounham B.C.L. to church of Kingston Deverill (*Kyngeston Deverell*), vac. by resig. of William Erl; patron, Peter Stantor. Ind.: archd. of Salisbury. London, 14 Dec. 1411.

303 Collation to Thomas Ayleward, chaplain, of a canonry in Salisbury cath. and the prebend of Maior pars altaris in the same. Mandate to the dean and chapter of Salisbury for his admission, and to the dean for his installation. Potterne (*Poterne*) manor, 24 Dec. 1411.

304 [Fo. 52^{v}/31^{v}] Exchange between Thomas Coyter, vicar of Box (*Boxe*); patrons, prior and conv. of Monkton Farleigh (*Farlegh*)—and Thomas Almerton, vicar of Iwerne Minster (*Iwerne Mynstr'*); patron, M. Adam Mottrum, rector or prebendary of Iwerne Minster. Ind. of Almerton: archd. of Wiltshire. Ind. of Coyter: archd. of Dorset. Potterne, 31 Dec. 1411.

305 Institution of Alexander Clympyng, chaplain, to the churches of St. John and St. Mary, Shaftesbury (*Shafton*); patrons, abbess and conv. of Shaftesbury. Ind.: archd. of Dorset. Potterne, 3 Jan. 1412.

306 Institution of Robert Curteys, chaplain, to church of Rampisham (*Ramsham*); patron, Robert Lovell, lord of Graunson [*sic*]. Ind.: archd. of Dorset. Potterne, 10 Jan. 1412.

[The barony of Grandison became extinct in 1375 (*Complete Peerage*, comp. G.E. Cokayne and others (13 vols., 1910–59), vi. 67).]

307 Institution of John Whyte M.A. to church of Lower Stirthill (*Netherstertill*); patron, Nicholas Coker, *domicellus*. Ind.: archd. of Dorset. Potterne, 18 Jan. 1412.

[For Lower Stirthill, in Burton Bradstock, see Hutchins, ii. 285–6.]

308 Institution of Nicholas Colnet, clerk, in person of John Bounde, chaplain, his proctor, to St. Catherine's chapel in Wanborough (*Wamburgh*) manor, vac. by resig. of John atte Water; patron, Maud, lady of Lovell and Holand. Ind.: archd. of Wiltshire. Potterne, 20 Jan. 1412.

309 Institution of Thomas Cryshale, chaplain, to church of Tockenham (*Tokenham*); patron, Edward, duke of York (*Ebor'*). Ind.: archd. of Wiltshire. Potterne, 23 Jan. 1412.

310 Collation to M. John Appulton B.Cn.L. in person of Oliver Dyngley, clerk, his proctor, of vicarage of Aldbourne (*Aldeborne*). Ind.: archd. of Wiltshire. Potterne, 31 Jan. 1412.

—

311 [Fo. 52/32] Exchange, by authority of Nicholas, bp. of Bath and Wells, between Geoffrey Ipplepenne, rector of Enborne (*Enedebourne*); patron, Lady Eleanor of St. Amand—and William Supplet of Egynton, rector of Norton sub Hamdon (*Norton subtus Hammedon*), dioc. Bath and Wells. Ind. of Supplet: archd. of Berkshire. Potterne, 15 Feb. 1412.

312 Exchange, by authority of Philip, bp. of Lincoln, between M. John Giles, rector of Tilbrook (*Tilbrok*), dioc. Lincoln, in person of John B [illegible], chaplain, his proctor—and Thomas Malton, rector of Lydiard Millicent (*Northlydyerd* alias *Lydyerd Milsent*), in person of William [?] Giles, his proctor; patron, King Henry. Ind. of Giles: archd. of Wiltshire. Potterne, 19 Feb 1412.

313 Collation to M. William Lyndewode D.Cn. & C.L. of a canonry in Salisbury cath. and the prebend of Ruscombe Southbury (*Roscompe*) in the same, vac. by resig. of M. John Fyton. Mandate for admission and installation to dean and chapter of Salisbury. Potterne, 23 Feb. 1412.

314 Collation to M. John Fyton B.Th. of a canonry in Salisbury cath. and the prebend of Grantham Borealis (*Grantham* alias *Grahamborial*) in the same, vac. by death of M. Roger Coryngham. Mandate for admission and installation to dean and chapter of Salisbury. Letters to the bp. of Lincoln for Fyton's induction into the *corpus* of the prebend, situated in dioc. Lincoln. Potterne, 23 Feb. 1412.

315 [Fo. 53^{v}/32^{v}] Institution of Nicholas Calton, to church of Brightwell (*Bryghtwell*); patron, Henry, bp. of Winchester. Ind.: archd. of Berkshire. Potterne, 28 Feb. 1412.

316 Exchange, by authority of Henry, bp. of Winchester, between John Palmer, vicar of Beedon (*Budene*); patrons, abbot and conv. of Abingdon (*Abyndon*)—and William [illegible], vicar of Wootton St. Lawrence (*Laurenswotton*), dioc. Winchester. Ind. of William: archd. of Berkshire. Potterne, 9 March 1412.

[This exchange is not recorded in the Winchester episcopal register, but William Langeton was instituted to Wootton St. Lawrence 2 Sept. 1409 (Hampshire Record Office, A1/12 fo. 56^{v}).]

317 Institution of M. William Nagard B.C.L. to church of Woodsford (*Wyrdesforde*); patrons, abbot and conv. of Cerne. Ind.: archd. of Dorset. Potterne, 21 March 1412.

REGISTRUM REVERENDI IN CHRISTO PATRIS ET DOMINI DOMINI ROBERTI DEI GRACIA SAR' EPISCOPI DE PERMUTACIONIBUS INSTITUCIONIBUS ET COLLACIONIBUS BENEFICIORUM DE ANNO DOMINI MILLESIMO QUADRAGINTESIMO DUODECIMO ETC.

318 Institution of [Robert Felton],[1] in person of Gilbert Oword, clerk, his proctor, to Athelhampton (*Athelhamston*) free chapel, vac. by death of William Werkeman; patron, Richard Martyn. Ind.: archd. of Dorset. Salisbury, bishop's palace, 4 Apr. 1412.

[1. Illegible in MS. Name supplied from Hutchins, ii. 588.]

319 [Fo. 54/33] Collation to William Trowghford, chaplain, of St. Mary's chantry in West Dean (*Westden*) church. Ind.: archd. of Salisbury. Potterne, 18 March 1412.

320 Exchange between Richard Coke, vicar of Marden (*Merden*); patrons, prior and conv. of Bradenstoke—and Thomas Exsale, vicar of Sutton Benger (*Sutton*); patron, the bp. of Salisbury. Ind. of both: archd. of Wiltshire. Woodford (*Wodeford*), 12 Apr. 1412.

321 Exchange between Thomas Stub, rector of Hazelbury (*Hasselbury*); patron, Richard Draper—and John Grenehulle, rector of St. Mary, Cricklade (*Criklade*); patrons, prior and conv. of Bradenstoke.[1] Ind. of both: archd. of Wiltshire. Sonning (*Sonnyng*) manor, 24 Apr. 1412.

[1. Margin, later 15th-century hand: *cave quod error est in scriptura patronorum. In alio loco per T. Berkley scilicet 23°* (i.e., fo. 44, **224**). This is itself an error, confusing Cricklade with Chicklade. Here the patrons are reversed, see **141**, **264**.]

322 Exchange, by authority of Nicholas, bp. of Bath and Wells, between Thomas Houchon, rector of Sulhampstead Abbots (*Silhampstede Abbatis*); patrons, abbot and conv. of Reading (*Radyng*)—and Henry Turpyn, rector of Priston (*Pryston*), dioc. Bath and Wells. Ind. of Turpyn: archd. of Berkshire. London, 6 May 1412.

323 Exchange, by authority of Thomas, bp. of Worcester, between Stephen Blanecombe, rector of Beechingstoke (*Bechynstoke*); patrons, abbess and conv. of Shaftesbury (*Shafton*)—and Walter Elyot, rector of St. Mary Redcliffe (*Beate Marie in Foco, ville de Brystoll*), dioc. Worcester. Ind. of Elyot: archd. of Wiltshire. London, 11 May 1412.

324 [Fo. 54ᵛ/33ᵛ] Collation to Thomas Mody, chaplain, of Membury free chapel. Ind.: vicar of Aldbourne (*Aldburne*). London, 11 May 1412.

325 Exchange, by authority of Nicholas, bp. of Bath and Wells, between William Play, vicar of Winterbourne Stoke (*Wynterburnestoke*); patron, for this turn, Queen Joan—and Richard Uphill, rector of Angersleigh (*Knyghteslee*), dioc. Bath and Wells. Ind. of Uphill: archd. of Salisbury. London, 16 May 1412.

[For Angersleigh, see Collinson, iii. 241.]

326 Exchange, by authority of Henry, bp. of Winchester, between Thomas Mody, chaplain of Membury free chapel; patron, the bp. of Salisbury—and William Goodsweyn, rector of Headley (*Heedley*), dioc. Winchester. [No ind. given.] London, 18 May 1412.

327 Exchange between M. John Pedewell, vicar of Bulbridge (*Bulbrygg*), in person of Oliver Dyngley, clerk, his proctor; patron, the bp. of Salisbury—and Richard Taunton, rector of St. Mary, West Dean (*Westdene*), in person of Richard Willesdon, clerk, his proctor; patron, Miles Stapulton, knight. Ind. of both: archd. of Salisbury. Sonning (*Sonnyng*), 21 May 1412.

328 Institution of John Calwe, chaplain, to chantry in Handley (*Henlegh*) chapel, dependent on prebendal church of Iwerne Minster (*Iwarn Mynstr'*); patron, M. Adam de Mottrum, prebendary of Iwerne Minster. Ind.: archd. of Dorset. Sonning, 26 May 1412.

329 [Fo. 55/34] Exchange, by authority of Henry, bp. of Winchester, between Laurence Howard, rector of Winterbourne Bassett (*Wynterborne Basset*); patrons, prior and conv. of St. Pancras, Lewes—and John Mascall, rector of Millbrook (*Mylbroke*), dioc. Winchester; patron, the bp. of Winchester. Ind. of Mascall: archd. of Wiltshire. Sonning, 2 June 1412.

330 Institution of John Michell, chaplain, to church or chapel with cure of souls of Norridge (*Norigge*), vac. by resig. of John Pert; patron, Nicholas Leye. Ind.: archd. of Wiltshire. Sonning, 7 June 1412.

331 Exchange between Henry Roys, vicar of Frampton, in person of Thomas Mascalsey, literate, his proctor; patrons, for this turn, Thomas, bp. of Durham, and Prince John, constable of England and warden of the East March on the Scottish border—and John Fysshemere, rector of East Chelborough (*Leucombe*); patron, John Chydyok, *domicellus*. Ind. of both: archd. of Dorset. Sonning, 23 June 1412.

[For Lewcombe and East Chelborough, see Hutchins, ii. 652.]

332 Exchange between Richard Benet, chaplain of Wootton Glanville (*Wotton Glamvile*) chantry; patron, Robert Moure, *domicellus*—and John Waleys, rector of Winterbourne Abbas (*Wynterbourne Abbatis*); patrons, abbot and conv. of Cerne. Ind. of both: archd. of Dorset. Sonning, 2 July 1412.

333 Institution of Richard Brook, chaplain, to church of West Stafford (*West Staforde*); patrons, abbot and conv. of Milton (*Middelton*). Ind.: archd. of Dorset. Sonning, 6 July 1412.

334 [Fo. 55v/34v] Exchange, by authority of Edmund, bp. of Exeter, between William Walsshe, rector of West Parley (*Westperlegh*); patron, Robert Derby—and John Hales, rector of Washfield (*Wasshefeld*), dioc. Exeter, in person of John Knyght, his proctor. Ind. of Hales, archd. of Dorset. Sonning, 8 July 1412.

335 Notarial instrument, drawn up by Richard de Petteworth, clerk (dioc. Chichester), public notary, attesting the resignation by M. Richard Dereham D.Th., papal protonotary, in the persons of John Wakeryng, archd. of Canterbury, John Bathe, canon of Wells, and Simon Flour, rector of St. Nicholas Cole Abbey (*Coldeabbey*), London, of Preston prebend in Salisbury cath., made in Chancery (in the upper part of the great hall of the king's palace of Westminster), 9 July 1412. Witnesses, M. John Stokes Inc.C.L., John Edmund, esquire (dioc. Norwich), and others.
Received by the bp. of Salisbury, Sonning, 11 July 1412.

336 [Fo. 56/35] Public instrument drawn up by Henry Lupi of Neuss (*Nussia*), clerk of dioc. Cologne (*Colonien'*), public notary, attesting M. Richard Dereham's appointment as his proctors of John Wakeryng, archd. of Canterbury, M. John Exworth D.C.L., John Bathe, canon of Wells, M. Robert Ely, John Thiryngton B.Cn.L. and Simon Flour, rector of St. Nicholas Cole Abbey, London.

The proctors, or any three of them, have power to approve and confirm the decisions of Thomas, abp. of Canterbury, in the business committed to him by King Henry. They are also to make an agreement with John Macworth in all matters concerning the archdeaconry of Norfolk in Norwich cath., apart from the case of the wounding of Edmund Lucas, Dereham's full brother (*frater germanus*), in the churchyard of Corton (*Corstone*), dioc. Norwich, united to the archdeaconry, which case has been unreservedly committed by King Henry to the abp. In addition, they are to promise in Dereham's name to accept all the decisions of the abp., except concerning the deanery of St. Martin-le-Grand royal free chapel, London. If necessary, they are to resign the archdeaconry and any other of Dereham's benefices (except the aforesaid deanery) in exchange for another benefice, or simply to resign it, if it seems right to the proctors or any three of them. They are to look after Dereham's interests in securing collation or institution, and possession of benefices, in collecting their revenues in the most advantageous manner, and generally to act on his behalf. Dereham promises to endorse the actions of his proctors. Witnesses, William Goodefadir, vicar of Sydenham (*Sidenham*), and Simon Northewe, rector of Southease (*Southese*), dioc. Chichester. Dereham's house, Boulogne (*Bononia*), 13 Oct. 1410.

337 [Fo. 56ᵛ/35ᵛ] Letter to John Macworth, archd. of Dorset, collating him, in the person of Thomas Elond, literate, his proctor, to a canonry in Salisbury cath. and the prebend of Preston in the same, vac. by resig. of M. Richard Dereham D.Th. Sonning, 11 July 1412.

338 Letter to dean and chapter of Salisbury for admission and installation of Macworth [as in **337**]. Sonning, 11 July 1412.

339 Institution of Henry Wegg, chaplain, to vicarage of Stockland (*Stoclond*); patrons, abbot and conv. of Milton (*Middelton*). Ind.: archd. of Dorset. Sonning, 17 July 1412.

340 [Fo. 57/36] Institution of John Paytesyn, chaplain, to church of Lacerton; patrons, prioress and conv. of St. Mary, Kington St. Michael (*Kyngton Michael*). Ind.: archd. of Dorset. Sonning, 21 July 1412.

341 Common pleas *admittatis*, concerning the church of Lacerton, because the prioress of Kington St. Michael has recovered the presentation from the bp. of Salisbury and Thomas Scovyle, clerk. *Teste* William Thrynnyng. Westminster, 18 June 1412.

342 Institution of Thomas Wyttyngton, chaplain, to church of Frilsham (*Fredlesham*); patrons, Richard Arches, knight, Edmund Hampdene, Richard Wyot, Thomas Bekyngham, Thomas Melreth and John Orwell. Ind.: archd. of Berkshire. Sonning, 23 July 1412.

343 Exchange, by authority of Henry, bp. of Winchester, between John Neve, rector of Cheddington (*Chedyngton*); patron, Thomas Bolour—and Nicholas Mylle, vicar of Portsmouth (*Portesmouth*), dioc. Winchester. Ind. of Mylle: archd. of Dorset. Ramsbury (*Remmesbury*), 31 July 1412.

344 Exchange, by authority of Edmund, bp. of Exeter, between John Botuler, rector of West Chelborough (*Chaulburth*); patron, John Golafore, *domicellus*—and John Harkecomb, rector of Jacobstowe (*Jacobystow*), dioc. Exeter. Ind. of Harkecomb: archd. of Dorset. Ramsbury, 31 July 1412.

345 Exchange, by authority of Thomas, bp. of Worcester, between William Buttys, vicar of Preshute (*Preschuut*); patron, George Louthorp, canon residentiary of Salisbury cath. and warden of the choristers, at the nomination of the bp. of Salisbury—and John Newent, rector of Tortworth (*Torteworth*), dioc. Worcester. Ind. of Newent: official of peculiar jurisdiction of Marlborough (*Marleburgh*). Note that George Louthorp put his obedience in writing.[1] Ramsbury, 31 July 1412.

[1. This sentence written in a different contemporary hand and underlined.]

346 [Fo. 57^{v}/36^{v}] Exchange, by authority of Thomas, abp. of Canterbury, between John Pomeray, vicar of Downton (*Dounton*); patrons, warden, fellows and scholars of St. Mary's college, Winchester—and Thomas Stratton, vicar of Upchurch (*Upchirche*), dioc. Canterbury. Ind. of Stratton: archd. of Salisbury. Ramsbury, 2 Aug. 1412.

347 Exchange, by authority of Richard, bp. of London, between John Wryght, rector of Shaw (*Schaw*); patrons, Stephen Anteswell and Nicholas North—and William Swaleclyve, vicar of Staines (*Stanys*), dioc. London. Ind. of Swaleclyve: archd. of Berkshire. Sherborne (*Schirborn*) castle, 12 Aug. 1412.

[Notification by archdeacon's official to bp. of the induction of Swaleclyve, 19 Aug. 1412, P.R.O., Exchequer K.R., E 135/21/30. This adds the information that the patrons were *domicelli*, and that William Maundevyle was Swaleclyve's proctor.]

348 Collation to William Bowtour, chaplain, of St. Mary's chantry in church of Whitchurch Canonicorum (*Whitchirch*); patron, for this turn, the bp. of Salisbury. Ind.: archd. of Dorset. Ramsbury (*Remmesbury*), 6 Aug. 1412.

349 Commission to the archd. of Wiltshire to hold a deanery inquiry before Michaelmas [29 Sept.] into the vacancy and patronage of Winkfield (*Wynfeld*) church, to which the abbot and conv. of St. Mary, Keynsham (*Keynesham*), dioc. Bath and Wells, have presented William Roberd, chaplain. If the inquiry is satisfactory, he is to admit, institute and induct Roberd. [Undated].

350 [Fo. 58/37] Collation to M. Thomas Teynton B.Cn.L. of church of West Kington (*Westkyngton*). Ind.: archd. of Wiltshire. Sonning (*Sonnyng*), 30 Aug. 1412.

351 Institution of M. John Ocley B.C.L. to church of Frome St. Quintin, vac. by resig. of M. Thomas Teynton; patrons, abbot and conv. of St. Mary, Tewkesbury (*Teukesbury*), order of St. Benedict, dioc. Worcester. Ind.: archd. of Dorset. Sonning, 4 Sept. 1412.

352 Collation to M. John Dygon B.C.L. of church of Bishop's Caundle (*Caundell Episcopi*). Ind.: archd. of Dorset. Sonning, 10 Sept. 1412.

353 Institution of John Boteler, chaplain, in person of M. William Nagard B.C.L., his proctor, to church of East Stoke (*Estoke*); patrons, John Jurdan and John Chyverell, esquire, as established by an inquiry. Ind.: archd. of Dorset. Sonning, 19 Sept. 1412.

354 Exchange, by authority of Philip, bp. of Lincoln, between Richard Cook, vicar of Sutton Benger (*Sutton*); patron, the bp. of Salisbury—and Thomas Caldewell of 'Eccleshale', vicar of Upton, dioc. Lincoln. Ind. of Caldewell: archd. of Wiltshire. London, 27 Sept. 1412.

[Cf. Lincolnshire Archives Office, Reg. XIV (Repingdon) fo. 451v for identification of Upton, Bucks.]

355 Exchange between John Lavyngton, rector of Draycot Cerne (*Draycote Cerne*); patron, Edward Cerne, *domicellus*—and John Humfray, rector of Didcot (*Dudecote*), in person of M. John Fyton, canon of Salisbury cath., his proctor; patron, Edmund Hamden, esquire. Ind. of Humfray: archd. of Wiltshire. Ind. of Lavyngton: archd. of Berkshire. London inn, 2 Oct. 1412.

356 [Fo. 58v/37v] Institution of John Gardener, chaplain, to church of Silton (*Sylton*); patron, for this turn, William Stourton, *domicellus*, guardian of William Bydyk, a minor, brother and heir of the late John Bydyk. Ind.: archd. of Dorset. London inn, 9 Oct. 1412.

357 Institution of M. John Well D.Cn.L. to church of Christian Malford (*Crystmalford*); patron, Nicholas, bp. of Bath and Wells. Ind.: archd. of Wiltshire. London inn, 11 Oct. 1412.

358 Institution of William Aas, clerk, to church of Broughton Gifford (*Broughton*), vac. by resig. of M. John Teffont; patrons, abbess and conv. of Shaftesbury (*Shafton*). Ind.: archd. of Salisbury. London inn, 12 Oct. 1412.

359 Institution of M. John Teffont B.C.L. to vicarage of Steeple Ashton (*Stepylasshton*), vac. by death of M. William Rodeburne; patrons, abbess and conv. of Romsey (*Romesey*), dioc. Winchester. Ind.: archd. of Salisbury. London inn, 12 Oct. 1412.

360 Institution of Hugh Sakerlegh, chaplain, to church of Chickerell (*Chykerell*), vac. by resig. of John Butiller; patron, Humphrey Stafford, knight. Ind.: archd. of Dorset. Sonning (*Sonnyng*), 15 Oct. 1412.

361 Exchange, by authority of Henry, bp. of Winchester, between John Malteby, rector of Belchalwill (*Belle*); patron, Henry FitzHugh, knight, lord of Ravensworth (*Raveneswath*)—and John Wyche *alias* Bathe, rector of Worthing (*Wortyng*), dioc. Winchester. Ind. of Wyche: archd. of Dorset. Ramsbury (*Remmesbury*), 23 Oct. 1412.

[For Belchalwill, see Hutchins, iii. 373–4.]

362 Institution of John Holston, chaplain, to church of Tockenham (*Tokenham*), vac. by resig. of Thomas Cryshale; patrons, for this turn, John Adam and William Gobion, attornies or proctors of Edward, duke of York (*Ebor'*), then abroad in the king's service. Ind.: archd. of Wiltshire. Ramsbury, 23 Oct. 1412.

363 [Fo. 59/38] Exchange, by authority of Henry, bp. of Winchester, between Robert Kene, vicar of Hannington (*Hanyngdon*); patrons, dean and chapter of the new collegiate church of St. Mary, Leicester (*Leycestrie*)—and Thomas Locke, rector of West Dean (*Westdeone*), dioc. Winchester. Ind. of Locke: archd. of Wiltshire. Ramsbury, 23 Oct. 1412.

364 Institution of Edmund Weston, chaplain, to church of Catmore (*Catmere*); patron, Walter Grendon, prior of hospital of St. John of Jerusalem in England. Ind.: archd. of Berkshire. Ramsbury, 24 Oct. 1412.

365 Institution of William Stokton, chaplain, to vicarage of Corsham (*Cosham*); patron, for this turn, Queen Joan. Ind.: archd. of Wiltshire. Ramsbury, 25 Oct. 1412.

366 Exchange between Andrew Swynesford, rector of Manston; patron, Thomas Manston of Manston—and Richard Tanton, vicar of Bulbridge (*Bulbrigge*); patron, the bp. of Salisbury. The archdeacons [unspecified] were ordered to induct. Ramsbury, 26 Oct. 1412.

367 Institution of John Selforde, chaplain, to church of Lockinge (*Loogenge*), vac. by death of M. Robert Ledefard;[1] patrons, abbot and conv. of Abingdon (*Abendon*). Ind.: archd. of Berkshire. Ramsbury, 1 Nov. 1412.

[1. He was murdered, **898**.]

368 Collation to M. Robert Dyneley M.A. of church of Boscombe. Ind.: archd. of Salisbury. Ramsbury, 2 Nov. 1412.

369 Collation to William Becke, chaplain, of church of Heddington (*Hedyngton*), in the bp. of Salisbury's collation for this turn *iure devoluto*. Ind.: archd. of Salisbury. Ramsbury, 2 Nov. 1412.

370 [Fo. 59v/38v] Institution of Adam Norton, chaplain, to vicarage of Frampton, vac. by resig. of John Fisshemere; patrons, Thomas, bp. of Durham, and Prince John, constable of England and warden of the East March on the Scottish border, custodians of the alien priory of Frampton. Ind.: archd. of Dorset. Ramsbury, 6 Nov. 1412.

371 Institution of John Stratford, chaplain, to vicarage of Colerne; patron, M. John Defford, rector of Colerne. Ind.: archd. of Wiltshire. Ramsbury, 8 Nov. 1412.

372 Letter of George Louthorp, canon residentiary of Salisbury and warden of the choristers, to the bp. of Salisbury, presenting M. Thomas Neweman, vicar of Stonehouse (*Stonehous*), dioc. Worcester, to the vicarage of Preshute (*Preschuyte*), in the warden's patronage, at the nomination of the bp. of Salisbury, by reason of an exchange with M. John Newent, vicar of Preshute. An annual pension of £20 is reserved to the warden and choristers from the church of Preshute. Salisbury, 30 Oct. 1412.

373 Exchange, by authority of Thomas, bp. of Worcester, between M. John Newent, vicar of Preshute—and M. Thomas Neweman, vicar of Stonehouse, dioc. Worcester [as in **372**]. Ind. of Neweman: official of peculiar jurisdiction of Marlborough (*Merleburgh*). Ramsbury, 16 Nov. 1412.

374 Exchange, by authority of Philip, bp. of Lincoln, between John Averey, rector of Up Cerne (*Upcerne*); patron, Ives FitzWaryn, knight—and John Roulond, rector of Great Munden (*Monden Magna*), dioc. Lincoln. Ind. of Roulond: archd. of Dorset. Ramsbury, 18 Nov. 1412.

375 [Fo. 60/39] Exchange, by authority of Henry, bp. of Winchester, between Richard Hamme, chaplain of Holy Trinity chantry in Hungerford church; patron, the bp. of Salisbury—and Thomas Lemyngton *alias* atte Fenne, rector of Sherfield English (*Schyrefeld*), dioc. Winchester. Ind. of Lemyngton: vicar of Hungerford. Ramsbury, 28 Nov. 1412.

376 Letters of archd. of Dorset's official, citing the bishop's commission of 14 Nov. 1412, to inquire into the right of presentation to Wareham (*Warham*) alien priory, to which Queen Joan and John Tibbey, clerk, have presented John Kyngeston, monk. The official certifies that an inquiry held in Holy Trinity church, Wareham, revealed that the office of prior has been vacant since the death of Stephen de Barra on 4 Nov. 1412. The queen and Tibbey are patrons, by grant of the king, during the war with France.

Stephen de Barra was formerly presented by the abbot and conv. of the alien monastery of Lyre (*Lira*). John Kyngeston is a monk of Westminster of good character, as seen in letters testimonial of his abbot. Present at the inquiry were the following rectors: Gilbert [Gavely] of Spettisbury (*Spettebury*), John [Sperhauk] of Holy Trinity, Wareham, John [Maylard] of Melcombe Horsey (*Melcombe*), John of Winterbourne Zelstone (*Wynterborn Zeleston*), William [Percy] of Winterbourne Houghton (*Houghton*), Stephen [Pope] of Lytchett Matravers (*Lychet Mautravers*), John of Shillingstone (*Okford Skyllyng*) and John [Gylot] of Burleston (*Burdeleston*). The following vicars were present: John of Puddletown (*Puleton*), Robert of Affpuddle (*Affepudell*), William [Dinant] of Spettisbury (*Spettebury*), John [Sampson] of Morden (*Mordon*), John of Milton (*Middelton*) and Thomas [Weye] of Tolpuddle (*Tolpudell*).[1] Wareham, 29 Nov. 1412. As a result, the bp. instituted John Kyngeston as prior.[2] Ind.: archd. of Dorset. Ramsbury, 2 Dec. 1412.

[1. Surnames supplied from Hutchins, except William Percy, see **265**.
2. It was later asserted that Queen Joan did not have the right of presentation and Kyngeston was ordered by the king 7 Apr. 1413 to hand over the issues of the priory (*CCR 1413–19*, pp. 15–16).]

377 [Fo. 60v/39v] Exchange between Robert atte Mylle, rector of Padworth (*Paddeworth*); patron, King Henry—and John Martyn, vicar of Bisham (*Bustlesham*); patron, Walter Grendon, prior of hospital of St. John of Jerusalem in England. Ind. of both: archd. of Berkshire. Ramsbury, 2 Dec. 1412.

378 Exchange, by authority of Henry, bp. of Winchester, between William Goldsmyth, rector of Easton Grey (*Eston Gray*); patrons, abbot and conv. of St. Peter, Gloucester—and Thomas Giffray, rector of St. John the Baptist, Southampton, dioc. Winchester. Ind. of Giffray: archd. of Wiltshire. Potterne, 9 Dec. 1412.

379 Institution of Henry Cowbrygge, chaplain, to church of Pangbourne (*Pangeborne*); patrons, abbot and conv. of Reading (*Radyng*). Ind.: archd. of Berkshire. Potterne, 12 Dec. 1412.

380 Institution of John Spynck, chaplain, to church of West Woodhay (*Westwodehay*), vac. by death of John Coupere; patron, Lady Eleanor of St. Amand. Ind.: archd. of Berkshire. Potterne, 15 Dec. 1412.

381 Exchange, on certificate of John Odiskyn, subdean of Hereford cath., between Richard Gode, vicar of Littleton Drew (*Litilton Drew*); patron, the bp. of Salisbury—and Thomas Whyte, vicar of St. Martin's church and All Saints' chapel, Hereford. Ind. of Whyte: archd. of Wiltshire. Potterne, 17 Dec. 1412.

382 Institution of William Marchall, chaplain, to vicarage of Market Lavington (*Chepyng Lavyngton*), vac. by resig. of John Bryd; patrons, rector and conv. of Edington (*Edyndon*). Ind.: archd. of Salisbury. Potterne, 21 Dec. 1412.

383 [Fo. 61/40] Institution of William Roberd, chaplain, in person of Thomas Don, clerk, his proctor, to church of Winkfield (*Wynfeld*); patrons, abbot and conv. of Keynsham (*Keynesham*). Ind.: archd. of Salisbury [*rectius* Wiltshire]. Ramsbury (*Remmesbury*), 24 Dec. 1412.

384 Exchange, by authority of Nicholas, bp. of Bath and Wells, between Henry Mory, rector of Tarrant Hinton (*Tarent Hynton*); patrons, abbess and conv. of Shaftesbury (*Shafton*)—and John Clere *alias* Smyth, rector of Limington (*Lymyngton*), dioc. Bath and Wells. Ind. of Clere: archd. of Dorset. Ramsbury, 27 Dec. 1412.

385 Institution of M. Roger Whelpedale B.Th., in person of John Ricardby, clerk, his proctor, to church of Stockton (*Stoketon*); patron, Henry, bp. of Winchester. Ind.: archd. of Salisbury. Ramsbury, 3 Jan. 1413.

386 Institution of William Batayle, chaplain, to chantry of St. Catherine and St. Margaret in Market Lavington (*Lavyngton Fore*) church, vac. by resig. of William Marchall; patron, Walter Beauchamp, esquire. Ind.: archd. of Salisbury. Ramsbury, 5 Jan. 1413.

387 Institution of John Dewy, chaplain, to church of Buckhorn Weston (*Bowkerne Weston*); patron, William Stourton. Ind.: archd. of Dorset. Ramsbury, 7 Jan. 1413.

388 Institution of Thomas Wyke, chaplain, to vicarage of St. Mary, Westport, Malmesbury, vac. by resig. of Walter Hatherleygh; patrons, abbot and conv. of Malmesbury. Ind.: archd. of Wiltshire. Ramsbury, 11 Jan. 1413.

389 Exchange between John Harekombe, rector of West Chelborough (*Chalborgh*); patron, John Golofre, esquire—and John atte Water, rector of Bremilham (*Bremelham*); patron, Walter Dauntesey, *domicellus*. Ind. of Harekombe: archd. of Wiltshire. Ind. of atte Water: archd. of Dorset. Ramsbury, 22 Jan. 1413.

390 Institution of William Horlok, chaplain, to church of Shaw (*Shawe*), vac. by resig. of William Swalclyve; patrons, Stephen Ansteswell and Nicholas North. Ind.: archd. of Berkshire. Ramsbury, 24 Jan. 1413.

391 [Fo. 61v/40v] Institution of Robert Blake, clerk, to church of Heddington (*Hedyngton*), vac. by resig. of William Becke; patrons, prior and conv. of Monkton Farleigh (*Farlegh*). Ind.: archd. of Wiltshire. Ramsbury, 30 Jan. 1413.

392 Institution of William Sumpter, chaplain, to church of Rollestone (*Rolveston*), vac. by resig. of Edmund Horsman; patron, Walter Grendon, prior of hospital of St. John of Jerusalem in England. Ind.: archd. of Salisbury. London inn, 13 Feb. 1413.

393 Exchange, by authority of Henry, bp. of Winchester, between William Dalton, vicar of East Garston (*Estgarston*); patrons, prioress and conv. of Amesbury (*Ambresbur'*)—and William Cotton, vicar of Wherwell (*Harewell, Wharewell*), dioc. Winchester. Ind. of Cotton: archd. of Berkshire. London inn, 21 Feb. 1413.

394 Exchange, by authority of Philip, bp. of Lincoln, between Robert atte Mille, vicar of Bisham (*Bustlesham*); patron, Walter Grendon, prior of hospital of St. John of Jerusalem in England—and John Inglewode, rector of Sutterby, dioc. Lincoln. Ind. of Inglewode: archd. of Berkshire. London inn, 22 Feb. 1413.

395 Institution of Thomas Coke, chaplain, to St. Michael's chantry, Bridport (*Brydeporte*), vac. by death of Edward Lowche; patron, M. Thomas Moyne, rector of Bridport. Ind.: archd. of Dorset. London inn, 24 Feb. 1413.

396 On receipt of royal letters presenting William Ingram, chaplain, to church of Castle Eaton (*Eton Maysy, Eton Moysy*), the bp. granted Ingram letters directed to archd. of Wiltshire to inquire into the vacancy and patronage, with power to admit Ingram if the inquiry established the king's right for this turn. London, 4 March 1413. The archdeacon's official certified that Ingram had been admitted after inquiry, 20 March.
[For Castle Eaton, see *Wilts. Place-names*, p. 24.]

397 [Fo. 62/41] Institution of William Colvyle, chaplain, to church of St. Peter, Old Sarum (*veter' Sar'*); patron, King Henry. Ind.: archd. of Salisbury. London, 5 March 1413.[1]
[1. Margin: *Nota*]

398 Institution of M. John Prophete, priest, to a canonry in Salisbury cath. and the prebend of Netherbury in Ecclesia in the same; patron, for this turn, King Henry, by reason of the temporalities of the bishopric of Salisbury lately in his hands after the death of bp. Richard. Mandate to the dean and chapter of Salisbury for his admission, and to the dean for his installation. London, 25 Feb. 1413.
[See *Fasti 1300–1541*, iii. 74.]

399 Institution of Thomas de Tibbay, clerk, to church of Devizes (*Devyses*); patron, Queen Joan. Ind.: official of peculiar jurisdiction of Devizes. London, 12 March 1413.

400 Exchange, by authority of Richard, bp. of London, between William Supplet of Egynton, rector of Enborne (*Enneborn*); patron, Lady Eleanor of St. Amand—and William Donne, rector of All Saints, Stock (*Herewardstok*), dioc. London. Ind. of Donne: archd. of Berkshire. London, 18 March 1413.

401 Exchange, by authority of Philip, bp. of Lincoln, between Richard atte Water, vicar of Purley (*Purlegh*); patrons, Provost Robert Busch and the fellows of St. Edmund's college, Salisbury—and Thomas Geffray, vicar of Stantonbury (*Stonton Barry*), dioc. Lincoln. Ind. of Geffray: archd. of Berkshire. London, 24 March 1413.

REGISTRUM REVERENDI IN CHRISTO PATRIS ET DOMINI DOMINI ROBERTI DEI GRACIA SAR' EPISCOPI PREDICTI DE INSTITUCIONIBUS PERMUTACIONIBUS ET COLLACIONIBUS ET DE ANNO DOMINI MILLESIMO QUADRINGENTESIMO TERCIODECIMO

402 [Fo. 62v/41v] Exchange, by authority of Henry, bp. of Winchester, between Thomas Hert, vicar of All Saints, Chitterne; patron, the bp. of Salisbury—and John Draper, rector of St. Nicholas, Guildford (*Gyldeford*), dioc. Winchester. Ind. of Draper: archd. of Salisbury. Sonning (*Sonnyng*),[1] 5 Apr. 1413.

[1. Possibly an error for London. Cf. **401**, **403**.]

403 Institution of Thomas Skern, chaplain, to vicarage of Bower Chalk (*Bourechalke*) chapel, in Chalk parish; patron, William Waltham, prebendary of Chalk in Wilton conventual church. Ind.: archd. of Salisbury [*rectius* Wiltshire]. London, 7 Apr. 1413.

404 Institution of John Dun, chaplain, to church of Batcombe (*Battecomb*); patron, Humphrey Stafford, knight. Ind.: archd. of Dorset. London, 10 Apr. 1413.

405 Collation to M. Thomas Teynton, priest, of a canonry in Salisbury cath. and the prebend of Maior pars altaris in the same, vac. by death of Thomas Ayleward. Mandate to the dean and chapter of Salisbury for his admission, and to the dean for his installation. London, 6 Apr. 1413.[1]

[1. Margin: *Nota*]

406 Exchange, by authority of Edmund, bp. of Exeter, between M. Thomas Speeke, rector of Grittleton (*Grydlyngton*), in person of John Speeke, his proctor; patrons, abbot and conv. of Glastonbury (*Glaston*)—and John Waryn, vicar of Liskeard (*Leskyrec*), dioc. Exeter, in person of Nicholas Ascheton, clerk, his proctor. Ind. of Waryn: archd. of Wiltshire. Sonning (*Sonnyng*), 14 Apr. 1413.

407 [Fo. 63/42] Institution of Robert Boveton, chaplain, in person of Robert Wylkyns, his proctor, to St. Mary's chantry, Marnhull (*Marunhull*);

patron, William Karent of Henstridge (*Hengstrygg*). Ind.: archd. of Dorset. Sonning, 20 Apr. 1413.

408 Institution of Simon Sloley, chaplain, in person of Thomas Barbor, his proctor, to church of Tarrant Gunville (*Tarent Goundeville*); patron, for this turn, King Henry, guardian of his brother Edmund, earl of March, a minor. Ind.: archd. of Dorset. Sonning, 21 Apr. 1413.

409 Exchange, by authority of Edmund, bp. of Exeter, between M. John Haget, canon and prebendary of Exeter cath., in person of M. Oliver Dyneley, clerk, his proctor—and M. Thomas Teynton, canon of Salisbury cath. and prebendary of Maior pars altaris in the same; patron, the bp. of Salisbury. Mandate to the dean and chapter of Salisbury for the admission of Haget, and to the dean for his installation. Sonning, 2 May 1413.

410 Institution of John Plente, priest, to church of Hemsworth (*Hemlysworth*); patrons, abbot and conv. of Milton (*Middelton*). Ind.: archd. of Dorset. Sonning, 4 May 1413.

411 Institution of John Bollam, clerk, in person of William Bygge, his proctor, to church of Steeple (*Steple*), vac. by resig. of John Marnham; patron, for this turn, King Henry. Ind.: archd. of Dorset. Sonning, 6 May 1413.

412 Institution of Thomas Dammet, clerk, to church of Stockton (*Stoketon*), vac. by resig. of M. Roger Whelpedale; patron, Henry, bp. of Winchester. Ind.: archd. of Salisbury. London, 16 May 1413.[1]

[1. Margin: *Nota*]

413 Institution of William Mulverton, chaplain, in person of John Knyght, his proctor, to chantry in church of Fisherton Anger (*Fissherton Ancher*) by Salisbury, for the souls of Stephen Cryour and Maud, his wife, and all the faithful, vac. by resig. of Thomas Heliere; patron, M. Simon Sydenham, archd. of Salisbury. Ind.: archd. of Salisbury. London, 18 May 1413.

414 [Fo. 63^{v}/42^{v}] Institution of John Lunyal, chaplain, to church of Yattendon (*Yatenden*); patron, John Coteron of Newbury. Ind.: archd. of Berkshire. London, 22 May 1413.

415 Institution of Richard Blythe, clerk, to church of Pulham; patrons, abbot and conv. of St. Mary, Cirencester, dioc. Worcester. Ind.: archd. of Dorset. London, 24 May 1413.

416 Institution of Richard Falus, chaplain, to vicarage of West Hendred (*Westhenreth*); patrons, prior and conv. of Holy Trinity, Wallingford (*Walyngford*). Ind.: archd. of Berkshire. London, 25 May 1413.

417 Institution of William Tame, chaplain, to St. Catherine the Virgin's chapel in Wanborough (*Wambergh*) manor; patron, Maud Lovell, lady of Lovell and Holand. Ind.: archd. of Wiltshire. London, 2 June 1413.

418 Exchange, by authority of Henry, bp. of Winchester, between William Bedford, vicar of Cookham (*Kocham*); patrons, abbot and conv. of Cirencester—and John Cook, rector of Albury (*Aldebury*), dioc. Winchester. Ind. of Cook: archd. of Berkshire. London, 8 June 1413.

419 Collation to Nicholas Calton, chaplain, of a canonry in Salisbury cath. and the prebend of Netheravon (*Netherhaven*) in the same, vac. by death of M. Nicholas Rixton. Mandate to the dean and chapter of Salisbury for his admission and to the dean for his installation. Canterbury (*Cantuar'*), 19 June 1413.

420 [Fo. 64/43] Exchange, by authority of Henry, bp. of Winchester, between M. Thomas Pyres, rector of Fittleton (*Fitelton*); patrons, Percival Soudan, knight, and Margaret, his wife—and Thomas Hert, rector of St. Nicholas, Guildford (*Gyldeford*), dioc. Winchester. Ind. of Hert: archd. of Salisbury. Horton Kirby (*Horton*) manor,[1] 22 June 1413.

[1. Bp. Hallum held the manor of Horton Kirby (Kent) (*CCR 1419–22*, pp. 47, 62, 64).]

421 Exchange, by authority of Henry, bp. of Winchester, between John Mascall, rector of Winterbourne Bassett (*Wynterborne Basset*); patrons, prior and conv. of St. Pancras of Lewes—and John Carpenter, rector of Headbourne Worthy (*Worthi Mortymer*), dioc. Winchester. Ind. of Carpenter: archd. of Wiltshire. Sonning (*Sonnyng*), 2 July 1413.

422 Institution of John Blomvill, clerk, in person of William Brugge, his proctor, to church of Upton Lovell (*Ubeton*); patron, Lady Maud, lady of Lovell and Holand. Ind.: archd. of Salisbury. Sonning, 10 July 1413.

423 Institution of John Jocy, chaplain, to vicarage of Toller Porcorum (*Tolre Porcorum*), vac. by resig. of Thomas Wyttyngton; patrons, abbot and conv. of Abbotsbury (*Abbodesbury*). Ind.: archd. of Dorset. Sonning, 20 July 1413.

424 Institution of John Abendon, chaplain, to church of Appleton (*Appulton*), vac. by resig. of Thomas Mason; patron, William FitzWaryn, esquire. Ind.: archd. of Berkshire. Sonning, 29 July 1413.

425 Institution of Nicholas Grave, chaplain, to vicarage of Upavon (*Uphaven*), vac. by death of John Messager; patrons, Queen Joan and John de Tibbay, clerk, as established by an inquiry. Ind.: archd. of Salisbury. Bradenstoke (*Bradenestoke*), 30 July 1413.

426 Institution of William Hogges, chaplain, to church of Fonthill Bishop (*Fountell*); patron, Henry, bp. of Winchester. Ind.: archd. of Salisbury. Ramsbury (*Remmesbury*), 2 Aug. 1413.

427 Letters received from M. Henry Corbrugge B.C.L., bishop's commissary, that he has instituted Thomas Bedull, chaplain, to the vicarage of Chieveley (*Chyveley*), vac. by resig. of John White; patrons, abbot and conv. of Abingdon (*Abendon*). Ramsbury, 4 Aug. 1413.

428 [Fo. 64v/43v] Institution of John White, chaplain, to church of Kingston Bagpuze (*Kyngeston Baggepiz*); patrons, prior and conv. of Poughley (*Poghle*). Ind.: archd. of Berkshire. Ramsbury, 4 Aug. 1413.

429 Collation to James Greny, chaplain, in person of John Greny, clerk, his proctor, of chantry in St. Edmund's church, Salisbury, for the souls of Reynold of Tidworth (*Tudeworth*), Joan, his wife, and all the faithful. Inductors: Robert Busch, provost of St. Edmund's collegiate church, the rector of Fisherton Delamere (*Fisherton*) and the chaplain of St. Edmund's. Ramsbury, 5 Aug. 1413.

[Reynold of Tidworth, mayor of Salisbury 1306; chantry founded 1305 (*VCH Wilts.*, vi. 152).]

430 Exchange, by authority of Henry, bp. of Winchester, between John Inglewode, vicar of Bisham (*Bustelesham*); patron, Walter Grendon, prior of hospital of St. John of Jerusalem in England—and Ralph Grove, vicar of Addington (*Adyngton*), dioc. Winchester. Ind. of Grove: archd. of Berkshire. Ramsbury, 12 Aug. 1413.

431 Institution of M. John Symondesborugh, chaplain, in person of John Symondesborugh, literate, his proctor, to church of Woodsford (*Wyrdesforde*), vac. by death of M. William Nagard; patrons, abbot and conv. of Cerne. Ind.: archd. of Dorset. Ramsbury, 16 Aug. 1413.

432 Institution of William Coudray, clerk, to church of Padworth (*Padeworth*), vac. by resig. of John Martyn; patron, for this turn, King Henry. Ind.: archd. of Berkshire. Ramsbury, 26 Aug. 1413.

433 Institution of Ralph Lambeden, chaplain, to vicarage of Upavon (*Uphavene*), vac. by resig. of Nicholas Grave; patron, King Henry, as established by an inquiry. Ind.: archd. of Salisbury. Woodford (*Wodeford*), 2 Sept. 1413.

434 Institution of Thomas Abel, chaplain, to vicarage of Hagbourne (*Hakebourne*); patrons, abbot and conv. of Cirencester, order of St. Augustine, dioc. Worcester. Ind.: archd. of Berkshire. Ramsbury (*Remmesbury*), 6 Sept. 1413.

435 [Fo. 65/44] Institution of William Palmer, clerk, to church of Buscot (*Berewardescote*), vac. by death of M. John Medford; patron, Simon Raileth, *domicellus*. Ind.: archd. of Berkshire. Ramsbury, 17 Sept. 1413.

436 Institution of M. Edmund Lacy D.Th., in person of Philip Lacy, his proctor, to church of Marnhull; patrons, abbot and conv. of Glastonbury (*Glaston*). Ind.: archd. of Dorset. Ramsbury, 24 Sept. 1413.

437 Institution of Roger Palmer, chaplain, in person of Simon Bradeford, rector of Ditteridge (*Ditheriche*), his proctor, to church of Hazelbury (*Haselbury*), vac. by resig. of John Grenhull; patrons, prior and conv. of Bradenstoke (*Bradenestoke*). Ind.: archd. of Wiltshire. Ramsbury, 4 Oct. 1413.

438 Institution of Simon Glyme, chaplain, to church of Charborough (*Charburgh*), vac. by death of John Stoke; patron, John Morvyle, senior. Ind.: archd. of Dorset. Ramsbury, 11 Oct. 1413.

439 Collation to M. Thomas Teynton, priest, of church of Poulshot (*Palesholte*). Ind.: archd. of Salisbury. Ramsbury, 11 Oct. 1413.

440 Collation to M. Gilbert Hallum, clerk, in person of M. Oliver Dyneley, clerk, his proctor, of a canonry in Salisbury cath. and the prebend of Highworth (*Hyworth*) in the same, vac. by death of M. Ralph Lovell. Mandate to the dean and chapter of Salisbury for his admission and to the dean for his installation. Ramsbury, 21 Oct. 1413.

441 Collation to M. Roger Basset D.Cn. & C.L. of a canonry in Salisbury cath. and the prebend of Netherbury in Terra in the same. Mandate to the dean and chapter of Salisbury for his admission and to the dean for his installation. Ramsbury, 24 Oct. 1413.

442 Exchange, by authority of Nicholas, bp. of Bath and Wells, between John Barkere, vicar of Minety (*Mynty*); patron, John Chitterne, archd. of Wiltshire—and Walter Clyve, vicar of Bathampton (*Hampton*), dioc. Bath and Wells. Ind. of Clyve: archd. of Wiltshire. Ramsbury, 5 Nov. 1413.

443 [Fo. 65v/44v] Institution of William Lawles, chaplain, to vicarage of Seagry (*Segre*), vac. by death[1] of Roger Palmer; patrons, prior and conv. of Bradenstoke (*Bradenestoke*). Ind.: archd. of Wiltshire. Theale (*Thele*), 17 Nov. 1413.

[1. Presumably an error for resignation. cf. **437**, **450**.]

444 King's bench *admittatis* concerning the church of Yattendon (*Yatenden*), because John atte Hyde and William Bruly have recovered the presentation from John Coteron and John Lunyal, chaplain, by reason of their default. *Teste* W. Hankeford. Westminster, 10 Nov. 1 Hen. V [1413]. Rotulet xxxvj Holgot.

[Enrolled P.R.O., KB 27/610.]

445 Institution of William Lynge, chaplain, to church of Yattendon; patrons, for this turn, John atte Hyde and William Bruly. Ind.: archd. of Berkshire. London, 19 Nov. 1413.

446 Exchange, by authority of Philip, bp. of Lincoln, between Simon Hermersworth, rector of the chapel with cure of souls of Crookham (*Crokham*); patron, Elizabeth, countess of Salisbury—and John Roper, vicar of Bradwell (*Bradewell*), dioc. Lincoln. Ind. of Roper: archd. of Berkshire. London, 27 Nov. 1413.

447 Exchange, by authority of Richard, bp. of London, between William Donne, rector of Enborne (*Endeburne*); patron, Lady Eleanor of St. Amand—and John Goodleef, rector of Aythorpe Roding (*Rothyng Aythrop*), dioc. London. Ind. of Goodleef: archd. of Dorset. London, 29 Nov. 1413.

448 Exchange, by authority of Robert, bp. of Chichester, between M. Thomas Lymyngton *alias* atte Fenne, chaplain of Holy Trinity chantry in Hungerford church; patron, the bp. of Salisbury—and John Yonge, vicar of Westbourne (*Westborne*), dioc. Chichester. Ind. of Yonge: vicar of Hungerford. London, 30 Nov. 1413.

449 [Fo. 66/45] Institution of M. Nicholas Colnet, clerk, in person of William Watton, priest, his proctor, to church of Sutton Courtenay, vac. by resig. of M. Walter Medeford; patron, Edward Courtenay, earl of Devon. Ind.: archd. of Berkshire. London, 10 Dec. 1413.

450 Exchange, by authority of Robert, bp. of Chichester, between Roger Palmere, rector of Hazelbury (*Hasulbury*); patrons, prior and conv. of Bradenstoke (*Bradenestok*)—and John Calvysberd, vicar of Barlavington (*Berlavyngton*), dioc. Chichester. Ind. of Calvysberd: archd. of Wiltshire. London, 11 Dec. 1413.

451 Exchange between M. Oliver Dyneley, clerk, porcioner of Haxton (*Hakeleston*); patron, Percival Sowdan—and Richard Blythe, rector of Pulham, in person of Thomas Batcombe, clerk, his proctor; patrons, abbot and conv. of Cirencester, dioc. Worcester. Ind. of Dyneley: archd. of Dorset. Ind. of Blythe: archd. of Salisbury. Potterne (*Poterne*), 17 Dec. 1413.

452 Institution of Henry Blakemore, chaplain, in person of M. John Morton, clerk, his proctor, to church of Long Bredy (*Langebridye, Langebrydie*), vac. by death of William Ekerdune; patrons, abbot and conv. of Cerne. Ind.: archd. of Dorset. Sherborne (*Schirborn*), 23 Dec. 1413.

453 Exchange, by authority of Richard, bp. of London, between John Umfrey, rector of Draycot Cerne (*Draycote Cerne*), in person of Thomas Kyrkeby, literate, his proctor; patron, Edward Cerne—and Edward

Mason, rector of Greensted (*Grenested*), dioc. London. Ind. of Mason: archd. of Wiltshire. Sherborne, 26 Dec. 1413.

454 Exchange, by authority of Thomas, bp. of Worcester, between John Rouland, rector of Up Cerne (*Upcerne*); patron, Ives FitzWaryn, knight—and Richard Martyn, rector of Naunton Beauchamp (*Newynton Beauchamp*), dioc. Worcester. Ind. of Martyn: archd. of Dorset. Sherborne, 28 Dec. 1413.

455 [Fo. 66v/45v] Institution of Richard Helihere *alias* Gerveys, chaplain, to church of Charborough (*Cherburgh*), vac. by death of Simon Glym; patron, John Morvile, *domicellus*. Ind.: archd. of Dorset. Sherborne, 29 Dec. 1413.

456 Collation to John Horewell, chaplain, of St. Mary's chantry in West Dean (*Westdene*) church. Ind.: archd. of Salisbury. Sherborne, 30 Dec. 1413.

457 Exchange, by authority of Edmund, bp. of Exeter, between M. John Waryn, rector of Grittleton (*Grydlyngton*); patrons, abbot and conv. of Glastonbury (*Glaston*)—and John Halsanger, rector of Cardinham (*Cardynan*), dioc. Exeter, in person of John Laurok, literate, his proctor. Ind. of Halsanger: archd. of Wiltshire. Sherborne, 31 Dec. 1413.

458 Institution of Richard Parys, chaplain, to church of Caundle Purse (*Caundell Purse*), vac. by resig. of William Pacere; patrons, abbess and conv. of Shaftesbury (*Shafton*). Ind.: archd. of Dorset. Sherborne, 4 Jan. 1414.

459 Institution of William Whitemere, subdeacon, to church of Compton Abbas (*Compton*), vac. by death of William Kelesey; patrons, abbess and conv. of Shaftesbury (*Shafton*). Ind.: archd. of Dorset. Sherborne, 9 Jan. 1414.

460 Institution of William Schirard, chaplain, to chapel of Little Mayne (*Lytelmayne*); patron, Henry Schirard, senior, *domicellus*. Ind.: archd. of Dorset. Sherborne, 9 Jan. 1414.

461 [Fo. 67/46] Institution of John Northefelde, chaplain, to church of Winterbourne Farringdon (*Wynterborn Germayn*); patron, Thomas Faryngdon. Ind.: archd. of Dorset. Sherborne, 11 Jan. 1414.

[Winterbourne Farringdon or St. German was 'entirely depopulated' by 1774, and is now incorporated into Winterbourne Came (Hutchins, ii. 519).]

462 Institution of M. John Symondesbourgh B.C.L., in person of John Symondesbourgh, literate, his proctor, to church of Hawkchurch (*Haukechurche*); patrons, abbot and conv. of Cerne. Ind.: archd. of Dorset. Sherborne, 12 Jan. 1414.

463 Exchange, by authority of Nicholas, bp. of Bath and Wells, between M. John Well, rector of Christian Malford (*Crystmalford*); patron, the bp. of Bath and Wells—and John Whitmere, rector of Chedzoy (*Chedesey*), dioc. Bath and Wells. Ind. of Whitmere: archd. of Wiltshire. Sherborne, 12 Jan. 1414.

464 Exchange, by authority of Robert, bp. of Hereford, between John Halys, rector of West Parley; patron, Robert Derby, esquire—and John Clerc, rector of Whitney (*Whyteney*), dioc. Hereford. Ind. of Clerc: archd. of Dorset. Sherborne, 17 Jan. 1414.

465 Institution of John Hanyle *alias* Kyng, chaplain, to vicarage of Bradford-on-Avon (*Bradford*); patrons, abbess and conv. of Shaftesbury (*Shafton*). Ind.: archd. of Salisbury. Sherborne, 18 Jan. 1414.

466 Notarial instrument drawn up by Wenceslas Swisiko, clerk (dioc. Brandenburg), notary public, certifying that the bp. of Salisbury has granted to William Boteler, formerly vicar of Bradford-on-Avon (*Bradford*), who has retired on account of his age and health, an annual pension of 12 marks [£9], to be paid out of the vicarage, with the agreement of John Hanyle *alias* Kyng, the present vicar. Boteler is also to have a high room in the east wing of the vicarage, facing the churchyard. Boteler and Hanyle are to share the hall, kitchen, gardens and orchard. Witnesses, John Luke B.Th., John Bernard, notary public, William Hanyle *alias* Kyng, priest (dioc. Canterbury and Bath and Wells). Chapel of Sherborne castle, 18 Jan. 1414.

467 [Fo. 67ᵛ/46ᵛ] Institution of Richard Netter, chaplain, to church of West Parley; patron, Robert Derby, esquire. Ind.: archd. of Dorset. Sherborne, 22 Jan. 1414.

468 Collation to John Conge, chaplain, of church of Poulshot (*Pawlesholt*). Ind.: archd. of Salisbury. Sherborne, 22 Jan. 1414.

469 [Fo. 68/47] Collation to Nicholas Sexpenne, chaplain, of church of Brixton Deverill (*Brixton Deverell*). Ind.: archd. of Salisbury. Sherborne, 22 Jan. 1414.

470 Institution of John Corbyn, chaplain, to vicarage of Toller Porcorum (*Tolre Porcorum*), vac. by resig. of John Jocy; patrons, abbot and conv. of Abbotsbury (*Abbodesbury*). Ind.: archd. of Dorset. Sherborne, 13 Feb. 1414.

471 Exchange, by authority of Edmund, bp. of Exeter, between Richard Taunton, rector of Manston; patron, Thomas Manston—and John Hele, vicar of Yarcombe (*Yartecombe*), dioc. Exeter. Ind. of Hele: archd. of Dorset. Sherborne, 27 Feb. 1414.

472 Institution of John Umfray, chaplain, to vicarage of Bucklebury (*Burghyldebury*), vac. by death of Thomas of Worthe; patrons, abbot and conv. of Reading (*Radyng*). Ind.: archd. of Berkshire. Sherborne, 5 March 1414.

473 Institution of John Kyng, clerk, in person of David Wyliam, chaplain, his proctor, to church of Woodsford (*Wyrdesforde*), vac. by resig. of M. John Symondesbergh; patrons, abbot and conv. of Cerne. Ind.: archd. of Dorset. Sherborne, 6 March 1414.

474 Letters of Thomas, prior of hermitage of Blackmore (*Blackmore Regis*), and the fellows of the same, presenting to the bp. John Adam of Okehampton, chaplain, with the request that he be admitted to their fellowship. [Undated.][1]

[1. Margin: *Nota*]

[Fo. 68ᵛ/47ᵛ] REGISTRUM REVERENDI IN CHRISTO PATRIS ET DOMINI DOMINI ROBERTI DEI GRACIA SAR' EPISCOPI DE COLLACIONIBUS INSTITUCIONIBUS ET PERMUTACIONIBUS BENEFICIORUM DE ANNO DOMINI MILLESIMO QUADRINGENTESIMO QUARTODECIMO

475 Institution of Robert Tolvey, chaplain, to vicarage of Brimpton (*Brympton*); patron, Walter Grendon, prior of hospital of St. John of Jerusalem in England. Ind.: archd. of Berkshire. Sonning (*Sonnyng*), 26 March 1414.

476 Institution of John Folyot, chaplain, to church of Alton (*Aleton*), vac. by resig. of John Comyn; patron, John Moyn, knight. Ind.: archd. of Salisbury. Salisbury, 5 Apr. 1414.

477 Collation to Robert Lovelych, chaplain, of vicarage of Idmiston (*Idemeston*). Ind.: archd. of Salisbury. Woodford (*Wodeford*), 14 Apr. 1414.

478 Letter to John Botston, chaplain, collating him to the status of a priest in St. Edmund's collegiate church, Salisbury. Woodford, 14 Apr. 1414.

479 Letter to Robert Busch, provost of St. Edmund's collegiate church, Salisbury, ordering the induction of John Botston [as in **478**]. Woodford, 14 Apr. 1414.

480 Collation to John Deynton and David Mychell, chaplains, of similar status in St. Edmund's collegiate church, with similar mandates for their induction. Woodford, 14 Apr. 1414.

481 Collation to Ranulph Rodely,[1] chaplain, in person of William Kegworth, his proctor, of church [*rectius* vicarage][2] of Winterbourne Whitchurch (*Whitchurche*). Ind.: archd. of Dorset. Woodford, 15 Apr. 1414.

[1. Cf. Thomas Rodeley, rector of Winterbourne Whitchurch 14 March 1416, **1054**.
2. Cf. Hutchins, i. 202.]

482 Collation to Robert Redeler, chaplain, of vicarage of Coxwell (*Cokes-well*). Ind.: archd. of Berkshire. Woodford, 15 Apr. 1414.

483 Exchange, by authority of Nicholas, bp. of Bath and Wells, between M. John Orum, rector of Rode, dioc. Bath and Wells, in person of William Orum, literate, his proctor—and William Fostbury, rector of Tarrant Keynston (*Kayneston*); patrons, abbess and conv. of Tarrant (*Tarente*). Ind. of Orum: archd. of Dorset. Woodford, 20 Apr. 1414.

484 [Fo. 69/48] Institution of John Chaas, chaplain, to St. Catherine's chantry in Gillingham (*Gyllingham*) church, vac. by death of Anselm [no surname]; patron, John Berkeley. Ind.: archd. of Dorset. Potterne, 22 Apr. 1414.

485 Exchange between Richard Synet, vicar of St. Mary, Marlborough (*Marleburgh*); patron, M. John Chaundeler, dean of Salisbury—and Andrew Gore *alias* Chalener, rector of Little Hinton (*Hyneton*); patron, Henry, bp. of Winchester. Ind. of Synet: archd. of Wiltshire. Ind. of Gore: official of peculiar jurisdiction of Marlborough. Leicester (*Leycestr'*), 11 May 1414.

486 Institution of Robert Osanne, clerk, to church of Steeple (*Steple*), vac. by resig. of John Bollam; patron, Edmund, earl of March and Ulster (*Marchie et Ultonie*), knight. Ind.: archd. of Dorset. Leicester, 12 May 1414.

487 Exchange, on certificate of Benet, bp. of Bangor (*Bangoren'*), between John Carpenter, rector of Winterbourne Bassett (*Wynterborn Basset*); patrons, prior and conv. of St. Pancras, Lewes—and William Canon, porcioner in church of Llandinam (*Landynan*), dioc. Bangor. Ind. of Canon: archd. of Wiltshire. Leicester, 13 May 1414.

488 Institution of William Fydyan, chaplain, to vicarage of Hagbourne (*Hakeborn*); patrons, abbot and conv. of Cirencester. Ind.: archd. of Berkshire. Leicester, 18 May 1414.

489 Exchange between Vincent Tydulsyde, rector of Burghfield (*Burghfeld*), in person of Oliver Dyneley, clerk, his proctor; patron, John Drayton, knight, lord of manor of Burghfield, and Isabel, his wife—and John Ropkyn, vicar of Shinfield (*Shynnyngfeld*); patrons, dean and chapter of Hereford. Ind. of both: archd. of Berkshire. Leicester, 15 May 1414.

490 [Fo. 69v/48v] Letter of M. Walter Medeford, canon of Salisbury cath. and prebendary of Bedwyn (*Bedewynd*) in the same, citing the bishop's commission, issued at Potterne (*Poterne*), 28 Apr. 1414, to inquire into the proposed exchange of benefices between John Whitham, rector of Ashley

(*Asshele*), and John Medmenham, chaplain and possessor of Crofton free chapel in Great Bedwyn prebendal church, and, if the inquiry is satisfactory, to carry out the exchange. Medeford, after learning from John Chaundeler, dean of Salisbury, that Crofton chapel was a free chapel and an exchangeable ecclesiastical benefice, has carried out the exchange, reserving the induction and obedience of Medmenham to the bp. Leicester, 22 May 1414.

491 Institution, on certificate of Walter Medeford, canon of Salisbury cath., bishop's commissary, of John Medmenham to church of Ashley (*Asshele*); patrons, for this turn, William Hankford, knight, William Poulet, William Besyle, esquires, and John Prat, rector of Hemington (*Hemyngton*), feoffees in all the lands and tenements of Walter Hungerford, knight. Ind.: archd. of Wiltshire. Leicester, 22 May 1414.

492 Institution of John Bonjon, chaplain, to church of Tidmarsh (*Tydmersh*); patron, Thomas Rothwell, junior. Ind.: archd. of Berkshire. Faringdon (*Faryndon*), 28 Apr. [*sic*] 1414.

493 Institution, on certificate of Geoffrey Crukadan, canon of Salisbury cath., of John Perlebyn, chaplain, to church of Thornton, after an inquiry into the vacancy and right of patronage; patron, William Elsander. Ind.: archd. of Dorset. Potterne (*Poterne*), 4 June 1414.

[For Thornton, formerly in Marnhull, see Hutchins, iv. 318–19.]

494 [Fo. 70/49] Exchange, by authority of Prior John and the chapter of Canterbury cathedral, *sede vacante*, between John Dreyn, rector of Sevington (*Sevyngton*), dioc. Canterbury, in person of Thomas Assheton, literate, his proctor—and John Godlefe, rector of Enborne (*Endeborne*); patron, Lady Eleanor of St. Amand. Ind. of Dreyn: archd. of Berkshire. Potterne, 8 June 1414.

495 Exchange between Adam Brystowe, rector of Studland (*Stodlonde*); patrons, William Alysaunder and Edith, his wife, Roger Stourton and Alice, his wife, and Elizabeth de la Bere, sister of the said Edith and Alice—and M. John Orum, rector of Tarrant Keynston (*Kayneston*), in person of M. Thomas Teynton, chaplain, his proctor; patrons, abbess and conv. of Tarrant (*Tarrente*). Ind. of both: archd. of Dorset. Potterne, 11 June 1414.

496 Institution of John Wylle, chaplain, to church of Studland, vac. by resig. of M. John Orum; patrons, [as in **495**]. Ind.: archd. of Dorset. Potterne, 17 June 1414.

497 Institution of Geoffrey Russell, chaplain, to church of Collingbourne Ducis (*Colyngbourne Ducis*), vac. by resig. of Thomas Norton; patrons, abbess and conv. of Wherwell (*Werewell*), dioc. Winchester. Ind.: archd. of

Wiltshire. A portion of 12 marks [£9] was assigned to Norton, to be paid by Russell and his successors as rectors. Potterne, 17 June 1414.

498 Exchange, on certificate of the abbot and conv. of Waltham Holy Cross, between William Broune, rector of Wormley (*Wormele*)—and Robert Hore, rector of Winterslow (*Wynterslewe*); patron, Edward, duke of York (*Ebor'*), earl of Cambridge (*Cantabrigg*), Rutland (*Rutlond*) and Cork (*Croac'*), and lord of the Isle of Wight (*Insula Vecta*). Ind. of Broune: archd. of Salisbury. Potterne, 22 June 1414.
[This exchange was reversed, 19 Oct. 1414, after an inquiry, **517**, **914**.]

499 [Fo. 70v/49v] Exchange, by authority of Henry, abp.–elect of Canterbury, between Robert Papulon, rector of Tollard Royal (*Tollard*); patron, Thomas Swanlond, esquire—and Alan Wombe, rector of Acrise (*Acryse*), dioc. Canterbury. Ind. of Wombe: archd. of Salisbury. Potterne, 28 June 1414.

500 Institution of John Wilthorp, chaplain, to church of Winterbourne Cherborough (*Wynterbourne Chirbourgh*), vac. by resig. of John Pynnok; patrons, William Alisandre and Robert Neweman. Ind.: archd. of Salisbury. A pension of 12 marks [£9] was assigned to Pynnok, to be paid by Wilthorp and his successors as rectors at the four terms of the year. Potterne, 6 July 1414.

501 Exchange, by authority of Nicholas, bp. of Bath and Wells, between William Coke, chaplain of chantry in Little Cheverell (*Chyverell Parva*) church; patron, William, lord of Botreaux, knight—and John Yveray *alias* Forde, rector of Christon (*Cricheston*), dioc. Bath and Wells. Ind. of Yveray: archd. of Salisbury. Potterne, 10 July 1414.

502 Institution of Thomas atte Mill, chaplain, to chapel of St. James of Philiberts in East Hanney (*Philbertescourt in Esthenney*), vac. by resig. of John Hardyng; patron, Robert Skeeram. Ind.: archd. of Berkshire. Potterne, 11 July 1414.
[For free chapel of St. James, see *VCH Berks.*, iv. 293.]

503 Exchange, by authority of Philip, bp. of Lincoln, between M. John Appulton, vicar of Aldbourne (*Aldeborne*); patron, the bp. of Salisbury—and William Goldyng, rector of moiety of Turvey (*Turveye*) church, dioc. Lincoln. Ind. of Goldyng: archd. of Wiltshire. Potterne, 12 July 1414.

504 Exchange, by authority of Philip, bp. of Lincoln, between Robert Garland, vicar of Milton Lilbourne (*Myddelton Lilbon*); patrons, abbot and conv. of Cirencester—and John Cryte, rector of Hardwick (*Herdewyk Audley*), dioc. Lincoln. Ind. of Cryte: archd. of Wiltshire. Potterne, 14 July 1414.
[For Hardwick, see J. C. Blomfield, *History of the Present Deanery of Bicester* (8 vols., 1882–94), iii. 42, 52.]

505 [Fo. 71/50] Institution of Richard Fletton, chaplain, to church of Winterbourne Steepleton (*Wynterbourne Stepulton, Wynterbourne Stypelton*); patron, Edmund, earl of March and Ulster (*Ulton*), knight. Ind.: archd. of Dorset. Potterne, 23 July 1414.

506 Institution of Robert de Tibbay, clerk, in person of Ellis Erlestoke, chaplain, his proctor, to church of Devizes (*Devyses*), vac. by resig. of Thomas de Tibbay; patron, Queen Joan. Ind.: official of peculiar jurisdiction of Devizes. Potterne, 26 July 1414.

507 Institution of John Wylly, chaplain, to church of Bremilham (*Bremelham*), vac. by resig. of John Harecombe; patron, Walter Dauntesey, esquire, lord of Dauntsey (*Dauntesey*). Ind.: archd. of Wiltshire. Potterne, 28 July 1414.

508 Exchange between John Freman, rector of East Shefford (*Estscheford*); patron, Thomas Estbury—and Richard Rayour, vicar of Basildon (*Bastelden*); patron, John Waver, warden of college of cantors of St. John the Baptist of Shottesbrook (*Shottesbrok*). Ind. of both: archd. of Berkshire. Potterne, 8 Aug. 1414.

509 Institution of William Bole, chaplain, to church of Easton Grey (*Eston Grey*); patrons, abbot and conv. of St. Peter, Gloucester. Ind.: archd. of Wiltshire. Sherborne (*Schirborn*), 26 Aug. 1414.

510 Exchange between Henry Shelford, rector of Cheselbourne (*Longe Cheselburne*); patrons, abbess and conv. of Shaftesbury (*Shafton*)—and John Mason, rector of Upway (*Upwey*); patron, the bp. of Salisbury. Ind. of both: archd. of Dorset. Sherborne, 31 Aug. 1414.

511 [Fo. 71v/50v] Exchange, by authority of Philip, bp. of Lincoln, between William Fydyan, vicar of Hagbourne (*Hakeborn*); patrons, abbot and conv. of Cirencester—and Robert Tunstall, rector of St. Clement, Oxford, dioc. Lincoln. Ind. of Tunstall: archd. of Berkshire. London, 26 Sept. 1414.

512 Institution of Thomas Marchaunt, chaplain, to church of Upton Lovell (*Ubeton*); patron, John Lovell, lord of Lovell, knight. Ind.: archd. of Salisbury. London, 30 Sept. 1414.

513 Institution of John Walden, chaplain, to St. John the Baptist's chapel, East Hendred (*Esthenreth*), vac. by resig. of William Strecher; patron, Ralph Arches, esquire. Ind.: archd. of Berkshire. London, 1 Oct. 1414.

514 Exchange between Walter Smyth, vicar of Compton; patron, John Chitterne, prebendary of Goodworth (*Godeworth*) in Wherwell (*Wherewell*) conventual church, dioc. Winchester, with the said church of Compton annexed to the prebend—and Thomas Radeford, vicar of Tilehurst (*Tylehurst, Tylherst*); patrons, abbot and conv. of Reading (*Radyng*). Ind. of both: archd. of Berkshire. London, 3 Oct. 1414.

515 Exchange, by authority of Edmund, bp. of Exeter, between Richard Batte, rector of Jacobstowe (*Jacobstawe*), dioc. Exeter—and John Corbyn, vicar of Toller Porcorum (*Tolre Porcorum*); patrons, abbot and conv. of Abbotsbury (*Abbotesbur'*). Ind. of Batte: archd. of Dorset. London, 10 Oct. 1414.

516 Institution of M. John Revell, chaplain, to vicarage of Ashbury (*Asshebury*); patron, M. Thomas Bubbewith, rector of Ashbury. Ind.: archd. of Berkshire. London, 11 Oct. 1414.

517 Exchange, on certificate of William, abbot of Waltham Holy Cross, dioc. London, between William Broune, rector of Winterslow (*Wynterslaw, Wynterslew*); patron, Edward, duke of York, earl of Rutland (*Ruteland*) and Cork, and lord of Wight (*Whyght*), knight—and Robert Hore, rector of Wormley (*Wormele*), dioc. London. Ind. of Hore: archd. of Wiltshire. London, 19 Oct. 1414.

[This reversed an earlier exchange of 22 June 1414, **498**, **914**.]

518 [Fo. 72/51] Exchange, by authority of Robert, bp. of Hereford, between M. Gilbert Stone, canon of Hereford cath. and prebendary of Eigne (*Yeyne*) in the same, in person of John Shudeford, chaplain, his proctor—and John Codeford, warden of Imber (*Ymmer*) free chapel; patron, William Rous. Ind. of Stone: archd. of Salisbury. London, 20 Oct. 1414.

519 Exchange, by authority of Henry, bp. of Winchester, between Thomas Milleward, rector of Huish (*Hewyssh*); patron, William Sturmy, knight—and William Preston, rector of Widley (*Wydeley*), dioc. Winchester. Ind. of Preston: archd. of Wiltshire. London, 22 Oct. 1414.

520 Exchange, by authority of Richard, bp. of London, between Richard Fygg, rector of Ufton Robert (*Ufton Roberd*); patron, William Perkynes—and Thomas West, rector of Greenford (*Parva Greneford, Parva Grenford*), dioc. London. Ind. of West: archd. of Berkshire. London, 23 Oct. 1414.

521 Exchange, by authority of Richard, bp. of Rochester, between Roger Longley, rector of Woolhampton (*Wolhampton*); patron, Walter Grendon, prior of hospital of St. John of Jerusalem in England—and John Gurry, vicar of Lessness (*Lesenes*), dioc. Rochester. Ind. of Gurry: archd. of Berkshire. London, 23 Oct. 1414.

522 Collation to Thomas Beke, clerk, of free chapel in Marlborough (*Marleburgh*) castle. Ind.: official of peculiar jurisdiction of Marlborough. London, 8 Nov. 1414.

523 [Fo. 72v/51v] Collation to M. Robert Holhan *alias* of Cork B.C.L. of church of Compton Bassett (*Compton Basset*). Ind.: archd. of Wiltshire. London, 9 Nov. 1414.

REGISTRUM REVERENDI IN CHRISTO PATRIS ET DOMINI DOMINI ROBERTI DEI GRACIA SAR' EPISCOPI HABITUM CORAM CIRCUMSPECTO VIRO MAGISTRO GALFRIDO CRUKADAN' UTRIUSQUE IURIS INCEPTORE ECCLESIE CATHEDRALIS SAR' CANONICO VICARIO IN SPIRITUALIBUS GENERALI, PREDICTO REVERENDO PATRE IN REMOTIS AGENTE ET DE ANNO DOMINI MILLESIMO QUADRINGENTESIMO QUARTODECIMO

524 Commission of Robert, bp. of Salisbury, to M. Adam de Mottrom, precentor of Salisbury cath., and M. Geoffrey Crukadan, canon, to act as vicars general during the bishop's absence abroad on matters concerning the English and the universal church [as **60**, omitting authority to collate to benefices in the bishop's gift]. Dover (*Dovor*), 19 Nov. 1414.

525 [Fo. 73/52] Commission of Robert, bp. of Salisbury, to Mottrom and Crukadan [as in **524**], to collate to benefices in the bishop's gift during the bishop's absence. Dover, 19 Nov. 1414.

[This authority is described in greater detail than in **60**, **60A.** Only Crukadan acted as vicar general during this absence of Hallum: Mottrom died July/Aug. 1415, **576**.]

[All the *acta* in the following section, **526–694**, are by M. Geoffrey Crukadan, vicar general.]

526 Exchange between John Boteler, rector of East Stoke (*Est Stoke, Estok*) by Bindon (*Byndon*); patrons, John Jurdan and John Cheverell—and Robert Ware, rector of Broadmayne (*Brodemayn*); patron, Thomas West, knight. Ind. of both: archd. of Dorset. Salisbury, 4 Dec. 1414.

527 Institution of John Taylor, chaplain, to church of Barford St. Martin (*Bereford*), vac. by death of John Sandon; patron, Lady Elizabeth Clynton. Ind.: archd. of Salisbury. Salisbury, 5 Dec. 1414.

528 Common pleas *admittatis* concerning the church of Barford St. Martin (*Bereford sancti Martini*), because Elizabeth, widow of John de Clynton, knight, has recovered the presentation from John Cornewayle, knight, and Elizabeth his wife, by reason of their default. *Teste* R. Norton. Westminster, 1 Dec. 1414.

529 [Fo. 73v/52v] Institution of John Westbury, chaplain, to moiety of church of Shillingstone (*Okeford Skyllyng*); patrons, Prior William Griche, and conv. of Montacute, dioc. Bath and Wells. Ind.: archd. of Dorset. Salisbury, 5 Dec. 1414.

[For Shillingstone, see **156**n.]

530 Exchange between John Ysoth, rector of Bexington (*Bexyngton*); patrons, abbot and conv. of Abbotsbury (*Abbodesbur'*)—and Richard *or* William Aversham, vicar of Abbotsbury; same patrons. Ind. of both: archd. of Dorset. Salisbury, 5 Dec. 1414.

531 Exchange, by authority of Philip, bp. of Lincoln, between Ralph Lambeden, vicar of Upavon (*Uphaven*); patron, King Henry—and William Rewe, rector of Tingrith (*Tyngreth*), dioc. Lincoln. Ind. of Rewe: archd. of Salisbury. Salisbury, 6 Dec. 1414.

532 Exchange between Ralph Grove, vicar of Bisham (*Bustlesham*); patron, Walter Grendon, prior of hospital of St. John of Jerusalem in England—and Richard Bitheham, vicar of White Waltham (*Waltham Abbatis*); patrons, abbot and conv. of Chertsey (*Chartesey*). Ind. of both: archd. of Berkshire. Salisbury, 7 Dec. 1414.

533 [Fo. 74/53] Vicar general's commission to the dean and chapter of Salisbury to inquire into the proposed exchange of benefices between Stephen Hulle, vicar of Norton Bavant (*Norton Bavent*); patrons, Prioress Maud and conv. of Dartford (*Derteford*), dioc. Rochester—and John Carlyl, vicar of Stourpaine (*Stourepayn, Stourpayne*); patrons, dean and chapter of Salisbury. If the inquiry is satisfactory, they are to carry out the exchange. Salisbury, 13 Dec. 1414.
M. John Chawndeler, dean, certifies that he has carried out the exchange, reserving the induction and obedience of Carlyl to the vicar general.

534 Institution of Roger Seliworth, chaplain, to free chapel of Little Sutton (*Parva Sutton*); patron, John Kyngeston, knight. Ind.: archd. of Salisbury. Salisbury, 8 Dec. 1414.

535 Exchange, by authority of Philip, bp. of Lincoln, between William Talbot, rector of Worth Matravers (*Worthe*) with Swanage (*Swanwyche*) chapel annexed, in person of William Gowrney, his proctor; patron, John Arundell, lord of Mautravers—and Robert Osanne, canon of Lincoln cath. and prebendary of Decem Librarum in the same. Ind. of Osanne: archd. of Dorset. Salisbury, 8 Dec. 1414.

536 Institution of M. John Coumbe, priest, to vicarage of Ramsbury (*Remmesbury*); patron, M. John Hurlhe, canon of Salisbury cath. and prebendary of Ramsbury in the same. Coumbe's induction ordered.[1] Salisbury, 24 Dec. 1414.

[1. Margin: *Nota de iurisdiccione domini in prebenda de Remmesbury*]

537 [Fo. 74v/53v] Exchange, by authority of Philip, bp. of Lincoln, between Richard Falus, vicar of West Hendred (*Westhenreth*); patrons, prior and conv. of Wallingford (*Walyngford*)—and Henry Viller, vicar of Aston Rowant (*Aston*), dioc. Lincoln. Ind. of Viller: archd. of Berkshire. Salisbury, 11 Jan. 1415.

[Cf. Lincolnshire Archives Office, Reg. XIV (Repingdon) fos. 401v–402 for identification of Aston Rowant, Oxon.]

538 Exchange, by authority of Henry, bp. of Winchester, between William Talbot, rector of Steeple (*Steple*); patron, Edmund, earl of March and Ulster (*Ulton*)—and Robert Leycester, rector of Wolverton (*Wolferton*), dioc. Winchester. Ind. of Leycester: archd. of Dorset. Salisbury, 12 Jan. 1415.

539 Exchange, by authority of Thomas, bp. of Worcester, between John Taylor, rector of Stanton St. Quintin (*Stawnton Quyntyn*); patron, Henry FitzHugh, knight—and William Buttus, rector of Tortworth (*Torteworth*), dioc. Worcester. Ind. of Buttus: archd. of Wiltshire. Salisbury, 15 Jan. 1415.

540 Institution of Henry Walbronde, chaplain, to vicarage of Winkfield (*Wynkefelde*); patrons, John Chaundeler, dean of Salisbury, and the chapter. Ind.: archd. of Berkshire. Salisbury, 16 Jan. 1415.

541 Institution of Brother Thomas Calne, chaplain, to vicarage of Canford Magna (*Caneford*); patrons, prior and conv. of St. Mary, Bradenstoke, order of St. Augustine. Ind.: archd. of Dorset. Salisbury, 19 Jan. 1415.

542 [Fo. 75/54] Exchange, by authority of Philip, bp. of Lincoln, between Peter Hasilmer, rector of Bucknall (*Bukenhull*), dioc. Lincoln—and Walter Tynker, vicar of St. James, Shaftesbury (*Schafton*); patrons, abbess and conv. of Shaftesbury. Ind. of Hasilmer: archd. of Dorset. Salisbury, 30 Jan. 1415.

543 Institution of Thomas Petite, chaplain, to vicarage of Gussage All Saints (*Gussych*); patron, John Makworth, archd. of Dorset. Ind.: archd. of Dorset. Salisbury, 31 Jan. 1415.

544 Exchange between James Grene, chaplain, of chantry in St. Edmund's collegiate church, Salisbury, for the souls of Reynold Tudeworth and Joan his wife, and all the faithful; patron, the bp. of Salisbury—and John Rasyn, vicar of Kington St. Michael (*sancti Michaelis de Westkyngton*); patrons, prioress and conv. of Kington St. Michael (*Estkyngton*). Ind. of Rasyn: provost of St. Edmund's collegiate church and M. William Dunham. Ind. of Grene: archd. of Wiltshire. Salisbury, 4 Feb. 1415.

545 Exchange, by authority of Thomas, bp. of Worcester, between Simon Sloley, rector of Tarrant Gunville (*Tarent Gondevile, Tarent Goundevile*); patron, Edmund, earl of March and Ulster (*Ulton*)—and Nicholas Touker or

Toutker, rector of Grafton Flyford (*Grafton super Fleford*), dioc. Worcester. Ind. of Touker: archd. of Dorset. Salisbury, 8 Feb. 1415.

546 [Fo. 75v/54v] Exchange between Walter Salesbury, vicar of Hullavington (*Honlavyngton, Hunlavyngton*); patron, King Henry—and Robert Redeler, vicar of Coxwell (*Cokeswell*); patron, the bp. of Salisbury. Ind. of Salesbury: archd. of Berkshire. Ind. of Redeler: archd. of Wiltshire. Salisbury, 9 Feb. 1415.

547 Exchange, by authority of Philip, bp. of Lincoln, between John Gurry, rector of Woolhampton (*Wolhampton*); patron, Walter Grendon, prior of hospital of St. John of Jerusalem in England—and William Rycheman, vicar of Potton, dioc. Lincoln. Ind. of Rycheman: archd. of Berkshire. Salisbury, 11 Feb. 1415.

548 Exchange, by authority of Henry, bp. of Winchester, between Robert Wantyng, rector of North Tidworth (*North Todeworth*); patron, Thomas de Monte Acuto, earl of Salisbury—and John Crufton, rector of Chiddingfold (*Chidyngfolde, Chyddyngfold*), dioc. Winchester. Ind. of Crufton: archd. of Salisbury. Salisbury, 15 Feb. 1415.

549 [Fc. 76/55] Exchange, by authority of Richard, bp. of London, between John Roo, vicar of Coombe Keynes (*Combecaynes*); patrons, Prior John and conv. of Merton—and Richard Figge, rector of Greenford (*Parva Greneford*), dioc. London. Ind. of Figge: archd. of Dorset. Salisbury, 18 Feb. 1415.

550 Institution of Aurelius Connewych, chaplain, to chaplaincy of Holy Trinity, Shaftesbury (*Shafton*); patrons, Abbess Cecily and conv. of Shaftesbury. Ind.: archd. of Dorset. Salisbury, 17 Feb. 1415.

551 Exchange between Richard Heryng, rector of Tyneham (*Tynham*); patrons, Prior Thomas and conv. of Tortington (*Tortyngton*), dioc. Chichester—and Richard Beck, rector of Critchell More (*Morekyrchill*); patron, Nicholas Cyfrewas, esquire. Ind. of both: archd. of Dorset. Salisbury, 24 Feb. 1415.

552 [Fo. 76v/55v] Institution of Thomas Bernard, chaplain, to vicarage of Market Lavington (*Chepynglavynton*), vac. by resig. of William Marchal; patrons, Rector Thomas Culmer and conv. of Edington (*Edyndon*). Ind.: archd. of Salisbury. The pension of 12 marks [£9] formerly assigned by the bp. to John Bryd, chaplain, was reserved. Salisbury, 24 Feb. 1415.

553 Exchange, by authority of the vicar general of Nicholas, bp. of Bath and Wells, then abroad, between William Caldewell, rector of South Perrott (*Southperot, Southperret*); patron, John Warre, esquire—and William

Causey, rector of North Perrott (*Northperot, Northperret*), dioc. Bath and Wells. Ind. of Causey: archd. of Dorset. Salisbury, 1 March 1415.

554 Exchange between John Hele, rector of Manston; patron, Thomas Manston, esquire—and John Yonge, chaplain of Holy Trinity chantry, Hungerford; patron, the bp. of Salisbury. Ind. of Yonge: archd. of Dorset. Ind. of Hele: vicar of Hungerford. Salisbury, 4 March 1415.

REGISTRUM HABITUM CORAM PRELIBATO MAGISTRO GALFRIDO VICARIO REVERENDI IN CHRISTO PATRIS ET DOMINI DOMINI ROBERTI DEI GRACIA SAR' EPISCOPI PREDICTI ET DE ANNO DOMINI MILLESIMO QUADRINGENTESIMO QUINTODECIMO

555 Institution of John Stone, king's secretary, to prebend or prebendal church of Fontmell (*Fountemell*); patrons, abbess and conv. of Shaftesbury (*Schafton*). Ind.: archd. of Dorset. Salisbury, 25 March 1415.

556 [Fo. 77/56] Institution of John Smyth, chaplain, to chantry in St. Thomas the Martyr's church, Salisbury, for the soul of Robert Godmaston, vac. by death of John Smyth [*sic*]; patrons, dean and chapter of Salisbury. Ind.: dean and chapter. Salisbury, 28 March 1415.

[Robert Godmaston or Godmanstone, mayor of Salisbury 1355; chantry founded 1380 (*VCH Wilts.*, vi. 148).]

557 Institution of Richard Hywet, chaplain, to vicarage of New Windsor (*Wyndesor nove*); patrons, abbot and conv. of Waltham Holy Cross, dioc. London. Ind.: archd. of Berkshire. Salisbury, 12 Apr. 1415.

558 Exchange between Robert Portisham, vicar of Bremhill (*Bremul*) [no patron given]—and Robert Sabyn, vicar of Avebury; patrons, abbot and conv. of Cirencester (*Cirencestrie*). Ind. of both: archd. of Wiltshire. Salisbury, 20 Apr. 1415.

559 Institution of John Horton, chaplain, to church of Monkton Farleigh (*Farlegh*), vac. by resig. of Thomas Nyhawe; patrons, prior and conv. of Monkton Farleigh. Ind.: archd. of Wiltshire. Salisbury, 22 Apr. 1415.

560 Institution of John Swytecok, chaplain, to church of Langley Burrell (*Langleyburell*); patrons, Thomas Sakavile, knight, Richard Wakehurst, John Broke and John Dryver. Ind.: archd. of Wiltshire. Salisbury, 25 Apr. 1415.

561 Exchange, by authority of John Rowlond, canon of Wells, vicar general of Nicholas, bp. of Bath and Wells, then abroad, between Richard Godyngton, rector of Warmwell; patron, Nicholas Coker, esquire—and William Lymyngton, rector of South Bradon, dioc. Bath and Wells. Ind. of Lymyngton: archd. of Wiltshire [*rectius* Dorset]. Salisbury, 8 May 1415.

562 [Fo. 77v/56v] Exchange, by authority of John Rowlond, canon of Wells, vicar general of Nicholas, bp. of Bath and Wells, then abroad, between Thomas Bugworth, rector of Littleton (*Lytelton*); patron, Avice Derby—and Thomas Scherde, rector of St. John, Ilchester (*Yelchester*), dioc. Bath and Wells. Ind. of Scherde: archd. of Dorset. Salisbury, 11 May 1415.

563 Institution of Geoffrey Skynner, chaplain, to church of Atworth (*Coteles Atteworth*), vac. by resig. of John Prodhome; patron, Thomas Beauschine, *domicellus*. Ind.: archd. of Wiltshire. Salisbury, 15 May 1415.

564 Exchange between Oliver Dyneley, rector of Pulham; patrons, abbot and conv. of Cirencester (*Sirencestrie*)—and Robert Canon, rector of Iwerne Courtnay (*Iwerne Cortenay*, *Iwerne Cowrtnay*); patrons, prior and conv. of Christchurch (*Crystchirche, Twynham*), order of St. Augustine, dioc. Winchester. Ind. of both: archd. of Dorset. Salisbury, 15 May 1415.

565 Institution of John Sanger, chaplain, to vicarage of Latton; patrons, abbot and conv. of Cirencester (*Sirencestrie*). Ind.: archd. of Berkshire [*rectius* Wiltshire]. Salisbury, 23 May 1415.

566 [Fo. 78/57] Exchange, by authority of Nicholas, bp. of Bath and Wells,[1] between William Rycheman, rector of Woolhampton (*Wolhampton*) [no patron given]—and John Saly, warden of chapel and chantry of St. John the Baptist in South Petherton (*Southpertton*), dioc. Bath and Wells; patron, for this turn, Queen Joan, guardian of Giles, son[2] and heir of the late Giles Daubeney, knight, a minor. Ind. of Saly: archd. of Berkshire. Salisbury, 15 July 1415.

[1. *Sic.* The commission was issued by the vicar general of Bubwith, who was at the council of Constance, see **562**.
2. *Sic, rectius* grandson (Collinson, iii. 108–9).]

567 Institution of William Scoch, chaplain, to church of Stapleford (*Stapulforde*), vac. by death of M. John Perche; patron, William Esturmy, knight. Ind.: archd. of Wiltshire. Salisbury, 27 July 1415.

[For Scoch's complaint about dilapidations, see *Reg. Chichele*, iv. 29, 59.]

568 Letter of Geoffrey Crukadan, citing commission of Robert, bp. of Salisbury, and collating to M. John Hurlegh B.Cn.L. a canonry in Salisbury cath. and the prebend of Ramsbury (*Remmesbury*) in the same, vac. by death of M. Richard Wyche. Salisbury, 23 Dec. 1414.

569 Institution of Thomas Marchal, chaplain, to vicarage of Woodford (*Wodeford*) prebendal church, vac. by death of Thomas Baker; patron, Ralph Repyndon, prebendary of Wilsford (*Wyvelisford*) and Woodford. Ind.: official of dean of Salisbury. Salisbury, 28 July 1415.

570 Institution of John Feryby, clerk, to church of Chisledon (*Chesulden, Chuseldene*), vac. by resig. of John Mynty; patrons, abbot and conv. of Hyde (*Hyda*). Ind.: archd. of Wiltshire. Salisbury, 28 July 1415.

571 [Fo. 78v/57v] Institution of John Chitterne, chaplain, to church of Newton Toney (*Neweton Tony*), vac. by resig. of John Perys, chaplain; patron, Thomas West, knight. Ind.: archd. of Wiltshire. Salisbury, 31 July 1415.

572 Institution of John Fovent, clerk, to church of Caundle Purse (*Caundell Pours, Caundell Purs*), vac. by death of Richard Parys; patrons, abbess and conv. of Shaftesbury (*Schafton*). Ind.: archd. of Dorset. Salisbury, 31 July 1415.

573 Institution of Richard Vincent, brother of the order of preaching friars, to chantry at altar of St. Catherine and St. Margaret in Market Lavington (*Stepullavynton*) church, vac. by resig. of William Marchall; patron, Walter Beauchamp, esquire. Ind.: archd. of Salisbury. Salisbury, 31 July 1415.

574 Institution of John Arundell, chaplain, to church of Stanton (*Stantun, Staunton*), vac. by death of M. John Perch; patrons, abbess and conv. of Wilton. Ind.: archd. of Wiltshire. Salisbury, 31 July 1415.

575 Exchange, by authority of Edmund, bp. of Exeter, between Robert Blake, rector of Heddington (*Hedyngton*); patrons, prior and conv. of Monkton Farleigh (*Farlegh*), order of Cluny—and William Walshe, rector of Washfield (*Wasshefeld*), dioc. Exeter. Ind. of Walshe: archd. of Wiltshire. Salisbury, 8 Aug. 1415.

576 [Fo. 79/58] Institution of Richard Prentys, chaplain, in person of his proctor, to prebendal church of South Newton (*Southnewton*), vac. by death of M. Adam Mottrom; patrons, Abbess Joan and conv. of Wilton. Ind.: archd. of Salisbury. Salisbury, 9 Aug. 1415.

577 Exchange, by authority of Philip, bp. of Lincoln, between John Longelegh, rector of Finchampstead (*Fynchampstede*); patrons, John Collee and Elizabeth, his wife—and John Ladd, rector of Westmill (*Westmulle*), dioc. Lincoln. Ind. of Ladd: archd. of Berkshire. Salisbury, 15 Aug. 1415.

578 Institution of John Lenyng, chaplain, to church of St. Michael, Wareham; patron, King Henry, custodian of the alien priory of Wareham during the war with France. Ind.: archd. of Dorset. Salisbury, 16 Aug. 1415.

579 Institution of Thomas Kynow B.A. (dioc. Winchester), to church of Alton Barnes (*Aulton Bernes*), vac. by death of Ralph Gardener; patrons, warden of the college of St. Mary of Winchester in Oxford, and the fellows and scholars of the same. Ind.: archd. of Wiltshire. Salisbury, 18 Aug. 1415.

580 [Fo. 79v/58v] Exchange between John Brygt, rector of Leigh (*Leygh, Lyegh*); patron, Reynold Curteys, lord of Leigh—and John Pere, rector of Wraxall (*Wroxale*); patron, Robert de Lovell. Ind. of Pere: archd. of Wiltshire. Ind. of Brygt: archd. of Dorset. Salisbury, 18 Aug. 1415.

581 Institution of John Alfred, chaplain, to church of Frome St. Quintin, vac. by death of M. John Ocley; patrons, abbot and conv. of Tewkesbury (*Tewkysbery*), dioc. Worcester. Ind.: archd. of Dorset. Salisbury, 18 Aug. 1415.

582 Collation to John Chitterne, chaplain, of a canonry in Salisbury cath. and the prebend of Hurstbourne (*Husseburne*) and Burbage (*Burbache*) in the same, vac. by resig. of M. John Luke. Admission by dean and chapter of Salisbury. Salisbury, 26 Aug. 1415.

583 The like to M. Simon Sidenham of the prebend of Yetminster (*Yatmyster*) Secunda. Salisbury, 11 Sept. 1415.

[For Sidenham's complaint about dilapidations, see *Reg. Chichele*, iv. 35.]

584 The like to Richard Lentwardyne, chaplain, of the prebend of Ratfyn (*Rotfen*). Salisbury, 12 Sept. 1415.

585 The like to John Frank, priest, of the prebend of Chisenbury (*Chesyngbury*) and Chute. Salisbury, 2 Oct. 1415.

586 The like to M. Henry Harburgh, chaplain, of the prebend of Beminster (*Bemister*) Prima. Salisbury, 2 Oct. 1415.

587 [Fo. 80/59] The like to M. John Luke, chaplain, of the prebend of Slape. Salisbury, 3 Oct. 1415.

588 Institution of Robert Letthe, chaplain, to vicarage of West Ilsley (*Westhildesle*), vac. by resig. of William Caddo; patrons, prior and conv. of Sandleford (*Sandelifforde*). Ind.: archd. of Berkshire. Salisbury, 4 Oct. 1415.

589 Institution of Richard Smithesende, chaplain, to vicarage of Cranborne (*Cranburne*); patrons, abbot and conv. of Tewkesbury. Ind.: archd. of Dorset. Salisbury, 4 Oct. 1415.

590 Institution of William Taylour, chaplain, to vicarage of Avebury; patrons, abbot and conv. of Cirencester (*Cirencestrie*). Ind.: archd. of Wiltshire. Salisbury, 13 Oct. 1415.

591 Collation to John Bathe, chaplain, of a canonry in Salisbury cath. and the prebend of Bedminster (*Bedmyster*) and Redclyffe (*Radeclyve*) in the same. Admission by dean and chapter. Salisbury, 25 Oct. 1415.

592 The like to William Werkeman, chaplain, of the prebend of Chardstock (*Cherdestoke, Cherdstoke*). Salisbury, 4 Nov. 1415.

593 Institution of Clement Ogmore, chaplain, to church of Stour Provost (*Stoureprewes*); patron, King Henry. Ind.: archd. of Dorset. Salisbury, 13 Nov. 1415.

594 [Fo. 80v/59v] Collation to M. Edmund Bekenham, priest, of a canonry in Salisbury cath. and the prebend of Axford (*Axforde*) in the same. Admission by dean and chapter. Salisbury, 16 Nov. 1415.

595 Institution of Thomas Dragon, chaplain, to church of Thoulstone (*Tholveston*); patron, Thomas Reyner, esquire. Ind.: archd. of Salisbury. Salisbury, 5 Dec. 1415.

[For Thoulstone, formerly in Warminster hundred, see *VCH Wilts.*, viii. 78–9, 89.]

596 Institution of M. William Gray, chaplain, to church of Pimperne (*Pymperne*); patron, Edmund, earl of March and Ulster (*Ulton*). Ind.: archd. of Dorset. Salisbury, 5 Dec. 1415.

597 Institution of Walter Eston, chaplain and monk, to priorate of Wareham; patron, for this turn, Queen Joan. Ind.: archd. of Dorset. Salisbury, 5 Jan. 1416.

598 Exchange, by authority of Henry, abp. of Canterbury, between Robert Pampilon, rector of Acrise (*Acres*), dioc. Canterbury—and Thomas Coyter, vicar of Iwerne Minster (*Werne*); patron, John Chitterne. Ind. of Pampilon: archd. of Dorset. Salisbury, 21 Jan. 1416.

599 Institution of John Colynnys, chaplain, to church of Bryanston; patron, John Rogeris, *domicellus*. Ind.: archd. of Dorset. Salisbury, 24 Jan. 1416.

600 Exchange, by authority of Henry, bp. of Winchester, between Thomas Caldewell, vicar of Sutton Benger (*Sutton Bengere, Sutton Bengeres*); patron, John Rober—and Henry Smalcombe, rector of Eastrop (*Estrope*), dioc. Winchester. Ind. of Smalcombe: archd. of Wiltshire. Salisbury, 2 Feb. 1416.

601 [Fo. 81/60] Institution of John Lodewell, chaplain, to church of Alton; patron, John Moigne, knight. Ind.: archd. of Salisbury. Salisbury, 10 Feb. 1416.

602 Exchange between John Saly, rector of Woolhampton (*Wolhampton*); patron, Walter Grendon, prior of hospital of St. John of Jerusalem in England—and Henry Walbronde, vicar of Winkfield (*Wynkefelde*); patrons, dean and chapter of Salisbury. Ind. of both: archd. of Berkshire. Salisbury, 16 Feb. 1416.

603 Exchange, by authority of John Blonham, precentor of Chichester cath., keeper of spiritualities of see of Chichester *sede vacante*, between John Yonge, rector of Manston; patron, Thomas Manston, *domicellus*—and Thomas Atkyn, rector of Eckington (*Hekenton*), dioc. Chichester. Ind. of Atkyn: archd. of Dorset. Salisbury, 26 Feb. 1416.

[For Eckington, in Ripe, see A. Mawer and F. M. Stenton, *The Place-names of Sussex* (English Place-name Soc., vi, vii, 1929–30), p. 404.]

604 Exchange, on certificate of Dean Thomas More and chapter of St. Paul's cath., London, between John Lavyngton, rector of Didcot (*Dudcote, Dudecote*); patron, Thomas Stonor, esquire—and John Carbura or Corbura, warden of St. Radegund's free chapel in crypt of St. Paul's. Ind. of Carbura: archd. of Berkshire. Salisbury, 2 March 1416.

605 [Fo. 81v/60v] Institution of M. Robert Maslyn, chaplain, to vicarage of Collingbourne Kingston (*Colingbourne Abbatis, Colyngborne Abbatis*), vac. by death of John Towker; patron, Nicholas Godwyn, rector of Collingbourne Kingston. Ind.: archd. of Wiltshire. Salisbury, 10 March 1416.

606 Institution of Robert Curteys, chaplain, to church of Haselbury Bryan (*Haselbere*); patron, Lady Alice de Bryene. Ind.: archd. of Dorset. Salisbury, 10 March 1416.

607 Institution of John Trafford, chaplain, to church of Rampisham (*Ramsham*), vac. by resig. of Robert Curteys; patron, Robert Lovell. Ind.: archd. of Dorset. Salisbury, 10 March 1416.

608 Institution of William Belman, chaplain, to church of Bradford Peverell (*Bradeforde Peverell*), vac. by death of John Best; patrons, Warden Robert Thurbern and the fellows and scholars of New College of St. Mary by Winchester, as established by an inquiry. Ind.: archd. of Dorset. A customary pension of 40 shillings owed to the college was reserved. Salisbury, 11 March 1416.

609 Institution of Thomas Illyng, chaplain, to church of Remenham (*Ramenham*); patron, William Mountford, esquire, lord of Coleshill (*Colshull*) in Arden (*Arderne*), county of Warwick. Ind.: archd. of Berkshire. Salisbury, 4 Apr. 1416.

610 [Fo. 82/61] Institution of John Wodegrene, chaplain, to vicarage of New Windsor (*Wyndesore Nove*); patrons, abbot and conv. of Waltham Holy Cross. Ind.: archd. of Berkshire. Salisbury, 4 Apr. 1416.

611 Institution of M. Thomas Baldyng, chaplain, to free chapel of Wytherstone (*Wythereston*), vac. by resig. of M. Walter London; patrons, abbot and conv. of Abbotsbury (*Abbodesbury*). Ind.: archd. of Dorset. Salisbury, 6 Apr. 1416.

612 Institution of Walter Bury, chaplain, to church of Lacerton (*Lasarton*), vac. by resig. of John Peyteveyn; patrons, prioress and conv. of Kington St. Michael (*Kyngton*). Ind.: archd. of Dorset. Salisbury, 11 Apr. 1416.

613 Institution of William Becke, chaplain, to church of Hilperton (*Hulpryngton*); patron, Edmund, earl of March and Ulster (*Ulton*), lord of Wigmore (*Wygmore*) and Clare. Ind.: archd. of Salisbury. Salisbury, 24 Apr. 1416.

614 Institution of Thomas Drewery, chaplain, to church of Brightwalton (*Brythwaltham, Brytwalton*); patrons, abbot and conv. of St. Martin, Battle. Ind.: archd. of Salisbury [*rectius* Berkshire]. Salisbury, 24 Apr. 1416.

615 Institution of John Spenser, chaplain, to vicarage of Charlton (*Charleton*); patron, Queen Joan. Ind.: archd. of Salisbury. Salisbury, 25 Apr. 1416.

616 Collation to M. Gilbert Hallum of a canonry in Salisbury cath. and the prebend of Netherbury in Ecclesia in the same. Salisbury, 25 Apr. 1416.

617 [Fo. 82ᵛ/61ᵛ] Collation to M. John Fyton, chaplain, of a canonry in Salisbury cath. and the prebend of Highworth (*Hyworth*) in the same. Admission by dean and chapter. Salisbury, 26 Apr. 1416.

618 Collation to M. Edmund Dutton, chaplain, of a canonry in Salisbury cath. and the prebend of Grantham Borealis (*Grantham Boriall*) in the same. Admission by dean and chapter. Salisbury, 26 Apr. 1416.

619 Institution of M. Peter de Alcobasso, in person of John Horlok, his proctor, to free chapel of St. James of Philiberts (*Fylberdescort*) [in East Hanney]; patron, Robert Skerne, *domicellus*, as established by an inquiry. Ind.: archd. of Berkshire. Salisbury, 16 May 1416.

620 Exchange, by authority of Henry, bp. of Winchester, between John Wilthorp, rector of Winterbourne Cherborough (*Wynterborne Chirbogh*); patron, William Alysandor—and Robert Everarde, rector of Grateley, dioc. Winchester. Ind. of Everarde: archd. of Salisbury. Salisbury, 20 May 1416.

621 Institution of Richard Prentys, chaplain, to prebendal church of Liddington (*Ludyngton*); patrons, abbess and conv. of Shaftesbury (*Shafton*). Ind.: archd. of Wiltshire. Salisbury, 2 June 1416.

622 Institution of M. Robert Langrisshe, priest, to vicarage of East Garston (*Estgarston*); patrons, prioress and conv. of Amesbury (*Ambresbury*). Ind.: archd. of Salisbury. Salisbury, 6 June 1416.

623 [Fo. 83/62] Exchange, by authority of Henry, bp. of Winchester, between Robert Stoyte, vicar of Norton; patrons, abbot and conv. of Malmesbury—and John Stoke, rector of Kingston (*Kyngeston*) chapel, Isle of Wight (*Insula Vecta*), dioc. Winchester. Ind. of Stoke: archd. of Wiltshire. Salisbury, 10 June 1416.

624 Exchange, by authority of Richard, bp. of London, between Henry Harburgh, rector of St. Bride, city of London; patrons, abbot and conv. of Westminster (*Westmon'*), dioc. London—and Thomas Faukys, precentor of Salisbury cath. Admission of Harburgh by dean and chapter of Salisbury. Salisbury, 13 July 1416.

625 Exchange, by authority of Edmund, bp. of Exeter, between John Corbyn, rector of Jacobstowe (*Jacobustow*), dioc. Exeter—and John Iveray, chaplain of chantry of Little Cheverell (*Cheverelle Parva*); patron, William Botreaux, knight. Ind. of Corbyn: archd. of Salisbury. Salisbury, 14 July 1416.

626 Institution of Thomas Clyve, chaplain, to church of Aston Priors (*Aston Prewys*) by Blewbury (*Blebury*), vac. by death of John Bleby; patrons, prior and conv. of St. Mary of Witham in Selwood (*Selewode*), Carthusian order, as established by an inquiry. Ind.: archd. of Berkshire. Salisbury, 14 July 1416.

[For Aston Priors, now part of Aston Tirrold, see *VCH Berks.*, iii. 455.]

627 Exchange between John Henton, rector of moiety of church of Shillingstone (*Ocford Skyllyng*); patrons, John Newman, Isabel, his wife, and Nicholas Caldecot—and Thomas Stratton, vicar of Downton; patrons, warden and fellows of New College, Winchester. Ind. of Henton: archd. of Wiltshire. Ind. of Stratton: archd. of Dorset. Salisbury, 15 July 1416.

[For Shillingstone, see **156**n.]

628 [Fo. $83^v/62^v$] Exchange between William Talbot, rector of Orcheston St. Mary (*Orcheston Marye*); patron, Richard Lytelcote, lord—and Thomas Attkyn, rector of Manston; patron, Thomas Manston, *domicellus*. Ind. of Attkyn: archd. of Salisbury. Ind. of Talbot: archd. of Dorset. Salisbury, 6 Aug. 1416.

629 Institution of John Jolyffe, chaplain, to church of Fifehead Neville (*Fyfede*); patron, Edmund Spersholt, *domicellus*, as established by an inquiry. Ind.: archd. of Dorset. Salisbury, 12 Sept. 1416.

630 Institution of John Malteby, chaplain, to church of Frome Billet (*Frome Belet*); patrons, abbot and conv. of Milton (*Middelton*). Ind.: archd. of Dorset. Salisbury, 14 Sept. 1416.

631 Exchange, by authority of M. Walter Medeford, vicar general in spirituals of Henry, bp. of Winchester, between Thomas Pencombe, rector of Chettle (*Chetill, Chetyl, Chetyll*); patrons, abbot and conv. of Tewkesbury (*Teukysbery*)—and John Brice, rector of Knight's Enham (*Enham*), dioc. Winchester. Ind. of Brice: archd. of Dorset. Salisbury, 18 Sept. 1416.

632 Institution of Walter Archer, chaplain, to church of Winterbourne Stickland (*Styklane*); patrons, abbot and conv. of Milton (*Middelton*). Ind.: archd. of Dorset. Salisbury, 23 Sept. 1416.
[For Winterbourne Stickland, see Hutchins, i. 330–4.]

633 Collation to John Conge, priest, of provostship of house or college of St. Edmund, Salisbury. Ind.: Geoffrey Crukadan. Salisbury, 8 Sept. 1416.

634 [Fo. 84/63] Grant to Laurence Fyton, substitute for M. John Hurlegh, proctor of Thomas Burton, canon of Salisbury cath. and prebendary of Torleton in the same, of a letter to the bp. of Worcester, for the induction of Burton into the *corpus* of the said prebend. Salisbury, 8 Sept. 1416.
[Admitted by dean and chapter of Salisbury 16 Aug. 1416. He had letters of collation of Bishop Robert, issued at Constance, on the death of William Loryng (Pountney, p. 41).]

635 Institution of M. John Chaundeler, priest, dean of Salisbury, to prebendal church of South Newton (*Southneuton*); patrons, abbess and conv. of Wilton. Ind.: archd. of Dorset. Salisbury, 4 Oct. 1416.

636 Letter of George de Louthorp, canon residentiary of Salisbury and warden of the choristers, to Geoffrey Crukadan, vicar general, presenting William Papelon, rector of Thruxton (*Throkelston*), dioc. Winchester, to the vicarage of Preshute (*Preshut*); patron, George Louthorp, at nomination of Geoffrey Crukadan, by authority of the bp. of Salisbury. Papelon is exchanging benefices with M. Thomas Newman, vicar of Preshute. An annual pension of £20 due to the wardens of the choristers from the vicars of Preshute is reserved.

637 Exchange, by authority of Henry, bp. of Winchester, between M. Thomas Newman, vicar of Preshute, and William Papelon, rector of Thruxton, dioc. Winchester, [as in **636**]. [No ind. given.] Salisbury, 5 Oct. 1416.

638 [Fo. 84v/63v] Exchange between John Colfote, rector of West Grimstead (*Westgrimestede*); patron, John Berkley, knight—and Richard Huphull, vicar of Winterbourne Stoke (*Wynterbornestoke*); patron, John, prior of new house of Jesus of Bedlem in Sheen (*Shene*), Carthusian order. [No ind. given.] Salisbury, 6 Oct. 1416.

639 Institution of John Whitmer, chaplain, to prebendal church of Liddington (*Ludyngton*); patrons, abbess and conv. of Shaftesbury (*Shafton*). Ind.: archd. of Wiltshire. Salisbury, 8 Oct. 1416.

640 Exchange between John Franke, rector of Gussage St. Michael (*Gussich, Gussyche*); patron, King Henry, custodian of the alien priory of Wareham during the war with France—and Henry Rodeman, rector of Pentridge (*Pentriche*); patrons, abbot and conv. of Tewkesbury (*Teukesbury*), dioc. Worcester. Ind. of both: archd. of Dorset. Salisbury, 9 Oct. 1416.

641 Institution of M. John Chaundeler, dean of Salisbury, priest, to prebendal church of Chalk (*Chalke*); patrons, abbess and conv. of Wilton. Ind.: archd. of Salisbury. Salisbury, 9 Oct. 1416.

[For Chaundeler's complaint about dilapidations, see *Reg. Chichele*, iv. 43.]

642 Institution of M. Edward Prentys, chaplain, to prebendal church of South Newton (*Southneuton*); patrons, abbess and conv. of Wilton. Ind.: archd. of Salisbury. Salisbury, 9 Oct. 1416.

[For Prentys's complaint about dilapidations, see *Reg. Chichele*, iv. 43, 56.]

643 Institution of John Conge, priest, to prebendal church of North Newnton (*Northneuton*); patrons, abbess and conv. of Wilton. [No ind. given.] Salisbury, 9 Oct. 1416.

644 [Fo. 85/64] Collation to M. William Clint, of a canonry in Salisbury cath. and the prebend of Netherbury in Terra (*Netherbery in Terra*) in the same. Admission by dean and chapter. Salisbury, 9 Oct. 1416.

645 Institution of John Foxholes, priest, to church of Bishopstone (*Byshopeston*) *alias* Ebbesborne (*Ebbesburne*); patron, bp. of Winchester. Ind.: archd. of Salisbury. Salisbury, 18 Oct. 1416.

646 Institution of M. John Hody, priest, to church of Brightwell (*Bryghtwell*), vac. by resig. of Nicholas Calton; patron, the bp. of Winchester. Ind.: archd. of Berkshire. Salisbury, 23 Oct. 1416.

647 Institution of John FitzRicharde, priest, to church of Pentridge (*Pentriche*), vac. by resig. of John Franke; patrons, abbot and conv. of Tewkesbury (*Teukesbury*). Ind.: archd. of Dorset. Salisbury, 5 Nov. 1416.

648 Exchange, by authority of Philip, bp. of Lincoln, between M. John Southam, rector of Loughborough (*Loughtburgh, Louthtburgh*), dioc. Lincoln; patron, King Henry, guardian of the son and heir of the late Henry, lord of Beaumont (*Beamont*)—and Thomas Enkeston, canon of Salisbury cath. and prebendary of Grantham Australis (*Grantham Australl*) in the same; patron, the bp. of Salisbury. Admission of Southam by dean and chapter. Salisbury, 6 Nov. 1416.

649 Collation to M. Oliver Dyneley, of a canonry in Salisbury cath. and the prebend of Yatesbury (*Yatysbury*) in the same, vac. by death of R. Busche. Admission by dean and chapter. Salisbury, 6 Nov. 1416.

650 [Fo. 85v/64v] Institution of Alan Leverton, chaplain, in person of William Symyngton, clerk, his proctor, to church of Chisledon (*Chesylden*), vac. by resig. of John Fereby; patrons, abbot and conv. of Hyde (*Hida*), dioc. Winchester. Ind.: archd. of Wiltshire. The proctor swore that his lord would observe the provision formerly made for the augmentation of Chisledon vicarage. Salisbury, 4 Dec. 1416.

[Cf. **927**, agreement made 23 Dec. 1412.]

651 Institution of Walter Wilkokes, chaplain, to church of Lydiard Millicent (*Lydyarde*); patron, King Henry. Ind.: archd. of Wiltshire. Salisbury, 1 Jan. 1417.

652 Institution of William Thame, chaplain, to church of Wroughton (*Elyndon*); patron, Henry, bp. of Winchester. Ind.: archd. of Wiltshire. Salisbury, 4 Jan. 1417.

[For Wroughton, see **3**n.]

653 Exchange, by authority of John Rolonde, canon of Wells, vicar general of Nicholas, bp. of Bath and Wells, between Simon Membery, rector of Long Critchell (*Langkyrchill*, *Longkyrchill*); patron, Thomas Swanlond, *domicellus*—and William Fostebery, rector of Rode (*Roode*), dioc. Bath and Wells. Ind. of Fostebery: archd. of Dorset. Salisbury, 9 Jan. 1417.

654 Institution of Richard Mowlam, chaplain, to church of Wimborne All Saints (*Wymborne Carentham*); patron, John Arundell, lord of Arundel (*Arundell*) and Mautravers. Ind.: archd. of Dorset. Salisbury, 12 Jan. 1417.

[For Wimborne All Saints, now united with Wimborne St. Giles, see Hutchins, iii. 600.]

655 Exchange, by authority of Henry, abp. of Canterbury, between Robert Benet, rector of Foxley; patrons, John Poulton and Richard Webbe, chaplain—and William Scurion, chaplain of Arundell's chantry (*Arundelleschauntry*) in Canterbury cath.; patron, the abp. Ind. of Scurion: archd. of Wiltshire. Salisbury, 15 Jan. 1417.

[For Benet, cf. **956** and Reg. Waltham fo. 101. He was Robert Benet de Bathe. This chantry had been founded by Thomas Arundell, abp. of Canterbury, 1396–7, 1399–1414 (*Reg. Chichele*, i. 200).]

656 [Fo. 86/65] Exchange, by authority of Stephen, bp. of St. Davids (*Meneven'*), between M. Edmund Lacy, rector of Marnhull (*Marnehull*), in person of M. Robert Browne, canon of Salisbury, his proctor; patrons, abbot and conv. of Glastonbury (*Glaston*)—and M. John Collis, chancellor of St. Davids cath. and prebendary of Llawhaden (*Lanvaden*) in the same, in person of Raymond Lancis, his proctor. Ind. of Collis: archd. of Dorset. Salisbury, 16 Jan. 1417.

657 Institution of M. Edward Prentys, priest, to church of Winterbourne Earls (*Wynterbourne Erlis, Wynterbourne Erlys*), vac. by death of William Cressy; patron, Thomas Montagu, earl [of Salisbury]. Ind.: archd. of Salisbury. Salisbury, 20 Jan. 1417.

658 Exchange between Richard Moryn, rector of Hampstead Marshall (*Hampsted Marchall, Hamsted Marchall*); patron, Queen Joan—and Robert Langrissch, vicar of East Garston (*Ergarston, Estgarston*); patrons, prioress and conv. of Amesbury (*Ambresbery*). Ind. of both: archd. of Berkshire. Salisbury, 4 Feb. 1417.

659 Institution of William Hayne, priest, to church of Bradford Peverell (*Bradeford Peverell*), vac. by death of William Belman; patrons, warden, fellows and scholars of New College of St. Mary, Winchester. Ind.: archd. of Dorset. An annual pension of 40 shillings due to the college from the church was reserved. Salisbury, 18 Feb. 1417.

660 Exchange between Walter Clyve, vicar of Minety (*Mynty*); patron, John Chitterne, archd. of Wiltshire—and John Calvesberde, rector of Hazelbury (*Haselbere, Hasilbury*); patrons, prior and conv. of Bradenstoke (*Bradenstok*). Ind. of both: archd. of Wiltshire. Salisbury, 18 Feb. 1417.

661 [Fo. 86v/65v] Institution of Richard Bele, clerk, to church of Church Knowle (*Knolle*); patron, Edmund, earl of March and Ulster (*Ulton*), lord of Wigmore (*Wyggemore*) and Clare. Ind.: archd. of Dorset. Salisbury, 20 March 1417.

662 Institution of John Chyppenham, chaplain, to vicarage of Brimpton (*Brympton*), vac. by resig, of Robert Frome; patron, Walter Grendon, prior of hospital of St. John of Jerusalem in England. Ind.: archd. of Berkshire. Salisbury, 20 March 1417.

663 Exchange, on certificate of M. Walter Bullok Lic.C.L., canon of Lichfield, vicar general of John, bp. of Coventry and Lichfield, then abroad, between John Wyndhill, rector of Cound (*Counde*), dioc. Worcester [*rectius* Coventry and Lichfield]—and John Osborn, rector or warden of free chapel of Kingston Russell (*Kyngeston Russell*); patron, Thomas, duke of Clarence (*Clarencie*), earl of Aumale (*Albemarlie*) and seneschal of England. Ind. of Wyndhill: archd. of Dorset. Salisbury, 21 March 1417.

664 Exchange, by authority of Henry, abp. of Canterbury, between M. Simon Sydenham D.C.L., rector of St. Mary-in-the-Marsh (*in Marisco de Rumnal*), dioc. Canterbury; patron, the abp.—and M. William Lyndewode D.Cn. & C.L., rector of Winfrith Newburgh (*Wynfred*), in person of M. Oliver Dyneley, his proctor; patron, the bp. of Salisbury. Ind. of Sydenham: archd. of Dorset. Salisbury, 21 March 1417.

665 [Fo. 87/66] Institution of Walter Rede, clerk, in person of Ralph Felice, his proctor, to church of Great Somerford (*Somerford Mautravers*); patron, John Arundell, lord of Arundel (*Arundell*) and Mautravers. Ind.: archd. of Dorset [*rectius* Wiltshire]. Salisbury, 22 March 1417.

REGISTRUM REVERENDI IN CHRISTO PATRIS ET DOMINI DOMINI ROBERTI DEI GRACIA SAR' EPISCOPI HABITUM CORAM MEMORATO MAGISTRO GALFRIDO IPSIUS REVERENDI PATRIS VICARIO GENERALI DE ANNO DOMINI MILLESIMO QUADRINGENTESIMO DECIMO SEPTIMO

666 Institution of Roger Prestecote, chaplain, to church of Biddestone St. Peter (*Sancti Petri de Budeston*), vac. by death of William Bryd; patrons, prior and conv. of Monkton Farleigh (*Farlegh*). Ind.: archd. of Wiltshire. Salisbury, 1 Apr. 1417.

667 Institution of Thomas Joye, chaplain, to church of Blunston St. Andrew (*Bluntesdon sancti Andree*); patron, Robert Andrewe, esquire. Ind.: archd. of Wiltshire. Salisbury, 5 Apr. 1417.

668 Exchange, by authority of M. Richard Bruton, chancellor of Wells, vicar general of Richard, bp. of London, then abroad, between Walter Wilcokkes, rector of Lydiard Millicent (*North'lydeyard Milsent*); patron, King Henry—and John Mankyn, rector of St. Margaret Moses (*Moysy*), Friday Street (*Frydaystrete*), city of London, in person of John Bowre, his proctor. Ind. of Mankyn: archd. of Wiltshire. Salisbury, 5 Apr. 1417.

669 [Fo. 87v/66v] Institution of John Waryn, chaplain, to vicarage of Steventon, vac. by death of Richard Botelere; patron, for this turn, King Henry, as established by an inquiry. Ind.: archd. of Berkshire. Salisbury, 22 Apr. 1417.

670 Institution of William Marshall, chaplain, to chantry at altar of St. Catherine and St. Margaret in Market Lavington (*Stepullavyngton*) church; patron, Walter Beauchamp, knight. Ind.: archd. of Salisbury. Salisbury, 27 Apr. 1417.

671 Exchange between Thomas West, rector of Ufton Robert (*Ufton Roberd*); patron, William Perkyn—and Ralph Growe, vicar of White Waltham (*Whitewaltham, Whitwaltham*); patrons, abbot and conv. of Chertsey (*Certesey*). Ind. of both: archd. of Berkshire. Salisbury, 11 May 1417.

672 Institution of Thomas Davy, chaplain, to vicarage of Kemble (*Kemel*), vac. by death of John Osberne; patrons, abbot and conv. of Malmesbury. Ind.: archd. of Wiltshire. Salisbury, 18 May 1417.

673 Exchange, by authority of M. John Rolond, canon of Wells, vicar general of Nicholas, bp. of Bath and Wells, then abroad, between John

Salford, rector of Lockinge (*Logenge*); patrons, abbot and conv. of Abingdon (*Abendon*)—and Ralph Lambeden, rector or minister of Kilve (*Culve*), dioc. Bath and Wells. Ind. of Lambeden: archd. of Berkshire. Salisbury, 23 May 1417.

674 [Fo. 88/67] Institution of Richard Richeman, priest, to free chapel of Imber (*Immere*), vac. by death of M. Gilbert Stone; patron, William Rous, esquire. Ind.: archd. of Salisbury. Salisbury, 1 June 1417.

675 Institution of William Lochard, clerk, to church of Clewer (*Clyware*), vac. by death of Ralph Thomas; patron, John Cifrewast, lord of Clewer, *domicellus*. Ind.: archd. of Berkshire. Salisbury, 15 June 1417.

676 Collation to John Waleys, chaplain, of free chapel in Marlborough (*Marleburgh*) castle, vac. by resig. of Thomas Beke, clerk. Ind.: official of peculiar jurisdiction of Marlborough. Salisbury, 15 June 1417.

677 Institution of Thomas atte Crouche, chaplain, to church of Easthampstead (*Esthampstede*), vac. by resig. of John Everdon; patrons, prior and conv. of Hurley, order of St. Benedict. Ind.: archd. of Berkshire. Salisbury, 18 June 1417.

678 Institution of John Dyere, chaplain, to church of Avington (*Avyngton*), vac. by resig. of Thomas Haynes; patron, William Coventre, *domicellus*. Ind.: archd. of Berkshire. A suitable portion of the fruits of the church was to be paid each year to Haynes. Salisbury, 23 June 1417.

679 Grant to Thomas Haynes, formerly rector of Avington, of an annual pension of £4, to be paid at Christmas, Easter, St. John the Baptist's day [24 June] and Michaelmas [29 Sept.] (40 shillings for the current year to be paid at St. John the Baptist's day and Michaelmas), by the express consent of John Dyere, present rector, with John Draper as witness. Salisbury, 24 June 1417.

680 [Fo. 88^{v}/67^{v}] Institution of William Hille, clerk, to free chapel of Wytherstone (*Wythereston*), vac. by resig. of Thomas Baldyng; patron, abbot of Abbotsbury (*Abbodesbury*). Ind.: archd. of Dorset. Salisbury, 26 June 1417.

681 Institution of William Kymyngton, chaplain, to vicarage of Norton, vac. by resig. of John Stokes; patrons, abbot and conv. of Malmesbury (*Malm'*). Ind.: archd. of Wiltshire. Salisbury, 28 June 1417.

682 Institution of Richard Blumhull, chaplain, to church of Remenham (*Ramenham*); patron, William Mountford, esquire. Ind.: archd. of Berkshire. Salisbury, 29 June 1417.

683 Institution of John Horton, chaplain, to vicarage of Box (*Boxe*), vac. by death of Thomas Aylmerton; patrons, prior and conv. of Monkton Farleigh (*Farlegh*). Ind.: archd. of Wiltshire. Salisbury, 2 July 1417.

684 Exchange, by authority of Edmund, bp. of Exeter, between William Derwent *or* Derewent, rector of Bratton Clovelly (*Bratton*), dioc. Exeter—and William Causey, rector of South Perrott (*Southperot*); patron, John Warre, *domicellus*. Ind. of Derwent: archd. of Dorset. Salisbury, 2 July 1417.

685 [Fo. 89/68] Institution of Thomas Clerk, chaplain, to church of Swyre (*Swere*), vac. by resig. of William Moor; patron, Morgan Gogh, esquire. Ind.: archd. of Dorset. Salisbury, 11 July 1417.

686 Exchange between John Plebs, rector of Great Chalfield (*Chaldefeld Magna*); patron, Constance de la Ryver, widow of Henry de la Ryver, knight—and William Beckebury, vicar of Seagry (*Segre*); patrons, prior and conv. of Bradenstoke. Ind. of Plebs: archd. of Wiltshire. Ind. of Beckebury: archd. of Salisbury. Salisbury, 17 July 1417.

687 Institution of Geoffrey Lyncolne, chaplain, to church of Monkton Farlegh (*Farlegh Monachorum*), vac. by resig. of John Horton; patrons, prior and conv. of Monkton Farleigh. Ind.:archd. of Salisbury. Salisbury, 18 July 1417.

688 Exchange, by authority of Richard, bp. of Rochester, between William Sandyacre, vicar of Aldworth (*Aldeworth*); patrons, prioress and sisters of Bromhall (*Bromhale*)—and John Baker, vicar of Chalk, dioc. Rochester. Ind. of Baker: archd. of Berkshire. Salisbury, 21 July 1417.

689 Exchange between Robert Orum, rector of Compton Beauchamp; patron, Richard de Beauchamp, earl of Warwick (*Warrewich*)—and Thomas Bedyll, vicar of Chieveley (*Chyvellee*), in person of Robert Sutton, his proctor; patrons, abbot and conv. of Abingdon (*Abendon*). Ind. of both: archd. of Berkshire. Salisbury, 21 July 1417.

[Fo. 89^{v}/68^{v}. A space of 10 cm. has been left, containing merely the place and date, Salisbury, 21 July 1417. In the margin is a heading referring to an exchange between the archd. of Berkshire and the dean of Wimborne (*Wymborne*), but the details were never entered. Peter de Alcobasso was dean of Wimborne since 1412, and Walter Medford was archd. of Berkshire since 1404.]

690 Institution of William Necke, priest, to church of Baverstock (*Babestoke*), vac. by resig. of Thomas Bonham; patrons, abbess and conv. of Wilton. Ind.: archd. of Salisbury. Salisbury, 25 July 1417.

691 Exchange, on certificate of the dean and chapter of St. Paul's cath., London, between Walter Stonyng, rector of Stoke Newington (*Stoke Neuton, Stoke Newton*), dioc. London, in the jurisdiction of the said dean and chapter—and John Wath, rector of St. Leonard, Wallingford (*Wallyngford*); patrons, prior and conv. of St. Frideswide (*Frideswyde*), Oxford (*Oxon*), dioc. Lincoln. Ind. of Stonyng: archd. of Berkshire. Salisbury, 2 Aug. 1417.

692 Institution of William Tayllor, chaplain, to St. Mary's chantry in Tisbury (*Tyssebury*) church; patrons, abbess and conv. of Shaftesbury (*Shafton*). Ind.: archd. of Salisbury. Salisbury, 4 Aug. 1417.

693 [Fo. 90A/69*] Institution of John May, chaplain, to vicarage of Bisham (*Brustellesham, Brustillesham Montagu*), vac. by death of Richard Bytham; patron, prior of hospital of St. John of Jerusalem in England. Ind.: archd. of Berkshire. Salisbury, 4 Aug. 1417.

694 Exchange between Richard Colne, vicar of Waltham St. Lawrence (*Waltham Laur'*); patrons, prior and conv. of Hurley (*Hurlegh*)—and Thomas Petyt, vicar of Gussage All Saints (*Gussich*); patron, M. John Macworth, archd. of Dorset. Ind. of both: archd. of Dorset. [*Rectius* Ind. of Colne: archd. of Dorset. Ind. of Petyt: archd. of Berkshire.] Salisbury, 4 Aug. 1417.

[Fo. 90A^{v}/69^{v} is blank.]

*This folio is a single odd sheet, the same width as the other folios, but only 15 cm. long.

Wills*

[All the wills are proved before Robert, bp. of Salisbury, unless otherwise stated.]

695 [Fo. 18/10] Will of Hugh Clyffort, rector of Newbury, dated 22 July 1408.
To be buried in the chancel of St. Nicholas's church, Newbury. Bequeathes 20*s* for the repair of the chancel, and 20*s* for the repair of the church; 40*d* to any priest serving in the church. Residue to William Tayllour, his parish chaplain, and Thomas Baylly, chaplain, to dispose of for the benefit of his soul.
Proved at bishop's London inn, 31 July 1408.
Acquittance of executors, Potterne manor, 3 Oct. 1408.

696 [Fo. 18^{v}/10^{v}] Will of Robert Hayward, rector of Upton Lovell (*Obeton*),[1] dated 23 Apr. 1409.
Bequeathes 1 breviary and his best surplice to Upton Lovell church; 6*d* to Salisbury cath.; 1 die stamp called 'Cuniothe'[2] to Sarah, wife of Thomas Rook; 3 silver spoons to Alice, wife of William Scherman; 3 silver spoons and 1 small chest to John Raynold; his best altar cloth to Upton Lovell church; 3 sheep to Edith, daughter of William Scherman; 1 sheep to Robert, son of John Pryns, senior; 1 bullock to John, son of William Scherman; 1 sheep to Maud, daughter of Thomas Soper; his best coverlet and 1 cow to John Kerdyff; 1 heifer with calf to Edith, daughter of William Scherman; 2 oxen to William Scherman; 2*s* 6*d* to John Pullyn. Residue to Thomas Rook and William Scherman, the rector's servant, who are appointed executors.
Proved before M. William Lyndewode D.Cn. & C.L., bishop's commissary, in Ramsbury (*Remmesbury*) prebendal church, 20 Dec. 1409.
Acquittance of executors by the same commissary, Ramsbury manor, 5 Jan. 1410.

[1. Not strictly speaking rector, as he had resigned 16 July 1408, **20**.
2. MS.: *cunium vocatum cuniothe*.]

697 Will of Robert Granereyn, rector of Bradfield (*Bradfeld*), dated 3 Sept. 1410.
To be buried in the churchyard of St. John the Baptist's church, Bradfield. Bequeathes 6*s* 8*d* to the fabric of Salisbury cath.; 2 quarters of corn and 5 quarters of barley or dredge[1] to the fabric of Bradfield church; 5 quarters of corn and 10 quarters of barley or dredge to Joan, his sister; his best gown and hood to Robert, his chaplain; 2 quarters of corn and 4 quarters of barley

*The wills cover fos. 18–22. They fill the remaining folios of the first institutions quire which were left empty when Hallum went to the council of Pisa and his vicar general began a new quire.

and dredge to John Kynge, clerk; 40*d* for the repair of the road from Bradfield town to Parkgate; 40*d* for the repair of the road in Bradfield from the bridge to the house of Peter Smith. Lucy Langford, lady of Bradfield, is appointed executrix (by permission of William de Langford, lord of Bradfield, at the rector's request), together with John Tanner, the rector's special friend. William de Langford is to be supervisor. The residue is to be disposed at the executors' discretion for the benefit of his soul, and those of his parents and benefactors. Witnesses, John Hode, rector of Englefield (*Inglefeld*), and Robert Clerc, rector's chaplain.[2]
Proved in Sherborne (*Shirborne*) castle, 2 Oct. 1410, and administration granted to John Tanner, saving the rights of Lucy Langford should she come to request it.

[1. A mixture of barley and oats.
2. Robert Clerc or Clerk succeeded Granereyn as rector of Bradfield, **189**.]

698 [Fo. 19/10a] Will of John Savage, dated 26 Feb. 1410.
To be buried in the north close of Tollard Royal (*Tollard*). Bequeathes 6*s* 8*d* to the fabric of Salisbury cath. Bequeathes £10 to the fabric of Tollard church, to build a new bell-tower at the end of the church: this is to be paid to the guardians of the work at its inception and completion and is to be used for no other purpose. Bequeathes 1 quarter of corn and 1 quarter of barley to the fabric of the church, apart from the previous legacy; the same to the fabric of Farnham (*Fernham*), Long Critchell (*Longcrushell*) and Hampreston (*Hunpreston*) churches respectively; 4 bushels of corn and 4 bushels of barley to the fabric of Church Knowle (*Knolle*) and Steeple (*Stypell*) churches respectively; 13*s* 4*d* to Robert Papilon, rector of Tollard Royal (*Tollard*), for tithes owed; 2*s* 6*d* each to Robert Papilion, rector of Tollard Royal, John Legge, rector of Farnham (*Fernham*), John [Haukesbury], rector of Ashmore (*Aschemere*), Laurence Maydenhith, rector of Holy Trinity, Shaftesbury (*Shafton*), Henry Redman, rector of Pentridge (*Pentriche*), John, chaplain of Handley (*Hanghle*) chapel, Thomas Geffray, chaplain of Hampreston, Robert [Porter], vicar of Shapwick (*Shapwyk*), Thomas Maundevile, rector of Durweston (*Dureweston*), Robert Curteys, rector of Upper Stirthill (*Upsterhill*),[1] John Den, rector of moiety of Tollard Royal, John, rector of Church Knowle (*Knolle*), and Robert Colyngborn, rector of Langton Long Blandford (*Langton*), for the celebration of a trental[2] for Savage's soul by each. A thousand masses to be celebrated for his soul and those of his parents and friends as soon as possible after his death in suitable places at the discretion of his executors: £4 5*s* 10*d* [*sic*] bequeathed for this purpose, namely 1*d* for each mass.

1 gown and hood, with hose and 1 pair of shoes for each of 8 poor men bearing torches on the day of his burial. 1½*d* each to be distributed on the same day to the most needy poor in neighbouring places. 4 bushels of corn and 4 of barley for the maintenance of the bridge of Hampreston (*Hambrygge*). 20*s* to Simon Talbot, 20*s* to John Chaldecot, 20*s* to John Barbor, 6*s* 8*d* to William Coniville, and 20*s* to William Cosmond, should they survive the testator. Thomas Rakyer is remitted his arrears of Critchell

(*Kyrkehyll*) and left 1 gown and hood. 1 gown and hood, 2 bushels of corn and 2 of barley to Richard Druet; 2 bushels of corn and 2 of barley respectively to Stephen Bonham, Richard Hurumhyll, Richard Okman and John Trub. 1 gown and hood to Robert Fouke. His black horse to his special friend, John Antyoche; his sorrel horse to Morgan Gof; his starred horse to John Fawnnteleroy. 20 marks [£13 6*s* 8*d*] for his eldest daughter Eleanor, as her share of all his goods and chattels, that she may be settled in a suitable religious house where she may be supported and find food and necessities for her life, at the executors' discretion. £20 for the expenses of his friends, chaplains and poor men on the day of his burial, to cheer them. £9 to his sister Maud; 40*s* to his brother John Hurdell; 40*s* and his better bastard sword to Robert Remmeston.

To Robert his son, 2 messuages with appurtenances in the parish of St. Martin, Shaftesbury, situated on the hill between the hospital of St. John on one side and a lane called Sorpustret on the other, which are worth 24*s* 6*d* a year rented out, above expenses, and one messuage in the same parish, situated between the tenement lately M. John Gray's on one side, and the tenement of Thomas Canvell on the other, which is worth 7*s* a year rented out, above expenses, and one close called Lordescroft in the parish of St. Laurence, worth 4*s* a year, above expenses, which is leased to Thomas Wyse and Margaret his wife for their lives. Also an annual revenue of 6*s* 8*d* [Fo. 19v/10av] from a tenement which Robert Pas Mason holds of him for his life in the parish of St. Mary, Shaftesbury, situated next to the north boundary of the abbess's long stable, together with the reversion of this messuage after the death of the said Robert Mason. Also one small house and yard in the parish of St. Martin, called Knapdel Hall, situated at the boundary of William Otle's tenement on the west side, which is worth 2*s* a year, rented out to William Otle, and 2 messuages with a yard in the parish of St. Oswald,[3] by the tenement of John Kynemer on the south side, which is worth 4*s* a year, rented out to Peter Auget. Also one messuage in the churchyard of Holy Trinity, on the north side of the parish church there, which is worth 10*s*. All these messuages, revenues and reversions with their appurtenances are to be held by Robert and his lawfully-begotten heirs for ever. Should Robert die without heir, they are to pass to Walter, the testator's son, and his lawfully-begotten heirs, or, should he die without heir, to Henry, the testator's son, and his lawfully-begotten heirs.

To Walter, the testator's son, 20*s* annual revenue coming from one messuage in Wimborne Minster (*Wymbornmynster*) situated in the Cockestret, which Laurence Taylor holds for his life, together with the reversion of this after Laurence's death; 16*s* annual revenue coming from one messuage situated opposite St. Peter's chapel, on the west, which Peter Jonewey holds, together with its reversion; 3*s* annual revenue from one burgage which Edward Baron holds in the same town, which is worth 7*s* thus rented out to him; one enclosed toft in the West Street, worth 2*s* a year after deductions, rented to William Chamburlayne; 2 acres of land in Leigh (*Leyfelde*),[4] worth 4*s* a year after deductions, rented to Walter Smyth. All these, with their appurtenances and reversions after the deaths of the tenants, are to be devised to Walter, and should he die without heir, they are to pass to Robert or to Henry.

If the testator dies when his children are under age, his executors are to put the revenues from the lands into the hands of some faithful friend, until the children reach maturity. If any child dies under age his portion is to be distributed equally among the others. Any residue is to be divided among his daughters.

All the lands and tenements formerly of John Sterre in Tarrant Gunville (*Tarrent Gowndevile*), together with those of Rodeberd in the same town, those of John Eyre at Duraco [uncertain reading], and those of the testator at Gussage All Saints (*Guschyt omnium sanc*[*t*]*orum*) are to be placed in the hands of certain of his friends (as is more clearly shown in the map made concerning them), on condition that they enfeoff the testator's son Henry and his heirs. If heirs fail, these lands are to pass to Walter and Robert.

As he has no land to devise to his eldest son John during the life of his parents, the testator's wife Eleanor promised in the presence of John Antyoche, Henry Redman and others, that if she survived her husband she would give John the manor of Long Critchell (*Gurchelfelde*) to support him during her lifetime.

Eleanor, his wife, Morgan Goff, John Antyoche, John Faunteleroy, [Fo. 20/10b] Robert Remston and Henry Kodoway appointed executors. Sealed by John Savage. 40*s* left to Joan, his bastard daughter. William Eyre is remitted all his debt, both in pence and sheep.
Proved in Sherborne (*Schirborn*) castle, 6 June 1410, and administration granted to John Antyoche, esquire, and Robert Reymston.

[1. The parish church was in fact at Lower Stirthill, cf. **307** & n.
2. 30 requiem masses.
3. St. Rowald or St. Rumbold, now united to St. Peter's church (Hutchins, iii. 3).
4. For Leigh, ½ mile east of Wimborne Minster, see *ibid.*, p. 242.]

699 Will of John Marleburgh, dated 31 Dec. 1410.
To be buried in the churchyard of St. Mary, Abingdon (*Abendon*). Bequeathes 12*d* to Salisbury cath.; 6*s* 8*d* to the vicar of St. Helen's for forgotten tithes; 6*s* 8*d* to the same church; 12*d* to each priest officiating there; 12*d* to each of the two parish clerks; 12*d* to each priest of St. John's; 12*d* to each chaplain of the churches of St. Nicholas and St. Edmund[1] and to the priest before the cross of the Abbey; 12*d* to each bed for the poor in the house of St. John, Abingdon; £10 for distribution to the poor on the day of his burial and for funeral expenses; £10 for two chaplains to celebrate for the souls of Marleburgh and his wife for one year at St. Catherine's altar in St. Helen's church; 10*s* for each of the mendicant orders of friars in Oxford; 35 marks [£23 6*s* 8*d*] for his anniversary days for seven years; 100*s* for 1000 masses for his soul to be celebrated in the fortnight after his death; 100*s* for the poor and needy of Abingdon.

20*s* to Margaret, his wife's daughter; 6*s* 8*d* to Joan, daughter of the same Margaret; 13*s* 4*d* to Robert Chaunden; 13*s* 4*d* to John, his son; 3*s* 4*d* to each of the sons of the same Robert; 13*s* 4*d* to Amice, his wife's sister; 6*s* 8*d* to each of her daughters; 10*s* to the brother of Thomas Marleburgh and 10*s* to the same Thomas; 3*s* 4*d* to the church of St. Nicholas; 3*s* 4*d* to Dry Sandford (*Sanford*) chapel;[2] all the debt owed by William Bullok and Robert Chamburleyn to be disposed in St. Catherine's chapel for masses and among the poor to pray for the souls of Marleburgh and his wife and all the faithful dead; 4 marks [£2 13*s* 4*d*] to the daughter of John [one or two illegible words]; 6 silver spoons, decorated with lions to Thomas Weston, clerk[3]; his manor and all the utensils of his house that she wishes to Maud his wife; 3*s* 4*d* to the fraternity of the Holy Cross of St. Helen's; 3*s* 4*d* to the fraternity of St. Thomas in Oxford; 6*s* 8*d* to the fraternity of the Holy Trinity, Coventry; 20*s* to John Clifton, canon of Dorchester (*Dork'*),[4] to pray for the souls of Marleburgh and all the faithful dead; 6*s* 8*d* to John Abendon, Carmelite of Oxford; 20*s* to Richard Sterihuppe to celebrate trentals of St. Gregory; 40*d* to Walter Barbor and 40*d* to John his son; 5 marks [£3 6*s* 8*d*] to Robert Bemond; 5 marks to John Kynge; 5 marks to John Bryt.

The residue to be disposed at the executor's discretion in celebration of masses, in alms and in other works of mercy for the souls of Marleburgh and his wife and all the faithful dead. Robert Bemond, John Kynge and John Bryt appointed executors. Sealed, with Richard Sterihuppe, chaplain, William Bullok, Richard Taylor and others as witnesses. 37 marks 6*s* 8*d* [£25] left for distribution to the poor for seven and a half years.
Proved in Sonning (*Sonnyng*) manor, 11 Feb. 1411.

[1. The chapel of St. Edmund was pulled down before 1554 (*VCH Berks.*, iv. 434).
2. The chapel of Dry Sandford dependent on the church of St. Helen, Abingdon existed in 1401 (*CPL 1396–1404*, p. 351), but seems to have fallen into decay by the 16th century (*VCH Berks.*, iv. 420).
3. Schoolmaster of Abingdon, *c.* 1388–1415 (*ibid.*, ii. 261–2).
4. Dorchester abbey, Oxon. John Clifton was later abbot (*VCH Oxon.*, ii. 90).]

[For commission on fo. 20^{v}/10b^{v}, see **60**.]

700 [Fo. 21/10c] Will of Thomas Oky, [rector] of the parish church of Brixton Deverill (*Brixton Deverell*), dated 14 July 1410.
To be buried wherever it pleases God. 13*s* 4*d* to the fabric of Brixton church. His best gown and cloak to John [Conge], chaplain in the same church. All his horses, his cart with all its equipment, 6 silver spoons, and all the wooden and pewter vessels, to his brother Nicholas. Also 1 oratory with a silver crucifix, all the linen and woollen clothes in his chamber, all the larder on the day of his death and 1 piece of woollen cloth. 25*s* to John, his servant. The residue to his executors. John, chaplain of Brixton, Nicholas Oky and William Cardewe are appointed executors and assigned 6*s* 8*d* each for their labour. Sealed, at London.
Proved at Sherborne (*Shirborn*), 23 July 1411. Administration committed to Nicholas Oky, in person of John Oky, his son.

701 Will of William Langford, knight, dated 24 Aug. 1411. To be buried in the church of Bradfield (*Brydefeld*), in St. Andrew's chapel. 6*s* 8*d* to the fabric of Salisbury cath. 40*s* for the repair of the said chapel.[1] Also I bequeythe to Lucy my wyf all my store and catell quikk and dede in Bradefeld' and Compton' wyth all the utensell of myn howse, that is to say in hall and chambur, in pantry and butrye, in larder and in kychin, wyth all hyr apparayr', that is to say in clothing rynges and all oyther ornamentis what so thei be, wyth all the hay and corn of this yere growyng, reserving the old graynes to myn executors to performe my will. Also I bequeth a kovor wyth the goodes therin in warde of Laurence Drewe in Southcot to the forseyd Lucy my wyf to hyr propre uyse. Also I bequeyth to Robert myn eldest son a rede bede of worstede wyth costoures that longeth thereto enbrawdue wyth white fete, wyth a canvace, a matras, a payr of blankkets, ij payre of shetis, also a basinet wyth a ventyle, a payre of vambrace and rerebracis, a payre of leg herneys, a hole brestplate, a paunce of stele, a payre gloves of plate white. Also to Elizabeth the wyf of the forseyd Robert a bord cloth whith ij towelles of devaunt of the sute. Also I bequeyth to William my son a haberion of stele wyth a palet coveryd with rede velvet, a payre of gloves of plate blak. Also to Herry my son a haberion, a ketill hatte. Also I bequeyth to Isabell by dowghter a C li. to hir mariage of wych some is owyng to me, C. mark [£66 13*s* 4*d*] by hondes of my Lady Lovell[2] and be the hand of William Tanner of Esgarston[3] xxvj marcas vj s. viij d. [£17 6*s* 8*d*] and the remmaynant be payed of my gudes that levey. Also I will at be gyvyn to pore men in almes to praye for me iiij marcas [£2 13*s* 4*d*], and in amendement of weyes lying aboute the manor of Bradefelde ij marcas [£1 6*s* 8*d*]. Also I bequeyth to Thomas Eyre my servant vj s. viij d., Henry Swon' xl d., William Herward' ij s., Jon Oxherde xl d., Pierys Smyth the younger xl d., Jon Shephird v s., Jon of the kechyn xl d., Robert Kocenyl xl d., Jon Coky xx d., William Chese ij s., Robert of the stuble xx d., Hugo Permay xl d., Jon Turnour carter v s., John Hayward vj s. viij d., William Burgeys and hys wyf xl s., Thomas Buclere vj s. viij d., William of Chessyre v s., Thomas Carpenter xl d., Mawde my servant to hir mariage xx s., John Oxhirde xl d., Beatryce my servant vj s. viij d. Also I will that all the londes and tenements in Sheffeld, Burfelde and Sulhampstede Abbatis,[4] wyth the mede clepyd Tibbeney in Ofton[5] of my purchace, stondyng in feffees hondes, [be sold,][6] and the silver thereof spendyd to the avance of my dowghter Lucy. And if she be convenably avansed wyth lasse somme, [Fo. 21^{v}/10b^{v}] I woll that the surplys be don for my soule. Also I woll that the forseyd sale of my londes and tenements in Sheffeld, Burfeld and Sulhampstede Abbatis be made princepaly to my wyf and my heires, giffyn therefor as another man will. Also I will that William my son have the manor of Chale wyth all the purtenaunts beyng in feffees hondes, wyth avowson of the chirche in the Ile of Wyght,[7] to hym and to his heires of his body lawfully begoton. And if he dye wythoute heires lawfully of his body begoton, thanne will I the forseyd manor wyth appurtenans remayne to Henry his brother and his heirs of his body lawfully begoton. And if the forseid Henry die [without heirs][8] lefull of his body goton, thanne will I that the forseid manor wyth appurtenans remayne to me and to myn heirs. Also I wyll that Henry my son have ten mark worth [£6 13*s* 4*d*] lond yerely to hym and to his heirs leffull of his body begoton, of the londes and rentes in the counte of Devonshire, beyng in feffees hondes, wyth avowisome of Mounkecampton.[9] And for defaut of issue commyng of the forseid Henry, I woll it remayne to William his brother and to his heirs of his body. And for defaute of issue of the forseyd William, I will the remaynder be to my rygh heirs. I pray yow also that bene myn feffees that ye mak estate unto my forsaid children, Lucye, Henry and William lyk as my will is before contenyd. Also I will that Thomas Rauf my servant have ij marc [£1 6*s* 8*d*] yerely duryng his lyf, takyng it of the londes and rentes in Deven shire beyng in feffees hondes, takyng a distresse in defaute of payment. Also my will is, that if my wyf or my children ascun hir resonabill part of my gudes after course of lawe, then will I that thei be excluded of all the avauntage of the ordenance of my will aboveseyde. Also my will is, that the silver that shall be receyved for the londes and tenements that I have before asyned for the avauncement of Lucye my dowter, that it abyde in the hondes of myn executors to fulfill my will. Also I will, towchand the londes the wyche I have asyned for William my son, that Lucie my wyf have governance thereof and profyt in to the forseyd William be of age of xviij yeres olde. And also of the londes that bene asyned to Henry, that my wyf have governance thereof and profyt in to the forseyd Henry be of age of xviij yeres olde. Also I will at the C li. wych I haf asyned for Isabell my doughter to hir avauncement and it fall that sche dy or she be avaunced, thane wyll I that the forseyd C li. be done for my soule. The residew of all my gudes, my dettes first payed and my will holy fulfylled as is before wrytyn, I will that it remayne to the forseyde Lucye my wyf. And I pray yow that bene enfeffed in my londes forseyde by me that ye fulfyll my forseyd will as ye will answere to fore God.

Laurence Drewe, William Stokes, Robert Clerk, rector of Bradfield, and John Jacob appointed executors.

Proved in Sonning (*Sonnyng*) manor, 24 Sept. 1411. Administration committed to Robert Clerk and John Jacob.

[This will was incorrectly proved before the bp. of Salisbury, as it involved property in more than one diocese. It was subsequently proved in the archbishop's court, 1 Oct. 1411 (P.R.O., Prerogative Court of Canterbury, PROB 11/2A, 24 Marche). It was printed from the P.C.C. version in *The 50 Earliest English Wills in the Court of Probate, London,* ed. F.J. Furnivall (Early English Text Soc., 1882), pp. 18–21.

1. From this point the will changes from Latin to English and is transcribed in full.
2. Either Maud, widow of John, Lord Lovel (d. 1408), or Eleanor, wife of John Lord Lovel (*Complete Peerage,* comp. G.E. Cokayne and others (13 vols., 1910–59), viii. 220–1).
3. East Garston.
4. Shefford, Burghfield and Sulhampstead Abbots.
5. Ufton Nervet, cf. *VCH Berks.*, iii. 440; *Berks. Place-names*, i. 225.
6. Words supplied from P.C.C. version.
7. In Carisbrook castle (*Calendarium Inquisitionum post mortem sive Escaetarum* (4 vols., 1806–28), iii. 337). For Chale, see *VCH Hants.*, v. 236–7.
8. Words supplied from the P.C.C. version. MS. has an omission mark, but the omitted words have not been interlined.
9. Monk Okehampton.]

702 Acquittance of William Parke, clerk, Giles Frensch, John Page and Thomas Chaumberleyn of New Windsor (*Nove Wyndesore*), administrators of the goods of the late Thomas Sy, esquire. Potterne, 10 Jan. [no year].
[Cf. **706**.]

703 [Fo. 22/10d] Acquittance of Robert Bemond, John Kyng, and John Bryt, executors of the late John Marleburwe of Abingdon (*Abendon*). Abingdon, 12 March 1412.
[Cf. **699**.]

704 Will of Roger Clap, rector of West Stafford (*Staford*), dated Stinsford (*Stytisford*), 28 March 1407.
To be buried in the churchyard of St. Michael, Stinsford (*Styftisford*). 12*d* to the fabric of Salisbury cath.; 20*s* to the fabric of West Stafford (*Staford*) church; 12*d* to the church of Stinsford (*Stytisford*). A ewe with lamb each to John Lagh and his wife; a ewe each to Thomas, the testator's servant, and to John Gentel, the testator's godson (*filiolo meo*); 2 bushels of barley to Thomas Golsi; 26*s* 8*d* to Nicholas Puri; 26*s* 8*d* to John Rok. The residue to be disposed by the executors for the use of Clap's mother. John Rok, clerk, and Nicholas Puri appointed executors.
Proved [no date]. Acquittance of executors, Sonning (*Sonnyng*), 15 June [1412].

705 Will of William Kyngton, rector of West Kington (*Westkyngton*), dated 11 July 1412.
To be buried in the chancel of his church before the altar. 13*s* 4*d* to the fabric of Salisbury cath.; 13*s* 4*d* for the tower of West Kington (*Kyngton*) church. A white coverlet, 1 pair of linen sheets, 1 pair of blankets, 1 green gown, 1 brass measure containing 3 gallons, 1 ox called Mayne, 1 bullock, 1 tod[1] of white and black wool, 3 bushels of malt, 20 sheep as they come from the flock and 3 silver spoons of minor value to Thomas, his brother. 1 new gown, 3 yards of blanket cloth and 1 yellow coverlet to John, clerk there. 1 gown of mixed colour, 1 tod of wool, 1 brass measure containing 3 gallons, 20 sheep as they come from the flock and 3 silver spoons of minor value to John, the testator's brother. 6*s* 8*d* to William, son of John Fynemor; 4 bushels of malt each to John Piers and Roger Kyng; 14 pounds of black and white wool to Edith Atteford. 40*s* for lights in the church; 40*s* for his obit to be held once a year, and at the request of the priest on any Sunday. 1 quarter of malt to William Tailor; 3*s* 6*d* to each of the 3 orders of friars in Bristol (*Bristoll*); 5*s* to the order of preachers; 5*s* to brother John and 8 yards of blanket cloth; 1 quarter of malt to John Wynter; 20 sheep as they come from the flock to Thomas Artour; 1 coverlet, 1 pair of new blankets, 1 pair of sheets and 20 sheep as they come from the flock to Nicholas, my kinsman. 4 bushels of malt and 4 fleeces to John Mulsent. 6*s* 8*d* to the church of Nettleton (*Nettilton*); 6*s* 8*d* to the chancel of St. Mary, Chipping Sodbury (*Chepyng Sobbury*).[2] 12*d* to every priest who comes on the day of the testator's

death to celebrate for his soul and the souls of all the faithful. 1*d* to every poor person coming on that day. 1 quarter of malt and 3 yards of russet to Alice Odam; 3 yards of russet cloth and 1 of white wool to Gillian Kyngton; 1 quarter of malt to William Symondes; 4 bushels of malt to Robert Smyth; 1 sheep and lamb to Robert Artour; 11*s* to the prioress of Kington St. Michael (*Estkyngton*) and the convent there; 1 sheep and lamb to William, son of John Kyngton his brother; all the fragments of wool, namely 60 pounds, to John Fynemor. 1 silk purse and 6*s* 8*d* to Gillian, daughter of William Symondes. The residue to be disposed by his executors for the good of his soul. John, rector of Nettleton,[3] and Thomas Pruet of West Kington are appointed executors. His sick bed with all its equipment, 1 old mattress, half a dozen best pewter vessels, 1 basin and ewer, a half share of the wooden vessels to Thomas, his brother. Half a dozen best pewter vessels, a half share of the wooden vessels, 1 bowl of the best brass, 1 basin and ewer and 1 black wine vat to John, his brother. His grey horse to Henry, vicar of Colerne[4]; 4 bushels of malt each to Thomas Hody and David Holway. 6½ marks [£4 6*s* 8*d*] left to brother John for masses for his soul and those of his father and mother for one year in West Kington church.
Proved in Sherborne (*Shirborn*) castle, 19 Aug. 1412.

[1. Old wood weight, about 28 lbs.
2. There was a chapel of St. Mary leading off the chancel of St. John the Baptist's church, Chipping Sodbury (*Trans. Bristol and Glos. Archaeol. Soc.*, xiii (1888–9), 38).
3. John Melton (cf. **1137**) or John Belton (Wiltshire Record Office, Reg. Neville, pt. i fo. 12/18).
4. Henry Hert (Reg. Medford fo. 112).]

706 [Fo. 22v/10dv] Commission appointing Simon Sy, Giles Frenshe and John Page administrators of the goods of Thomas Sy, esquire, who died intestate. The bishop's London manor in the parish of St. Bride, Fleet Street (*Fletstrete*), 24 March 1412.
[Cf. **702**.]

Licences, Letters and Commissions

[A space of 10 cm. has been left at the top of this folio, presumably for a heading to the quire of licences, letters and commissions started at the beginning of the episcopate.*
All the letters, **707–56**, are issued by Robert, bp. of Salisbury.]

707 [Fo. 90B/1] Licence to William Fostbury, rector of Tarrant Keynston (*Kayneston*), according to the clause 'Cum ex eo',[1] to be absent from his benefice for one year's study at Oxford university, with permission not to proceed further than subdeacon's orders, provided that his church is properly served and that he distributes alms. Sealed with the seal which we used to use in the office of archd. of Canterbury, which we have to hand.[2] Abingdon (*Abendon*) monastery, 20 Apr. 1408.

[1. *Corpus Iuris Canonici*, ii, col. 964, *Sext* I, 6, c. 34. This allowed ordination to be delayed for a maximum of 7 years, provided the benefice-holder were ordained subdeacon within a year of the licence's being granted.
2. Hallum continued to use this seal for the first few months of his episcopate, cf. **43**, **928**. By 12 May he seems to have possessed an episcopal great seal, cf. **708**.]

708 Licence to Nicholas Kentewode, *domicellus*, and Maud his wife, to have divine service privately celebrated by a suitable chaplain in the oratory or chapel of West Shefford (*Shyfford*) manor. Sealed with our seal.[1] Welford, 12 May 1408.

[1. This is the earliest date on which Hallum refers to 'our seal', and by this time Hallum presumably had his own episcopal great seal, cf. **707** n. 2. The only example of a seal of Hallum (and that one is in a bad condition) is attached to British Library, Additional Charter 19648, of 10 Jan. 1411, described in W. de G. Birch, *Catalogue of Seals in the British Museum* (1887), i. 344, and J. Wordsworth, 'On the seals of the bishops of Salisbury', *Wilts. Archaeol. and Natural Hist. Mag.*, xxiv (1889), 220–43. This is probably the seal *ad causas* rather than the great seal.]

709 Licence to Robert de la Maare, esquire, and Catherine his wife, to have divine service privately celebrated by a suitable chaplain in the chapel of Aldermaston (*Aldermerston*) manor. Welford, 12 May 1408.

710 Licence to M. John Symondesburgh B.C.L., rector of Stoke Abbott (*Stoke Abbatis*), to be absent from his benefice for two years' study anywhere in England. Welford, 19 May 1408.

711 [Fo. 90B^{v}/1^{v}] Licence to M. Thomas Teynton B.Cn.L., subdeacon, rector of Frome St. Quintin (*Frome sancti Quintini*), to be absent from his benefice for two years' study anywhere, without proceeding to higher orders. Welford, 19 May 1408.[1]

[1. MS. margin (same hand): *non habet litteras*]

*In the top right-hand corner is written in a 15th-century hand *quaternus primus*. The half quire, fos. 152–157^{v}, **928–49**, was used concurrently for longer letters.

712 Licence to John Haukesbury, chaplain, rector of Ashmore (*Asche*), at the request of the aforesaid M. Thomas Teynton, to be absent from his benefice for one year from Michaelmas [29 Sept.]. Welford, 19 May 1408.
[For Ashmore, Dors., see Hutchins, iii. 369.]

713 Letters dimissory to M. Thomas Teynton, subdeacon, B.Cn.L., rector of Frome St. Quentin, permitting him to receive the orders of priest and deacon from any Catholic bp., despite the fact that he is beneficed in dioc. Salisbury. Culham, 4 June 1408.

714 Licence to Ralph de la Stane, *domicellus*, to have divine service celebrated in the oratory of his house of Stainswick (*Staneswyke*). Welford, 31 May 1408.
[For Stainswick, in Ashbury, Berks., see *Berks. Place-names*, ii. 347–8.]

715 The like to Richard Colyngborn, *domicellus*, and Joan his wife, in the oratory of their house in Great Bedwyn (*Bedewynd*) parish. Culham, 12 June 1408.

716 Licence to John [Chiveley], bp. of Callipolis (*Calipolen'*),[1] to reconcile the church of Childrey (*Chelrey*), polluted by bloodshed. Culham, 13 June 1408.[2]
[1. *Handbook of British Chronology*, p. 268; *Hierarchia Catholica*, i. 158.
2. MS. margin (contemporary hand): *Commiss'* and *Nota*]

717 [Fo. 91/2] Licence to John Wykham, rector of Bishopstone (*Busshoppeston*), to be absent from his benefice for two years' study. Culham, 5 July 1408.

718 The like to Robert Bemynstre, rector of 'Brutton', for one year's study. Culham, 5 July 1408.

719 Licence to Godfrey, vicar of Hurley, to celebrate divine service, either himself or by a chaplain, in the chapel of Holy Trinity upon Altishorn, in Hurley parish. Culham, 14 June 1408.
[For the field called Altishorn or Alteshore (1360), see *Berks. Place-names*, i. 65.]

720 Licence to Reynold Kyngbrygge, rector of St. Martin, Shaftesbury (*Shafton*), to be absent from his benefice until the bishop's next visitation, at the request of (*contemplacione*) John Gaweyn, *domicellus*. Culham, 11 July 1408.
[Hallum held a visitation of the archdeaconry of Dorset *c.* Sept. 1410, **862**.]

721 Licence to M. William Rodborn, vicar of Steeple Ashton (*Asshton*), and John Compton, chaplain, to hear the confessions of the abbess and nuns of Lacock (*Lacok*), and to grant absolution even in cases reserved to the bp. This grant revokes any previous ones. Culham, 14 July 1408.

722 Licence to John Wynterburne, rector of Woodborough (*Wodebergh*) to be absent from his benefice for one year. Culham, 14 July 1408.

723 Licence to William Langford, knight, and Lucy his wife to have divine service celebrated in any fit place in Bradfield (*Bradefeld*) manor. Sonning (*Sonnyng*), 20 July 1408.

724 [Fo. 91^{v}/2^{v}] Licence to Walter Lambard, rector of Brinkworth (*Brynkworthe*), to be absent from his benefice for one year. London, 26 July 1408.

725 The like to John Newton, rector of Compton Valence (*Compton Valens*). London, 29 July 1408.

726 Licence to John Adam, *domicellus,* to have divine service celebrated in the oratory of his house in Pangbourne (*Pangburne*) parish. London, 29 July 1408.

727 The like to John Brouns, *domicellus,* and Maud his wife, in the chapel or oratory of their house in Harwell (*Harewell*) parish. Culham, 24 Aug. 1408.

728 The like to Richard Brouns, *domicellus,* and Gillian his wife, in Sutton Courtenay (*Sutton*) parish. Culham, 24 Aug. 1408.

729 Letters dimissory to William Trenerth, rector of Pewsey (*Peuesey*), first tonsure, permitting him to receive all orders from any Catholic bp. London, 3 Aug. 1408.

730 Licence to Thomas Rothewell and Alice his wife to have divine service celebrated in the oratory of their manor of South Moreton (*Southmorton*). Salisbury, bishop's palace, 11 Sept. 1408.

731 Licence to Philip Helemor, rector of moiety of church of Child Okeford (*Schylddokeford*), to be absent for one year. Salisbury, bishop's palace, 11 Sept. 1408.

732 The like to Robert Stanford, rector of Berwick St. James (*Berewyk sancti Jacobi*). Woodford (*Wodeford*), 14 Sept. 1408.

733 [Fo. 111/21] The like to William Dunham, rector of Hampreston. Woodford, 16 Sept. 1408.

734 Licence to Thomas Bonham, *domicellus,* and his wife to have divine service celebrated in the oratory of their house of Welford (*Wellford*). Potterne (*Poterne*), 22 Sept. 1408.

735 Licence to Thomas Norton, rector of Collingbourne Ducis (*Colyngborn Ducis*), to be absent from his benefice for one year. Potterne, 29 Sept. 1408.

736 The like to Richard Hamme, rector of Boxford (*Boxore*). London, 20 Oct. 1408.

737 The like to Laurence Howard, rector of Winterbourne Bassett (*Wynturburn Basset*). London, 21 Oct. 1408.

738 Licence to Thomas Trewyn, *domicellus*, to have divine service celebrated in the oratory or other suitable place in his house of Woodrow (*Woderow*) in the parish of Melksham (*Melkesham*). London, 21 Oct. 1408.

739 The like to Richard Welham, citizen of London, in the chapel of his inn in the town of Reading (*Redyng*). London, 23 Oct. 1408.

740 Letters dimissory to Thomas Shelford, subdeacon, rector of Piddlehinton (*Hynepydele*), to receive the orders of deacon and priest from any Catholic bp., notwithstanding he has a benefice in dioc. Salisbury. London, 2 Nov. 1408.

741 Licence to John Wotton, rector of St. Sampson, Cricklade (*Crekelade*), to be absent from his benefice for one year. London, 2 Nov. 1408.

742 [Fo. 111v/21v] Licence to Nicholas Sannburn, junior, and Catherine his wife to have divine service celebrated in the oratories of their houses of Farnham (*Fernham*) and Ludgershall (*Lusteshull*). London, 9 Nov. 1408.

743 Licence to Thomas Roberd, rector of Studland (*Stondlond*, *Stonelond*), to be absent from his benefice for one year. Salisbury, 10 Dec. 1408.

744 Licence to Robert Andrew, *domicellus*, and his wife to have divine service celebrated in the chapel or oratory of their manors of Chapel Eaton (*Chappell Eton*) and Castle Eaton (*Castell Eton*) in the parish of Cricklade (*Crekkelade*). Potterne (*Poterne*), 13 Dec. 1408.

745 Licence to John Bradeby, rector of Okeford Fitzpaine (*Ocford Fytz Payn*, *Ocford Fyzt Payn*), to be absent from his benefice for one year. Sherborne (*Schirborn*), 22 Dec. 1408.

746 The like to Henry Wetherby, priest, rector of Semley (*Semble*), for two years' study at the university of Oxford (*Oxon*) or Cambridge (*Cantabrig*). Salisbury, 9 Jan. 1409.

747 Licence to Maud Wythe to have divine service celebrated in chapels or oratories anywhere in dioc. Salisbury. London, 15 Jan. 1409.

748 Licence to Simon Kynat, rector of Brixton Deverill (*Bryghston Deverell, Bryghtston Deverell*), to be absent from his benefice for one year, with the relaxation of the sequestration imposed on account of his non-residence. London, 31 Jan. 1409.

749 Indulgence of forty days promised to all who say the Lord's Prayer for the soul of Robert Walyngford, monk of Winchester (*Wynton*) cath.[1] London, 24 Jan. 1409.

[1. Formerly subprior (*Register of the Common Seal of the Priory of St. Swithun, Winchester, 1345–1497*, ed. J. Greatrex (Hants Record Ser., ii, 1978), nos. 68–9).]

750 Indulgence of forty days promised to all who contribute within the next year to the construction and maintenance of the hospital of St. Thomas the Martyr of Acon, London. London, 26 Jan. 1409.

751 [Fo. 112/22] Commission to the dean of Bridport (*Brydeport*), Robert Axmothe, chaplain, and Morgan Gough, *domicellus,* to sequestrate the revenues of Symonsbury (*Symmysburgh*) church and the goods of the late Thomas Terry, formerly rector, on account of the dilapidations left by him in the chancel of the church and in the buildings belonging to it. They are to report by the feast of the Annunciation of the B.V.M. [25 March]. London, 28 Jan. 1409.

752 Licence to William Brygthwell, rector of Remenham, at the request of Richard, bp. of Rochester, to be absent from his benefice indefinitely in the service of the said bp. London, 30 Jan. 1409.

753 Letter to the abbess and conv. of Lacock (*Lacok*) nominating as nun Agnes, daughter of Thomas Guch, *domicellus,* in accordance with Salisbury custom. London, 12 Feb. 1409.

[For the bishop's right to nominate on appointment, cf. *VCH Wilts.*, iii. 310–11.]

754 Mandate to the archd. of Salisbury for the execution of the mandate of Thomas, abp. of Canterbury (dated Lambeth (*Lamheth*), 30 Nov. 1408), transmitted by Richard, bp. of London (dated Fulham, 2 Dec.), summoning the clergy of the province to a convocation at St. Paul's, London, 14 Jan. 1409, and the following days, [Fo. 112^{v}/22^{v}] to authorize a delegation to attend a council at Pisa to end the schism of the Church. The bishops, or the vicars general of any absent, are to be summoned, and through them, the deans and priors of cath. churches, archdeacons, abbots, priors and other prelates of churches, exempt or not exempt, all of whom are to appear in person; the clergy of each dioc. who are to be represented by two proctors; and the cath. chapters who are to be represented by at least one proctor. [Fo. 113/23] An indulgence of forty days is promised to those praying for the council. Potterne (*Poterne*) manor, 14 Dec. 1408.
Similar mandates were sent to the archdeacons of Wiltshire, Dorset and Berkshire, and to the dean and chapter of Salisbury cath.

[The archbishop's summons is printed in *Reg. Bubwith*, i. 42–6; *Concilia*, iii. 311–13 (in part). The bishop's mandate to the dean and chapter is entered in Vyring, pp. 25–6.]

755 [Fo. 113^{v}/23^{v}] Notification to the abp. of Canterbury of the execution of his mandate. Those cited in dioc. Salisbury are as follows: in Salisbury cath., M. John Chaundeler, dean, and the chapter; in the archdeaconry of Salisbury, M. Simon Sydenham, archd., Thomas, rector of Edington (*Edyngdon*), William, prior of Monkton Farleigh (*Farlegh*); in the archdeaconry of Wiltshire, John Chitterne, archd., Thomas, abbot of Malmesbury, William, abbot of Stanley, Robert, prior of Bradenstoke, Walter, prior of St. Margaret, Marlborough (*Marleburgh*); in the archdeaconry of Berkshire, M. Walter Medeford, archd., Richard, abbot of Abingdon (*Abyndon*), Richard, abbot of Reading (*Radyng*), Adam, prior of Bisham (*Bustelesham*); in the archdeaconry of Dorset, John Macworgh, archd., Robert, abbot of Sherborne (*Schirborn*), Walter, abbot of Milton (*Myddelton*), Robert, abbot of Abbotsbury (*Abbodesbury*), Robert, abbot of Cerne, William, abbot of Bindon (*Byndon*). The proctors appointed for the clergy of dioc. Salisbury are M. Simon Sydenham, archd. of Salisbury, and John Chitterne, archd. of Wiltshire. Salisbury, bishop's palace, 9 Jan. 1409.

756 [Fo. 114/24] Mandate to the archd. of Salisbury for the execution of the mandate of Thomas, abp. of Canterbury (dated Lambeth (*Lamhith*), 31 Jan. 1409), transmitted by Richard, bp. of London (dated London, bishop's palace, 4 Feb)., for the collection of four pence in the pound on all ecclesiastical goods and benefices, granted by the convocation of Canterbury province meeting in St. Paul's, London, 14–30 Jan., for the support of the English delegation going to the council at Pisa to end the schism of the Church. [Fo. 114^{v}/24^{v}] The money is to be paid to M. Richard Brynkley, dean of the Arches, or M. John Perche, registrar of the court of Canterbury, at London, by the feast of St. Gregory [12 March]. London, bishop's inn, 7 Feb. 1409.
Similar mandates to the archdeacons of Wiltshire, Dorset and Berkshire.
[The archbishop's mandate is printed in *Reg. Bubwith*, i. 48–9.]

REGISTRUM REVERENDI IN CHRISTO PATRIS ET DOMINI DOMINI ROBERTI DEI GRACIA SAR' EPISCOPI HABITUM CORAM CIRCUMSPECTO VIRO MAGISTRO ADAM DE MOTTRUM PRECENTORE ECCLESIE SAR' VICARIO IN SPIRITUALIBUS GENERALI DICTI REVERENDI PATRIS

[All the letters, **757–97**, are issued by M. Adam de Mottrum, vicar general.]

757 Letters dimissory to William Saivyrnak, first tonsure, to receive the minor orders and those of subdeacon and deacon. Salisbury, 16 March 1409.

758 The like to M. Edward Prentys, subdeacon, B.C.L., canon of Salisbury cath. and prebendary of Stratford in the same, to receive all orders. Salisbury, 22 March 1409.

759 The like to Robert Colerne, acolyte of dioc. Salisbury, to receive all orders. Salisbury, 22 March 1409.

760 [Fo. 115/25] Licence to Fulk Stafford, subdeacon, rector of Ditchampton (*Dichampton*), to be absent from his benefice for one year's study at Oxford university. Salisbury, 4 Apr. 1409.

761 The like to Stephen Morpath, rector of East Knoyle (*Knoel*), for three years' study at any English *studium generale*. Salisbury, 12 Apr. 1409.

762 Letters dimissory to John Doll, subdeacon of dioc. Salisbury, to receive all orders. Salisbury, 23 Apr. 1409.

763 The like to John Turner, subdeacon, to receive all orders. Salisbury, 23 Apr. 1409.

764 The like to Roger Clottham, subdeacon, to receive all orders. Salisbury, 25 Apr. 1409.

765 The like to John Trusser, first tonsure, to receive all minor and holy orders. Salisbury, 25 Apr. 1409.

766 Letters testimonial certifying that John Lucas, priest, was ordained deacon by Nicholas [Burbache], bp. of Christopolis (*Christipolitan*),[1] by authority of John Waltham, bp. of Salisbury, in Tisbury (*Tyssebury*) church, during Lent about fifteen years previously. Sealed with the precentor's seal, which is also used in the office of vicar general. Salisbury, 30 Apr. 1409.
[The ordination lists are missing from the bound Reg. Waltham.
1. *Handbook of British Chronology*, p. 267.]

767 Commission to the official of the archd. of Berkshire and the vicar of Liddington (*Ludyngton*) to hold an inquiry into the dilapidations which Thomas Shelford, rector of Ashbury (*Asshebury*, *Aysschebury*), alleges have been left by his predecessor at the time of his death. The goods of the previous rector are to be sequestrated, and his executors are to be summoned to appear before the vicar general in Salisbury cath. on the twentieth day after being cited. Sealed [as in **766**]. Salisbury, 1 May 1409.
[The previous rector was Thomas Byssebury (*Reg. Bubwith*, i. 52).]

768 [Fo. 115v/25v Mandate to the archd. of Salisbury for the execution of the mandate of Thomas, abp. of Canterbury (dated Lambeth (*Lamheth*), 20 Apr. 1409), transmitted by Richard, bp. of London (dated Fulham, 30 Apr.), and received by the vicar general 9 May, for greater efforts in collecting the subsidy for the delegates to the council of Pisa. Two months after the money should have been paid, only one seventh has been received. [Fo. 116/26] Collectors are to be appointed with full powers in each diocese, and the money is to be paid to M. Richard Brynkele, dean of the Arches,

and M. John Perche, registrar of the court of Canterbury, at London, by the Sunday after Ascension Day [i.e. by 19 May]. The archd. of Salisbury is appointed collector in his archdeaconry. Sealed [as in **766**]. Salisbury, 10 May 1409.
Similar mandates to the archdeacons of Wiltshire, Dorset and Berkshire.
[The archbishop's mandate is printed in *Concilia*, iii. 320–1.]

769 [Fo. 116v/26v] Notification to the abp. of Canterbury of the execution of his mandate. The archdeacons of Salisbury, Wiltshire, Dorset and Berkshire have been appointed collectors in their archdeaconries. Sealed [as in **766**]. Salisbury, 14 May 1409.

770 Letters dimissory to Robert Redeler (Rodeler), deacon of dioc. Salisbury, to receive all orders. Salisbury, 6 May 1409.

771 The like to John Gully, to receive all orders. Salisbury, 20 May 1409.

772 The like to Nicholas Sexpenne, clerk, to receive all orders. Salisbury, 20 May 1409.

773 [Fo. 117/27] Licence granted to Ralph Gardyner, priest, rector of Alton Barnes (*Aulton Berners*), to be absent from his benefice for one year in the service of the abbot of St. Albans, dioc. Lincoln. Salisbury, 20 May 1409.

774 Licence granted to John Crukerne of Childhay (*Cheldehey*) and Alice his wife to have divine service celebrated in the oratory of their house of Childhay in the parish of Broadwinsor (*Brodewyndesore*). Salisbury, 20 May 1409.

775 Letters dimissory granted to John Daley, deacon, to receive the order of priest. Salisbury, 22 May 1409.

776 The like to Edmund Penne, acolyte, to receive all orders. Salisbury, 22 May 1409.

777 The like to John Daley, deacon, to receive the order of priest. Salisbury, 24 May 1409.
[Cf. **775**: grant entered twice.]

778 The like granted to the abbot of Abbotsbury (*Abbodesbury*) to permit John Byry, monk of Abbotsbury, to receive the order of priest. Salisbury, 25 May 1409.

779 The like granted to the prior of Bradenstoke (*Bradenestoke*) to permit William Compton, Thomas Thornbury, John Laurens and John Chynnoc, canons of Bradenstoke, to receive all orders. Salisbury, 28 May 1409.

780 The like to Robert Gryme, deacon, to receive the order of priest. Salisbury, 30 May 1409.

781 The like to William Wyntyrborne, acolyte, to receive all orders. Salisbury, 30 May 1409.

782 The like to William Dalderby, deacon, to receive the order of priest. Salisbury, 31 May 1409.

783 Licence to John Anton, rector of Langton Matravers (*Langton in Purbyk*), to be absent from his benefice for one year. Salisbury, 8 June 1409.

784 [Fo. 117v/27v] Commission to William [Yeurde], bp. of Selymbria (*Salubrien'*),[1] to act as suffragan in the city and diocese of Salisbury, with power of reconciling, whenever need arises, conventual, collegiate and parish churches, churchyards having burials, and church altars, whether fixed to the ground or portable; of seeking and receiving procurations due; of confirming children (*parvulos*) and adults; of consecrating chalices and patens; of blessing priestly vestments and other ecclesiastical ornaments; and of conferring all orders, even minor ones, at suitable times, on persons of dioc. Salisbury or others with letters dimissory from their diocesans, who are found fit and suitable. Sealed with the precentor's seal, which is also used in the office of vicar general. Salisbury, 20 June 1409.

[1. *Handbook of British Chronology*, p. 268; *Hierarchia Catholica*, i. 431.]

785 Licence granted to William Fynamor and Agnes his wife to have divine service celebrated in the oratory of their house of Whetham in the parish of Calne. However, they are to attend the parish church at the great festivals if possible. Salisbury, 11 July 1409.

786 Commission to the official of the archd. of Dorset and the rector of Bradford Peverell (*Bradeford*) to inquire into the dilapidations which John Waleys, rector of Winterbourne Abbas (*Wynterborn Abbatis*), alleges have been left by his predecessor. Salisbury, 27 July 1409.

787 Notification to the clergy of Shaftesbury (*Shafton*) deanery that William Smyth, chaplain, is licensed to preach there, when invited by the clergy, until the arrival of the bp. of Salisbury, or until this licence is revoked. Salisbury, 27 July 1409.

[This is the earliest example in the register of a licence to preach after the publication of the constitutions against Lollardy, in the convocation of 24–30 Jan. 1409 (cf. Constitution I, **955**). This licence was issued even before Adam de Mottrum had notified the abp. of Canterbury of the publication of the constitutions in Salisbury dioc., 1 Aug. 1409, **954**, and its wording suggests that he was not entirely certain as to procedure.]

788 Letters dimissory granted to Thomas Gerard of Bray (*Braye*) to receive all orders. Salisbury, 31 July 1409.

789 The like to John Colas, deacon, to receive the order of priest. Salisbury, 5 Sept. 1409.

790 The like to William Savernake, deacon, to receive the order of priest. Salisbury, 12 [August][1] 1409.

[1. MS: *die duodecimo mense loco et anno predictis.* This may be a slip as Savernake was ordained priest by Richard Clifford, bp. of London, 1 Sept. 1409, in the chapel of Much Hadham manor, at the title of Ivychurch priory (British Library, Campbell Charter xxii/12).]

791 [Fo. 118/28] The like to Thomas Salford, deacon, and Hugh Lowdelow, subdeacon, monks of Abingdon (*Abyndon*), to receive all orders. Salisbury, 16 Sept. 1409.

792 Licence to John Framton, esquire, senior, to have divine service celebrated in the oratory of his house of Moreton (*Morton*) in the parish of Moreton, during his illness. Salisbury, 18 Sept. 1409.

793 Licence granted to John Forde, rector of Cholderton (*Cheldryngton*), to be absent from his benefice for one year in the service of M. John Eclomor D.C.L. Salisbury, 24 Sept. 1409.

794 Licence granted to John Teffont, rector of Broughton Gifford (*Browgton*), to be absent from his benefice for one year's study at Oxford university. Salisbury, 24 Sept. 1409.

795 Letters testimonial certifying that John Teffont, rector of Broughton Gifford (*Browgton*), was ordained acolyte and subdeacon by Robert, bp. of Salisbury, 9 June 1408 in Sutton Courtenay (*Sutton*) church, and deacon 22 Sept. 1408 in the chapel of Potterne (*Poterne*) manor, at the title of his benefice. Salisbury, 27 Sept. 1409.

796 Letters testimonial certifying that Richard Curteys received the order of priest from Richard [Medford], bp. of Salisbury, 18 Sept. 1400, at the title of Ivychurch (*Ederosis*) priory. Salisbury, 27 Sept. 1409.

[Cf. Reg. Medford fo. 170.]

797 Licence granted to William Fostbury, subdeacon, rector of Tarrant Keynston (*Kayneston*), to be absent from his benefice for one year's study at any English *studium generale*. Salisbury, 12 Oct. 1409.

[Fo. 118v/28v, the outside one of a gathering, has been rendered largely illegible by damp. The top half appears to contain two licences for absence and two indulgences. The bottom half is clearer and is calendared below. All the letters, **798–918**, are issued by Robert, bp. of Salisbury.]

798 Indulgence granted to all contributing to the support and relief of Robert Cork [reading uncertain] of Ramsbury (*Remmesbury*) parish. Ramsbury, 18 Nov. 1409.

799 Licence granted to Thomas Robard, rector of Studland (*Stokeland*), for certain reasons, to be absent from his benefice for one year. Salisbury, 2 Dec. 1409.

800 Letters dimissory granted to Gilbert [? Spenser], clerk, to receive all orders. Salisbury, 4 Dec. 1409.

801 Licence granted to M. William Swyft, rector of Boyton, to be absent from his benefice for one year's study at Oxford university. Salisbury, 4 Dec. 1409.

802 Letter of William Somerhill, subdean of Salisbury cath., to Robert, bp. of Salisbury, asking him to invoke the secular authority for the capture of four citizens of Salisbury, namely Walter Simond, tailor, John Hill, hellier (*heliere*),[1] Roger Porter and Robert Michell, excommunicated by the subdean for contumacy, who have remained obdurate for forty days and more. Salisbury, 2 Dec. 1409.

[1. A tiler or thatcher.]

803 [Fo. 98/9] Signification to the Crown of the excommunication of four persons [as in **802**], with a request for their capture by the secular authority. Woodford (*Wodeford*) manor, 4 Dec. 1409.

[Original, P.R.O., Chancery significations of excommunication, C 85/148/21, in a different hand from the register copy.]

804 The like concerning Margery Coterell and Gillian Ferman, of the parish of Hungerford, who have remained obdurate for forty days and more, as appears in letters of the official of the dean of Salisbury. Woodford, 4 Dec. 1409.

[Original, P.R.O., C 85/148/22, in a different hand from the register copy.]

805 Letters dimissory to John Fer, clerk, of dioc. Salisbury, to receive the orders of acolyte and subdeacon. Ramsbury (*Remmesbury*) park, 10 Dec. 1409.

806 Confirmation, by the bp., of the ordinance of John Mercand, vicar of Cumnor (*Comnore*), made 26 Apr. 1408 at Cumnor, granting permission to the parishioners of Wytham (*Wyghtam*) to bury their dead in Wytham churchyard instead of at Cumnor. The bp. of Salisbury and Richard, abbot of Abingdon (*Abendon*), patron of Cumnor vicarage, have given their consent, and the official of the archd. of Berkshire has added his seal to that of the vicar. The bp. confirms the ordinance with letters sealed with his seal, with the impression of his signet on the dorse. Ramsbury park, 10 Dec. 1409.

807 [Fo. 98^{v}/9^{v}] Licence, for five years, to Thomas More and Christine his wife to have divine service celebrated in the oratory of their house in the parish of East Hendred (*Esthenreth*), provided that they attend the parish church on Sundays and the great festivals if possible. Ramsbury, 15 Dec. 1409.

808 Letters testimonial to the effect that on 30 May 1403 at Salisbury, M. John Snap D.Cn.L. was instituted by Richard [Medford], bp. of Salisbury, to the church of Pewsey (*Peuesey*), vac. by the resig. of M. Thomas Polton; patrons, abbot and conv. of Hyde (*Hyda*). He was inducted by the archd. of Wiltshire. Ramsbury park, 19 Dec. 1409.

809 Licence, for three years, to Edith, widow of John Remston, to have divine service celebrated in the oratory of her house in the parish of Corfe Castle (*Corff*). Ramsbury park, 21 Dec. 1409.

[For the Remston or Rempston family, see Hutchins, i. 533, 667.]

810 Commission to the official of the archd. of Wiltshire to inquire before 2 Feb. 1410 into the dilapidations which Henry Pyke, vicar of Purton (*Purynton*), alleges have been left by his predecessor, John Burnet, at the time of his death, and to sequestrate the latter's goods. Ramsbury park, 2 Jan. 1410.

811 [Fo. 99/10] Mandate to the prioress of Amesbury (*Ambresbury*) to ensure that those postulants whom the bp. is to consecrate on 12 Jan. shall duly prepare themselves. She is to report to the bp. on the action taken. Ramsbury park, 2 Jan. 1410.

812 Mandate to the vicar of Lambourn (*Lambourne*) to solemnize the marriage between Robert Cook, of the parish of Highworth (*Hyworthe*), and Alice Clerkes, of the parish of Lambourn. Their banns have been published in the churches of Highworth and Ashbury (*Assh'bury*), and in the chapel of Eastbury (*Isbury*) in the parish of Lambourn, but their marriage has been delayed on account of the short time that Alice Clerkes has lived in Lambourn. The vicar is to perform the marriage by 9 Feb. on pain of excommunication. Ramsbury park, 14 Jan. 1410.

813 Appointment of M. John Turry B.Cn. & C.L. as sequestrator and commissary general in the archdeaconries of Wiltshire and Berkshire, with power of investigating, punishing and correcting crimes. [Ramsbury park,] 14 Jan. 1410.

814 Appointment of M. John Turry as official of the peculiar jurisdiction of Potterne (*Poterne*), Marlborough (*Marleburgh*), Devizes (*Devyses*) and Lavington (*Lavyngton*), with power of correcting and punishing crimes. [Ramsbury park,] 14 Jan. 1410.

815 Letter to M. Ralph Lovell, prebendary of Highworth (*Heworthe*) in Salisbury cath., Richard, vicar of Highworth, and Ingram Hampton and

John Henton, proctors of the community of Little Blunsdon (*Bluntesdon*), in the parish of Highworth, granting permission, in accordance with their request, for a churchyard to be consecrated next to Little Blunsdon chapel, so that the inhabitants may be buried there instead of at Highworth. Ramsbury park, 20 Jan. 1410.

816 [Fo. 99v/10v]. Licence to John Wotton, rector of St. Sampson, Cricklade (*Crekelade*), to be absent from his benefice for one year from Easter [23 March], on condition that he appoints a proctor in his place. London, bishop's inn, 28 Jan. 1410.

817 Commission to M. Geoffrey Crukadan, bishop's official and canon of Salisbury cath., to appoint penitenciaries in each deanery of dioc. Salisbury, to whom the clergy can make confession, in accordance with the constitutions. He is to certify the names of those appointed. London, bishop's inn, 5 Feb. 1410.

[Cf. Lyndwood, pp. 326, 335, 340; V, 16, c. 1, 9, 13.]

818 Licence to Laurence Howard, rector of Winterbourne Bassett (*Wynterbourne Basset*), to be absent from his benefice for one year, on condition that he appoints a substitute. London, 5 Feb. 1410.

819 Letters dimissory to Thomas Jon, clerk, of dioc. Salisbury, to receive the orders of acolyte and subdeacon. London, 6 Feb. 1410.

820 The like to Walter Bagge, acolyte, of dioc. Salisbury, for the orders of subdeacon and deacon. London, 12 Feb. 1410.

821 The like to John Plomer for the order of acolyte. London, 12 Feb. 1410.

822 [Fo. 110/20*] Mandate to the archd. of Salisbury for the execution of the mandate of Thomas, abp. of Canterbury (dated Dartford, 12 Jan. 1410), transmitted by Richard, bp. of London (dated Much Hadham (*Hadham*) manor, 20 Jan.), summoning the clergy of the province to a convocation at St. Paul's, London, 17 Feb. 1410, in accordance with a royal writ to the abp. dated Eltham, 3 Jan.

[No other details are legible. The archbishop's summons is printed in *Reg. Bubwith*, i. 71–3. Those summoned are as in **754**, except that in addition to cath. chapters, colleges and convents are specified, each to be represented by one proctor.]

823 [Fo. 110v/20v] Similar mandates to the archdeacons of Wiltshire, Dorset and Berkshire, and to the dean and chapter of Salisbury cath.

[The chapter received the bishop's mandate 4 Feb. 1410 (Vyring, p. 38).]

*In the top right-hand corner is written in a 15th-century hand *quaternus quartus*, a quire originally consisting of fos. 110, 92–7, 101, **822–58**. This outside folio has been badly affected by damp and is almost illegible.

824 Notification to the clergy of the city and diocese of Salisbury that M. John Symondesbergh B.C.L., treasurer of St. Paul's cath., London, has been granted a licence to preach throughout the diocese. London, 21 March 1412.

[This entry and **825** were added in 1412 to fill up a space on this folio.]

825 Licence to Brian Stapulton, knight, and Cecily his wife, of North Moreton, to choose their own confessor for one year. London, 21 March 1412.

[See **824**n.]

826 [Fo. 92/3] Licence to the vicar of Calne prebendal church to hear the confessions of his parishioners, and to grant absolution even in some reserved cases, until the octave of Easter [30 March]. London, bishop's inn, 13 Feb. 1410.

827 Commission to M. Geoffrey Crukadan, the bishop's official and canon of Salisbury, to inquire into the proposed exchange of benefices between Robert Bochard, rector of Hardenhuish (*Hardynghuwyssh*), patron, King Henry—and John Scot, vicar of Compton Chamberlayne (*Compton Chaumberleyn*); patron, provost of St. Edmund's collegiate church, Salisbury. If the inquiry is satisfactory, he is to effect the exchange. London, bishop's inn, 8 Feb. 1410.

[This exchange was effected (see **164**, **274**) but was not recorded among the exchanges of benefices.]

828 Indulgence of forty days promised to all who contribute within the next year to the relief and support of William Selby, who has been impoverished by frequent hostile invasions into England and by payment of his ransom from a foreign land. London, bishop's inn, 13 Feb. 1410.

829 [Fo. 92v/3v] Licence to William Brytby, subdeacon, rector of the chapel with cure of souls of Over Compton, to be absent from his benefice for two years' study anywhere in England, with permission not to proceed to further orders. London, 21 Feb. 1410.

830 Letters testimonial certifying that Thomas Welyn, acolyte, was ordained subdeacon by Robert [Wyville], bp. of Salisbury, at the title of Littlemore (*Litelmore*) monastery, 16 June 1375, in the church of St. Edmund, Salisbury; was ordained deacon by Ralph [Erghum], bp. of Salisbury, at the same title, 29 March 1376, in Maiden Bradley (*Maydenbradelegh*) conventual church; and was ordained priest by the same 20 Sept. 1376, in Reading (*Radyngie*) conventual church. London, 21 Feb. 1410.

[The ordination lists are missing from the bound registers of Wyville and Erghum in the Wiltshire Record Office.]

831 Commission to the dean of Wimborne Minster (*Wynburnmynstre*) free chapel to inquire into the proposed exchange of benefices between William Marnhull, prebendary of Crantock (*Karentisbern*) in the free chapel of Wimborne Minster—and John Langhorn, vicar of Sturminster Marshall (*Sturmynstre Marschall*); patron, Queen Joan. If the inquiry is satisfactory, he is to effect the exchange, reserving the obedience of Marnhull to the bp. London, 25 Feb. 1410.

832 [Fo. 93/4] Licence to M. John Possell, provost of the college of St. Mary of Oriel (*Oriell*), Oxford, to preach throughout the city and diocese of Salisbury. London, bishop's inn, 3 March 1410.

833 The like to M. Richard Stabull, vicar of St. Peter in the East, Oxford. London, bishop's inn, 5 March 1410.

834 Commission to the warden of Shottesbrook (*Schotesbrok*) collegiate church and John Cerne, vicar of St. Laurence, Reading (*Redyng*), to hear and determine a suit for divorce brought by Catherine Chalk of Reading against Thomas Gyles, her husband. Sonning (*Sonnyng*), bishop's manor, 17 March 1410.

835 Monition to John Jocy, chaplain, at the complaint of John [Mason], rector of Batcombe (*Batecombe*), ordering him to serve his cure of souls in Batcombe church and not to officiate elsewhere for money. Salisbury, [undated.]

836 Commission to the dean of Shaftesbury (*Schaffton*) and William Broke, parish chaplain of Marnhull (*Marehull*), on complaint of William Staunton, rector of Marnhull, to excommunicate those who have defrauded the church of tithes and other payments, unless they make payment within thirty days. Woodford (*Wodeford*), bishop's manor, 30 March 1410.

837 [Fo. 93v/4v] Commission to the subdean of Salisbury cath. and all parish curates and chaplains of the city of Salisbury to order the proper observance of Sundays and feast days. People are engaging in business, shops are open for trade, the tavern is frequented rather than the church, feasts and drunkenness abound rather than tears and prayers. All parishioners are to be warned to abstain from all secular business and manual work, in public and in private, and to attend their parish churches. The clergy are to notify the bp. of the action taken and of the names of any disobeying the warnings. Woodford, bishop's manor, 1 Apr. 1410.
[Preamble given in full in Appendix D.]

838 [Fo. 94/5] Licence to M. John Luke B.Th. to preach throughout the city and diocese of Salisbury. Potterne (*Poterne*), bishop's manor, 5 Apr. 1410.

839 The like to M. Roger Welpedalle B.Th. Potterne, 5 Apr. 1410.

840 Commission to M. John Wellis D.Cn.L., M. Edmund Werham Lic.Cn.L., and M. John Turry B.Cn. & C.L., bishop's commissary, to hear the purgation of Brother John Paunteley D.Th. from alleged incontinence, adultery and incest with the wife of William FitzWaryn of Appleton (*Appulton*), his kinswoman, or, if he is unable to purge himself, to punish him. Potterne, 7 Apr. 1410.

[Paunteley was a monk of St. Peter's abbey, Gloucester, ordained priest in 1375, who was at Gloucester College in Oxford in 1410 (*Register of the Diocese of Worcester*, ed. J. W. Willis Bund (Worcs. Hist. Soc., 1897), p. 341; *BRUO*, iii. 1437).]

841 Commission to the abbot of Sherborne (*Schirborn*) to hear before Whitsun [11 May] the complaint of Alice Amisell of Sherborne, in the abbot's jurisdiction, daughter of William Amisell, against Stephen Carlell *alias* Scryneyn, her husband, who, she alleges, has committed adultery with Joan, wife of John Iveyn, tailor of Sherborne. The abbot is to certify the bp. before Trinity Sunday [18 May]. Potterne, 8 Apr. 1410.

842 [Fo. 94v/5v] Mandate to the prior of Llanthony (*Lanton*), dioc. Worcester, ordering the reception of Hugh Raulyn, canon of Bradenstoke (*Bradenastoke*), who wishes to move to Llanthony where he thinks he will serve God more acceptably. The bp. testifies to his good character and approves his wish. The prior is to certify the prior and conv. of Bradenstoke after the arrival and profession of Raulyn. Potterne, 16 Apr. 1410.

843 Commission to M. William Rodebourn B.C.L., vicar of Steeple Ashton (*Asshton*), and M. Thomas Speke, rector of Grittleton (*Grytlyngton*), to supervise the administration of the conventual church of Kington St. Michael (*Kyngton*), and to correct any abuses. Potterne, 19 May 1410.

844 [Fo. 95/6] Commission to the rectors of Winterbourne Monkton (*Wynterburnewast*) and All Saints, Dorchester (*Dorcestre*), and the vicar of Stinsford (*Stentisford*) to sequestrate the goods of Robert Whityng, rector of Winterbourne Came (*Wynterburnecame*), who died intestate, and to summon any who violate the sequestration to appear before the bp. in Salisbury cath. on the tenth day after their citation. The commissaries are to notify the bp. of the action taken. Sherborne (*Shirborn*) castle, 7 June 1410.

[For Winterbourne Monkton, formerly Winterbourne Wast, see Hutchins, ii. 530.]

845 Commission to John Rok, vicar of Stinsford (*Stantisford*), and Henry Osteler of Dorchester, to administer the goods of Robert Whityng [as in **844**]. Sherborne, 13 June 1410.

846 Commission to M. William Rodeborn B.C.L., vicar of Steeple Ashton (*Asshton*), to examine and determine the suit of Robert Napper, vicar of Hungerford, against William Whitgat, who, he alleges, has failed to pay the tithes of wool, lambs, calves, pigs and other small tithes on the lands within the parish of Hungerford which he holds at farm of the monastery of St. Frideswide, Oxford. The case has been partially heard before the bp., but because of the inconvenience and expense of appearing before him, he has agreed to the parties' request that he appoint a commissary before whom they may bring witnesses and documents. The prior and conv. of St. Frideswide are to be summoned, and the commissary is to hear the case and report to the bp. by 21 Sept. 1410. The parties are to appear before the bp. on 22 Sept. Sherborne, 25 June 1410.

847 [Fo. 95v/6v] Letters testimonial certifying that John Lenyng of dioc. Salisbury was ordained priest, at the title of Cerne abbey, by Nicholas [Burbache] bp. of Christopolis (*Christipolitan*),[1] by authority of Richard [Medford], bp. of Salisbury, 10 Apr. 1406, in Bulbridge (*Bulbrygge*) church. Sherborne, 8 June 1410.

[There is no record of this ordination in Reg. Medford. Lenyng was ordained deacon by Bp. Nicholas, at the title of Cerne abbey, on 27 March 1406 in Sherborne conventual church (Reg. Medford fo. 178v).
1. See **766**n.]

848 Mandate to the official of Salisbury, ordering prayers and processions to be made for the good estate of the realm. An indulgence of forty days is promised to those complying. The official is to notify the bp. by Michaelmas [29 Sept.] of the action taken. Chardstock (*Cherdestok*), bishop's manor, 14 July 1410. Similar mandate to the dean of Salisbury.

849 [Fo. 96/7] Commission to M. John Fyton B.Th., M. John Turry B.Cn. & C.L. and M. John Hurll B.Cn.L. to examine and determine the dispute between the prioress and conv. of Amesbury (*Ambresbury*) and the vicar of Preshute (*Preschute*) over the tithes of rabbits in the land called le Temple, in the parish of Preshute. Chardstock, 15 July 1410.

[For le Temple, formerly owned by the Templars, see *Wilts. Place-names*, p. 309.]

850 [Fo. 96v/7v] Mandate to the archd. of Dorset or his official, demanding that he hold a second and more careful inquiry by the clergy of the deanery into the patronage of the church of Winterbourne Came (*Wynterbourn Caam*), to which various people have claimed the right to present. Sherborne (*Shirborn*) bishop's castle, 22 Aug. 1410.

851 Commission to the archd. of Dorset or his official to institute the rightful presentee to the church of Winterbourne Came (*Wynterbourn Caam*), after he has held an inquiry into the rights of the various people claiming to present. He is to notify the bp. of the action taken by 8 Sept. Sherborne, 25 Aug. 1410.

852 [Fo. 97/8] Letter to the rector and parishioners of Moreton (*Morton*) in response to their petition that, for certain good reasons, the day of the church's dedication be changed from the feast of St. Magnus the Martyr [19 Aug.]. The bp. grants permission for it to be celebrated instead on the Sunday after the octave of the Assumption of the B.V.M. [Sunday after 22 Aug.]. An indulgence of forty days is promised to those who hear the divine office in the church on that day. Sherborne, 28 Aug. 1410.

853 Letters patent announcing the purgation on 19 Aug. before the bishop's commissaries in the chapel of St. Mary Magdalen by Sherborne (*Shirborn*) castle of Richard Fyssher, rector of Stock Gaylard (*Stoke Colard*), from the alleged crime of adultery with Christine, wife of Thomas Hykes, of the same parish. Sherborne, 28 Aug. 1410.

[Cf. **1139**. Nevertheless, Fyssher exchanged his benefice 6 Nov. 1410, Appendix A VII.]

854 Mandate to the vicar of Bradford-on-Avon (*Bradeford*), on petition of Ralph Dornam and Joan Russhell of the same parish, that he solemnize their marriage, after publication of the banns, if there is no impediment. Sherborne, 31 Aug. 1410.

855 Commission to the vicar of Wilsford near Pewsey (*Wylsford*), on petition of M. John Holaund, rector of Dauntsey (*Daundesey*), to sequestrate the goods of John Selman, deceased, who defrauded the church of Dauntsey of the revenues of its portion in Wilsford, and to cite any who violate the sequestration to appear before the bp. on the twelfth day after the citation. The vicar is to report to the bp. on the action taken. Sherborne, 31 Aug. 1410.

[For the rector of Dauntsey's right to certain great and small tithes on the Wilsford Dauntsey estate, see *VCH Wilts.*, x. 212.]

856 [Fo. 97^{v}/8^{v}] Monition to the dean of Salisbury cath. to correct before Michaelmas [29 Sept.] certain abuses in the parish of the prebendal church of Bere Regis (*Beer*), in the dean's jurisdiction. William Dukke, chaplain of the church, is alleged to have consorted with several women, including Margaret, nurse of Walter Inkeberghe of Puddletown (*Pudell*), and a servant of Robert Turvyle, knight; and John Dudde, though married, has lived for seven years with Alice Dynes. The dean is to report to the bp. within eight days after Michaelmas concerning the action taken. [Undated].

[This entry is in a different shade of ink from that which precedes it. It was entered later, probably in 1412, to fill an empty space.
The dean had visited the prebendal church of Bere Regis 6 June 1412. One entry among the *detecta* mentions John Dodde's alleged adultery with Alice, wife of Richard Dyne. Dodde appeared before the dean 16 June 1412 (Decanal Reg. Chandeler, pt. i fo. 139^{r-v}).]

[Fo. 100 is a piece of parchment of different shape and size from the other folios of the register. It contains a will belonging to the episcopate of John Chandeler, which is given below, **1148**.]

857 [Fo. 101/11] Commission to the official of the archd. of Dorset and the rector of Broadway (*Brodewey*), on the petition of Joan Sekrystine *alias*

Benevyle, to inquire into her marriage. She was married at a tender age to a certain Alfonso of Lisbon (*Lussh'bone*), a Portuguese man, and after he had left her and had been abroad many years, thinking him dead, she married John Benevyle, with whom she begat sons and daughters. She has now received information that her first husband may be still alive. The commissaries are to ascertain all the facts and notify the bp. Sherborne, 5 Sept. 1410.

858 Notarial instrument confirming the composition between the inhabitants of Ranston (*Randelston*) in Iwerne Courtnay *or* Shroton (*Shereston*) parish, and Robert Canon, rector of Iwerne Courtnay, that a chaplain be provided at the rector's expense to celebrate divine service in Ranston chapel three days a week (on Sunday, Wednesday and Friday).
[Fo. 101v/11v, formerly the outside folio of a quire, has been seriously affected by damp so that the top half is virtually illegible. This contains the oath of Robert Canon and of the proctors, followed by the agreement between them. The lower half of the page is more legible.]
Maurice Bruyn, *domicellus,* lord of Ranston hamlet, and Robert Waltham were appointed proctors of Richard Prest, senior, Richard Prest, junior, John Prest, William Muleward, John Baron, John Magge, Maud Prest and all the other inhabitants of Ranston, by letters dated 14 May 1410 and sealed with the seal of the dean of Dorchester (*Dorcestrie*) deanery. [Fo. 102/12*] The bp. approves the composition, in the presence of M. William Lyndewode D.Cn. & C.L., M. Thomas Tenton B.Cn. & C.L. and M. John Appulton, notary public, and the notarial instrument is drawn up by Wenceslas Swisiko, clerk (dioc. Brandenburg), notary public by papal and imperial authority. Chapel of Potterne (*Poterne*) bishop's manor, 15 May 1410.

859 Commission to the clergy of the city of Salisbury to publish the sentence of excommunication passed on John Golapyn and Edith Payns of the city of Salisbury, for contumacy when summoned to appear before the bp. The clergy are to denounce them in their churches, when most people are present, and are not to admit them to their company, on pain of excommunication. They are to continue to do this until they hear further from the bp., and are to certify him of the action taken before Christmas. Woodford (*Wodeford*),[1] 3 Nov. 1410.

[1. Cf. **860** n. 2.]

860 [Fo. 102v/12v] Request to Philip, bp. of Lincoln, to cite Robert Marchall *alias* Wythum, a chaplain, living in dioc. Lincoln, executor of the will of William Kyrkeby,[1] formerly rector of Knighton (*Knyghton*), to appear before the bp. of Salisbury in an inquiry into the dilapidations which Adam

*In the top right-hand corner is written in a 15th-century hand *quaternus quintus*, a quire consisting of fos. 102–9, **859–90**.

Raceton, the present rector, alleges were left by his predecessor. Shaftesbury (*Shafton*),[2] 3 Nov. 1410.

[1. Error for *Wryghte*? Cf. **967**; Reg. Medford fo. 96ᵛ.

2. Cf. place of **859**. Woodford and Shaftesbury are 18 miles apart as the crow flies, and though it is possible, it seems scarcely probable that letters were issued in both these places on the same day.]

861 Commission to M. John Chaundeler, dean of Salisbury cath., M. Adam Mottrum, precentor, and M. Geoffrey Crukadan, canon, to hear the purgation of William Colvyle, chaplain, and Agnes, wife of John Mason, of the city of Salisbury, from the alleged crime of incontinence and adultery, or, if they are unable to purge themselves, to punish them. Ramsbury (*Remmesbury*), bishop's manor, 22 Nov. 1410.

862 Mandate to the clergy of the archdeaconry of Dorset not to admit the archd. of Dorset, who has disobeyed the bishop's inhibition of inferior jurisdictions during the episcopal visitation of the archdeaconry. The bishop's letter or a copy of it is to be displayed publicly by the rural deans in the principal places of each deanery. Sherborne (*Shirborn*) castle, 16 Sept. 1410.

863 [Fo. 103/13] General notification that William FitzWaryn of Appleton (*Appulton*) has been excommunicated for contumacy when summoned to appear before the bp. Sonning (*Sonnyng*), bishop's manor, 20 Jan. 1411.

864 Notarial instrument drawn up at the petition of John Jocy of Seagry (*Segre*), chaplain, incorporating letters testimonial concerning his orders. [Fo. 103ᵛ/13ᵛ] Peter, bp. of Grado (*Graden'*), primate of Dalmatia (*Dalmacie*), papal confessor, in letters dated at Rome, 9 Dec. 1398, testified that he had that day ordained Jocy (then an acolyte of dioc. Salisbury) subdeacon, by special verbal command of Pope Boniface IX, in the chapel of his house in the Parione district (*regione Parionis*)[1] at Rome. Conrad [Caraczolus], abp. of Nicosia (*Nicosien'*),[2] papal chamberlain, in letters dated St. Peter's, Rome, 18 Dec. 1398, testified that John, abp. of Naupactus (*Neapoten'*),[3] had that day ordained Jocy deacon, by his command and by special verbal commission of the pope, in the church of St. Maria supra Minervam in the Pigna district (*regione Pinee*).[4] Conrad, abp. of Nicosia, in letters dated St. Peter's, Rome, 21 Dec. 1398, testified that Anthony [de Samudia], bp. of Melfi (*Melfien'*)[5] had that day ordained Jocy priest, by his command and by special verbal commission of the pope, in the chapel of St. Andrew in St. Peter's, Rome. The notarial instrument is drawn up with the bp. of Salisbury's approval by Wenceslas Swisiko, clerk (dioc. Brandenburg), notary public by papal and imperial authority, who has examined the original letters and found them genuine, in the presence of M. William Lyndewode D.Cn. & C.L. and M. John Fyton B.Th. (dioc. Lincoln, and Coventry and Lichfield). Chapel of Sonning (*Sonnyng*) manor, 17 Feb. 1411.

[1. Cf. *Stradario Romano*, ed. B. Blasi (Rome, 1933), p. 226.

2. *Hierarchia Catholica*, i. 366.

3. Probable identification, cf. *ibid.*, i. 362.

4. *Stradario Romano*, p. 239.

5. *Hierarchia Catholica*, i. 335.]

865 [Fo. 104/14] Dispensation to the abbot of Milton (*Middelton*) to eat meat during Lent on the advice of the doctors and others assisting him, on account of his illness, provided he does it discreetly. London, 14 March 1411.

[The abbot, Walter Archer, was suffering from gout and kidney stones in 1408, **939**, but he lived until 10 Jan. 1418 (Reg. Chandeler, pt. ii fo. 11).]

866 General notification that the bp. has granted a licence to John Goweyn to give land and houses in the city of Salisbury to Richard Holhurst, chaplain, proctor of the vicars choral of Salisbury cath., for their support, and that he has granted a licence to the vicars to receive it, despite the statute of mortmain.[1] The property consists of a certain corner tenement, inn or messuage called the Rose in Minster Street (*Munstret*)[2] and four[3] shops next to it, situated between the messuage or tenement of the vicars choral in New Street on the west and the tenement of Reynold Glover in Minster Street on the north; also two shops with appurtenances in Brown Street (*Brounestret*) between the tenement of Laurence Goweyn on the north and that lately belonging to Richard Juell on the south. These properties are at present held of the bp. in chief, and are to be held by the vicars choral in the same way.[4] Sonning (*Sonnyng*), bishop's manor, 5 March 1411.

[1. Royal licence granted 9 Apr. 1411 (*CPR 1408–13*, p. 290).
2. The Rose in Minster Street (present High Street) became the Rose and Crown in the 17th century and subsequently the Crown Hotel (C. Haskins, *The Ancient Trade Guilds and Companies of Salisbury* (Salisbury, 1912), pp. 309–10).
3. The royal licence has five (*CPR 1408–13*, p. 290).
4. The vicars choral had received a formal charter of incorporation from Henry IV 18 Nov. 1409 (*ibid.*, p. 152). This included the right to acquire and hold property in common, whereas formerly grants for the maintenance of the vicars choral were made to the dean and chapter.]

867 Commission to the rector of Wasing (*Wasyng*) to publish the bishop's relaxation of the sequestration imposed on the revenues of Aldermaston (*Aldermanston*) church. No one is to hinder the rector from disposing of them as he wishes. Sonning, 3 Apr. 1411.

868 Notification to the treasurer and barons of the king's exchequer that the abbot and conv. of Hyde (*Hyda*) (dioc. Winchester), who have various possessions in dioc. Salisbury, have been appointed collectors of the tax of one tenth and a half granted by the convocation of Canterbury province meeting in St. Paul's, London. They are to collect it in the archdeaconries of Wiltshire and Berkshire in place of the abbot and conv. of Cirencester (*Cirencestr'*) (dioc. Worcester), who are heavily burdened. The benefices of the following are exempted: the poor nuns of Lacock (*Lacok*) and Kington St. Michael (*Estkyngton*) in Wiltshire archdeaconry, and of Bromhall (*Bromhale*) in Berkshire archdeaconry. [Undated.][1]

[1. The abbot and conv. of Cirencester were appointed 8 Oct. 1410, **1086**.]

869 [Fo. 104v/14v] General notification that William Streccher, chaplain, has been excommunicated for contumacy. Potterne (*Poterne*), [undated].

870 Mandate to the official of Salisbury for the execution of a citation by Marcellus de Strozis D.C.L., papal nuncio and collector, dated London, 19 March 1411, summoning certain persons to appear before him at his inn in the parish of St. Mary at Hill, London, by 12 June 1411, on pain of excommunication, to pay in full the papal procurations which they owe or to explain their reasons. They are the dean and chapter of Salisbury cath., the abbots of Abingdon (*Abendon*), Milton (*Middilton*), Abbotsbury (*Abbotesbury*), Bindon (*Bynedon*), Sherborne (*Shirborn*), Malmesbury, Reading (*Radyng*) and Stanley (*Stanleye*); the priors of Monkton Farleigh (*Farlegh*), Bradenstoke (*Bradenstok*), Ogbourne (*Okeburne*) and Hurley (*Hurle*); the abbesses of Wilton, Shaftesbury (*Shafton*), Tarrant (*Tarent*) and Lacock (*Lacok*); the prioress of Amesbury (*Ambresbury*); and the priors of Frampton, Loders, Poughley (*Poghley*) and Wareham (*Warham*). The prior of Wallingford (*Wallyngford*) owes procurations for the year 1410. The bp. is to notify the papal collector by 12 June 1411, and the official is to notify the bp. by 1 June, of the action taken. [Undated.]

871 [Fo. 105/15] Commission to the archd. of Salisbury to publish in his archdeaconry the bishop's order forbidding collectors of alms to be admitted to the diocese. It has been reported that many people have claimed to be collecting on behalf of poor hospitals and individuals, in contravention of the statute of the general council,[1] and have been offering spurious indulgences. The archd. is to inform all parish curates and their chaplains and they are to publish the bishop's order in their churches. No collectors are to be admitted unless they can show the bishop's special permission, sealed with his signet on the dorse. Any collectors are to be summoned to appear before the bp. The archd. is to notify the bp. by the feast of St. Peter ad vincula [1 Aug.] of the action taken. Potterne, 9 May 1411.

[1. Fourth Lateran Council (1215), constitution 62 (*Conciliorum Oecumenicorum Decreta*, ed. J. Alberigo and others (3rd edn., Bologna, 1973), p. 263).]

872 Letters testimonial for John Newerke or Newwerke who was admitted to the bishop's household, when the bp. was at the Roman curia as abp.-elect of York.[1] He is to enjoy the privileges which have been granted to the bp. by the pope for the benefit of those in his service.[2] [Undated.]

[1. Papal provision, 14 May 1406 (*CPL 1404–15*, p. 84).
2. Hallum had the right 25 May 1410 to keep in his service clerks of any kind, even regular, or those holding perpetual benefices (*ibid.*, p. 213). Newerke was rector of Skirpenbeck, Yorks., **1037**.]

873 [Fo. 105^{v}/15^{v}] Notification to the clergy of the diocese of an indulgence of forty days promised to all who contribute within the next year to the repair and construction of the hospital of St. Thomas the Martyr of Acon, London, and the support of the master and brothers and the needy who flock there. Roger Chalkepole, proctor of the hospital, has permission to visit the diocese, notwithstanding the bishop's mandate of 9 May 1411 against collectors of alms. The letter is sealed with the bishop's signet on the dorse. Potterne, 12 May 1411.

874 General notification that William FitzWaryn of Appleton (*Apulton*) has been absolved from sentence of excommunication in the person of Geoffrey Wrexham, his proctor, subject to the imposition of a suitable penance when he is summoned by the bp. Potterne, 28 May 1411.

875 Commission to M. John Turry B.Cn. & C.L., bishop's commissary, and the rector of Newbury (*Neubury*), who is skilled in the law, to hear and determine a case of alleged withdrawal and detention of goods belonging to the church of Welford. John Whiteway and John Cerney, proctors of the church's goods, are on the one side, and Geoffrey Elston, Ralph Neele, John Smyth and other parishioners of Welford are on the other. Potterne, 3 July 1411.

876 [Fo. 106/16] General notification that William Strecher, chaplain of St. John the Baptist's chapel, East Hendred (*Esthenreth*), has been freed from the sentence of suspension imposed during the bishop's visitation, and has been restored to his former status. The letter is sealed with the bishop's seal *ad causas*. Potterne, 3 July 1411.

877 Letters testimonial for Henry de Buddeworth, chaplain, who has lived twelve years in the diocese, is of good character and reputation, and does not hold any opinions deviating from the Catholic faith. [Undated.]
[Cf. Constitutions against Lollardy, **955**, sections II, X.]

878 Commission to the archd. of Wiltshire or his official to hold an inquiry into the revenues of Corsham (*Cossham*) vicarage, which Richard Pere, vicar, has petitioned should be augmented on account of their inadequacy. The archd. is to go in person to the church of Corsham, and to summon the rector and the rectors and vicars of the neighbouring churches and other people, and to ascertain the true value of all the types of revenues belonging to the church and vicarage, together with the common estimate of their annual value and their charges, so that the bp. can decide whether the vicarage should be augmented. The archd. is to notify the bp. before the feast of All Saints [1 Nov.] of the action he takes. Chardstock (*Cherdestok*), 1 Sept. [1411.]

879 [Fo. 106v/16v] Mandate to the abbot, prior, subprior and conv. of Abingdon (*Abyndon*), where the bp. is in process of holding a visitation, forbidding them to seal anything important with the common seal without previous consultation with him. It has been discovered that the seal has been used carelessly of late to the possible prejudice of the conv., and it is not to be used until they receive the bishop's injunctions at the end of his visitation. Sonning (*Sonnyng*), 27 Sept. 1411.

880 Copy made from the register of Nicholas [Longespee],[1] bp. of Salisbury, of a grant by the bp. to Geoffrey de Turbevile, knight, and Isabel his wife, at their request, that they may have a chapel with a chaplain on their manor of East Hendred (*Esthenreth*) for the use of their household. The chaplain is to be supported by the tithes owed from the manor and is to be presented for institution by the bp. He is to swear that he will pass on to the parish church all offerings and revenues other than the tithes, that he will obey the rector, that he will admit no parishioner to any sacrament in the chapel unless he be of the Turbevile household, and that he will not allow anything prejudicial to the parish church. The chapter of Salisbury gives its assent. Sealed with the bishop's and the chapter's seals in form of a chirograph. Woodford (*Wodeford*), 30 March 1293. This ordinance of St. John's chapel, East Hendred, was copied into the register at the bishop's command, when a suit arose between the rector and the chaplain.[2]

[1. The register of Longespee (1291–7) is no longer in existence. The earliest extant Salisbury episcopal register is that of Simon de Gandavo, 1297–1315.
2. Agreement between them confirmed 11 June 1412, **918**.]

881 [Fo. 107/17] Notification of the archd. of Berkshire's official that on 12 July 1411 he received the bishop's commission dated at Potterne (*Poterne*), 6 July, and has executed it. In the course of his visitation, the bp. discovered that William Streccher, chaplain of St. John the Baptist's chapel within the parish of East Hendred (*Esthenreth*), had been withholding certain offerings and tithes which belonged to the parish church, apart from the tithes from the manor in which the chapel was situated. He ordered Streccher to restore these to John Robtot, rector. The tithes of the following were specified as belonging to the parish church: eighteen acres of arable land of Edmund Spersold in the Castle Furlong (*Castelfurlong*); lands called 'Poghleylond' or 'Laurencelond'; the croft or garden of the same tenure; four acres of land lately belonging to John Canons; 125 sheep of the abbot and conv. of Reading (*Radyng*) pastured in a separate pasture within the parish; forty-five sheep pastured in the same pasture belonging to the parish church and to John Robtot and his successors. The bp. ordered the archd. or his official to publish this sentence, and to warn Streccher and others whom it might concern to restore the offerings and tithes, under pain of excommunication if they disobeyed, to be published in the church of East Hendred and at least six neighbouring churches. He was to notify the bp. of the action taken before Michaelmas [29 Sept.]. The official published this sentence in East Hendred church and other suitable places on 19 July between masses, and has found no one disobeying it. Sealed with his seal of office. Abingdon (*Abendon*), 22 Sept. 1411.

882 [Fo. 107v/17v] Commission to the rector of G.[1] for the reconciliation by any Catholic bp. of his church, which has been polluted by bloodshed. London, 20 Nov. 1411.

[1. Probably Grittleton, cf. **1004**.]

883 Licence to Robert Cammell M.A., rector of Tidpit (*Tudeput, Tudput*), to be absent from his benefice for two years' study at any English *studium* *generale*, with permission not to proceed beyond the order of subdeacon. London, 11 Dec. 1411.

884 Commission[1] ordering the denunciation as excommunicate of the unknown persons who have violated the sequestration imposed by the bp. on the revenues of the church of Lacerton (*Laserton*). The sentence is to be published in the churches on the Sundays and feast days immediately following the receipt of this mandate, between masses, when most people are present, and inquiry is to be made concerning the identity of the violators. The bp. is to be notified of the names of any suspects, and of the action taken, before the feast of St. Andrew the apostle [30 Nov.]. Sonning (*Sonnyng*), 4 Nov. 1411.

[1. Recipients not stated.]

885 [Fo. 108/18] Notification to the bp. by John, rector of East Stoke (*Stoke*), that he has received the bishop's commission (dated Potterne, 9 May 1411) addressed to the rectors of Chaldon Herring (*Chalvedon*), Moreton (*Morton*) and East Stoke, to sequestrate two parts of the tithes and revenues of the church of Winfrith Newburgh (*Wynfred*), which the abbot of Bindon (*Byndon*) claims as his portion, since the abbot has failed to produce evidence of his right to them in the course of the bishop's visitation. The rectors are to publish this sentence in their churches, and in the church of Winfrith Newburgh and the dependent chapel of West Lulworth (*Lulleworth*), warning people not to violate the sequestration, and they are to keep the sequestrated portion until further notice, not obstructing the rector of Winfrith Newburgh's disposal of the third part of the tithes and revenues. They are to notify the bp. before Whitsun [31 May] of the action taken. The rector reports that he published the sequestration in Winfrith Newburgh church and West Lulworth chapel 16 May, and has carried out the other orders. [Undated.]

886 General notification that in the course of the bishop's visitation of Salisbury cath.,[1] M. Thomas Polton was summoned to prove his title to the canonry and prebend of Grimston (*Grymston*).[2] He appeared before the bp. and demonstrated that he had received a papal provision of a canonry with expectation of a prebend in either Salisbury or Lincoln cathedral, that he had accepted the prebend of Grimston when it was vacant by the death of M. Thomas Wrofton, had been admitted in person by the chapter and had taken possession.[3] The bp. confirms his title. London, 20 May 1412.

[1. In Oct. 1411 (cf. Vyring, p. 69).

2. The bp. had collated M. William Pylton to the prebend 23 Apr. 1408, cf. **2**.

3. Polton showed the chapter 17 March 1408 two papal bulls (of 21 Dec. 1406 and 14 May 1407) and a royal licence of July 1407 (Salisbury, Dean and Chapter Archives, Chapter Act Book, Dunham, p. 328). He was admitted to the prebend of Grimston by the dean and chapter 7 June 1408, on the death of M. Thomas Wrofton (Vyring, pp. 4, 15).]

887 [Fo. 108v/18v] Commission to the archd. of Wiltshire or his official to denounce as excommunicate (in accordance with the canon 'Si quis suadente diabolo'[1]) the unknown persons who wounded the vicar of St. Mary, Westport, Malmesbury.[2] The sentence is to be published in the churches of the deanery of Malmesbury on the Sundays and feast days immediately following the receipt of this mandate, between masses, when most people are present. The archd. is to notify the bp. before the feast of St. Peter and St. Paul [29 June] of the action taken and of the names of any of the guilty. [Undated.]

[1. *Corpus Iuris Canonici,* i, col. 822, *Decreti Secunda Pars,* 17, 4, c. 29.
2. The vicar, Walter Hatherleygh, resigned by 11 Jan. 1413, **388**.]

888 [Fo. 109/19] General notification that the bp. has held an inquiry into the petition of the abbot and conv. of Abingdon (*Abendon*), patrons of the church of St. Nicholas, Abingdon, that the vicarage there be reunited and consolidated with the church, since the church's revenues are insufficient to maintain both a rector and a vicar, and several vicars in turn have left to the detriment of the divine worship. As a result, the bp. has united the vicarage with the church, the vicar having previously tendered his resignation, with the consent of the parishioners and of the rector, Henry Cromp. An annual pension of eight pence is reserved to the bp., one of four pence to the chapter of Salisbury and one of four pence to the archd. of Berkshire, all to be paid on the feast of Annunciation of the B.V.M. [25 March] in Salisbury cath. Potterne, bishop's manor, 20 May 1410.[1]

[1. This entry was made much earlier than the other entries in the quire, which were subsequently written before and after it.]

889 [Fo. 109^v/19^v] Commission to the archd. of Berkshire or his official, and to Richard Stanley and Thomas Bernesley, clerks, to warn Robert de Lamare who has withdrawn tithes and other dues owed to the provost and fellows of Queen's College, Oxford, and to the church of Sparsholt (*Sperholt*), which is annexed to the college. He is to pay them within fifteen days of the warning, on pain of excommunication, or to appear before the bp. on the twelfth to explain his conduct. Sonning (*Sonnyng*), 9 Sept. 1412.

890 General notification that on 19 Dec. 1412 John Dun of Coulston (*Culey*) purged himself before the bishop's commissaries in Potterne prebendal church from the alleged crime of stealing a cow belonging to John Bulluk of Steeple Ashton (*Esshton*). Potterne, bishop's manor, 19 Dec. 1412.

891 [Fo. 119/29*] Licence to Ralph Thomas, rector of Clewer (*Clewere*), to be absent from his benefice for two years. London, 12 Oct. 1412.

892 Commission to the vicar of Pewsey (*Peuesey*) and the rector of Manningford Abbots (*Manyngford*) to sequestrate the revenues of Pewsey church, on account of the dilapidations left by the rector. Ramsbury (*Remmesbury*), 20 Oct. 1412.

*This folio, the outside one of the quire consisting of fos. 119-26, has been badly affected by damp. In the top right-hand corner is written in a 15th-century hand *quatermus tertius.*

893 General notification that the bp. has granted an indulgence of forty days to those visiting and venerating the shrine of King Edward the Martyr in the monastery of Shaftesbury (*Shafton*), on his four principal feasts, from the beginning of the first vespers to the end of the second. [Undated.]

[Preamble given in full in Appendix D. Only 3 feasts of St. Edward are generally celebrated, commemorating his death, 18 March, and the 2 translations of his body, 18 Feb. and 20 June (*Acta Sanctorum, March*, ii (Antwerp, 1668), pp. 639–40).]

894 General notification that the bp. has granted an indulgence of forty days to those saying the Lord's Prayer for the souls of John Wede, abbot of Cerne, William and Alice his parents, and his brothers and sisters who are buried in the churchyard of P. (dioc. Salisbury). [Undated.][1]

[1. After 26 Sept. 1411, **1114**.]

895 Mandate to the abbess and conv. of Shaftesbury (*Shafton*) forbidding the nuns to leave their house except for good cause, approved by the superior, and in the company of senior nuns of proved character. It has been reported that several nuns have often been wandering outside the house in various places longer than is seemly and for frivolous reasons. The abbess and prioress are enjoined to consider the punishment that overtook Dinah the daughter of Jacob for yielding to the desire to go abroad, so that the bp. is not forced to impose punishment himself. [Undated.]

[Given in full in Appendix D.]

896 [Fo. 119v/29v] Commission to M. Richard Carcy, clerk, Giles Frenche, William Benfeld and John Kylby of the parish of Winkfield (*Wynkefeld*) to sequestrate the revenues of Winkfield church, on account of the failure of the dean and chapter of Salisbury to pay the annual pension of forty shillings due to Richard Wyton, the vicar. This should be paid in equal parts at the feasts of All Saints [1 Nov.] and the Annunciation of the B.V.M. [25 March], but sixty shillings are owed, despite frequent requests by the vicar. Any violators of the sequestration are to be summoned to appear before the bp. on the fifteenth day after the summons to explain why they should not incur sentence of excommunication. [Undated.][1]

[1. As Wyton was instituted 3 Apr. 1411 and 3 payments were owing, this commission was probably issued in Nov. 1412.]

897 Commission to certain clergy to denounce as excommunicate the unknown persons who have stolen documents (*cartas, evidenciam et alia munimenta*) of M. John Daunvers, chaplain, relating to an annuity granted him by Alice Aderbury, widow of Edmund Daunvers, for the term of her life. Without these documents, he believes he will be unable to recover the annuity. They are to publish the sentence in their churches between masses, when asked by M. John to do so, ordering the return of the documents within fifteen days. [Undated.]

[For Alice, widow of Edmund Daunvers (d. 1381), and wife of Richard Aderbury, see *VCH Berks.*, iv. 64, 282, 508—'Edmund Danvers', 'Richard Abberbury'; and cf. **918**. For John Daunvers, see *BRUO*, i. 542—'John Danvers'.]

898 [Fo. 120/30] Commission to the archd. of Berkshire or his official to denounce as excommunicate (in accordance with the canon 'Si quis suadente diabolo'[1]) the unknown persons (and any aiding or abetting them) who recently came to the church of Lockinge (*Lokynge*) by night, broke down the doors, stole books, money and various goods, and murdered M. Robert Lydeford, the rector. The sentence is to be published in the vulgar tongue in all the conventual, collegiate and other churches of the archdeaconry, between masses, when most people are present, until further notice from the bp. [Undated.][2]

[1. See **887** n. 1.
2. The new rector was instituted 1 Nov. 1412, **367**.]

899 Letters dimissory granted to John Langman, Thomas Jon and Ralph Hykes, deacons, to receive the order of priest, and to Thomas Marlyng, subdeacon, to receive the orders of deacon and priest. London, 16 March 1413.

900 The like to M. William Nagard, subdeacon, rector of Woodsford (*Wyrdysford*), to receive the order of deacon. London, 17 March 1413.

901 The like to John Gray, clerk, first tonsure, to receive all orders. London, 19 March 1413.

902 Licence to William Aas, subdeacon, rector of Broughton Gifford (*Broughton*), to be absent from his benefice for one year. London, 19 March 1413.

903 [Fo. 120v/30v] Commission to the archd. of Salisbury or his official, at the request of John Juyl, rector of Milston (*Myldeston*), to inquire whether there is any reason why the church, which is not dependent on any other, and is perfectly constructed of old, should not be consecrated. The archd. is to notify the bp. [Undated.]

[Commission for the church's consecration, 3 Oct. 1413, **952**.]

904 Commission to M. John Welles D.Cn.L., rector of Christian Malford (*Crystenmalford*), to hear and determine a matrimonial case between Joan Peverell and John Latenner, which was begun before the bishop's official in the consistory court of Salisbury. London, 11 Apr. 1413.

905 Commission to M. Richard Leyot D.C.L., M. John Holand D.C.L., Richard Cassy Lic.C.L. and M. Henry Corbryg B.C.L. to examine the witnesses in a case of disputed tithes between the provost and scholars of Queen's College, Oxford, to whom the church of Sparsholt (*Spresholt*) is annexed, and Robert Dalamar, esquire, lord of Sparsholt. The parties have been ordered to bring their witnesses to the church of Sparsholt on the Saturday after the feast of St. Augustine, bishop and confessor [2 Sept. 1413] and the two juridical days following. The commissaries, or at least two of them to whom the parties consent, are to examine the witnesses in the presence of one or two notaries who are to swear publicly on the gospels to record the depositions faithfully. [Incomplete.][1]

[1. Cf. **889**. The next folio is missing, and must have been removed from the quire before 1415, since entries for that year run consecutively from fo. 124^{v} to fo. 125, where the other half of the missing folio originally came.]

906 [Fo. 121/31] Indulgence of forty days granted to all who contribute to the cost of a pilgrimage of a certain Henry. [Incomplete.][1]

[1. This entry began on the missing folio, cf. **905**n.]

907 Commission to M. Thomas, chaplain of Holy Trinity chantry in Hungerford church, and William Clerk of the same, to inhibit the jurisdiction of John, rector of Ashley (*Aschle*), official of the peculiar jurisdiction of Ogbourne (*Okeborne*), who has declared a sentence of excommunication on Robert Napper, vicar of Hungerford, who had previously appealed to the apostolic see and for the protection of the court of Canterbury, and has now appealed to the bp. The official is to be cited to appear before the bp. or his commissaries on the next juridical day after Michaelmas [29 Sept.]. M. Thomas and William Clerk are to notify the bp. of the date of receipt of this commission and of the action taken. [Undated.]

908 General notification that John Flemmyng of Great Somerford (*Brodesomerford*) has been absolved from sentence of excommunication imposed for his support of heretics. Flemmyng has sworn that he will obey the bishop's mandates and not associate with nor defend any suspected of heresy or error, and the bp. has enjoined suitable penance. Ramsbury (*Remmesbury*), bishop's manor, 25 Aug. 1413.

909 Commission to M. John Hurle B.Cn.L. and John Pedewell, skilled in the law, to receive the revenues of St. Mary's chantry in the church of West Dean (*Westdene*), in the bishop's collation, and use them for the repair of the chantry buildings. The commissaries are to have a written report made of their receipts and expenses. Woodford (*Wodeford*), bishop's manor, 31 Aug. 1413.

910 [Fo. 121^{v}/31^{v}] General notification of Thomas, abp. of Canterbury, that William Strecchere, chaplain, has been restored to the chapel of St. John the Baptist, East Hendred (*Esthenreth*), after the invalidation by M. Henry Ware, auditor of causes in the archbishop's court of audience, of an alleged exchange with Walter Frost, vicar of Wendover, dioc. Lincoln. Oxford (*Oxon'*), 7 Aug. 1411.

911 Licence to John Kyng, clerk, rector of Woodsford (*Wyrdesforde*), to be absent from his benefice for one year's study anywhere in England, on condition that he be ordained subdeacon at the statutory time. Potterne (*Poterne*), 4 July 1414.

912 Letters dimissory to John Mayheu to receive all orders. Potterne, 6 July 1414.

913 Commission[1] to cite Thomas Smewen, chaplain of Little Sutton (*Parva Sutton*) chapel, to appear before the bp. or his commissaries on charges of having failed to produce a title to his benefice or to serve it. He is to be cited in person if he can be found, or any proctor appointed by him is to be cited in his place, and the summons is to be made in the chapel and in the parish church of Sutton Veny (*Sutton*), and at the houses where Smewen used to live. The bp. intends to take proceedings against him whether or not he appears.[2] [Undated.]

[1. Recipients not stated.
2. A new chaplain was instituted 8 Dec. 1414, **534**.]

914 Commission,[1] at the petition of Robert Hore, chaplain, lately rector of Winterslow (*Wynterslewe*), to cite William Broune, present rector, who by fraud and deceit induced Hore to exchange his benefice, which is worth more than £20 a year, for the church of Wormley (*Wermole*), dioc. London, worth less than ten marks [£6 13*s* 4*d*] a year. Broune is to appear before the bp. or his commissaries, and the bp. intends to take proceedings against him whether or not he appears.[2] The commissaries are to notify the bp. of the date of receipt of this commission and of the action taken. [Undated.]

[1. Recipients not stated.
2. The exchange took place 22 June 1414, **498**. Hore and Broune returned to their original benefices 19 Oct. 1414, **517**.]

915 [Fo. 122/32] Commission[1] to cite John Taylor, rector of Winterbourne Stickland (*Stykelane*), who, John Norton, literate, alleges, made an agreement with Thomas Haytur, lately rector, to pay him an annual pension of eight marks [£5 6*s* 8*d*] for his lifetime, on condition that Haytur resigned his benefice in Taylor's favour, without the authority or licence of the bp. In addition, Taylor bound himself to Haytur in a bond of £200 and obtained the presentation to the benefice from the patrons, the abbot and conv. of Milton, who were aware of all this. Taylor is to be cited to appear before the bp. to answer these charges.[2] [Undated.]

[1. Recipients not stated.
2. A new rector was instituted 23 Sept. 1416, **632**.]

916 Commission to the archd. of Salisbury or his official to hold an inquiry into the advowson of Barford St. Martin (*Bereford*) church, vac. by the death of John Sandon. An earlier commission for inquiry was sent to the archd. after Elizabeth, lady of Clynton, had presented John Taylor to the church. Subsequently John Cornewaill, knight, presented Philip Pope to the same church, claiming to be patron for this turn. The archd. is now to hold a thorough inquiry into Cornewaill's right and all the circumstances, in full chapter of the place, even though this is the time of harvest, by the rectors and vicars of the deanery. He is to notify the bp. of the rightful patron, together with the names of the jurors. [Undated.][1]

[1. Royal writ of *ne admittatis*, 26 June 1414, **1109**; Taylor instituted 5 Dec., **527**.]

917 [Fo. 122^{v}/32^{v}] Mandate to the prioress and conv. of Bromhall (*Bromehale*) to receive Alice Boyton, nun of Kington St. Michael (*Kyngton*), who is to be transferred on account of her bad behaviour. She is to be in the special custody of a mature, God-fearing nun and is to be kept from communication with secular or religious people except in the presence of this guardian. She is not to go outside the monastery until further notice. The house will be paid for her stay by the priory of Kington St. Michael. [Undated.]

918 General notification of the bishop's confirmation of an agreement between John Robtot, rector of East Hendred (*Esthenreth*), and William Streccher, chaplain of St. John the Baptist's chapel on the manor of Ralph Arches in the parish of East Hendred, concerning the tithes belonging to the manor for the support of the chaplain. It cites the grant of Nicholas [Longespee], bp. of Salisbury, to Geoffrey Turbevile, knight, to have divine service said by a chaplain in the chapel [as in **880**].

[Fo. 123/33] The chaplain is to have all the greater and lesser tithes of the following lands belonging to the manor:

In North-east Field in Kilman Knoll Down (*Estnorthfeld in Kynmanside*), a piece of land called the Butts (*le Buttus*), containing an estimated fifteen acres lying towards Tomkin's Land (*Tomkynnezlond*) on the south; a piece of land containing an estimated five acres lying between the road called the Ambling Way (*Amblyngwey*) and the land of Robert Frankleyn; one capital acre called Smoke Acre (*Smokacre*), abutting on the Ambling Way; a piece of land called the Butts (*le Buttes*) containing six butts lying between the land of Frankeleyn on one side and the land called the Farthings (*Ferthingeslond*) which Annabel Saundres holds and which abuts on the Ambling Way on the east; a piece of land containing eight acres lying in the Heath Furlong (*le Hethforlong*) between the land of John Warner on one side and the land of Roger Remmesbury on the other; a piece of land containing two acres lying in the Middle Furlong (*le Middelforlong*) by the land of Walter le Bagnore; one stich containing an estimated half acre lying by the Ambling Way in the Down (*le Den*); a piece of land containing six butts lying in 'Smalcombe' between the land of John Fox on either side and abutting on the land of John Sturne [Fo. 123^{v}/33^{v}] on the east; a piece of land called 'le Schad' lying in 'le Pawmer' containing an estimated five acres lying by the land called 'le Haryngdon'; one acre lying in the Bottom Meadow 'Pawmer' (*le Bottomedel Pawmer*); all the demesne land of the same manor which lies in the severalty of 'Haryngdon'; except two acres which lie by the path leading from the village of East Hendred towards Harwell (*Harewell*) on the north, which pay tithes to the parish church; one other acre lying in the Bottom Meadow 'Pawmer' (*le Bottemede Pawmer*) on which stands a sheepfold; a piece of land called the Short Butts (*Shortbuttes*) lying by the North Breach (*le Northbreche*) between the land of the abbot of Reading (*Radyng*) on either side and abutting on the land of John Harnham on the north; a piece of land lying at 'Manithorne' which contains an estimated eight acres and abuts on Aldfield (*Aldefelde*).

In South-east Field in Kilman Knoll Down, one piece of land called the Gores lying by the land of Boxworth (*Boxwatthes*) and abutting on Abbot's Breach (*Abbotes breche*); a piece of land lying in the Breach land (*le Brichlond*) containing an estimated three acres, between the land of Annabel Sawndres on the south and the land of Farthings (*Ferthing*) which Nicholas Paddebury holds; one piece of land called Six Butts (*vj bottes*) lying between the land of the abbot of Reading at South Breach (*Southbreche*) on one side and the land of John Whiche on the other and abuts on the land of John Sturne; one acre called Foxacre by the land of Walter Bagnore on the east and called 'Forshetter'; one capital acre called Link Acre (*Linkaker*) or Smoke Acre; one piece of land called 'Fynegoryn' lying by the Golden Mile (*Gyldenmyle*) on the east; a piece of land containing an estimated four acres of which two belong to 'Forshettres' lying by the land of William le Wyke on the east and abutting on the land of John Sturne which lies by the Golden Mile; one piece of land containing an estimated eleven acres, lying by the land of John Sturne on the east and abutting towards the Down (*le Downe*); a piece of land containing an estimated six acres lying at Meashill (*Meshull*) and abutting on the lands of John Sturne and John Whiche on the west; two acres which lie in the same Redlands (*Redelonde*) by the land of John Warner on the west; one piece of land containing an estimated six acres, lying at Meashill and abutting on the capital acre called Smoke Acre on the north, and on the capital acre of William Wyke on the south; a piece of land containing an estimated six acres, abutting on the capital acre called 'Mudyus Lynkacre' on the north; a piece of land containing an estimated four acres lying between the land of Roger Snelle on the west and the land of the abbot of Reading on the east.

In South Field, one capital acre lying in Gosspath (*Gospath*) by the land of John Fynamor and abutting on the land of William Scherwod; two half-acres lying in 'le Berwforlong' between the land of John Cosyn on the west and the land of Kyppynges on the east.

In North Field, a piece of land containing two acres lying between the land of the prior of Noyon (*Noion*) on the east and the land of William Schirwod on the west, abutting on the road called the Broadway (*Bradewey*); one acre lying between the land of William Pinifolde on the west and the land of Richard Adderbury, and abutting on the Broadway; two acres lying between the land of the rector on the west and the land of Keynes Mill (*Kenysmulle*) on the east; one acre lying in Water Slade (*Watrislade*) between the land of Jurdan on the west and of Harmes on the east; two acres lying in the Eastworth (*le Estworth*) by the land of Harmes's tenant on the west and abutting on the capital acre of William Scyrwod; two acres lying in the Quab (*le Quabbe*), between the land of Richard Adderbury on the south and the land of Jordan on the north; a piece of land called St. James Butt lying by the land of John Chambrer on the south; one and a half acres lying at Cuckhamsley (*Quengyneseline*) between the land of the abbot of Reading on the east and the land of [the prior of] Frampton (*Fremton*) on the west; one acre lying at 'le Ferne' between the land of the rector on the east and the land of the prior of Noyon on the north; [Fo. 124/34] one acre lying at 'le Ferne' called 'Ketys' between the land of Canons on the south and the land of Richard Adderbury on the north; one half acre lying by the Pound of Buller's Mill (*Bolurusmylle*) on the east.

In 'Yowryngeslond', one acre lying in the west field between the land of John Skyrmare on the north and the land of John Mascall on the south, called Picket Acre (*Pykeacre*); one acre lying in the Chapel Furlong (*Chapelforlong*) between the land of Walter Bagnore on the west and the land of the prioress of Littlemore (*Lytelmore*); one acre lying by Pater Noster Cross (*Pater Noster Crosse*) by the land of Walter Bagnore on the west; one acre lying by the half-acre which lies by the Pound of Buller's Mill (*Bulresmulle*), and abutting on the half-acre of Harmes on its northern boundary; of the lands of Walter Bagnore, one acre lying at Farthings Cross (*Ferthinggus Crosse*) by the land of the prior of Frampton and abutting on the Broadway; one half-acre in 'Lofforlong' between the land of John Fynamor on the east and the land of David Jones on the west; one half-acre lying in 'Rysbroke' by the land of David Jones and abutting on the road which leads towards Steventon (*Stevynton*).

In South-east Field, one acre lying in Stonyland (*Stenylonde*) between the land of David Johannis on the west and the land of Harmes on the east; one acre lying in Lockland (*Loklond*) between the land of Jordan on the west and the land of John Basset on the east; one half-acre lying in Broadland (*Brodlond*) between the land of David Jones on the east and the land of Hulmannys on the west; one and a half acres lying on Blacknell Hill (*Blakenhyll*) between the land of David Jones on the east and the land of John de Twychen on the west; one acre lying in 'le buttine' between the land of David Jones on the south and the land of Thomas More on the north; one acre lying in 'Luttenhulle' between the land of Coles on the south and the land of John Fynamore on the north and abutting on the road which leads to Cuckhamsley (*Quichameslew*).

In South-west Field, one acre lying at Pater Noster Cross (*Pater Noster Croys*) between the land of Adderbury on the east and the land of Yowryng on the west; one half acre lying in Stonyland (*Stonylonde*) between the land of David Jones on the south and the land of John Keppyng on the north; one and a half acres lying on Blacknell Hill between the land of David Jones on the south and the land of William Scherwod on the north; one acre lying in the same culture between the land of Richard Addurbury on the north and the land of Harmes on the south; one acre lying at 'Doggetiscros' between the land of David Jones on the south and the land of the chapel on the north; two acres lying in 'le butine' in Broadland by the land of Jackman's Place (*Jakemannesplace*).

In North-east Field in Kilman Knoll Down, one acre lying above 'Luttonhull' by the land of Jordan on the north; two acres lying in the Middle Furlong (*Middelfurlong*) between the land of Arches on the east and the land of Pypercornez on the west.

In South-east Field, one and a half acres lying in 'le Hamme' between the land of Harmes on the north and the land of Richard Adderbury on the south, called Flax Acre (*Flexacre*); one acre lying in the Heath Furlong abutting on 'le Ryxen' between the land of Richard Adderbury on the south and the land of Harmes on the north.

In North-east Field in Kilman Knoll Down, one acre lying in the Heath Furlong between the land of Pypercornes on the south and the land of John Whiche on the west; one acre abutting above 'Haryndon' between the land of John Warner on either side; one acre lying in Humberdean (*Humberden*) between the land [Fo. 124^{v}/34^{v}] of Roger Remmesbury on the west and the land of Annabel Sawndres on the east; one capital acre lying above Meashill called Link Acre, abutting on the land of William Wyke on its eastern boundary.

In South-east Field in Westman Knoll (*Estsouthfelde in Westmanside*), one acre lying in Stonyland between the land of Thomas More on the east and the land of the prior of Noyon on the west; one acre lying in the Middle Furlong between the land of John Cosyn on the south and the land of Kyppyng on the north.

In South-west Field in Westman Knoll, one acre lying above 'le Berwe' towards Runnington (*Wronnyngdon*) by the land of the rector of Hendred on the north and abutting on the capital acre of William Schirwod; one acre lying in Gosspath between the land of Walter Bagnore on the north and the land of Kyppyng on the south, abutting on the land of Frampton; one acre lying in 'le Butune' between the land of John Cosyn on the north and the land of Harmes on the south; one capital acre in the Drove, abutting on the land of Walter Goldny on the northern boundary.

Of the lands of Matthew Fuller in South-east Field in Westman Knoll, one acre lying in Portway Furlong (*Portweyforlong*) between the land of Thomas More on the east and the land of Jordan on the west; one half-acre lying above 'Luttonshull' by the land of the prior of Noyon on the west.

In South-west Field in Westman Knoll, one half-acre lying at 'Scychthorne' between the land of the rector on the south and the land of Frampton on the north; one half-acre lying in Gosspath between the land of the prior of Noyon on the south and the land of the prior of Frampton on the north; one acre lying above 'Luttunhulle' between the land of Harmes on the north and the land of the prior of Noyon on the south; one half-acre lying in the Drove between the land of Harmes on the west and the land of John Childe on the east.

In Farthingland North Field, two acres lying in 'Loffurlong' by the road called Farthings Mill Way (*Ferthynges Mulwey*) on the east; one acre lying in 'Lofforlong' between the land of Richard Aderbury on the west and the land of Harmes on the east; two acres lying in 'le Worth' between the land of Harmes on the south and the land of the prior of Noyon on the north.

In North-west Field, one acre lying in the Marsh (*le Merssh*) between the land of Pater Noster on the south and the land of William Shirwode on the north; two acres lying in the same culture between the land of the prior of Noyon on the south and the land of Jordan on the north; two half-acres lying in the same culture and abutting on the land of Harmes on the southern boundary; one acre lying in the same culture by the land of the prior of Noyon on the north and abutting on the pasture of Edmund Spersholt on the western boundary.

In Spersholt's land, two small capital acres of Edmund Spersholt, lying between eighteen acres called Castle Furlong (*Castelforlong*) on the west and the land of the abbot of Westminster on the east.

Of the meadows of the same manor, one acre lying in Folks Mead (*Folkesmede*) between the meadow of the rector of East Hendred on the south and the meadow of Harmes on the north; one acre lying in the same meadow between the meadow of Skirmare on the south and the meadow of Harmes on the north; one acre lying in the same meadow, between that of Pater Noster on the south and that of Harmes on the north; one acre lying in the same meadow by the meadow of Harmes on the north; one meadow called Knights Moor (*Knyttesmore*), ditched around, lying by 'le Mullehammes' of Buller's Mill (*Bullersmull*) on the southern boundary and abutting on the western boundary of one acre of land of John Fynamor on the north.

There are two cottages [Fo. 125/35] built within the manor, from which the chaplain shall receive greater and lesser tithes, namely on the things maintained or renewed within the cottages, except the parish tithes of the tenants living there which shall be paid in entirety to the parish church. The chaplain of the chapel shall receive half of the tithe of the produce of the garden lying between the churchyard of the parish church on one side and the tenement that lately belonged to David Jones on the other.

The rector and his successors shall receive and have all the greater and lesser tithes from any lands within the boundaries of the parish.

As regards tithes of wool, lambs, pigs and other lesser tithes, the parties agreed that if the lord of the manor shall have ninety or fewer sheep anywhere within the boundaries of the parish (in a separate pasture or in the common pasture), the rector shall receive and have all the tithe of their wool. But if the lord shall have between 90 and 480 sheep, the rector shall have the tithe of the ninety (or nine fleeces), and the chaplain the tithe of the rest, as soon as convenient after the shearing, and the rector is to take the fleeces as they come to hand, not choosing individually. If the lord shall have more than 480 sheep, the tithe of all those over 480 shall go to the rector. If the lord shall take in other sheep for grazing up to 480, the tithe of them shall be divided as already described, but if he shall take in sheep of parishioners their tithe shall be paid to the rector. If the lord has the pasture of Farthing or holds it at farm, the sheep or other animals in it shall be tithed to the rector.

In addition, the twenty-four cows which the lord has in a separate pasture of the abbot of Reading, shall be tithed in the following way: if they winter on manor land, then the chaplain shall have the tithe of milk or cheese throughout the year, but he shall not receive the tithe of calves unless they are born on manor land. If the cows do not winter on the manor, the rector shall have all the tithe from them, even if the calves are born on the manor. [Fo. 125v/35v] If the lord shall sell his pasture of cows or hand it over to farm, or receive other cows for grazing, the tithes are to be paid to the rector.

If any animals are born on the manor (other than the twenty-four cows and the sheep from which the chaplain has the tithe of wool), they shall be tithed to the rector. And if young of any kind are born outside the manor but within the parish they shall be tithed to the rector.

Other greater and lesser tithes from the manor, offerings and mortuary payments (apart from the tithes assigned above to the chaplain) shall be paid in full to the rector without hindrance by the lord or chaplain.

This agreement was confirmed by the bp. in Sonning (*Sonnyng*) manor, 11 June 1412, in the presence of M. John Luke B.Th. and Robert Reynel, clerk (dioc. Canterbury), and many other witnesses.

[Identification of field names based on A. L. Humphreys, *East Hendred: a Berkshire Parish* (1923), pp. 3–6; *Berks. Place-names*, ii. 480–5.

In the right-hand margin of fo. 123 a 16th-century hand has written a bull of Pope Alexander IV granting permission to the bp. of Salisbury to allow John de Turbelvyle, lord of Hendred, to build a private chapel. This is given below, **1149**.]

919 [Fo. 126/36] Notarial instrument incorporating the sentence given by John Cosham, prior of Bruton, papal judge delegate, in Corsley parish church 13 June 1415, in a dispute over burial rights between Henry Willyn, John atte Rigge and Walter Frensshe and other parishioners of Corsley and all the inhabitants of the neighbouring vills and hamlets, in the person of John Harewell their proctor, on the one hand, and William Fovent, vicar of Warminster (*Wermestre*), on the other. After a thorough inquiry, the judge delegate declared that the inhabitants of Corsley should have the churchyard consecrated and that the rectors of Corsley should then be allowed to bury the dead of Corsley and the neighbouring hamlets. The vicar of Warminster is to receive the offerings with wax at the first mass when the corpse is present, and the personal tithes of people of both sexes of the vills of Great Corsley (*Corsley Magna*), Little Corsley (*Corsley Parva*), Whitbourne (*Wytebourne*) and Chapmanslade (*Chepmanslade*) by way of tithes of wool, lambs, pigs, geese, calves, milk, cheese, chickens, doves, gardens, orchards and mortuary dues.

The instrument cites Cosham's commission as judge delegate by Pope John XXIII, dated Constance (*Constancie*), 16 March 1415, on petition of the inhabitants of Corsley, etc., who requested that their churchyard should be consecrated because of the distance to Warminster and the difficulties of carrying bodies there especially in winter.[1] [Fo. 126v/36v] It also cites the appointment, sealed with the seal of the official of the [peculiar] jurisdiction of Banwell (*Banewell*) and dated in Corsley church, 13 June 1415, by Henry Willyum, John atte Brigge, Walter Frensshe and the other inhabitants, of Thomas Landaff and John Koke, laymen, John Turnepeny and John Harewell, clerks, or any one of them, as their proctors in this matter.

The following were present as witnesses: M. Thomas Frome, canon of Wells, M. Thomas Harewell B.C.L., John Merlond, Thomas Bathe, Thomas Blaneford and Robert de Legh, esquires.

M. William Brett, clerk (dioc. Salisbury), notary public by papal authority, drew up the instrument. Sealed at Bruton priory, 16 June 1415.

[1. *CPL 1404–15*, p. 491. Corsley is 3 miles from Warminster.]

[All the letters, **920–6**, are addressed to, or issued by, M. Geoffrey Crukadan, vicar general.]

920 [Fo. 127/37] Mandate of Richard, bp. of London, to M. Geoffrey Crukadan, vicar general of Robert, bp. of Salisbury, then abroad, transmitting the mandate of Henry, abp. of Canterbury (dated Otford (*Otteford*), archbishop's manor, 3 July 1416), to publish the constitutions concerning heretics drawn up in the convocation of Canterbury province meeting in St. Paul's, London. All bishops and archdeacons of the province are to make inquiries in their jurisdictions and in each rural deanery at least twice a year, in person or by their officials or commissaries. Three or more reliable men are to report on oath and in writing if there are any heretics or secret conventicles, or people with suspect books written in English, or any receiving people suspected of heresy or error. The archdeacons or commissaries are to send the names and details of such people to their bishops, who are to proceed against them and imprison them, as the case requires, either for life or at least until the next convocation of Canterbury province. The bishops are to give a full account to the abp. at the next convocation and this is to be inserted in the records of the court of Canterbury for reference. This constitution is to be published throughout the city and diocese. The bp. of London is to notify the abp. by the feast of St. Peter ad vincula [1 Aug.] of the action taken. He orders the execution of the mandate in dioc. Salisbury. London, bishop's palace, 6 July 1416.

[The archbishop's mandate is printed in *Reg. Chichele*, iii. 18–19.]

921 [Fo. 127v/37v] Mandate of Richard, bp. of London, to M. Geoffrey Crukadan, vicar general, transmitting the mandate of Henry, abp. of Canterbury (dated London, archbishop's inn, 1 July 1416), to publish the ordinance concerning probate drawn up in the convocation of Canterbury province meeting in St. Paul's, London, as a result of popular complaints concerning the indiscreet commission of administration of goods and excessive charges for probate and acquittance of executors. [Fo. 128/38] Each bp., or person with probate jurisdiction, is to sequestrate the deceased's goods immediately and not commit the administration of the estate until the executors named in the will have submitted an accurate and clear inventory. The executors are not to meddle with any goods other than those named in the inventory, on pain of excommunication, but are to produce another inventory of any goods newly found. They are to administer the goods according to the deceased's will within one year if possible, and to give a full account, not retaining any goods unlawfully. For the next year after the date of the present mandate, fees taken for probate or hearing the account or the final acquittance of the executors are not to exceed five shillings in all. The goods of people dying intestate are to be disposed as quickly as possible for the benefit of their souls and in accordance with the provincial statutes. This ordinance is to be published throughout the city and diocese. The vicar general is to notify the abp. before the feast of St. Peter ad vincula [1 Aug.] of the action taken. London, bishop's palace, 9 July 1416.

[The archbishop's mandate is printed in *Reg. Chichele*, iii. 16–18.]

[Fo. 128v/38v. A space of half a folio is left blank, possibly intended to contain the execution of the mandate.]

922 Mandate of Richard, bp. of London, to M. Geoffrey Crukadan, vicar general, transmitting the mandate of Henry, abp. of Canterbury (dated Saltwood (*Saltwode*), archbishop's castle, 2 Aug. 1416), who has heard that his earlier mandate for prayers has not been properly obeyed, and therefore reiterates his order for prayers and processions on Wednesdays and Fridays for the peace and unity of the Church, the king's good estate, favourable weather and the success of the Emperor Sigismund. [Fo. 129/39] He quotes biblical and historical examples of the efficacy of prayer, and ordains that the intercessions prescribed continue until further notice. An indulgence of forty days is promised by the abp. to those who engage in them in his diocese, and the bishops are to promise similar ones in their dioceses. London, bishop's palace, 11 Aug. 1416.

[The archbishop's mandate is printed in *Reg. Chichele*, iv. 158–9.]

[The remaining quarter of the folio is left blank, possibly intended to contain the execution of the mandate. Fo. 129v/39v. The top third of the folio is left blank.]

923 Mandate of Richard Bruton, chancellor of Wells cath. and vicar general of Richard, bp. of London, then abroad,[1] to the bp. of Salisbury's vicar general, transmitting the mandate of Henry, abp. of Canterbury [Fo. 130/40] (dated Calais (*Calesius*), archbishop's inn, 20 Sept. 1416),[2] summoning the clergy of the province to a convocation at St. Paul's, London, 9

Nov. 1416, and the following days, to deal with important matters concerning the Church and realm of England.[3] London, 13 Oct. 1416.

[1. Richard Clifford was appointed ambassador to the council of Constance, 20 July 1416 (*Foedera*, IV. ii. 168).
2. Printed in *Reg. Chichele*, iii. 22–3.
3. Those summoned are as in **754**, except that after prelates, 'not mendicants' is specified, and that cath. chapters are to be represented by one proctor.]

[The remaining half of the folio is left blank, possibly intended to contain the execution of the mandate.]

924 [Fo. 130v/40v] Mandate of Richard, bp. of London, to the bp. of Salisbury or his vicar general, transmitting the mandate of Henry, abp. of Canterbury (dated Otford (*Otteford*), archbishop's manor, 4 Jan. 1416),[1] proclaiming the feast of St. George [23 Apr.] as a greater double, and ordering the observance of the feasts of St. David [1 March], St. Cedd [2 March] and St. Winifred [3 Nov.] with choral services of nine lessons. The bp. of London is to notify the abp. before the feast of St. Matthew the apostle [24 Feb.],[2] of the action taken, and the vicar general is to notify the abp. before Easter [19 Apr.]. Fulham, bishop's manor, 20 Jan. 1416.

The vicar general notified each archd. of dioc. Salisbury,[3] and he notified the abp. in customary form.

[1. Printed in *Reg. Chichele*, iii. 8–10.
2. *Reg. Chichele* has the feast of the Purification of the B.V.M., i.e. 2 Feb.
3. Notification to the dean and chapter of Salisbury, Pountney, p.33.]

925 [Fo. 131/41] Notification of the vicar of Bere Regis (*Byr*) and the rector of Holy Trinity, Wareham (*Warham*), to M. Geoffrey Crukadan, vicar general, that they have executed his commission (dated Salisbury, 1 Feb. 1416) to hold an inquiry into the extent of the dilapidations of the chancel of Sturminster Marshall (*Stourmynstr' Marchall*) church, and whether the farmers of the church or the vicar are responsible for their repair. The commissaries report that they held an inquiry in the church 7 May 1416 by trustworthy senior parishioners and neighbours, summoning William Warr, farmer of the church, William Marnhull, vicar, and others. They discovered that the chancel is totally ruined and almost collapsed, and that divine service cannot be held there. The jurors said that responsibility for the repair of the chancel has always belonged to the rector. Sealed with the seals of the commissaries, the jurors and that of the dean of Dorchester (*Dorcestr'*) deanery. The names of the jurors were John Carsy, John Scot, John Albold, John Threscher, John Janwey, Edward Hyle, Nicholas Atteyerde, Peter Champayne, Robert Chynne, Edward Holle, Robert Govayr, John Shoyle, John Floke, William Joye, John Priour, William Lake, junior, John Dyer and William Basket. Sturminster Marshall, 7 May 1416.

926 [Fo. 131v/41v] Mandate of Richard Bruton, chancellor of Wells cath. and vicar general of Richard, bp. of London, then abroad, to the bp. of Salisbury's vicar general, transmitting the mandate of Henry, abp. of

Canterbury (dated Otford (*Otteford*), archbishop's manor, 16 Dec. 1416), concerning the feast of St. John of Beverley (*de Beverlaco*). As it was on the day of his translation [25 Oct.] that King Henry V was victorious at Agincourt [*Agyncourt*], it is ordained that his deposition [7 May] be celebrated annually throughout the province with choral service, according to the Use of Salisbury. On 25 Oct., the feast of St. Crispin and St. Crispinian is already celebrated, but now, in memory of this notable victory, that day is to be observed with services of nine lessons, three concerning St. Crispin and St. Crispinian, three concerning the translation of St. John of Beverley and the last three concerning many martyrs, according to the Salisbury Use. Bruton is to notify the abp. before the feast of the Purification of the B.V.M. [2 Feb.] of the action taken. The bp. of Salisbury's vicar general is to publish this throughout the city and diocese. London, 8 Jan. 1417.

[The archbishop's mandate is printed in *Reg. Chichele*, iii. 28–9.]

927 [Fo. 132/42] Agreement between Thomas Beworthy, vicar of Chisledon (*Chesulden*), and John Mynty *alias* Smyth, rector, by his proctor, Simon Unwyn, skilled in the law, made before M. Thomas Teynton B.Cn. & C.L., bishop's chancellor, with M. John Kempe B.C.L. and M. William Radeborn B.C.L. as mediating friends, to augment the revenues of the vicarage of Chisledon. The rector is to receive all the tithes of corn sheaves and hay, lambs and wool, within the parish (excluding the lands and pastures of the vicar), and the small tithes of animals and gardens of the rectory, and the mortuary fees. The vicar is to receive all other small tithes and personal tithes and all offerings (except any specifically made to the rector). [Fo. 132^{v}/42^{v}] The rector is to pay the vicar five marks [£3 6*s* 8*d*] annually, in equal portions at Michaelmas [29 Sept.] and Easter, in place of the aforesaid tithes which formerly belonged to the vicar. If the rector is more than one month late in paying, the revenues of the church are to be sequestrated until he pays the vicar and also pays 3*s* 4*d* to the bp. as punishment. Witnesses, Wenceslas Swysico, notary public, and William Torlinton, clerk. Ramsbury (*Remmesbury*) prebendal church, 23 Dec. 1412.

The bp. confirmed this agreement, at the request of the proctor and vicar, in the presence of M. John Appulton, notary public, and John Brewnyng, chaplain. Chapel of Sonning (*Sonnyng*) bishop's manor, 4 Feb. 1413.

[Most of the next folio, which is blank, has been cut away, leaving a strip 10 cm. wide. Two folios following it have been cut away entirely. Fo. 133/43^{r-v} is blank.]

[All the letters, **928–53**, are issued by, or addressed to, Robert, bp. of Salisbury.]

928 [Fo. 152/62*] Commission to M. Simon Sydenham D.C.L., canon of Salisbury cath., to preside over the consistory court of Salisbury until the

*The half quire, fos. 152–157, **928–49**, was begun at the beginning of the episcopate for longer letters than those entered in *quaternus primus*, **707** ff., with which it was used concurrently. The latter half of this quire was used for ordination lists.

feast of St. John the Baptist [24 June]. He is to hear all cases that pertain to the bp., both instance cases and cases *ex officio*, and to hear appeals.[1] Sealed with the seal which we used to use in the office of archd. of Canterbury.[2] London, 31 March 1408.

[1. A much fuller commission was given 22 Sept. 1408 to William Lyndewode, **945**. 2. Cf. **707** n. 2.]

929 Mandate to the archd. of Salisbury or his official to warn all non-resident rectors and vicars in his archdeaconry to return to their cures within two months. He is to notify the bp. before the feast of St. John the Baptist [24 June] of the names of such. Welford, 14 May 1408.

Similar letters were sent to the archdeacons of Dorset, Wiltshire and Berkshire, or their officials.

930 Notification to all the tenants and residents of the city of Salisbury of the appointment of William Westbury as bailiff of the bishop's demesne and liberty in the city. They are to co-operate in everything pertaining to his office. [? Welford], 12 May 1408.

931 [Fo. 152^{v}/62^{v}] General notification that the bp. has granted an indulgence of forty days to those saying the Lord's Prayer for the soul of Margaret Holden, who has recently died and is buried in Hunton church (dioc. Canterbury) before the altar of St. Peter the apostle and St. Petronella. Culham, 14 June 1408.

932 Notification to the clergy of the diocese that the bp. has granted an indulgence of forty days (in addition to the indulgences granted by several popes[1]) to those contributing to the support of the hospital of St. Anthony, when its proctors visit the diocese. The clergy are to announce this to the people. Sealed with the bishop's signet on the dorse. London, bishop's inn, 1 Aug. 1408.

[1. R. Graham, 'The order of St. Antoine de Viennois and its English commandery, St. Anthony's, Threadneedle Street', *Archaeol. Jour.*, lxxxiv (1927), 341–406.]

933 Commission to M. Adam Mottrum, precentor of Salisbury cath., and M. Simon Sydenham, archd. of Salisbury, to relax the sentence of suspension imposed on John Taillour *alias* FitzRichard, priest with cure of souls of Stratford Toney (*Stratford Tony*) church, on account of his incontinence with Margaret Clement and Agnes Bukden of the parish, after enjoining suitable penance. Welford, 1 June 1408.

934 [Fo. 153/63] Notification of the dean of Reading (*Redyng*) that he has executed the bishop's commission (dated Culham, 12 June 1408) addressed to him and the vicar of Aldermaston, to sequestrate the revenues of

Woolhampton (*Wolhampton*) church, in which the cure of souls and divine service have been neglected, and to notify the bp. before the feast of the translation of St. Thomas the martyr [7 July] of the action taken. The dean reports that he has published the sequestration and that the sequestrated revenues are in the custody of John Clerk, farmer of the church. Sealed with his seal of office. Woolhampton, 21 June 1408.

935 General notification that John Frye of dioc. Salisbury has been excommunicated for contumacy to certain monitions. Culham, 17 July 1408.

936 Commission to John Markydstide, priest, to commit the administration of the goods of Thomas Kentewode who died intestate to Isabel, his wife. He is to receive her oath to administer the goods faithfully and to make a reliable inventory, saving the portion belonging to the son of Thomas and Isabel, concerning which John Preston and William Buggynges, chaplain, have given their guarantee to the bp. London, bishop's inn, 28 July 1408.

937 [Fo. 153^{v}/63^{v}] Commission to Adam Mountrum [*sic*], precentor of Salisbury cath., and Simon Sydenham, archd. of Salisbury, to hear the purgation of Richard Sterlyng, vicar of Pewsey (*Peuesey*), from the alleged crime of adultery with Joan, wife of Thomas Hert, or, if he is unable to purge himself, to punish him. Culham, 27 June 1408.

938 Notification of the official of the archd. of Wiltshire that he has executed the bishop's commission (dated London, bishop's inn, 24 July 1408) to hold an inquiry into the dilapidations in Pewsey (*Peuesey*) church, which William Trenerth, rector, alleges have been left by his predecessor, M. John Snapp and others, in the chancel and buildings of the rectory, and the cost of their repair. The official reports that the jurors say that it would cost at least ten marks [£6 13*s* 4*d*] to repair the chancel wall, twenty shillings to repair the stonework and glass of some windows on the south side of the chancel, forty pence to repair the ceiling, forty shillings to repair the damage between the chancel and the nave, forty pence to repair the door on the south side of the chancel, [Fo. 154/64] twenty marks [£13 6*s* 8*d*] to repair the damage in the walls of the hall of the rectory and of the rooms at the upper and lower ends of the hall, twenty pounds to repair the roof of the hall and rooms, twenty pounds to repair the two barns, dovecot, stable, byre and cook-house (*coquina*), and that all these repairs are the responsibility of the rector. M. John Snap,[1] the previous rector, was there for more than four years. Before him, M. Thomas Polton[2] was rector for two years and received forty marks [£26 13*s* 4*d*] a year. He also received twenty-five pounds for dilapidations from the goods of M. Stephen Vaggescombe,[3] his immediate predecessor, but kept twenty marks [£13 6*s* 8*d*] for himself and used only 27½ marks [£18 3*s* 4*d*] on repairs in the whole of his time. The names of the jurors were William Edeshale, rector of

Huish (*Hewyssch*),[4] John Noter, rector of Everley (*Everle*); John Wygge, rector of Manningford Bruce (*Manyngforde Petri*); John Dorse, rector of Wotton Rivers (*Wotton*); Richard Sloughtre, rector of Mildenhall (*Mildenhale*); Robert Gayland, vicar of Milton Lilbourne (*Milton*); John Colynes; John Beneg, senior; John Beneg, junior; John Kepenhull; John Orcharde and William Beneg. Sealed with the seals of the official and the jurors. Pewsey, 30 July 1408.

[1. Instituted 30 May 1403, on the resig. of Thomas Polton, **808**; cf. Reg. Medford fo. 91ᵛ. He died by 17 Nov. 1407, *ibid.* fo. 189.
2. Instituted 7 March 1402, on the death of Richard Ketel (error for Stephen Vaggescombe), *ibid.* fo. 83.
3. Instituted 12 March 1390, on the resig. of Richard Ketul, Reg. Waltham fo. 115.
4. Probably error for William Swayn, cf. **122**.]

939 Mandate of Richard, bp. of London, transmitting the mandate of Thomas, abp. of Canterbury (dated Lambeth (*Lamhith*), archbishop's manor, 25 June 1408),[1] which he received after vespers on 25 June, summoning the clergy of the province[2] to a convocation in St. Paul's, London, 23 July 1408, and the following days, to discuss the ending of the Schism, which has now lasted for thirty years. [Fo. 154ᵛ/64ᵛ] Nine cardinals, who have withdrawn from the pope at Lucca (*civitas Lucana*) and gone to Pisa, have written to the king of England and have appealed from the pope to a general council. [Fo. 155/65] Prayers and religious observances are enjoined for the unity of the Church, and an indulgence of forty days is granted to those engaging in them. The bp. of London orders the execution of this mandate in dioc. Salisbury. London, bishop's palace, 25 June 1408.

[Fo. 155ᵛ/65ᵛ] Mandate to the dean of Salisbury,[3] transmitting the above letters, which were received 1 July, and ordering their execution. The dean is to notify the bp. before the feast of St. Swithin [15 July] of the action taken. Culham, 2 July 1408.

Mandate to the archd. of Salisbury, ordering the execution of the archbishop's letters in his archdeaconry. He is to cite the heads of religious houses to attend the convocation, and is to summon the clergy to assemble and choose one or two proctors who are to meet with the proctors of the other archdeaconries of dioc. Salisbury in Salisbury cath. on the morrow of St. Swithin [16 July], before the bishop's commissaries, to choose two proctors to represent all the clergy at the convocation. He is to enjoin prayers and religious observances and to publish the indulgence. He is to notify the bp. 16 July of the action taken. Culham, 2 July 1408.

Similar mandates were sent to the archdeacons of Wiltshire, Berkshire and Dorset.

[Fo. 156/66] Notification to the abp. of Canterbury that the mandate has been executed in dioc. Salisbury. A list of those cited is appended. London, bishop's inn, 22 July 1408.

In Salisbury cath.: M. John Chaundeler, dean; the chapter of the cath. of St. Mary, Salisbury. In Salisbury archdeaconry: M. Simon Sydenham, archd. of Salisbury; William, prior of Monkton Farleigh (*Farlech*). In Wiltshire archdeaconry: John Chytterne, archd. of Wiltshire; Thomas, abbot of

Malmesbury; William, abbot of Stanley (*Stanleygh*); Robert, prior of Bradenstoke (*Bradyngstoke*). In Berkshire archdeaconry: M. Walter Medeford, archd. of Berkshire; Richard, abbot of Abingdon (*Abyndon*); Richard, abbot of Reading (*Redyng*). In Dorset archdeaconry: John Macworgh, archd. of Dorset; Robert, abbot of Sherborne (*Shirborn*); Robert, abbot of Cerne; Robert, abbot of Abbotsbury (*Abbotysbury*); William, abbot of Bindon (*Byndon*); Walter, abbot of Milton, was also cited, but is said to be suffering from gout and kidney stones. Proctors appointed for the clergy of the whole of dioc. Salisbury: M. Simon Sydenham, archd. of Salisbury, and John Chytterne, archd. of Wiltshire.[4]

[1. The archbishop's mandate is printed in *Concilia*, iii. 306.

2. Those summoned as in **754**, with the addition of other sensible and mature men of great learning of each dioc., whom the suffragans consider necessary to be present at the discussion of the union. These were to be summoned to attend in person.

3. Entered in Vyring, p. 11.

4. This was the first summons to convocation during Hallum's episcopate, and the mandates in execution of it are entered more fully than for any subsequent convocation, possibly to serve as precedents.]

940 General notification that John Elys *alias* Elyot of Aldbourne (*Aldebourne*) has been excommunicated since 16 July for contumacy when summoned to appear before the bp. to answer charges of breach of faith and perjury, at the instance of Hugh Vicary of Aldbourne. Sealed with our seal. Salisbury, bishop's palace, 11 Sept. 1408.

941 Letter to the abbess and conv. of Shaftesbury (*Shaftesbyry*) nominating as nun Catherine, daughter of John Brombelegh of Sherborne (*Schirborn*), a young girl, in accordance with the bp. of Salisbury's customary right on appointment. She will be sent by the bp. and is to be received and put into the company of Agnes Poney, who is to instruct her in the regular disciplines. They are to notify the bp. of the action taken. Woodford (*Wodeford*), bishop's manor, 14 Sept. 1408.

942 [Fo. 156v/66v] Letter to the abbess and conv. of Wilton (*Wylton*) nominating as nun Eleanor Cokkyng, *domicella*, in accordance with Salisbury custom. They are to receive her with sisterly love, assigning to her the position and rights due, and are to notify the bp. of the action taken, when asked on behalf of Eleanor. London, bishop's inn, 24 Jan. 1409.

943 Commission to M. Richard Burgh B.C.L. to act as the bishop's sequestrator and commissary general in the archdeaconries of Wiltshire and Berkshire, with power of investigating, correcting and punishing crimes, of testamentary jurisdiction, and of seeking and receiving the bishop's spiritual revenues. Culham, 17 Aug. 1408.

The same day M. Richard Burgh received the bishop's commission to hold chapters and synods in the peculiar jurisdiction of Marlborough (*Marleburgh*), Lavington (*Lavyngton*), Devizes (*Devysys*) and Potterne (*Poterne*).

944 Commission to M. William Lyndewode D.Cn. & C.L., president of the consistory court of Salisbury, and M. Richard Burgh B.C.L., bishop's commissary, to receive the oath of canonical obedience of certain rectors, vicars and other lower clergy in dioc. Salisbury who are bound by law or custom to give it. Sonning (*Sonnyng*), bishop's manor, 12 Jan. 1409.

945 [Fo. 157/67] Commission to M. William Lyndewode D.Cn. & C.L. to preside over the consistory court of Salisbury.[1] He is to hear all cases that pertain to the bp., both instance cases and cases *ex officio*; to hear appeals; to investigate, correct and punish crimes; to exercise testamentary jurisdiction; to appoint a general confessor who may grant absolution except in reserved cases; to seek and receive all the bishop's spiritual revenues; and to appoint a clerk as official who will seek clergy convicted in the secular courts and transfer them to the bishop's prison.[2] Sealed with the bishop's seal. Potterne (*Poterne*), bishop's manor, 22 Sept. 1408.

[1. This is the office of bishop's official, which Lyndewode himself describes, Lyndwood, pp. 104–5, 14. He maintains there that the official does not normally have powers of investigating, punishing and correcting crimes, unless they be specially committed to him, as was the case in Hallum's commission. He became official of the abp. of Canterbury by 1420 (*Reg. Chichele*, iv. 77).

2. Cf. temporary commission of 31 March 1408 to Simon Sydenham, **928**. Lyndwood was succeeded as official by Geoffrey Crukadan, whose commission is not entered in the register, but who occurs as official by December 1409, **1076**. Lyndwood was the bishop's chancellor by June 1410 and possibly earlier, **129**, **166**.]

946 Licence to the vicar and parishioners of Sparsholt (*Spersot*), at their petition, to change the day of the feast of the church's dedication from the morrow of St. Tecla [24 Sept.], on which date for certain reasons it has not hitherto been celebrated with due solemnity, to the Sunday after the feast of St. Martin [11 Nov.]. An indulgence of forty days is promised to all who hear the divine offices on that day in the church. London, bishop's inn, 1 Nov. 1408.

947 [Fo. 157v/67v] Commission to the vicar of Sutton Benger (*Sutton*) and the chaplain of the church of Christian Malford (*Crismaleford*) to warn the unknown persons who have stolen tithes, offerings and other goods from John Morhay, rector of Christian Malford, and his proctor, John Spencer, to make satisfaction within fifteen days. If they fail to do so, the commissaries are to denounce them and any who aid and abet them as excommunicate. London, 8 Feb. 1409.

948 General notification that the bp. has granted to John de Merssh, acolyte of dioc. Lichfield, a title to be promoted to all orders by any Catholic bp. London, 12 Feb. 1409.

949 Commission to John Cathelyn, rector of Fisherton Anger (*Fyssherton iuxta civitatem nostram Sar'*), and John Pedewell, vicar of Bulbridge (*Bulbrygg*), to seek and receive any clergy imprisoned by the royal justices in

Wiltshire or the city of Salisbury, so that they may be dealt with in the ecclesiastical courts. Sealed with our seal. Canterbury (*Cantuar'*), 27 Feb. 1409.

Similar commission to the rectors of St. Peter and St. Leonard, Wallingford (*Walyngford*) for clergy in the town of Wallingford and in Berkshire.

Similar commission to John Marchant, rector of All Saints, Dorchester (*Dors'*), and Walter Byngham, rector of Upway (*Weghe*) for Dorset.

Similar commission to the dean of Reading (*Radyng*) and all the curates of the deanery for Berkshire.*

950 [Fo. 142/52†] Commission,[1] at the request of John Rygges, rector of Holy Trinity, Dorchester (*Dors*), who complains that although he is resident in his church, no chaplain is willing to serve in the parish church of St. Peter, Dorchester, which is dependent on Holy Trinity, preferring to celebrate anniversaries. The commissaries are to compel some suitable chaplain to leave private services and serve the cure of souls in St. Peter's church, at a suitable salary, to be paid by the rector of Holy Trinity. If he refuses, after twenty days he is to be suspended. The commissaries are to notify the bp. of the receipt of this commission and of the action taken, when asked to do so by the rector. [Undated.][2]

[1. Recipients not stated.
2. Probably *c.* Sept. 1413, cf. **951**, Appendix A x.]

951 Signification to the Crown that William Godfray of Potterne (*Poterne*), excommunicated for contumacy to the bishop's monitions in a matrimonial case between him and Agnes atte Nesshe of Potterne, has remained obdurate for forty days and more, with a request for his capture by the secular authority. Ramsbury (*Remmesbury*), bishop's manor, 17 Sept. 1413.

952 Commission to John Juyll, rector of Milston (*Mildeston*), to have his church and the area designated for a churchyard consecrated by any Catholic bp. Ramsbury, 3 Oct. 1413.

953 Commission to Thomas Mounk, chaplain, of dioc. Salisbury, to act as coadjutor to Robert Porter, vicar of Shapwick (*Schapewyke*), on account of his age and infirmity, with the latter's express consent. [Undated.]

[Mounk was instituted as vicar 5 Feb. 1418, on the resig. of Porter, who received a pension as old and infirm (Reg. Chandeler, pt. i fo. 2^v).]

*On the completion of this half quire, subsequent business was recorded in *quaternus primus*, which had hitherto been used concurrently with it. For just over one year (from **754**), letters of all types were recorded together, apart from the constitutions against Lollardy, **955**.

†**950–3** were entered later to fill an empty space in the gathering containing the constitutions against Lollardy of 1409.

[Fo. 142v/52v. The top three-quarters of this folio are blank.*]

954 Notification of Adam de Mottrum, precentor of Salisbury cath., vicar general of the bp. of Salisbury, then abroad, to Thomas, abp. of Canterbury, that he has executed the archbishop's mandate which he received 7 June to publish the constitutions against Lollardy. On 18 June he had them published in full consistory in Salisbury cath. to the clergy and people, and then, having sent copies to the archdeacons' officials, they were similarly published in their chapters. Sealed with the precentor's seal. Salisbury, 1 Aug. 1409.

955 [Fo. 143/53] Mandate of Richard, bp. of London, to the bp. of Salisbury or his vicar general, transmitting the mandate of Thomas, abp. of Canterbury (dated Queenborough (*Qweenburgh*), archbishop's castle, 13 Apr. 1409),[1] to publish the constitutions against Lollardy drawn up in the provincial council held at Oxford[2] and confirmed in the recent convocation of Canterbury province meeting in St. Paul's, London.[3] The bishops are to publish them in each city and diocese, in their synods and chapters. The bp. of London is to notify the abp. before the feast of St. John the Baptist [24 June] of the date of receipt of this mandate and of the action taken. The bp. of London sends copies of the constitutions, and orders that the abp. be notified by the same feast of St. John the Baptist of the action taken. Fulham, bishop's manor, 20 May 1409.

[Constitutions against Lollardy][4]

Introduction: A concern for uniform pure doctrine in the province of Canterbury and for the extermination of perverse preaching and doctrine which imperil souls has caused these constitutions to be drawn up.

I. [Fo. 143v/53v] No priest is to preach in Latin or in English without prior examination and authorization by the ordinary of the place, under pain of excommunication, and, for a second offence, denunciation as a heretic.[5] Parish priests in their churches are to preach only those things contained in the provincial constitution, 'Ignorantia sacerdotum'.[6]

II. [Fo. 144/54] No clergyman and no parishioners shall admit anyone to preach without such a licence, or the church or place shall receive an interdict.

III. Preachers shall chiefly deal with the vices common to their hearers, and not with other matters, under pain of punishment by the ordinary of the place.

IV. [Fo. 144v/54v] Preachers shall not deal with the sacrament of the altar, matrimony, confession, nor preach anything contrary to the teaching of the Church, on pain of excommunication and, for a second offence, denunciation as a heretic.

*There is a strong possibility that fo. 142 (which is a single sheet) originally followed the Constitutions, as **954** refers back to them. This space may have been intended to contain the letter to the archdeacons and their officials for execution of the archbishop's mandate.

v. Schoolmasters or teachers are not to teach anything contrary to the Church's teaching, nor allow exposition of Scripture or disputes concerning the Catholic faith, under pain of punishment by the ordinary.
vi. No treatise of John Wyclyff or his contemporaries is to be copied by the stationers unless approved by at least twelve doctors chosen by the university of Oxford (*Oxon'*) or Cambridge (*Cantebrigg*).[7] Anyone reading such a work without approval is to be punished.
vii. No one is to translate Scripture into English on his own authority. Anyone reading such a translation is to be punished with excommunication.
viii. [Fo. 145/55] No one shall defend in the schools or elsewhere any proposition against the sound doctrine of the Church.
ix. No disputing is to be allowed on the articles of the Church, especially concerning the adoration of the cross, images, saints and pilgrimages, and no one is to question their authority, under penalty as a heretic.
x. No chaplain is to celebrate outside his own diocese without letters of his orders and letters of his ordinary testifying to his character.[8]
xi. Inquiries are to be made monthly throughout the colleges and halls of the university of Oxford for any holding Lollard opinions, who are to be expelled.[9] Negligent wardens are to be deprived and excommunicated.
xii. [Fo. 145v/55v] Anyone disobeying these constitutions is to be ineligible for any benefice for three years.
xiii. Anyone suspected of heresy is to be cited to appear before the ordinary of the place, who is to punish him.[10]

[1. Printed in *Concilia*, iii. 320.
2. 28 Nov.–10 Dec. 1407, *ibid.*, iii. 306; cf. **1059**.
3. 14–31 Jan. 1409, *Concilia*, iii. 311; cf. **754**.
4. Only an abbreviated summary is given in this calendar. The constitutions are printed in *Concilia*, iii. 314–19; *Sacrorum Conciliorum Nova et Amplissima Collectio*, ed. G. D. Mansi and others (54 vols. in 59, Paris, 1901–27, repr. Graz, 1960–1), xxvi, cols. 1031–41; English translation in *Acts and Monuments of John Foxe*, ed. S. R. Cattley (8 vols., 1837–41), iii. 242–8.
5. For examples, see **787**, **824**, **832–3**, **838–9**, **965**, **970**, **981**, **988**, **990**.
6. Lyndwood, p. 54: I, II, c. I.
7. See **1126**.
8. See **877**, **1013**.
9. See **1126**.
10. See **1131**, **1133**, **1142**.]

[All the letters, **956–1026**, are issued by, or addressed to, Robert, bp. of Salisbury.]

956 [Fo. 134/44*] Notification of the official of the archd. of Wiltshire that on 27 Apr. 1410 he received the bishop's commission (dated Potterne (*Poterne*), bishop's manor, 24 Apr. 1410), to inquire into the right of

*This folio, the outside one of a quire consisting of fos. 134–41, **956–1013**, has been badly affected by damp. In the top right-hand corner is written in a 15th-century hand *quaternus secundus*, although it was not the second quire to be started for letters. It was used concurrently, *c.* Apr. 1410—*c.* Sept. 1412, with the quires later called *quaternus quartus*, **822–58**, and *quaternus quintus*, **859–90**.

presentation to the vicarage of Hannington (*Hankynton*) chapel, to which John Thornbury, rector of Crudwell (*Cruddewell*) has presented Edward Hunte, in an exchange of benefices for the church of Evesbatch (*Esbache*), dioc. Hereford. He is to make inquiry by the rectors and vicars of the deanery, and to notify the bp. of the result and of the names of the jurors, in letters sealed with his and their seals. The official reports that he summoned the rector of Crudwell to appear before him in . . . [illegible] church in Malmesbury deanery on 28 Apr., and there the rector declared to the clergy of the deanery that the chapel was dependent on Crudwell church, and he and his predecessors had always presented the vicar. The jurors agreed that this was so, and added that the rector had last presented one Ralph Spurner, and that the chapel had the cure of souls as the vicars had ministered to the inhabitants of the vill of Hannington as long as they knew, and some of them had known the chapel for thirty years. The rector of Crudwell was able to minister in the chapel, and the vicar had a manse in the vill of Hannington. This vill was more than half a mile distant from Crudwell church and in winter the road was so muddy and there were so many floods that the inhabitants of Hannington were unable to get there, even if they wanted to. The rector would repair the chancel if necessary. The names of the jurors were Robert Herman, rector of Long Newnton (*Newenton*); Robert Bathe,[1] rector of Foxley (*Foxle*); William Colbat, rector of Bremilham (*Bremelham*); John Comley, vicar of St. Paul, Malmesbury; and John Osborne, vicar of Kemble (*Kemele*). Sealed with the official's and jurors' seals. 28 Apr. 1410.

[1. Cf. **655**. He was Robert Benet de Bathe (Reg. Waltham fo. 101).]

957 [Fo. 134v/44v] Licence to Thomas Myleward, rector of Huish (*Hewyssch*), to be absent from his benefice for one year to make a pilgrimage to Rome, provided that his church is properly served and that he appoints a proctor. Potterne, bishop's manor, 8 May 1410.

958 Licence to John Shottesbruk, esquire, and Alice his wife to have divine service celebrated in their oratories or chapels anywhere in the city or diocese of Salisbury, provided that it is quietly done (*submissa tamen voce*) and that there is no prejudice to the parish churches. Potterne, 9 May 1410.

959 Commission to the dean of Salisbury, the archd. of Salisbury and his official, and all the rural deans, rectors, vicars and parish chaplains of the archdeaconry of Salisbury to denounce as excommunicate Richard Wade of Heytesbury, who maliciously and falsely accused John Dunnyng, vicar of Chitterne, of adultery with Joan Wade, his wife, from which allegation Dunnyng has purged himself. They are to announce these facts in their churches on Sundays and feast days, between masses, when most people are present, until further notice. They are to notify the bp. or his commissaries of the action taken. Potterne, 8 May 1410.

960 [Fo. 135/45] General notification of an indulgence of forty days promised to all who contribute towards the rebuilding of the church of Laverstock (*Laverkestok*), which, together with the manse of the vicarage and other neighbouring buildings, has recently been entirely destroyed by a sudden fire at night. [Undated.]

961 Licence to William Chamber, *domicellus*, to have divine service celebrated in the oratory of his house in Abingdon (*Abyndon*), on account of his illness. Potterne, 16 May 1410.

962 Mandate to the sheriff of Wiltshire for the release from prison of Margery Coterell and Gillian Ferman of the parish of Hungerford, who have been absolved from sentence of excommunication on their submission. Sherborne (*Shirborn*), 2 June 1410.
[Given also in Decanal Reg. Chandeler, pt. ii fo. 35.]

963 Licence to William Ekerdon, rector of Long Bredy (*Langebridie*), to be absent from his benefice for one year. Sherborne, 11 June 1410.

964 [Fo. 135v/45v] Notification of the official of the archd. of Dorset that he has executed the bishop's commission (dated Sherborne (*Shirbourn*), bishop's castle, 28 June 1410) to hold an inquiry into the dilapidations which M. Richard Betty, rector of Stalbridge (*Stalbrugge*) alleges have been left by his predecessor, M. Benet Nycoll, bp. of Bangor, in the chancel, books, ornaments and buildings of the church and in the manse of the rectory, to estimate the cost of their repair and to sequestrate the goods of Nycoll. The official reports that he cited Nycoll to appear in the church on 17 July, and on this day, in the presence of Betty, although Nycoll failed to appear, he has held a careful inquiry. The jurors say that the chancel has defects in the roof which would cost at least twenty shillings to repair. The great barn of the rectory has defects in its woodwork, walls and roof which would cost £38 14*s* 4*d* to repair. The second barn and the stable adjacent have defects in their walls, woodwork and roof which would cost twenty marks [£13 6*s* 8*d*] to repair. The bakehouse (*pistrinum*) and brewhouse (*domus ad pandoxandum*) have defects in their walls which would cost twenty shillings to repair. Other boundary walls would cost 6*s* 8*d* to repair. The principal room of the rectory has defects in the roof which would cost 13*s* 4*d* to repair. The other rooms of the rectory have defects in the doors, windows, walls and other appurtenances which would cost forty shillings to repair. The names of the jurors are Hugh Weston, Baldwin Thornhull, William Clement, Richard Carpenter, Nicholas Hargrave, Walter atte Hulle, Robert Lokke, senior, William Pyard, Robert Honyman, Robert Baker, Robert Knygh, Reynold Phelpe, Richard Corscombe and Richard Frych. After this inquiry, the official summoned John Gaunt, recently farmer of the church for Nycoll, and he sequestrated some revenues of the church which were in his hands, as no other goods of Nycoll are known in the bp. of

Salisbury's jurisdiction. Sealed with the official's seal. Stalbridge, 17 July 1410.

965 [Fo. 136/46] Licence to Walter Bexhampton of Bridport, chaplain, to preach anywhere in dioc. Salisbury. Chardstock (*Cherdestok*), 5 Aug. 1410.

966 Licence to Robert Mere, rector of Little Wittenham (*Wytnam Abbatis*), to be absent from his benefice for one year in the service of the dean of Salisbury. Sherborne (*Shirborn*), 14 Aug. 1410.

967 Commission to the archd. of Dorset or his official to hold an inquiry into the dilapidations which Adam Raceton, rector of Knighton (*Knyghton*), alleges have been left by his predecessor, William Wryghte, and are now the responsibility of his executors. Sherborne, 17 Aug. 1410.

968 Licence to Thomas Ringwod and his wife to have divine service celebrated in the oratory of their house in the parish of Downton (*Dunton*). Sherborne, 19 Aug. 1410.

969 Indulgence of forty days granted to all who contribute to the support of the leper-house or hospital of St. Catherine of Lusty (*Lysty*) by Bruton. Sherborne, 24 Aug. 1410.

[Very little is known about this hospital beyond the fact of its existence (*VCH Som.*, ii. 156; D. Knowles and R. N. Hadcock, *Medieval Religious Houses* (1971), pp. 316, 348; R. M. Clay, *Medieval Hospitals of England* (1909), pp. 318–19). This indulgence adds information as to its dedication and situation. Lusty is south-west of Bruton.]

970 Licence to Thomas Loot M.A. to preach anywhere in dioc. Salisbury. Sherborne, 4 Sept. 1410.

971 Resignation by Thomas Shelford, in the person of William Purs, his proctor, of the church of Ashbury (*Asschbury*), on account of his presentation and institution a fortnight previously to the church of Buckland Newton (*Bokelond*), provided that if the latter church is taken from him for any reason he may return to Ashbury. The bp. received and approved this resignation, in the presence of M. Thomas Tenton B.Cn. & C.L., M. John Luk B.Th. and M. John Appulton B.C.L. Sherborne, 23 Sept. 1410.

972 [Fo. 136v/46v] Licence to M. John Hopton, rector of Great Cheverell (*Cheverell Magna*), at the request of John, bp. of Coventry and Lichfield, to be absent from his benefice in the service of the said bp. Sherborne, 26 Sept. 1410.

973 The like to M. John Teffont, rector of Broughton Gifford (*Browgton*), for one year's study at Oxford university. Sherborne, 10 Oct. 1410.

974 The like to William Fostbury, rector of Tarrant Keynston (*Kayneston, Kaynston*), subdeacon, for one year's study at any English *studium generale*, according to the clause 'Cum ex eo'. Salisbury [*sic*], 7 Oct. 1410.

975 Licence to Ellen Cerne, widow of Edward Cerne, knight, to have divine service celebrated in her oratory in the parish of Melcombe Horsey (*Melcombe*). Woodford (*Wodeford*), 28 Oct. 1410.

976 The like to John Whytyng and Isabel his wife, in the oratory of their house in the parish of Melbury Abbas (*Melbury Abbatisse*). Shaftesbury (*Shafton*), 5 Nov. 1410.

977 The like to Thomas Bonham and Alice his wife, in the oratories of any of their houses in the city and diocese of Salisbury. Shaftesbury, 5 Nov. 1410.

978 Letters dimissory to John Dun, subdeacon, to receive the orders of deacon and priest. Edington (*Edyngdon*), 7 Nov. 1410.

979 The like to Thomas Uppenere, subdeacon, to receive the orders of deacon and priest. Sonning (*Sonnyng*), 20 Dec. 1410.

980 The like to Peter Hert and William Boner, clerks, to receive all further minor and major orders. Abingdon (*Abendon*), 14 Jan. 1411.

981 Licence to Masters Nicholas Wyldobor, Richard Southbrok, Thomas Moston and Thomas Tynkelden, masters of arts, to preach anywhere in the city and diocese of Salisbury. Abingdon, 15 Jan. 1411.

982 [Fo. 137/47] Letters dimissory to Ralph Hogele, deacon, to receive the order of priest. Sonning (*Sonnyng*), 28 Feb. 1411.

983 Commission to the vicar of Bray (*Brey*), to sequestrate the goods of Walter Snell, vicar of Winkfield (*Wynkfeld*), who recently died intestate. He is to notify the bp. before Easter [12 Apr.] concerning the goods, and to keep them until further notice. Sonning, 28 Feb. 1411.

984 Letters dimissory to John Seward, clerk, to receive all orders. London, 13 March 1411.

985 The like to John Bollam, clerk, to receive all orders. London, 13 March 1411.

986 The like to John Gobet, acolyte, to receive all further orders. London, 14 March 1411.

987 The like to John Alfred, clerk, to receive all further orders. London, 20 March 1411.

988 Licence to M. John Sarger M.A. to preach anywhere in the city and diocese of Salisbury. Potterne, 22 May 1411.

989 Licence to John Kirton or Kreton and Alice his wife to have divine service celebrated in their oratory in the parish of [blank]. Potterne, 25 May 1411.

990 Licence to David Michell M.A. to preach anywhere in the city and diocese of Salisbury. Potterne, 29 May 1411.

991 Licence to the abbess of Wilton to have divine service celebrated in the oratories of her houses anywhere in dioc. Salisbury. Potterne, 29 May 1411.

992 Licence to Elisha Pese, chaplain of Wilton, to hear the confessions of Alice Hallum, the bishop's kinswoman (*consanguinee*). Potterne, 29 May 1411.

993 Indulgence of forty days granted to all who contribute to the support of the hospital of St. John the Baptist, Malmesbury. Potterne, 2 June 1411.

994 [Fo. 137v/47v] Licence to John Turpyn, rector of Whaddon, to be absent from his benefice for one year's study at a *studium generale*. Potterne, 20 June 1411.

995 Letters dimissory to Nicholas Capron, clerk, to receive all further orders. Potterne, 18 June 1411.

996 The like to M. Nicholas Colnet M.A. to receive all further orders. Potterne, 29 June 1411.

997 The like to Alexander Lenne and Stephen Colman, deacons, to receive the order of priest. London, 16 Sept. 1411.

998 The like to Ralph Thomas, acolyte, rector of Clewer (*Clewere*), to receive all orders. London, 16 Sept. 1411.

999 The like to John Patrych, deacon, to receive the order of priest. London, 16 Sept. 1411.

1000 The like to Ralph Hyckys, acolyte, to receive the order of subdeacon. London, 16 Sept. 1411.

1001 The like to John Craas, subdeacon, to receive the orders of deacon and priest. London, 16 Sept. 1411.

1002 General notification that John Spenser, the bearer of these letters, has, at his own request, received from the bp. the habit of a hermit. Potterne. [Undated.][1]

[The bp. was at Potterne 22 Apr.—*c.* 6 July 1411 (see Itinerary, Appendix C).]

1003 Mandate of Richard, bp. of London, transmitting the mandate of Thomas, abp. of Canterbury (dated Charing (*Charryng*), archbishop's manor, 23 Oct. 1411), which he received on the eve of the feast of St. Simon and St. Jude [27 Oct.], summoning the clergy of the province[1] to a convocation in St. Paul's, London, 1 Dec. 1411, and the following days, at the command of the king (dated Beauregard manor, 29 Sept.) that he assemble the clergy before the feast of St. Martin [11 Nov.] to discuss certain weighty and urgent matters concerning the realm and Church. The bp. of London orders the execution of this mandate in dioc. Salisbury. Much Hadham (*Hadham*), bishop's manor, 31 Oct. 1411.

[Fo. 138/48] The bp. of Salisbury received this mandate 10 Nov. 1411, and a mandate was directed to M. Geoffrey Crukadan, canon of Salisbury and official of Salisbury, for its execution. Crukadan was to notify the bp. by the feast of St. Andrew the apostle [30 Nov.] of the action taken.

When Crukadan's notification was received, the bp. notified the abp. of Canterbury in the customary way, with the names of those cited in an attached schedule: [Fo. 138v/48v] M. John Chaundeler, dean of Salisbury; the chapter of Salisbury cath.; M. John Macworth, archd. of Dorset; M. Simon Sydenham, archd. of Salisbury; John Chitterne, archd. of Wiltshire; M. Walter Medford, archd. of Berkshire; Robert, abbot of Sherborne (*Shirborn*); Robert, abbot of Abbotsbury (*Abbotesbury*); John, abbot of Cerne; Walter, abbot of Milton; Thomas, rector of Edington (*Edyndon*); Thomas, abbot of Malmesbury; Robert, prior of Bradenstoke; Richard, abbot of Abingdon (*Abyndon*); Thomas, abbot of Reading (*Radyng*). Proctors for the clergy of dioc. Salisbury: M. Geoffrey Crukadan and M. John Medford.

[1. Those summoned as in **754**, except that cath. chapters are to be represented by one proctor.]

1004 Commission to the archd. of Wiltshire or his official to denounce as excommunicate, in accordance with the canon and constitution of the holy fathers,[1] the unknown persons, and any aiding or abetting them, who recently broke into the church of Grittleton (*Grydlyngton*), and killed a certain Robert who had fled there for sanctuary. The sentence is to be published in all the churches of the archdeaconry, between masses, and in the synods and chapters of the clergy, when most people are present, on Sundays and feast days. Any guilty people found as a result of their inquiry are to be cited to appear before the bp. or his commissaries in Salisbury cath. on the eighth day after the citation. They are to notify the bp. of the names of any such, and of the action taken. Potterne, 30 Oct. 1411.

[1. 'De abstrahentibus confugientes ad ecclesiam', *Constitutiones Legatinae D. Othonis et D. Othoboni* (Oxford, 1679), p. 101: Constitution of Ottobono, Tit. 12.]

1005 [Fo. 139/49] Commission to the dean of Salisbury or his locumtenens to supervise the penance imposed by the bp. on N. Webbe, R. Esporner, John atte Courte, W. Bayly and John Knyght, who removed Robert Jordan from the sanctuary of Grittleton (*Grytlyngton*) church. They are to present themselves at the west door of Salisbury cath. before the beginning of high mass on the feast of the Circumcision [1 Jan.], wearing only linen shirts, in the sight of the people and in the dean's presence, and are to prostrate themselves until the dean has said over them the psalm, 'Have mercy on me, O Lord', with customary discipline as seems good to him. If they are suitably humble and contrite, they may enter the cathedral at the dean's command, each bearing a candle costing two pence and genuflecting to the font, and should solemnly offer the candle into the hands of the celebrant at the step of the high altar after the reading of the gospel. The dean is to summon them to perform this penance, and if they perform it devoutly he is to notify the bp. before the feast of the Epiphany [6 Jan.]. [Undated.][1]

[1. This mandate is also entered in Vyring, p. 73, where the date is given as Potterne (*Poterne*), 30 Dec. 1411.]

1006 Licence to William Brytby, subdeacon, rector of the chapel with cure of souls of Over Compton (*Overcompton*), to be absent from his benefice for two years' study at any *studium generale*, in accordance with the clause 'Cum ex eo'. Potterne, 18 Feb. 1412.

1007 Licence to John Deen, rector of Tollard Royal (*Tollard*), to hear the confessions of his parishioners, and to grant absolution even in some reserved cases, until the octave of Easter. He may also choose a suitable priest as his own confessor. [Undated.]

1008 Notification of the official of the archd. of Wiltshire that he has executed the bishop's commission (dated Potterne, bishop's manor, 10 Feb. 1412), which he received 14 Feb., to hold an inquiry into the dilapidations which M. John Appulton, vicar of Aldbourne (*Aldeborne*), alleges have been left by his predecessor, the late John Croke, in the chancel, books and ornaments of the church and in the buildings and enclosure of the vicarage, to estimate the cost of their repair and to sequestrate the goods of Croke. [Fo. 139v/49v] The official reports that on 15 Feb. he sequestrated the goods of Croke in the custody of John Dier, chaplain, and John Godard, his executors, and cited the executors to appear before him in the church of Aldbourne on 23 Feb., together with M. John Appulton. On this day he has held an inquiry by jurors, who say that John Croke was vicar for more than thirty-six years and that the vicarage is worth forty marks [£26 13*s* 4*d*] annually. The vicar has a farm (*fundus*) with one virgate of land, which all the vicars have possessed in living memory, situated in Aldbourne between the tenement of John Lovoryng on the north and the tenement which used to belong to Alice Budstone on the south, and the vicar for the time being is accustomed to live here. On this farm, there is only a fairly dilapidated

stable for keeping horses and hay, so that if the vicar wanted to live here he would have to build a new hall, chambers, kitchen, brewhouse and barn, which would cost at least forty pounds, and is the responsibility of the executors. However, the books and ornaments of the church have been competently repaired. The names of the jurors are William Brygthlampton, rector of St. Peter, Marlborough (*Marleburgie*); William Buttys, vicar of Preshute (*Preschut*); William Holtham, vicar of Ramsbury (*Remmesbury*); John Bedewynde, vicar of Froxfield (*Frokysfeld*); William Walrond; James Combe; John Sapere; John Amys; Richard Schayll; John Wheler; John Cok, tailor; and Simon Rasell. Witnesses: M. Nicholas [Borugh] B.Cn.L., vicar of Wroughton (*Elyndon*);[1] John Denby, clerk; and many others. Sealed with the official's and jurors' seals. Aldbourne, 23 Feb. 1412.
The official further notifies the bp. that the parties have made an agreement between them.
[1. Cf. Reg. Chandeler, pt. i fo. 17.]

1009 Notarial instrument confirming the dispensation granted by Anthony de Pireto M.Th., minister general of the friars minor, nuncio of Pope John XXIII in England, [Fo. 140/50] to Thomas Hulle of Britford (*Brydford*) and Emmot Randolf, of dioc. Salisbury (sealed with his seal and dated London, house of the friars minor, 1 May 1412), permitting them to marry although they are related in the third and fourth degrees of consanguinity. The papal licence to Pireto to grant dispensations to sixty men and women within these degrees, excluding kings and queens and their children (dated St. Peter's, Rome, 23 Oct. 1411)[1] is included. The bp. endorses the dispensation, in the presence of M. Thomas Teynton B.Cn.L., rector of Frome St. Quintin, M. John Lavyngton, rector of Draycot Cerne (*Draycote Cerne*), M. John Dygon and M. Oliver Dyngley (dioc. Exeter and Winchester), notaries public by papal authority, and other witnesses. The notarial instrument is drawn up by Wenceslas Swisiko, clerk (dioc. Brandenburg), notary public by papal and imperial authority. Chapel of Sonning (*Sonnyng*) bishop's manor, 7 June 1412.
[1. *CPL 1404–15*, p. 171.]

1010 [Fo. 140v/50v] Licence to the proctors whom the parishioners of St. Mary's church, Wallingford (*Walyngford*), have appointed to attend to the fabric and repair of the church, permitting them to use the timber and stones of St. Martin's church, Wallingford, which collapsed long ago and is ruined, without a rector and almost entirely without parishioners, provided that the patron and any parishioners agree and that the churchyard is suitably enclosed on all sides. Future responsibility for the churchyard is placed on the parishioners of St. Mary's church and their successors. Sonning, 23 June 1412.

1011 Letters of commendation of Pope John XXIII to the bp. of Salisbury, cardinal priest elect,[1] on behalf of Anthony de Pireto M.Th., minister general of the friars minor, and Paul de Caputgrassis of Solmona (*Sulmona*)

D.Cn.L., papal chamberlain and clerk, who are appointed papal nuncios in England. St. Peter's, Rome, 23 Oct. 2 John [XXIII] [1411].

[1. Cf. **1125**; *Hierarchia Catholica*, i. 33.]

1012 Mandate received by the bp. of Salisbury at Sonning, 1 Sept. 1412 of Richard, bp. of London, transmitting the mandate of Thomas, abp. of Canterbury (dated Canterbury (*Cant'*), archbishop's palace, 14 Aug. 1412),[1] at the king's request, for processions to be made every Wednesday and Friday in all cathedrals and churches, with seven penitential psalms and litany, and with prayers, fasting and tears, for the good estate of the realm and for the expedition of the duke of Clarence to recover Aquitaine (*Acquitan', Aquitan'*).[2] [Fo. 141/51] As the time of harvest is near, when it is not convenient to gather people for processions, they may be held on Sundays, but after the harvest is over, they are to be held on Wednesdays and Fridays without fail until further notice. An indulgence of forty days is granted to those taking part in dioc. Canterbury and is to be granted by the bishops in their dioceses. The bp. of London is to notify the abp. before the feast of the exaltation of the Cross [14 Sept.] of the action taken. The bp. of London orders the execution of this mandate in dioc. Salisbury. The bp. of Salisbury is to notify the abp. by 14 Sept. Wickham Bishops (*Wykham*), bishop's manor, 26 Aug. 1412.

[Fo. 141^{v}/51^{v}] Mandate to the dean of Salisbury, transmitting the above letters and ordering their execution in Salisbury cath. An indulgence of forty days is granted. Sonning, 1 Sept. 1412.

A similar mandate was sent to M. Geoffrey Crukadan, canon of Salisbury, to execute the archbishop's mandate in respect of the archdeaconries and the clergy and people of the diocese.

Notification to the abp. of Canterbury that the mandate has been executed in dioc. Salisbury. Sonning, 7 Sept. 1412.

[1. Printed in *Concilia*, iii. 337.
2. It set out *c.* 15 Aug. 1412 (*Thomae Walsingham . . . Historia Anglicana*, ed. H. T. Riley (2 vols., Rolls Ser., 1863–4), ii. 288).]

1013 Letters testimonial for John Corndon, chaplain of dioc. Exeter, who is of good character and reputation, not suspended nor excommunicate, not involved in any known crime, and not suspected of any opinions contrary to the Catholic faith. He has lived for more than three years in dioc. Salisbury, at first in minor orders, then in holy orders, and is reported to have behaved laudably in the office and ministry of the priesthood. Sealed with the bishop's seal. Sonning, 16 Sept. 1412.

[This conforms to the requirements of the constitutions against Lollardy published May 1409, **955**, XI. Corndon presumably wanted to officiate in another diocese.]

1014 [Fo. 146/56*] Commission to the archd. of Wiltshire or his official and all the clergy of Malmesbury deanery to denounce as excommunicate

*The quire, fos. 146–51, **1014–27**, was used concurrently, autumn 1412–Feb. 1415, with the quire later called *quaternus tertius*, **891–919**.

those who violently withdrew a certain John Hobkoc from the porch of St. Paul's church, Malmesbury, where he had fled for sanctuary, and any who aided or abetted them. They are to announce this in all the monasteries and churches of the deanery, between masses, when most people are present, ordering those who are holding Hobkoc prisoner to return him to the sanctuary immediately. They are to notify the bp. of the action taken before Christmas. [Undated.]

1015 Request to the king to order the sheriff of Wiltshire and the royal bailiffs and servants to restore to sanctuary John Hobcok, who has been removed from St. Paul's church, Malmesbury, and is being held prisoner in Salisbury castle, in defiance of ecclesiastical privilege. [Undated.]

1016 Commission to the rural dean and clergy of Malmesbury to denounce as excommunicate, in accordance with the constitution of Ottobono,[1] Thomas Pye of Malmesbury, who withdrew John Hobcok from sanctuary in St. Paul's church, Malmesbury. The sentence is to be published in their churches on Sundays and feast days until Pye makes satisfaction to God and the Church and deserves absolution. [Undated.]

[1. See **1004** n. 1.]

1017 [Fo. 146ᵛ/56ᵛ] General notification that the bp. has declared the feast of the translation of King Edward the Martyr, who is buried in Shaftesbury (*Shafton*) monastery, viz. 20 June, to be observed annually as a solemn feast throughout the archdeaconry of Dorset. An indulgence of forty days is granted to those observing the feast in any church of the archdeaconry. Ramsbury (*Remmesbury*) manor, 22 Jan. 1413.

[Cf. **893**. Given in full in Appendix D.]

1018 [Fo. 147/57] Mandate of Marcellus de Strozis D.C.L., papal nuncio and collector, to the bp. of Salisbury, to cite certain persons to appear before him at his inn in London by 15 May 1413 to pay in full the papal procurations which they owe. The bp. is to notify the collector by 15 May of the action taken. Sealed with his seal, London, 20 Feb. 1413.

Richard Salford, abbot of Abingdon (*Abendon*), Sibyl Montagu, prioress of Amesbury (*Ambresbury*), the priors of Frampton and Wareham, and John Lamborn, prior of Poughley: these owe procurations for many years and are to be pronounced excommunicate. They are to be cited to appear in person and the revenues of their benefices are to be sequestrated. The bp. is to notify the collector of the names of the priors of Frampton and Wareham. The possessor or farmer of Ogbourne (*Okeburn*) priory is to be warned to pay on pain of excommunication: he is to be cited, his revenues sequestrated, and his name and surname notified. The abbots of Milton (*Middelton*), Reading (*Radyng*) and Stanley, the dean and chapter of Salisbury, the priors of Monkton Farleigh (*Farlee*), Bradenstoke (*Bradenestoke*), Wallingford (*Walyngford*) and Hurley (*Hurlee*), the abbesses of Wilton (*Wylton*), Shaftesbury (*Shafton*) and Tarrant (*Tarenta*) and the prior of Loders: these are to be warned to pay on pain of excommunication and cited etc. In addition, the bp. is to notify the collector of any churches in his diocese appropriated to monasteries, priories and other ecclesiastical places or persons from the time of Popes Alexander V and John XXIII, and their occupiers are to be warned, cited and sequestrated.

On 8 March 1413, the bp. transmitted this letter for execution to M. Geoffrey Crukadan, official of Salisbury.

1019 Mandate of Richard, bp. of London, transmitting the mandate of Thomas, abp. of Canterbury (dated London, archbishop's inn, 20 Jan. 1413), which he received 21 Jan., summoning the clergy of the province[1] to a convocation in St. Paul's, London, 6 March 1413, and the following days, at the command of the king (dated Westminster, 19 Jan.) that he assemble the clergy before the octave of the Purification of the B.V.M. [9 Feb.] to discuss certain weighty and urgent matters concerning the realm and Church. [Fo. 147^{v}/57^{v}] The bp. of London orders the execution of this mandate in dioc. Salisbury. Wickham Bishops (*Wykham*), bishop's manor, 23 Jan. 1413.

[Fo. 148/58] The bp. of Salisbury notified the abp. of Canterbury of the execution of his mandate, with the names of those cited in an attached schedule: M. John Chaundeler, dean of Salisbury; the chapter of Salisbury cath.; M. Simon Sydenham, archd. of Salisbury; Thomas, rector of Edington (*Edyngdon*) conventual church; William, prior of Monkton Farleigh (*Farlegh*); John Macworth, archd. of Dorset; Robert, abbot of Sherborne (*Shirborn*); John, abbot of Cerne; Walter, abbot of Milton (*Middelton*); Robert, abbot of Abbotsbury (*Abbotesbury*); William, abbot of Bindon (*Byndon*); John Chitterne, archd. of Wiltshire; Thomas, abbot of Malmesbury; Robert, prior of Bradenstoke (*Bradenestoke*); William, abbot of Stanley (*Stanleye*); M. Walter Medeford, archd. of Berkshire; Richard, abbot of Abingdon (*Abendon*); Thomas, abbot of Reading (*Radynge*), Adam, prior of Bisham (*Bustelesham*). John Chitterne is the chapter of Salisbury cathedral's proctor. Masters Simon Sydenham and Geoffrey Crukadan are proctors of all the clergy of dioc. Salisbury.

[1. Those summoned as in **754**, except that cath. chapters are to be represented by one proctor.]

1020 Ordinance of Robert[1] [Bingham], bp. of Salisbury, confirming the foundation by Warin, king's chaplain, of a hospital at Cricklade (*Crikelad*), with its lands, possessions and liberties.[2] This place, with its chapel and dwellings (some built and others yet to be constructed) is intended especially for the needs of poor priests, in particular those unable to carry out their office through age or infirmity. However, hospitality is also to be extended as much as possible to poor travellers, who are to have a night's lodging and refreshment. The inmates are to have the right, after seeking a licence from the bp., of choosing their own rector from among themselves or from outside, and the bp. will institute him. He is to be a discreet man, who will be responsible for the spiritual care and temporal administration of the house, to whom the inmates shall promise obedience and respect. They may call him prior, rector or provost, as seems best to them, and he is to live as a regular. With him, he is to have two priests, also living as regulars, one a deacon and the other a subdeacon, if the resources of the house permit, one of whom is to celebrate the daily office and the other the mass for the dead, and the rector is to take his turn. As the resources of the house grow, the number of those serving God there should grow also, so no restriction of number is placed on the congregation. The chaplains are to be chosen without conditions or simony. The priests are to live and sleep in common, wearing a uniform regular habit, without personal possessions, attending the masses and other canonical hours unless ill. They are not to go outside the house without the provost's licence, and feasts and drinking in the town are forbidden to them, as are too frequent conversations with secular people. Rather they should pray assiduously with special prayers twice a day for the benefactors of the house, namely after lunch and at compline. The ordinance is confirmed with the assent of the chapter of Salisbury. Sealed with the bishop's and chapter's seals, saving their rights. London, 16 Apr. 1237. Witnesses, M. Luke Barth de Cameseya; Valentine, canon of Salisbury; William de Leycestre and Geoffrey, chaplains; M. Roger Robert de Eston, dean of Cricklade (*Crickelad*); Miles de Cerneia; Luke, the king's treasurer; M. Nicholas de Farnham; Ralph, the king's chaplain; Walter de Brackele; M. Walter de Leuth; William de Wynton, clerk; Thomas de Wynton, clerk; and many others.

[1. MS. has Richard, corrected in a later hand to Robert.
2. Cf. *Close Rolls 1227–31*. p. 487; *Calendar of Charter Rolls 1226–57*, p. 130.]

1021 [Fo. 148v/58v] Mandate of Marcellus de Strozis D.C.L., papal nuncio and collector, to the bp. of Salisbury, to cite certain persons to appear before him at his inn in London by 28 Feb. 1414 to pay in full the papal procurations which they owe. The bp. is to notify the collector by 28 Feb. of the action taken. Sealed with his seal, London, 1 Dec. 1413.

The abbot of Milton (*Middelton*), the prior of Monkton Farleigh (*Farlee*), the abbess of Shaftesbury (*Schafton*), the abbess of Tarrant (*Tarent*) and Ralph de Nubibus, prior of Frampton, owe procurations of various years, and are therefore to be denounced as excommunicate in Salisbury cath. and their own churches, to be cited and to have their revenues sequestrated. The abbots of Abbotsbury (*Abbottesbury*), Bindon (*Bynedon*), Cerne and Sherborne (*Schirborn*), the dean and chapter of Salisbury, the priors of Bradenstoke (*Bradenstok*) and Hurley (*Hurlee*), the abbesses of Wilton (*Wylton*) and Lacock (*Lacok*), the priors of Poughley (*Poughlee*) and Wareham (*Warham*) and William Coventre, farmer of Ogbourne (*Okeborne*) priory, are to be warned to pay the procurations owed on pain of excommunication and cited etc. Careful inquiry is to be made concerning the goods and chattels of John [Mortymer],[1] rector of Langley Burrell (*Langele Burell*), who recently died there, and of Stephen, who died at Mere in Wiltshire, honorary papal chaplains: their goods are to be sequestrated and those holding them are to be cited to appear before 28 Feb. In addition, the bp. is to notify the collector of any churches in his diocese appropriated to monasteries, priories and other ecclesiastical places or persons from the time of Popes Alexander V and John XXIII, and their occupiers are to be warned, cited and sequestrated.

[1. Instituted 23 Sept. 1396 (Reg. Medford fo. 42v).]

1022 [Fo. 149/59] Commission to M. John Colles B.Cn.L. to act as official of the peculiar jurisdiction of Potterne, Marlborough (*Marleburgh*), Devizes (*Devyses*) and Lavington (*Lavyngton*). He is to have power of holding chapters and synods, of hearing and determining all cases in the bishop's jurisdiction, both instance and *ex officio*, of correcting and punishing crimes, of testamentary jurisdiction, of declaring sentences of suspension, excommunication and interdict, and of imposing sequestrations in cases permitted by law. [Undated.]

1023 Commission to M. John Colles B.Cn.L. to act as the bishop's sequestrator and commissary general in the archdeaconries of Wiltshire and Berkshire. He is to have power of correcting and punishing crimes, of testamentary jurisdiction, of seeking and receiving the bishop's spiritual revenues, of inquiring concerning the non-residence of clergy, of sequestrating the revenues of clergy who let their benefices to farm without licence or who fail to keep the buildings of their benefices in repair or who transfer money for repairs received from their predecessors into other uses, or of citing such clergy to appear before the bp. [Undated.]

1024 Commission to the parish priest of St. Martin, Salisbury, John Laurence and Richard Hyllarye, at the petition of Robert Crome of Salisbury, to cite the subdean of Salisbury cath. who has no jurisdiction over Crome yet has falsely accused him of adultery with Elizabeth, wife of Henry Suthwyk of Salisbury. When Crome successfully purged himself from the alleged crime with the number of compurgators required by the subdean, the latter continued to summon him to appear before him at each of his chapters or sessions until he should pay at least twenty shillings for a letter of purgation, whereupon Crome appealed to the bishop's court of audience. The commissaries are to inhibit the subdean's jurisdiction in this case and to cite him to appear before the bp. [Undated.]

1025 [Fo. 149v/59v] Commission[1] for the sequestration of the revenues of Beechingstoke (*Bychyngstok*) church, whose rector, Walter Elyot, the parishioners complain has gone to remote places unknown to them and has neglected the cure of souls for a long time, leaving the church without a suitable chaplain to minister there. Now that various public warnings to reside have been made to Elyot, the bp. has decided to sequestrate the revenues of the church. The commissary is to publish this sentence and to sequestrate the revenues, reserving a portion for the maintenance of a suitable chaplain to serve in the church in the absence of the rector. [Undated.][2]

[1. Recipient not stated.
2. Between Elyot's institution 11 May 1412 (**323**) and Hallum's departure for the council of Constance 19 Nov. 1414 (**525**); probably in 1414.]

1026 Commission to M. John Aylmer D.C.L., canon of Chichester, and M. Simon Sydenham D.C.L., canon of Salisbury, to inquire into the proposed appropriation of the church of Blandford Forum (*Blaneford*) in Dorset to the priory of Christchurch (*ecclesie Christi de Twynham*), dioc. Winchester. Henry Lacy, earl of Lincoln, gave the canons by charter certain lands, tenements, rents and services within his manor of Kingston Lacy (*Kyngeston Lacy*) and Holt, until he or his successors should provide them with lands of greater value or an ecclesiastical benefice, on condition that the canons find two chaplains to celebrate at a chantry in the chapel of the earl's manor of Kingston Lacy. The value of the grant has never exceeded ten marks [£6 13*s* 4*d*] a year, [Fo. 150/60] yet the canons have faithfully provided two chaplains as stipulated, until now this is beyond their resources. Although the priory was formerly sufficiently endowed, yet because it is situated on a public route, the burden of hospitality to a large number of visitors has become too great for it. Moreover, the priory's revenues have been reduced by floods, epidemics, fires and storms, until now they are insufficient to fulfil the terms of its foundation. King Henry has therefore granted the priory the advowson of the church of Blandford Forum, which was in the patronage of his duchy of Lancaster (*Lancastrie*),[1] and has asked the bp. to incorporate, annex and unite it to the priory. Its annual value is not more than eight pounds of English money, according to the taxation of the tenth. As the bp. has no certain knowledge of the foregoing and cannot personally proceed in the business, as he is occupied with other serious matters,[2] the commissaries are to summon the rector of Blandford Forum and others, and to make a full inquiry by trustworthy clergy and laymen into the proposed union. If they find the reasons to be true and the union justified, they are to unite, incorporate and annex the church and all its appurtenances to the priory with the bishop's authority, so that when the rector resigns or dies, the prior and conv. shall have possession of the church and its revenues. The bp., the chapter of Salisbury cath. and the archd. of Dorset are to be indemnified, and a suitable portion is to be reserved for the maintenance of a vicar, to be instituted by the bp. London, bishop's manor in the parish of St. Bride, Fleet Street (*Fletestret*), 12 Nov. 1414.

[1. *CPR 1413–16*, p. 225 (25 May 1414).
2. He left the same month for the council of Constance, **525**.]

1027 [Fo. 150^v/60^v] Notification of M. Simon Sydenham D.C.L., canon of Salisbury and commissary of the bp. of Salisbury, at present abroad, to

Thomas Talbot, prior of Christchurch (*ecclesie Christi de Twynham*), dioc. Winchester, and the same conv., concerning the appropriation of the church of Blandford Forum (*Blaneford*). The commissary summoned the rector of Blandford Forum and others to an inquiry into the proposed appropriation and found the reasons for it to be true. After thorough discussion with the chapter of Salisbury and after weighing all considerations, with the express agreement of the chapter and with the king's licence, at the request of M. John Morton B.C.L., the convent's proctor, he decreed and pronounced in favour of the appropriation, and he incorporated, appropriated, annexed and united the church with all its appurtenances to the priory. A portion was reserved for a vicar who should be presented by the conv. to the bp. for admission and institution. The conv. is granted the right of taking full possession of the church on its voidance by the present rector, and of using the revenues for the priory, without anyone's permission or licence.

[Fo. 151/61] With the consent of the dean and chapter of Salisbury and the prior and conv., an annual pension of eight shillings is reserved for the bp. of Salisbury, to be paid in the cath. at the feast of the Annunciation of the B.V.M. [25 March], to compensate for the revenues of the church which he used to receive at every vacancy. An annual pension of 6*s* 8*d* is reserved for the dean and chapter of Salisbury, to be paid on the same day, to compensate for the revenues of the vacant church which they used to receive during a vacancy of the see. An annual pension of forty pence is reserved for the archd. of Dorset, to be paid on the same day, to compensate for his share in the revenues of the church in time of vacancy. Two shillings are to be distributed among the poor parishioners of Blandford Forum every 25 March. If the prior and conv. fail to make these payments, the revenues of the church will be *ipso facto* sequestrated until payment is made with damages. The law of precedence, jurisdiction (both ordinary and diocesan), special rights and customs due to the bp. and the chapter are safeguarded. Sealed with the seals of the archdeaconry of Salisbury, the dean and chapter of Salisbury and the official of the archd. of Dorset. Salisbury cath., 21 Feb. 1415. Those present were John Smyth, vicar in Salisbury cath., M. John Warham B.C.L. and M. Peter Upaven B.C.L., notaries public, and other specially summoned witnesses.

These letters were drawn up in public form by William de Dunham, clerk (dioc. Lincoln), notary public by papal authority, who has subscribed his name and affixed his seal. He agrees that four small mistakes in the letters were made not deliberately but by error. [Fo. 151v/61v] The dean and chapter of Salisbury approve the appropriation, give their common consent and have affixed their common seal.[1] The archd. of Dorset consents to all the foregoing and has affixed the seal of his office which he has to hand.

[1. Cf. Pountney, p. 14, dean and chapter's agreement, 23 Feb. 1415.]

Ordination Lists*

[All the ordinations are by Robert, bp. of Salisbury, unless otherwise stated.]

1028 [Fo. 158] Orders celebrated in the church of St. Nicholas, Abingdon (*Abendon*), 13 Apr. 1408.

Exorcist

John Wyly, dioc. Salisbury

Acolytes

Bartholomew Gore, dioc. Salisbury

William Casbard, dioc. Salisbury

John Herward, rector of Winterbourne Farringdon (*Wynterburn German*)

Thomas Moston, rector of Aston Flamville (*Aston Flamvyl*), dioc. Lincoln, lett. dim.

John Colne, rector of Methley (*Methelay*), dioc. York (*Ebor'*), lett. dim.

John Wyly [as above]

Thomas Ewesham, Thomas Canon, Thomas Salford and Richard Henreth, monks of Abingdon

Thomas Blysset and Thomas Hoggenorton, canons of Osney (*Osneye*), dioc. Lincoln

John Love, dioc. Bath and Wells

William Grover, dioc. Winchester, and William Estecourt, dioc. Worcester, fellows of New College, Oxford

John Wymbelton

Thomas Trevergy, dioc. Salisbury

Thomas Coyne, dioc. St. Davids, lett. dim.

Subdeacons

Thomas Ewesham, Thomas Canon, Thomas Salford, Richard Henreth, Thomas Blysset and Thomas Hoggenorton [as above]

Thomas Moston, rector of Aston Flamville (*Aston Flamvil*), dioc. York [*rectius* Lincoln], lett. dim. by chapter *sede vacante*, title of benefice [cf. above]

Robert Whittok, vicar choral of Salisbury cath., title of benefice

John Daley, dioc. Salisbury, title of abbot and conv. of Sherborne (*Shirburn*)

David John, dioc. St. Davids, rector of Llangynllo (*Llangenllo*), lett. dim., title of benefice

Bartholomew Gore, dioc. Salisbury, title of abbess and conv. of St. Mary, Winchester

*In this edition, details relating to an ordinand given on his first occurrence are not repeated subsequently, if they are the same. Fresh information and variants of names on second and later occurrences are noted. The order of names in the lists has been preserved. The appellation 'frater' for regular clergy, which is appended in the register with some inconsistency, has been omitted when there is other evidence of status.

John Wakerffeld, dioc. Durham, title of his office of perpetual vicar in St. Davids cath., lett. dim.

John Nanskelly, dioc. Exeter, title of Rewley abbey (*de Regali loco iuxta Oxon*), lett. dim.

William Sudbury, dioc. Norwich, title of Hailes abbey (*Hayles*), dioc. Worcester, lett. dim.

John Wymbelton [cf. above], dioc. Winchester, title of his patronage (*patronatus sui*), lett. dim.

Thomas Norman and [Fo. 158ᵛ] John Smalbon, dioc. Salisbury, title of hospital of St. John, Lechlade (*Lecchelade*)

John Maynolf, dioc. Lincoln, title of prioress and conv. of Sopwell (*Soppewelle*), lett. dim.

William Festbury, rector of Tarrant Keynston (*Kayneston*), title of benefice

Deacons

John Bemond, monk of Abingdon (*Abyndon*)

Roger Capytane, rector of Hopesay (*Hopesaye*), dioc. Hereford, lett. dim. title of benefice

Thomas Walter, dioc. Worcester, title of hospital of Elsingspital (*Elsyngspitell*), London, lett. dim.

William Selke, dioc. Salisbury, title of abbot and conv. of Abbotsbury (*Abbottysbiry*)

William Westgate, dioc. Coventry and Lichfield, title of hospital of St. John the Baptist, Oxford, lett. dim.

M. Stephen Brakeley, rector of Ayot St. Lawrence (*Ayot*), dioc. Lincoln, lett. dim., title of benefice

Richard Stourton, dioc. Salisbury, rector of Milton Podimore (*Mydelton in Pudemore*), dioc. Bath and Wells, title of benefice

Thomas Perys, rector of Fittleton (*Fytelton*), dioc. Salisbury, title of benefice

John Newent, dioc. Hereford, rector of Tortworth (*Torteworth*), dioc. Worcester, lett. dim., title of benefice

Philip David, rector of Llansadurnen (*Lansdorney*), dioc. St. Davids, by papal lett. dim., title of benefice

Priests

Roger Radeclyf, rector of Yoxall (*Yoxhale*), dioc. Coventry and Lichfield, lett. dim., title of benefice

John Kemp, dioc. Lincoln, title of hospital of Scalthwaiterigg (*Kyrkeby Kendale*), dioc. York, lett. dim.

Thomas Lange, rector of Instow (*Yenstowe*), dioc. Exeter, lett. dim., title of benefice

John Besewyle, dioc. Salisbury, title of Lacock (*Lacok*) abbey

Philip Payne, dioc. St. Davids, title of Alcester (*Alcestr'*) abbey, dioc. Worcester, lett. dim. of abp. of Canterbury, *sede vacante*

Henry Person, title of fellowship of New College, Oxford, by papal privilege

John Inelyth, rector of Oldcastle (*Aldestre*), dioc. Coventry and Lichfield, lett. dim., title of benefice

1029 Orders celebrated in the church of Sutton Courtenay (*Sutton*), 9 June 1408.

Acolytes

Edward Wych, dioc. Salisbury

John Teffont, rector of Broughton Gifford (*Browgton*)

John Stowgton, dioc. Salisbury, rector of Newnham (*Newham*)

William Penbegyl and William Grene, dioc. Exeter, lett. dim.

William Payne, dioc. Salisbury

Thomas Chakendene, Stephen de Bray and Thomas Henle, monks of Reading (*Redyng*)

John Martyn, dioc. Salisbury

John Oxenford and John Witnay, monks of Rewley (*de Regali loco*)

William Hoper, rector of Aberedw (*Aberedwy*), dioc. St. Davids, lett. dim.

James Vyttelton, dioc. Salisbury

Robert Redyng, Thomas Burcestre, Nicholas Redyng and Edward London, canons of Notley (*Nottele*), dioc. Lincoln, lett. dim.

Subdeacons

Edmund Eyr, dioc. Salisbury, canon of Poulton (*Polton*)

[Fo. 159] John Colne [as **1028**]

John Kendale, dioc. York, title of prior and conv. of Rochester cath., lett. dim.

William Forster, dioc. Ely (*Elien'*), title of abbess of Godstow, dioc. Lincoln, lett. dim.

William Dalderby, dioc. Salisbury, title of abbot and conv. of Eynsham (*Eynesham*), dioc. Lincoln

Richard Eustace, dioc. London, title of hall or college of Merton, Oxford, lett. dim.

John Oxenford, John Witnay, William Hoper, Thomas Chakendene, Stephen de Bray, Thomas Henle, Robert Redyng, Thomas Burcestre, Nicholas Redyng, Edward London, John Stowgton and John Teffont [as above]

Deacons

John Smalbon, Thomas Norman, Bartholomew Gore, John Daley, John Nanskelly and John Maynolf [as **1028**]

John Kyng, dioc. Norwich, title of Osney (*Osneya*) abbey, dioc. Lincoln, lett. dim.

John Wymbelton, dioc. Winchester, title of his patrimony, lett. dim. [cf. **1028**]

Thomas Evesham [as Ewesham, **1028**]

Thomas Canon and Thomas Salford [as **1028**]

Richard Henred [as Henreth, **1028**]

Priests

Walter ap David, rector of Llanychaer (*Llannerchaeth*), dioc. St. Davids, lett. dim., title of benefice

Stephen Brakeley [as **1028**]

Robert Chiltenham, monk of Reading
David ap Rys, rector of Brightwalton (*Brythwalton*), title of benefice
John Newent [as **1028**]

1030 Orders celebrated in the chapel of Potterne (*Poterne*) manor, 22 Sept. 1408.

[Fo. 159v] *Acolytes*
John Dolle, dioc. Salisbury
Robert Bergham, dioc. Canterbury, lett. dim.
John Preston, dioc. Salisbury
William Wynterborne, clerk of Salisbury
John Douke, dioc. Salisbury
John Pulton, dioc. Coventry and Lichfield, lett. dim.
Thomas Plomptre, dioc. York, lett. dim.
John Taylur, dioc. Salisbury
Hugh Ludelow, monk of Abingdon (*Abyndon*)
Thomas Gloucestre, monk of Stanley

Subdeacons
David Wyllyam, dioc. St. Davids, lett. dim. of Thomas, abp. of Canterbury, *sede vacante*, title of abbot and conv. of Cerne
Richard Bere, dioc. Salisbury, title of abbot and conv. of Abbotsbury (*Abbodesbury*)
Robert Bergham [as above], title of hall or college of Merton, Oxford
William Walsh *alias* More, dioc. Cloyne (*Clonen'*), lett. dim., title of master and conv. of hospital of St. John the Baptist, Bridgwater (*Bryggewater*), dioc. Bath and Wells
John Preston [as above], title of New College, Oxford
John Pulton [as above], title of prior and conv. of St. Margaret, Marlborough (*Marleburgh*)
John Tourner, dioc. Salisbury, title of abbot and conv. of Abbotsbury
Richard Wyseman, dioc. Bath and Wells, lett. dim., title of abbot and conv. of Vaudey (*Vallis Dei*), dioc. Lincoln
Hugh Ludelow and Thomas Gloucestre [as above]

Deacons
Richard Eustace M.A. [as **1029**]
John Kandale [as Kendale, **1029**]
John Teffont [as **1029**]
William Rooke, dioc. Salisbury, title of abbot and conv. of Abbotsbury
Thomas Freman, dioc. Bath and Wells, lett. dim., title of prior and conv. of Montacute (*domus Montis Acuti*)
Nicholas Sexpenne, dioc. Salisbury, title of his free chapel of Frome Whitfield (*Fromewhafeld*)
Nicholas Hale, dioc. York, lett. dim., title of hospital of St. John, Lechlade (*Lecchelade*), dioc. Worcester
William Dalderby [as **1029**]

John Chesham, friar minor of Salisbury
Roger Lye, brother of conventual church of Edington (*Edyngdon*)

Priests
John Clerk, dioc. Salisbury, title of abbot [*rectius* prior] and conv. of Ivychurch (*de Ederose*)
John Nanskelly [as **1028–9**]
Robert Cardemaker, dioc. Salisbury, title of priory of Bradenstoke (*Bradenestoke*)
John Kyng [as **1029**]
John Strecche, dioc. Salisbury, title of prioress and conv. of Bindon (*Byndedon*)
John Maynolf [as **1028–9**]
[Fo. 160] John Sorell, dioc. Salisbury, title of priory of Easton (*Eston*)
Laurence Geffray, dioc. Salisbury, title of priory of Ivychurch
Bartholomew Gore and John Smalbon [as **1028–9**]
Richard Lane, dioc. Salisbury, title of master and brothers of the house or hospital of St. John the Baptist, Wells
William Westage [as Westgate, **1028**]
Thomas Norman [as **1028–9**]
John Bisley and William Chipstede, friars minor of Salisbury
Thomas Evesham [as Ewesham, **1028–9**]
Thomas Chepman, monk of Stanley

1031 Orders celebrated in the conventual church of Sherborne (*Schirborn*), 22 Dec. 1408.

Acolytes
Robert atte the Chapell, dioc. Lincoln, lett. dim.
Thomas Coll, William Hoser, Walter Byschop and William Wutton, dioc. Salisbury
Thomas Colman and William Thyrlby, vicars choral of Salisbury cath.
William Boure, dioc. Salisbury
George Radeclif, rector of dioc. [Coventry and] Lichfield, lett. dim.
Peter Partrich, dioc. London, lett. dim.
William Wychrym and Bartholomew Nyell, dioc. Salisbury

Subdeacons
John Dolle [as **1030**], title of abbot and conv. of Abbotsbury (*Abbodesbury*)
Richard Bothum, vicar choral of Salisbury cath., title of benefice
Nicholas Rowdys of Calne, dioc. Salisbury, title of abbot and conv. of Stanley (*Stanlegh*)
Roger Clottham, dioc. Salisbury, title of priory and conv. of Poughley (*Poghele*)
Thomas Aleyn, dioc. Rochester, lett. dim., title of prior and conv. of Tonbridge (*Tonebrigg*)
Peter Partrich [as above], title of monastery of St. Frideswide, Oxford
William Thyrlby [as above]

William Savage, friar preacher of Salisbury
Thomas Gardyner, John Boskeir, Henry Trente and William Prechour, monks of Sherborne
Henry Brydport, monk of Abbotsbury (*Abbotesbury*)
George Radeclif [cf. above], rector of Eccleston
Robert atte the Chapell [as above], title of the patrimony of John Golefir, esquire

Deacons
Edmund Dotton, rector of Aston-on-Trent (*Aston super Trent*), dioc. [Coventry and] Lichfield, lett. dim., title of benefice
William Walsh *alias* More [as **1030**]
[Fo. 160^{v}] John Pulton [as **1030**]
William Laurence, vicar choral of Salisbury cath., title of benefice
Richard Bere [as **1030**]
David Willyam [as Wyllyam, **1030**]
Robert Whyttok [as Whittok, **1028**]
Thomas Sampson, vicar choral of Salisbury cath., title of benefice
John Covte and John Wynter, monks of Milton (*Middelton*)
John Byri, monk of Abbotsbury

Priests
John Kendale [as **1029–30**]
John Comyn *alias* Felys, rector of Alton (*Aleton*), dioc. Salisbury, title of benefice
William Rooke [as **1030**]
William Forster of Tydd St. Giles (*Tyd sancti Egidii*) [as **1029**]
Nicholas Hale [as **1030**]
Thomas de Moston [as **1028**]
Nicholas Newton, friar minor of Dorchester (*Dorcestrie*)
John Aspelon and Thomas Chesham, friars minor
John Chesham and Roger Lye [as **1030**]
Robert Clopton, monk of Montacute (*Mountagu*)
William Selke [as **1028**]

1032 Orders celebrated by John [Greenlaw], bp. of Sultaniyek (*Soltanien'*),[1] by authority of Robert, bp. of Salisbury, while Adam de Mottrum was vicar general, in the conventual church of the friars minor, Salisbury, 21 Sept. 1409.

Exorcists
Thomas Robyn, Richard Mey, Ralph Bredford and John Burell, dioc. Salisbury

Acolytes
Richard Horn, Walter Bagge, Henry Bedwyn and John Krundon, dioc. Salisbury
John Burstow, friar minor of Salisbury

Subdeacons

Roger Smyht, dioc. Salisbury, title of the provost and fellows of St. Edmund's college, city of Salisbury

John Croft, friar preacher of Salisbury

John Burstow [as above]

Deacons

Thomas Chakenden, Stephen Brey and Thomas Henley [as Chakendene, Bray and Henle, **1029**]

Hugh Lowdelow [as Ludelow, **1030**]

James Man, friar preacher of Salisbury

Henry Trynt [as Trente, **1031**]

William Thyrlby and Richard Bothum [as **1031**]

[Fo. 161] *Priests*

John Grymsell, friar preacher of Salisbury

Thomas Clyve, canon of Ivychurch (*Yvekirche*)

Thomas Salford [as **1028–9**]

Thomas Mor, friar minor of Salisbury

John Teffont [as **1029–30**]

John Colas, dioc. Salisbury, title of abbot and conv. of Abbotsbury (*Abbodesbury*)

[1. *Handbook of British Chronology*, p. 267.]

1033 Orders celebrated in the chapel of Ramsbury (*Remmesbury*) manor, 21 Dec. 1409.

Exorcist

John Henton, dioc. Salisbury

Acolytes

Simon Whitrat, dioc. Ely, lett. dim.

David Smyth *alias* Presse, dioc. Hereford, lett. dim.

Ralph Kyngysford, dioc. Exeter, lett. dim.

John Craas, dioc. Salisbury

William Ulff, dioc. Lincoln, lett. dim.

John Henton [as above]

Thomas Yarwell, monk of Marlborough (*Marleburgh*)

Subdeacons

John Sherman, dioc. Lincoln, lett. dim., title of prior and conv. of Poughley (*Pogheley*)

Henry Bedewynd [as Bedwyn, **1032**], title of prior and conv. of Poughley

Thomas Hancok, dioc. Salisbury, title of monastery of Milton (*Middelton*)

M. William Ulff [as above], rector of Playden, dioc. Chichester, title of his benefice

William Draper, rector of Kirk Bramwith (*Bramwyth*), dioc. York, title of his benefice, lett. dim.

David Smyth *alias* Presse [as above], title of abbot and conv. of Medmenham

Deacons

John Trusser, dioc. Salisbury, title of abbot and conv. of Dorchester (*Dorckacestre*)

Nicholas Rowdys [as **1031**]

William Compton, Thomas Dornby, John Laurens and John Chynnok, canons of Bradenstoke (*Bradenestoke*)

Nicholas Stodley, monk of Stanley (*Stanlegh*)

Thomas Glosester [as Gloucestre, **1030**]

Priests

M. Roger Capytayne [as Capytane, **1028**]

Robert Bregham [as Bergham, **1030**]

William Payn [as Payne, **1029**], title of abbot and conv. of Osney (*Oseney*), dioc. Lincoln

Hugh Lowdelow [as Ludelow, **1030**, **1032**]

1034 Orders celebrated in Salisbury cath., 22 March 1410.

[Fo. 161v] *Acolytes*

John Westmore, Hugh Rede and Richard Wayneman, vicars choral of Salisbury cath.

Thomas Manssell, William Seybod, Richard Fendor, John Grey, William Knell, Robert Gylle and Peter Massy, dioc. Salisbury

Thomas Elme and Thomas Remmesbury, brothers of the house of Bonhommes, Edington (*Edyngdon*)

Subdeacons

John Westmore and Hugh Rede [as above], title of their benefices

William Hende and William Love, vicars choral of Salisbury cath., title of their benefices

William Ingram, dioc. Salisbury, title of abbot and conv. of Milton (*Middelton*)

John Baker, dioc. Salisbury, title of abbess and conv. of Tarrant (*Tarent*)

Walter Buschump, dioc. Salisbury, title of abbot and conv. of Cerne

William Hoyser [as Hoser, **1031**], title of abbot and conv. of Sherborne (*Schirborn*)

William David of Melksham (*Melkesham*), dioc. Salisbury, title of abbot and conv. of Stanley (*Stanlegh*)

Richard Huchyn, dioc. Salisbury, title of abbot and conv. of Bindon (*Bynedon*)

Thomas Isabell, dioc. Salisbury, title of hospital of St. John, Bridgwater (*Bruggewater*), dioc. Bath and Wells

John Brone, dioc. Salisbury, title of abbess and conv. of Tarrant

John Wayte, dioc. Salisbury, title of prior and conv. of St. Margaret, Marlborough (*Marleburgh*)

John atte Welle, dioc. Bath and Wells, lett. dim., title of abbot of Muchelney (*Muchelnyne*)

Ralph Hogele, dioc. Salisbury, title of the patrimony of Thomas Tyrewyn, esquire

William Knapp, dioc. Bath and Wells, title of Ivychurch (*de Ederose*)

John Wilyam, dioc. Salisbury, title of abbot and conv. of Sherborne

Thomas Elme and Thomas Remmesbury [as above]

Deacons

M. John Turry, rector of Handborough (*Hannebergh*), dioc. Lincoln, lett. dim., title of benefice

Clement Pittys, dioc. Lincoln, lett. dim., title of hospital of St. John the Baptist outside the East Gate, Oxford

Thomas Hancok [as **1033**]

William Spenser, dioc. Salisbury, title of abbess and conv. of Tarrant

Roger Smyth [as Smyht, **1032**]

John Croft [as **1032**]

John Cerne, friar minor of Salisbury

Priests

Henry Bedewynde [as Bedwyn, **1032–3**]

Thomas atte Mylle, dioc. Salisbury, title of prior and conv. of Poughley (*Poghley*)

Nicholas Rowdys [as **1031**, **1033**]

Richard Stourton, rector of Milton Podimore (*Middelton*), dioc. Salisbury [*rectius* Bath and Wells, cf. **1028**]

William Mere, dioc. Bath and Wells, title of hospital of St. John the Baptist, Wells

Richard Bothum [as **1031–2**]

William Compton [as **1033**]

Thomas Thornbury [as Dornbry, **1033**]

1035 [Fo. 162] Orders celebrated in the chapel of Potterne manor, 17 May 1410.

Acolytes

Nicholas Edward, Walter Smyth, John Donne, Richard Panyse, John Hele, Thomas Walter, Thomas Clement, William Berbryt and John Jerveys

Subdeacons

Nicholas Brook, dioc. Exeter, title of monastery of Dunkeswell, same dioc., lett. dim.

William Casberd [as Casbard, **1028**], title of abbot and conv. of Reading (*Radyng*)

William Bracer, dioc. Salisbury, title of abbot and conv. of Cerne

John Bemestre and Thomas Brydport, monks of Cerne

Deacons

William David [as **1034**]

John Marchall, dioc. York, lett. dim., title of prioress and conv. of Studley (*Stadle*), dioc. Lincoln

Richard Huchyn [as **1034**]
Thomas Isabell [as **1034**, variant *Bregewater*]
John Wyllyam [as Wilyam, **1034**]
John atte Wylle *alias* Baker [as atte Welle, **1034**]
William Hosier [as Hoser, Hoyser, **1031**, **1034**]
William Hende, dioc. Exeter, lett. dim. [as **1034**]
William Love [as **1034**]
Ralph Hogele [as **1034**, variant *Tyrwyn*]
Nicholas Ockombe, John Sutton, John Trent and William Trent, monks of Montacute (*de Montagu*)
William Prechur [as Prechour, **1031**]
John London, monk of Cerne
Thomas Elme and Thomas Remmesbury, monks of Stanley [cf. **1034**, where said to be of Edington]

Priests
Clement Pyttys [as Pittys, **1034**]
Walter Bagge [as **1032**], title of abbot and conv. of Cerne
John Colne [as **1028–9**, variant *Metheley*]
M. John Turry [as **1034**]
Henry Trent [as Trente, Trynt, **1031–2**]
Nicholas Stodeley [as Stodley, **1033**]
Thomas Gloucett [as Gloucestre, Glosester, **1030**, **1033**]
John Frome, canon of Longleat (*Langlete*)

1036 [Fo. 162^{v}] Orders celebrated in the conventual church of Sherborne (*Shirborn*), 20 Sept. 1410.

Acolytes
Gilbert Hallum, M. John Stone, Walter Peynter, William Chapman, Edward Veyser, Walter Folde, John Corneys, William Mayne, William Servyngton, John Yorke, Thomas Hardy, William Symone and Thomas Hyllard, dioc. Salisbury

Subdeacons
Nicholas Edward [cf. **1035**], dioc. Salisbury, title of prior and conv. of St. Frideswide, Oxford, dioc. Lincoln
John Taylour [as Taylur, **1030**], title of abbot and conv. of Milton (*Middelton*)
Thomas Bernard of Crudwell (*Crudewell*) and John Gerard, dioc. Salisbury, title of prior and conv. of Bradenstoke (*Bradenestok*)
John Dun [cf. Donne, **1035**], dioc. Salisbury, title of abbot and conv. of Milton
Richard Weyneman [cf. Wayneman, **1034**], dioc. Exeter, lett. dim., title of his benefice
Richard Walton, dioc. York, lett. dim., title of rector and conv. of Ashridge (*Assherigg*), dioc. Lincoln

Deacons

John Dyer, dioc. Bath and Wells, lett. dim., title of abbot and conv. of Muchelney

John Broune [as Brone, **1034**]

John Baker [as **1034**]

Thomas Scherde, dioc. Bath and Wells, title of prior and conv. of Montacute (*Montis Acuti*), lett. dim.

Walter Buschump [as **1034**]

William Casberd [as Casbard, **1028**, **1035**]

Nicholas Broke [as Brook, **1035**]

Walter Clay, dioc. Bath and Wells, lett. dim., title of monastery of Muchelney

Priests

William David [as **1034–5**]

Richard Hawen, dioc. Bath and Wells, lett. dim., title of prior and conv. of Montacute

Thomas Isabell [as **1034–5**, variant *Brygewater*]

Richard Huchyn [as **1034–5**]

John Hobbes, dioc. Bath and Wells, lett. dim., title of hospital of St. John the Baptist, Bath (*Bathon'*) [*rectius* Wells]

Thomas Hancok [as **1033–4**]

Richard Mason, dioc. Bath and Wells, lett. dim., title of hospital of St. John the Baptist, Bath (*Bathon'*) [*rectius* Wells]

William Oke, dioc. Bath and Wells, lett. dim., title of abbot and conv. of Muchelney

John Willyam [as Wilyam, Wyllyam, **1034–5**]

John Smyth, dioc. Bath and Wells, lett. dim., title of abbot and conv. of Muchelney

Laurence Brystow, dioc. Bath and Wells, lett. dim., title of prior of St. Frideswide, Oxford

William Spenser [as **1034**]

William Love [as **1034–5**]

John Kyngton, canon of Keynsham (*Kenesham*), dioc. Bath and Wells, lett. dim.

William Eretage and Richard Shirborn, monks of Abbotsbury (*Abbotesbury*)

Nicholas Otecombe, John Sutthon, William Trente and John Trente [as Ockombe, Sutton and Trent, **1035**]

William Prechur [as Prechour, **1031**, **1035**]

1037 [Fo. 163] Orders celebrated in the chapel of Sonning (*Sonnyng*) manor, 20 Dec. 1410.

Acolytes

John Arteys, dioc. Durham, lett. dim.

Stephen Colman, Thomas Uppenore and John Walmyster, dioc. Salisbury

John Coryngdon, dioc. Exeter, lett. dim.

John Ychenden, John Newman and William Hukevyll, canons of Bisham (*Brustlesham*)
Thomas Barvot, Walter Andenere, Thomas Yarnemowthe and John Fynchamstede, monks of Reading (*Radyng*)
Robert Wodyll, John Borstall, William Welton, William Grene and Peter de Gystella, friars minor of Reading

Subdeacons
M. John Stone [cf. **1036**] B.C.L., rector of Berwick St. John (*Berewyk sancti Johannis*), title of benefice
John Asley, monk of Reading
Thomas Barvot and Walter Andenere [as above]
William de Staneley, dioc. Coventry and Lichfield, lett. dim., title of abbot and conv. of Whalley (*Whallay*)
Thomas Uppenore [as above], title of warden and college of the free chapel of St. George, Windsor (*Wyndesore*)
William Taylour, dioc. Salisbury, title of prior and conv. of Longleat (*Langley*)
William Servyngton [as **1036**], rector of Whatley, dioc. Bath and Wells, title of benefice
John Tylbery, canon of Bisham
John Ychenden [as above]

Deacons
Nicholas Edward [as **1035–6**]
Thomas Bernard [as **1036**, variant *Bradenastok*]
Robert Stopford, dioc. Coventry and Lichfield, lett. dim., title of abbot and conv. of Vale Royal (*de Valle regali*)
Thomas Penreth, dioc. Carlisle, lett. dim., title of prior and conv. of Lanercost
John de Capella and John de Mota, friars minor of Reading
John Newerk, rector of Skirpenbeck (*Skirpenbek*), dioc. York, lett. dim., title of benefice

Priests
Nicholas Brooke [as Brook, Broke, **1035–6**]
William Bryt, monk of St. Albans

1038 Orders celebrated in the chapel of Sonning (*Sonnyng*) manor, 28 March 1411.

Subdeacons
Thomas Yarnemowthe and John Fynchamstede [as **1037**]

Deacons
John Hassele, Thomas Barwot and Walter Andener [as Asley, Barvot and Andenere, **1037**]
John Chyveley and John Chaddesle, canons of Notley, dioc. Lincoln, lett. dim.

Priests
William de Staneley [as **1037**]
Edward London [as **1029**]

[This is followed by an incomplete entry, consisting only of the date 5 Apr. 1411, Palm Sunday.]

1039 [Fo. 163v] Orders celebrated in the chapel of Sonning (*Sonnyng*) manor, 11 Apr. 1411.

Acolytes
John Bawdewyn and Ralph Hyckys, dioc. Salisbury
M. Nicholas Bildeston, dioc. Exeter, lett. dim.

Subdeacons
Stephen Colman [as **1037**], title of abbot and conv. of Bindon (*Bynedon*)
John Corndon, dioc. Exeter, lett. dim., title of prior and conv. of Hurley
John Patrych, dioc. Salisbury, title of abbess and conv. of Tarrant (*Tarent*)
Alexander Lenne, dioc. Salisbury, title of abbot and conv. of Milton (*Middelton*)
Simon Younge, dioc. Salisbury, title of prior and conv. of Ivychurch (*de Ederose*)
William Underwode, dioc. Salisbury, title of prior and conv. of Bradenstoke (*Bradenstok*)
John Queynton, dioc. Lincoln, lett. dim., title of abbot and conv. of Reading (*Radyng*)
Robert Stamford, dioc. Salisbury, title of abbot and conv. of Forde (*Ford*), Bath and Wells dioc.
M. Nicholas Bildeston [as above], rector of Phillack (*sancte Felicitatis in Cornubia*), title of benefice
Robert Raynhill, dioc. Coventry and Lichfield, lett. dim., title of prior and conv. of Upholland (*Holond*)

Deacons
M. Richard Baron and M. Thomas Martyn, dioc. Salisbury, and M. Roger Gates, dioc. Chichester, fellows of Merton (*Martonhall*), Oxford, title of benefice
M. John Stone [as **1036–7**]
John Taylour [as Taylur, **1030**, **1036**]
John Gerard [as **1036**]
William Nychol, dioc. Lincoln, lett. dim., title of monastery of St. Frideswide, Oxford

Priests
M. Richard Stapulton, dioc. York, lett. dim., title of Balliol Hall (*aula Ballioli*), Oxford, dioc. Lincoln
Richard Falus, dioc. York, lett. dim., title of hospital of St. John the Baptist outside the East Gate, Oxford

Peter Hert, dioc. Salisbury, title of priory of Christchurch (*ecclesie Christi de Twynham*), dioc. Winchester
John Artays [cf. Arteys, **1037**], dioc. Durham, lett. dim., title of house of canons of 'Assheley', same dioc.
William Taillour [as Taylour, **1037**]
Walter Buschump [as **1034**, **1036**]
William Casberd [as Casbard, **1028**, **1035–6**]
M. John Herward [as **1028**, variant *Wynterborne Germayn*], title of benefice

1040 Orders celebrated in the chapel of Potterne (*Poterne*) manor, 6 June 1411.

Exorcists
John Baron and John Baker, dioc. Salisbury

Acolytes
Thomas Chireton, Thomas Ferour, John Donyton, Hugh Hakker, Robert Flechar, William Barbour and James Chydyok, dioc. Salisbury
William Mewsham, dioc. Exeter, lett. dim.
Robert Hete, dioc. Lincoln, lett. dim.
William Bristow and Thomas Lather, canons of Maiden Bradley (*Bradley*)
Philip Osmond, friar of Marlborough (*Marleburgh*)
John Porter, Peter Saresbury and Richard Marleburg, canons of Easton (*Eston*)

Subdeacons
John Lovell, dioc. Salisbury, title of prior and conv. of Longleat (*Langlete*)
[Fo. 164] William Mayne [as **1036**], title of abbot and conv. of Milton (*Middelton*)
Thomas Rothwell, Carmelite friar of Marlborough (*Marleberg*)
Richard Horne [as Horn, **1032**], title of St. Edmund's college, city of Salisbury
Robert Hete [as above], title of New College, Oxford
Peter Massy [as **1034**], vicar choral of Salisbury cath., title of benefice

Deacons
Stephen Colman [as **1037**, **1039**, variant *Byndon*]
Alexander Lenne [as **1039**]
John Partrich [as Patrych, **1039**]
Thomas Cowlyng, dioc. Exeter, lett. dim., title of priory of Launceston (*Lancestrii*)
William Bracer [as **1035**]
John Lavendry, dioc. Bath and Wells, lett. dim., title of priory of Bruton
M. John Love B.Cn. & C.L. [as **1028**], title of New College, Oxford
Edward Bradley, dioc. Salisbury, title of New College, Oxford
John Corndon [as **1039**, variant *Hurle*]
Richard Wayneman [as Weyneman, **1034**, **1036**]
Walter Bryggewater, dioc. Salisbury, Carmelite friar of Marlborough
John Oxonford and John Wytteney [as Oxenford, Witnay, **1029**], lett. dim.

Thomas Blysset [as **1028**] and Thomas Hognorton [as Hoggenorton,] **1028**], lett. dim.
John Queynton and Robert Raynhill [as **1039**]

Priests
M. John Stone [as **1036–7**, **1039**]
John Brownne [as Brone, Broune, **1034**, **1036**]
John Baker [as **1034**, **1036**]
John Alfrede, dioc. Salisbury, vicar of Cranborne, title of benefice
John Taylour [as Taylur, **1030**, **1036**, **1039**]
Thomas Sampson [as **1031**], dioc. Bath and Wells, lett. dim.
M. William Fryth, dioc. Winchester, title of New College, Oxford
William Houde, dioc. Exeter, and Robert Watford, dioc. London, lett. dim., vicars choral of Salisbury cath., title of benefice
John Gerard [as **1036**, **1039**]
George Radeclyf [as Radeclif, **1031**, variant *Ecleston*]

1041 Orders celebrated in the chapel of Potterne manor, 27 Feb. 1412.

Exorcists
John Dyryng, William Cendale, John Colyn, William Henlove, William Newman, Walter Edyndon, John Whathord, Thomas Elneworth and Henry Kene, dioc. Salisbury

Acolytes
John Langeman, Hugh Yonge, Thomas Boner, Thomas Merlyng, John Smyth, John Hill, Robert Cammell, John Chaundeler, Matthew Baker and Stephen Abraham, dioc. Salisbury
[Fo. 164[v]] John Yatesbury, Henry Baker and John Hay, dioc. Salisbury
John Harde, dioc. Exeter, lett. dim.

Subdeacons
Robert Dryffeld, dioc. Lincoln, lett. dim., title of prior and conv. of Caldwell
William Mewsham [as **1040**], title of prior and conv. of St. Germans
Thomas Ferur [as Ferour, **1040**], title of prior and conv. of Longleat (*Longelete*)
Nicholas Palmer, dioc. Worcester, lett. dim., title of prior and conv. of Bradenstoke
John Skynner, dioc. Salisbury, title of prior and conv. of Maiden Bradley (*Maydenbradlegh*)
Henry Burgeys, dioc. Salisbury, title of prior and conv. of St. Margaret by Marlborough (*Marleburgh*)
William Spiser, dioc. Salisbury, title of monastery of Stanley
M. Peter Payne, dioc. Lincoln, lett. dim., title of John [St. John], knight, lord of Paulerspury (*Paulespury*)
Richard Hale, dioc. York, lett. dim., title of prior and brothers of the hospital of St. John, Lechlade (*Lechelade*), dioc. Worcester

Stephen Wysbeche and John Blanford, brothers of Edington (*Edyndon*)
William Brystow [as Bristow, **1040**]
Thomas Lather [as **1040**]
John Hamstede and Reynold Neubury, monks of Stanley

Deacons

John Howell, dioc. Bath and Wells, lett. dim., title of prior and conv. of Barlynch (*Berlich*), same dioc.
John Lovell [as **1040**]
John Cornewale, dioc. Salisbury, title of abbess and conv. of Tarrant (*Tarent*)
John Donyton [as **1040**], title of prior and conv. of Ivychurch (*de Ederose*)
John Rayny, dioc. Salisbury, title of abbess and conv. of Tarrant
John Craas [as **1033**], title of hospital of Lechlade (*Lechelade*)
William Mayne [as **1036**, **1040**]
John Malmesbury and John Wodestok, canons of Poulton (*Pulton*)
Thomas Stodeley, monk of Stanley
Thomas Stokton, canon of Maiden Bradley

Priests

William Hosier [as Hoser, Hoyser, **1031**, **1034–5**]
Thomas Gardener [as Gardyner, **1031**]
John Basker, monk of Sherborne (*Shirborn*)
Edmund Eyr [as **1029**]

1042 Orders celebrated in Salisbury cath., 2 Apr. 1412.

Exorcists

John Bot, William du Port and Thomas Blundell of Jersey (*de Insula Garsei*), dioc. Winchester, lett. dim.

Acolytes

Thomas Edmund, Roger Prytman, John Carter, Nicholas Baker, Thomas Hymbury, John Bradford, William Tuker and John Preston, dioc. Salisbury
John Whitfeld and William Benetland, vicars choral of Salisbury cath.
John Bemynstre and Clement Consell, friars preacher of Salisbury
John Strotto, friar minor of Salisbury

Subdeacons

John Uphille, dioc. Salisbury, title of prior and conv. of Cerne
John Bodyn, dioc. Salisbury, title of prior and conv. of Breamore (*Brimmor*), dioc. Winchester
William Boner, dioc. Salisbury, title of prior and conv. of Christchurch (*ecclesie Christi de Twynham*), dioc. Winchester
M. William Chery, dioc. York, lett. dim., title of prior and conv. of Haltemprice (*Hautemprys*)

M. Robert Cammell [cf. **1041**], rector of Tidpit (*Tudput*), dioc. Salisbury, title of benefice

Thomas Dyrydaunt, dioc. Bath and Wells, lett. dim., title of monastery of Bindon (*Bynedon*), dioc. Salisbury

John Sombrok, dioc. [Coventry and] Lichfield, papal lett. dim., title of hospital of St. Nicholas by Salisbury

William Benetland [as above], title of benefice

John Bakeller, vicar choral of Salisbury cath., title of benefice

[Fo. 165] M. William de Mottrum, canon of St. Probus collegiate church, dioc. Exeter, lett. dim., title of benefice

William Whitfeld, vicar choral of Salisbury cath., title of benefice

John Herward, friar preacher of Salisbury

John Haye [cf. Hay, **1041**]

Deacons

M. Ralph Lovell, canon of Salisbury cath., title of benefice

Ralph Hykes [as **1039**], title of abbot and conv. of Abbotsbury (*Abbodesbury*)

Nicholas Palmer [as **1041**, variant *Bradenestok*]

William Underwode [as **1039**]

Thomas Ferour [as Ferur, **1040–1**]

William Westmore, vicar choral of Salisbury cath., title of benefice

Peter Russell, dioc. St. Davids, lett. dim., title of his patrimony

Peter Payne M.A. [as **1041**]

John Clerk, dioc. Exeter, lett. dim., title of abbot and conv. of Forde

John Jerbard, rector of Roborough (*Rowburgh*), dioc. Exeter, title of benefice

John Harde [as **1041**], title of priory of St. Nicholas, Exeter

Walter Throp, dioc. Lincoln, lett. dim., title of house of Littlemore (*Litilmor*)

John Lund, dioc. York, lett. dim., title of master of hospital of St. John the Baptist, near Oxford

John Skynner [as **1041**]

William Mewsham [as **1040–1**]

William Ingram [as **1034**]

Robert Ramsey and Thomas Somerton, brothers of the hospital of St. John the Baptist outside the East Gate, Oxford, lett. dim.

William Brystow and Thomas Lather [as **1040–1**]

Priests

John Rayny and John Cornewale [as **1041**]

William Bracer [as **1035**, **1040**]

John Donyton [as **1040–1**]

John Howell [as **1041**]

William Mayne [as **1036**, **1040–1**]

William Hancok, dioc. Exeter, vicar choral of Salisbury cath., title of benefice

Thomas Stokton [as **1041**]

John Cerne [as **1034**]

1043 Orders celebrated in the church of Sonning (*Sonnyng*), 28 May 1412.

Acolytes

M. William Nagard, Richard Whitthorn, Hugh Forde, John Croffte and John Blake, dioc. Salisbury

John Shirborne, John Haselbere and John Pedyll, monks of Milton (*Middelton*)

Subdeacons

Richard Harwdon, dioc. Lincoln, lett. dim., title of prior and conv. of Canons Ashby (*Assheby*), same dioc.

John Bulluk, dioc. Salisbury, title of abbot and conv. of Abbotsbury (*Abbodesbury*)

John Lorde, dioc. Lincoln, lett. dim., title of prior and conv. of Thurgarton, dioc. York

John Langman [as Langeman, **1041**], title of abbot and conv. of Abbotsbury

Stephen Abraham [as **1041**], title of prior and conv. of Bradenstoke (*Bradenestoke*)

James Chydyok [as **1040**], title of abbot and conv. of Bindon (*Bynedon*)

M. William Nagard [cf. above], rector of Woodsford (*Wyrdysforde*), title of benefice

[Fo. 165v] John Shirborne, John Haselbere and John Pedyll [as above]

Deacons

Nicholas Assheleghe, dioc. Bath and Wells, lett. dim., title of abbot and conv. of Sherborne

Richard Waryn, dioc. St. Davids, lett. dim., title of abbot and conv. of St. Dogmell (*sancti Dogmael*)

Thomas Dyrydaunt [as **1042**]

John Bodyn [as **1042**, variant *Brymmor*]

William Chery and John Sombrok [as **1042**]

Robert Saxton, dioc. York, lett. dim., title of prioress of Clementhorpe (*Clementthorpe*)

Thomas Yarnemowthe and John Fynchamstede [as **1037–8**]

M. John Haye [cf. Hay, **1041–2**]

Priests

William Badenam, dioc. Worcester, lett. dim., title of monastery of St. Frideswide, Oxford

John Lund [as **1042**]

Robert Dryffeld [as **1041**]

Thomas Ferour [as Ferur, **1040–2**]

M. Thomas Peres [as Perys, **1028**]

Walter Thorp [as Throp, **1042**, variant *Lytelmore*]

John Luffenham, dioc. Salisbury, title of prior and conv. of Bisham (*Bristelesham*)

John Wynter [as **1031**]

William Brystow and Thomas Lather [as **1040–2**]

John Hychynden [as Ychenden, **1037**]
John Newman [as **1037**]
William Clere, canon of Bisham (*Brystelesham*)
John Preshore and John Sonyngwell, monks of Bruern (*Bruare*)
Thomas Chakenden, Stephen Bray and Thomas Hendley [as Chakendene, de Bray, Brey, Henle, Henley, **1029**, **1032**]
John Horsley, monk of Reading (*Radyng*)
Thomas Nortone, monk of Osney (*Oseneye*)
Robert Ramesey [as Ramsey, **1042**]
Thomas Somerton [as **1042**]
John Oxenford and John Wytteney [as Oxonford, Witnay, **1029**, **1040**]

1044 Orders celebrated in the chapel of Potterne manor, 17 Dec. 1412.

Exorcists
Walter Godyng, dioc. Salisbury
Miles Morley, dioc. Coventry and Lichfield
John Drew, dioc. Exeter

Acolytes
William Hardyng, John Spenser and M. Robert Dynkley, dioc. Salisbury
Robert Lulworth and Thomas Vynt, monks of Bindon (*Byndon*)
Thomas Hopwas, dioc. Coventry and Lichfield
John Gyles, William Pateney, William Hawke, Richard Dore and William Whitmer, dioc. Salisbury
John Radele, Robert Comnore, Thomas Abyndon, Robert Fermesworth and John Thomeley, monks of Abingdon (*Abyndon*)

Subdeacons
John Fox, dioc. Salisbury, title of abbot and conv. of Milton (*Middelton*)
William Sadler, dioc. York, lett. dim., title of abbot and conv. of St. Mary, Barlings (*Berlesden*), dioc. Lincoln
Richard Bredon, dioc. York, lett. dim., title of abbot and conv. of Notley (*Notteley*)
Thomas Wyborne, dioc. York, lett. dim., title of prior and conv. of St. Frideswide, Oxford
John Smyth, dioc. Salisbury, title of abbot and conv. of Hailes (*Heyles*), dioc. Worcester
Thomas Boner [as **1041**], title of prior and conv. of Bradenstoke (*Bradenestok*)
[Fo. 166] Richard Pavy, dioc. Salisbury, title of abbot and conv. of Malmesbury
Thomas Marlyng, dioc. Salisbury, title of abbot and conv. of Abbotsbury (*Abbodesbury*)
Thomas Coll [as **1031**], title of prior and conv. of Montacute (*Montis Acuti*), dioc. Bath and Wells
M. John Ocley B.C.L., rector of Frome St. Quintin (*Frome sancti Quintini*), title of benefice

M. Robert Dynkley M.A. [as above], rector of Boscombe, title of benefice
William Whitmer, dioc. Coventry and Lichfield, lett. dim., title of prior and conv. of Ivychurch (*de Ederose*)
M. John Corfe, dioc. Salisbury, scholar and fellow of New College, Oxford, title of the college
William Schirborn, monk of Sherborne (*Schirborn*)
Thomas Hillarde [as Hyllard, **1036**]
William Scheftesbury and Thomas Boclond, monks of Sherborne
Robert Lulworth and Thomas Vynt [as above]
John Radele, Robert Comnore, Thomas Abyndon, Robert Fermesworth and John Thomeley [as above]
Peter Salysbury and Richard Marleburgh [as Saresbury, Marleburg, **1040**]
William Pateneye [as above, Pateney], vicar choral of Salisbury cath., title of benefice

Deacons
M. William de Mottrom [as Mottrum, **1042**]
John Lorde [as **1043**]
John Langeman [as Langman, **1041**, **1043**]
John Bulluk [as **1043**]
William Spiser [as **1041**]
Henry Burgeys [as **1041**]
John Whittefeld, dioc. Lincoln, lett. dim. [as Whitfeld, **1042**]
Stephen Abraham [as **1041**, **1043**]
John Bakeler, dioc. Exeter, lett. dim. [as Bakeller, **1042**], title of benefice
Thomas Jon, dioc. Salisbury, title of monastery of Chertsey (*Chertesey*), dioc. Winchester
Stephen Wysbeche [as **1041**]
John Blaneford [as Blanford, **1041**]
John Bemestere [as Bemestre, **1035**]

Priests
John Jerbard [as **1042**]
Richard Harwdon [as **1043**]
M. William Chery [as **1042–3**]
M. Thomas Rodebourne, rector of Stainton (*Staunton*), dioc. York, title of benefice
James Chydyok [as **1040**, **1043**]
John Skynner [as **1041–2**]
Robert Fleccher, dioc. Coventry and Lichfield, lett. dim., title of abbot [*rectius* prior] and conv. of Stone, same dioc.
William Ingram [as **1034**, **1042**]
M. John Hey [as Hay, Haye, **1040–3**]
John London [as **1035**]
Richard Hale [as **1041**, variant *Lychelad*]
John Uphille [as **1042**]
Thomas Remesbury, brother of the house of Edington (*Edyngdon*) [cf. Remmesbury, **1034–5**]

John Laurence [as Laurens, **1033**]
John Chynnok [as **1033**]
Thomas Stodeley [as **1041**]
John Brystoll and Francis de Bustoducis, friars minor of Reading (*Radyng*)
Nicholas Palmer [as **1041–2**, variant *Bradynstok*]

1045 [Fo. 166v] Orders celebrated in the chapel of Sonning (*Sonnyng*) manor, 22 Apr. 1413.

Acolytes

Thomas Trendle and John Trendle, monks of Reading
Thomas Kynow, dioc. Winchester, title of New College, Oxford

Subdeacons

M. Gilbert Hallum, canon and prebendary of Netherbury in Terra in Salisbury cath., title of benefice
Thomas Maunsell [as Manssell, **1034**], title of prior and conv. of Longleat (*Langa Lette*)
Thomas Trendle and John Trendle [as above]
Richard Godryluyge, canon of St. Frideswide, Oxford, lett. dim.

Deacons

M. John Ocley and M. Robert Dynkley [as **1044**]
John Suyfmore, dioc. Bath and Wells, lett. dim., title of monastery of Dunkeswell, dioc. Exeter
Walter Belle, dioc. Carlisle, lett. dim., title of M. Richard Courtenay, lord of the manors of Yealmpton (*Yelton*) and Powderham (*Pouderam*) in Devon
Thomas Collis [as Coll, **1031**, **1044**]
John Nowers, dioc. Lincoln, lett. dim.
William Oxonford and John Mountagu, canons of St. Frideswide, Oxford, lett. dim.
Peter Salesbury [as Saresbury, Salysbury, **1040**, **1044**]

Priests

M. William de Mottrom [as Mottrum, **1042**, **1044**]
John Heyre, dioc. Salisbury, title of prior and conv. of Sandleford (*Sandylford*)
William Cok, vicar of Hennock (*Hanok*), dioc. Exeter, lett. dim., title of benefice
John Legh, dioc. Coventry and Lichfield, lett. dim., title of prior of St. Frideswide, Oxford
William Herryson, dioc. Coventry and Lichfield, lett. dim., title of monastery of St. Mary, Keynsham (*Keynesham*)
John Lorde [as **1043–4**]
M. William Twyte M.A., dioc. Bath and Wells, lett. dim., title of monastery of St. Peter and St. Paul, Dorchester (*Dork'*)
Peter Warde, dioc. York, lett. dim., title of priory of St. Frideswide, Oxford, dioc. Lincoln
John Bulluk [as **1043–4**]

John Rampney, dioc. Llandaff, lett. dim., title of Ievan ap Lowys ap Morgayn
John Westmore [as **1034**]
John Baccaler [as Bakeller, Bakeler, **1042**, **1044**]
Robert Langryssh and Henry Clerk, fellows and scholars of New College, Oxford, title of same college
Walter Andener [as **1037–8**]

1046 Orders celebrated in the prebendal church of Ramsbury (*Remmesbury*), 23 Sept. 1413.

Acolytes
M. John Clerk, William Smyth, John Berawe, John Carpenter, Peter Hynden, Thomas de Tibbay, Richard Clerk, John Hert and John Loundener, dioc. Salisbury
Thomas Grenam and Simon Ildesle, monks of Abingdon (*Abendon*)
Edward Watton, monk of Abbotsbury (*Abbodesbur'*)
Robert Vyse, monk of Monkton Farleigh (*Farlegh*)
William Roude, dioc. Coventry and Lichfield, lett. dim.
John Rabasse, dioc. Lincoln, lett. dim.
William Deyster, John Norton and John Roudon

[Fo. 167] *Subdeacons*
Thomas de Tibbay [as above], rector of Devizes (*Devyses*), title of benefice
William Lawndener, dioc. Salisbury, title of prior and conv. of Ivychurch (*de Ederose*)
Simon Whytrat [as Whitrat, **1033**], title of abbess and conv. of St. Mary de la Pré (*de Pratis*), by Northampton
John Pecok, vicar choral of Salisbury cath., title of benefice
William Deyster, dioc. Lincoln, lett. dim., title of abbot and conv. of Warden (*Wardon*)
Walter Shaftesbury, of the house of Edington (*Edyngdon*)
Thomas Grenam and Simon Ildesle [as above]
Edward Watton [as above]
Robert Vyse [as above]
John Norton and John Roudon [cf. above], fellows and scholars of New College, Oxford, lett. dim., title of same college

Deacons
M. Gilbert Hallum [as **1045**]
Thomas Boner [as **1041**, **1044**]
Thomas Derlyngton, dioc. Durham, lett. dim., title of abbot and conv. of Osney (*Oseneye*)
Thomas Bagley, dioc. Chichester, lett. dim., title of prior and conv. of Shulbrede (*Schulbrode*)
John Smyth and Richard Pavy [as **1044**]
Thomas Maunsell [as Manssell, **1034**, **1045**]
William Pateneye [as Pateney, **1044**]

John Wyete, dioc. Salisbury, title of priory of St. Margaret by Marlborough (*Merleburgh*)
John Fox [as **1044**]
John Haselbere and John Shirborn [as **1043**]
John Pyddyll [as Pedyll, **1043**]
John Radele, Robert Comenore, Robert Fremusworthe, Thomas Abendon and John Thomele [as Radele, Comnore, Fermesworth, Abyndon, Thomeley, **1044**]
William Shirborn [as Schirborn, **1044**]
Thomas Hyllard [as Hillarde, **1036**, **1044**]
William Shaftesbury and Thomas Bocland [as Scheftesbury, Boclond, **1044**]
Henry Heyde, monk of Abbotsbury
Thomas Brydport [as **1035**]
William Talbot, friar minor of York

Priests
Walter Belle [as **1045**]
Henry Burgeys [as **1041**, **1044**]
William Spyser [as Spiser, **1041**, **1044**]
John Spynk, dioc. York, lett. dim., title of house of Studley (*Stodeley*)
M. Robert Dynkley [as **1044**, **1045**]
Stephen Abraham [as **1041**, **1043–4**]
John Craas [as **1033**, **1041**]
Laurence Wyllyng, dioc. Salisbury, title of abbot and conv. of Milton (*Middelton*)
Thomas Collis [as Coll, **1031**, **1044–5**]
John Cothe [as Covte, **1031**]
Peter Salesbury [as Saresbury, Salysbury, **1040**, **1044–5**]
John Malmesbury [as **1041**]
John Bemynstre [as Bemestre, Bemestere, **1035**, **1044**]

1047 Orders celebrated in the conventual church of Sherborne (*Schirborn*) abbey, 23 Dec. 1413.

[Fo. 167v] *Tonsured*
John Pecket, John Corneys, Thomas Tollard, Thomas Dollyng, Robert Morys, John Morton, Thomas Mapuder, John Bareth, John Knyght, John Martyn, John Knap, Martin Bronyng, William Hoper, Peter Dounton, Richard Jons and William Hampton

Acolytes
M. Oliver Dyneley, M. John Banham, M. John Morton, John Waryn, John Rydele *alias* Gate, Robert Parfyt, William Stiklan, Walter Iwerne and William Montagu, monk of Montacute (*de Montagu*), dioc. Salisbury

Subdeacons
Robert Parfyt [cf. above], title of abbot and conv. of Sherborne

Thomas Bolter, dioc. Worcester, lett. dim., title of abbot and conv. of Sherborne

John Martyn, dioc. Salisbury, title of abbot and conv. of Sherborne

Thomas Gylmyn, dioc. Salisbury, title of abbot and conv. of Milton (*Middelton*)

John Yatesbury [as **1041**], title of abbess and conv. of Wherwell (*Wherewell*)

William Vaym, dioc. Salisbury, title of abbot and conv. of Abbotsbury (*Abbodesbury*)

Richard Chestre, dioc. Durham, lett. dim., title of prior and conv. of Elsham

John Spenser [as **1044**], title of prior and conv. of the house of St. Margaret, outside Marlborough (*Marleburgh*)

Edward Veyser [as **1036**], title of abbot and conv. of Abbotsbury

John Smale, dioc. Bath and Wells, lett. dim., title of prioress and conv. of Amesbury (*Ambresbury*)

Richard Lawe, dioc. Exeter, lett. dim., title of monastery of Dunkeswell

M. John Banham [cf. above]

Deacons

William Lawndener [as **1046**]

Walter Donne, friar preacher of Salisbury

Edward Watton [as **1046**]

Priests

Thomas Boner [as **1041**, **1044**, **1046**]

Richard Pavy, John Smyth and William Schirborn [as **1044**, **1046**]

Thomas Hyllard [as Hillarde, **1036**, **1044**, **1046**]

William Cheftesbury [as Scheftesbury, Shaftesbury, **1044**, **1046**]

Thomas Bokeland [as Boclond, Bocland, **1044**, **1046**]

John Montagu and John Muchelney, monks of Montacute

John Herward [as **1042**]

Henry Hyder [as Heyde, **1046**]

1048 Orders celebrated in the conventual church of Sherborne (*Schirborn*) abbey, 3 March 1414.

Tonsured

James Hyllarye, John Mulinth, Robert Burgeys, William Champ, Thomas Broun, Thomas Harwell, William Jocy, Peter Jolith and William Maschall

Acolytes

Roger Suthworth, dioc. Coventry and Lichfield, lett. dim.

Thomas Stork, Thomas Salter, John Baret, Oliver Sanders, Robert Roper and Richard Cathe, dioc. Salisbury

Richard Faukys and John Pedell, monks of Abbotsbury (*Abbodesbury*)

Thomas Roude, canon of Ivychurch (*Iwechirche*)

[Fo. 168] *Subdeacons*

M. Oliver Dyneley [as **1047**], rector of Pulham, title of benefice

John Lowys, dioc. Salisbury, title of prior and conv. of Breamore (*Bremmore*), dioc. Winchester

M. Henry Boner, dioc. Lincoln, lett. dim., title of prioress and conv. of St. Mary, Clerkenwell (*Clerconwell*)

John Carpynter [as Carpenter, **1046**], title of prior and conv. of Holy Trinity, Mottisfont (*Motesfonte*), dioc. Winchester

Walter Dashont, dioc. Salisbury, title of abbot and conv. of Milton (*Middelton*)

Nicholas Baker [as **1042**], title of abbot and conv. of Bindon (*Bynedon*)

John Hert [as **1046**], title of abbot and conv. of Stanley

John Dralans, dioc. Salisbury, title of abbot and conv. of Cerne

Oliver Sanders, Richard Faukys, John Pedell and Thomas Roude [as above]

Deacons

John Smale, Thomas Bolter, William Vaym and Robert Parfyt [as **1047**]

Edward Veyser [as **1036**, **1047**]

Thomas Gylmyn [as **1047**]

John Watkynnys, dioc. Salisbury, title of abbot and conv. of Milton

John Yatesbury [as **1041**, **1047**]

John Martyn [as **1047**]

M. John Banham [cf. **1047**]

Robert Lolworde and Thomas Vynce [as Lulworth, Vynt, **1044**]

Priest

John Fox [as **1044**, **1046**]

1049 Orders celebrated in Salisbury cath., 7 Apr. 1414.

Acolytes

Henry Sywell, William Vuell, Thomas Mannyng, John Gofys and Robert Holewey

William Corscombe and Robert Were, brothers of the house of Edington (*Edyngdon*)

Subdeacons

M. John Clerk M.A. [as **1046**], scholar of De Vaux (*de Valle*) college, Salisbury, title of the same house

Robert Boneknol, dioc. Salisbury, title of abbot and conv. of Bindon (*Bynedon*)

William Smyth [as **1046**], title of prior and conv. of Ivychurch (*de Ederose*)

Thomas Stork [as **1048**], title of abbot and conv. of Cerne

John Lawndener [as Loundener, **1046**], title of abbot and conv. of Sherborne (*Schirborn*)

Thomas Farlegh, dioc. Salisbury, title of patrimony of William Palton, knight

Philip Raukyn, dioc. Salisbury, title of prior and conv. of Ivychurch

William Wyke and John Gofys, vicars choral of Salisbury cath., title of benefice

Roger Suthworth [cf. **1048**]
John Sutton, friar of Marlborough (*Marleburgh*)
Robert Cole, friar preacher of Salisbury

[Fo. 168v] *Deacons*
M. Oliver Dyneley [as **1047–8**]
John Spenser [as **1044**, **1047**]
John Carpynter [as Carpenter, **1046**, **1048**]
John Lowes [as Lowys, **1048**]
William Whitemere [cf. Whitmer, **1044**], rector of Compton Abbas (*Compton*), title of benefice
John Hert [as **1046**, **1048**]
Walter Shaftesbury [as **1046**]
John Salesbury, canon of Bristol, lett. dim.
Thomas Roude [as **1048**]
John Meriot, friar preacher of Salisbury

Priests
M. John Holand D.C.L., rector of Dauntsey (*Daundesey*), title of benefice
Thomas de Tibbay [as **1046**]
Robert Parfyt, Thomas Bolter, John Martyn and John Smale [as **1047–8**]
William Pateney [as Pateneye, **1044**, **1046**]
John London *alias* Dukkeslee, dioc. London, title of abbot and conv. of Sherborne
John Watkynnys [as **1048**]
John Wayte [as **1034**]
William Underwude [as Underwode, **1039**, **1042**]
John Bodyn [as **1042–3**]
M. Henry Boner [as **1048**]
John Quenerton, monk of Eynsham (*Enesham*), dioc. Lincoln, lett. dim.
Stephen Wisbeche [as Wysbeche, **1041**, **1044**]

1050 Orders celebrated in the chapel or oratory of the bishop's inn in Abingdon (*Abendon*), 2 June 1414.

Acolyte
Thomas Harkynden, dioc. York, lett. dim.

Deacons
M. John Clerk [as **1046**, **1049**]
M. William Gray B.C.L., rector of Swanscombe, dioc. Rochester, lett. dim., title of benefice

1051 Orders celebrated in the chapel of Sonning (*Sonnyng*) manor, 22 Sept. 1414.

Acolytes
John Henle, Thomas Tylhurst, John Clere and John Cholsey, monks of Reading (*Radyng*)
Edward Rede and John Sothe, dioc. Salisbury

Subdeacons

M. Henry Clee, dioc. London, lett. dim., title of abbot and conv. of Notley (*Nottelee*)

Edward Rede [cf. above]

Deacons

Roger Suthworth [cf. **1048–9**]

Thomas Trenle and John Trenle [as Trendle, **1045**]

[Fo. 169] *Priests*

M. Oliver Dyneley [as **1047–9**]

M. John Ocley [as **1044–5**]

M. John Clerk [as **1046**, **1049–50**]

Thomas Barvet [as Barvot, Barwot, **1037–8**]

1052 Orders celebrated by Richard [Belmer], bp. of Achonry (*Caten'*),[1] by authority of Robert, bp. of Salisbury, then abroad, in the conventual church of the friars preacher at Fisherton (*Fyscherton*) by Salisbury, 23 Feb. 1415.

Acolytes

John Hay, John Carpenter, Richard Seward and John Struton, dioc. Salisbury

John Davy, dioc. Worcester, lett. dim.

John Holyn, Thomas Suddon, William Eweyn, John Norton, Richard Skylour and Walter Gay, dioc. Salisbury

Subdeacons

Thomas Trevergi [as Trevergy, **1028**], title of prioress and conv. of Littlemore (*Litelmor*)

Thomas Wodyngton, dioc. Salisbury, title of priory of Maiden Bradley (*Maydenbradley*)

John Sothe [as **1051**], title of abbot and conv. of Reading (*Radyng*)

Peter Fader, dioc. Bath and Wells, lett. dim., title of prioress of Stratford-le-Bow (*Stratford atte the Bowe*)

John Henlegh and Thomas Tylherst [as Henle, Tylhurst, **1051**]

John Clere and John Cholsey [as **1051**]

Thomas Phillipe, dioc. Lichfield, lett. dim., title of prior and conv. of Breamore (*Bremmore*)

Thomas Lambard and Philip Shirbourne, monks of Cerne

William Hauke [as Hawke, **1044**], title of house of Easton (*Eston*)

Walter Archer, dioc. Salisbury, title of abbot of Milton (*Middelton*)

Robert Osanne, rector of Swanage (*Swanwich*)

John Hasard, dioc. Salisbury, title of monastery of Abbotsbury (*Abbotesbury*)

John Kyng *alias* Knapp, rector of Woodsford (*Wirdeford*)

[Fo. 169v] *Deacons*

John Yatesbury [as **1041**, **1047–8**]

Nicholas Baker [as **1042**, **1048**]

Thomas Trendele [as Trendle, Trenle, **1045**, **1051**]

David Pontan, dioc. St. Davids, title of monastery of Talley
William Lyne, friar minor of Salisbury

Priests

John Warrayn, dioc. Salisbury, title of monastery of Milton
Thomas Sure, monk of Cerne
Gilbert Hallum [as **1045–6**]
Roger Suthworth [cf. **1048–9**, **1051**], vicar of Broadwinsor (*Brode Wyndesore*)
Edward Veiser [as Veyser, **1036**, **1047–8**]
Thomas Grenham [as Grenam, **1046**]
Robert Lolworth [as Lulworth, Lolworde, **1044**, **1048**]
Philip Rawkyn [as Raukyn, **1049**]
Robert Gylle [as **1034**], title of hospital of St. John, Wilton
John Yatesbury [as **1041**, **1047–8**, **1052**, *Deacons*]
Thomas Trendel [as Trendle, Trenle, Trendele, **1045**, **1050**, **1052**, *Deacons*]
John Wilton, dioc. Salisbury

[1. *Handbook of British Chronology*, p. 269. He also acted as a suffragan bishop in dioc. Bath and Wells, 1414–18 (*Reg. Bubwith*, i, pp. xxxv, 236, 296, ii. 510–27).]

1053 Orders celebrated by Richard, bp. of Achonry (*Caten'*), by authority of Robert, bp. of Salisbury, then abroad, in the conventual church of the friars preacher at Fisherton (*Fyssherton*) by Salisbury, 22 Sept. 1415.

Acolytes

M. Robert de Corke, rector of Compton Bassett (*Compton*)
John Perot and Andrew Forde, dioc. Salisbury
John Spernyn, monk of Witham (*Selwod*)
Thomas Bonde and Nicholas Bradestoke, dioc. Salisbury
Thomas Grene, friar preacher of Salisbury
William Borde, canon of Keynsham (*Keynesham*), dioc. Bath and Wells
John Fovent, John Flecchere and Philip Goffe, dioc. Salisbury
Robert Bolte, canon of Maiden Bradley (*Bradelegh*)

[Fo. 170] *Subdeacons*

M. Robert de Corke [as above]
Robert Staunton, friar of Marlborough (*Marlebrigg*)
John Frysdon, friar preacher of Salisbury
John Helier, friar preacher
John Duke, subdeacon [*sic*], dioc. Salisbury, title of prior and brothers of the hospital of St. John, Lechlade (*Lichelade*)
Thomas Bristowe and Ralph Alderley, canons of Bradenstoke (*Bradestoke*)
Edmund Hende, dioc. Exeter, lett. dim., title of hospital of St. Nicholas by Salisbury

Deacons

John Kyng *alias* Knapp [as **1052**], title of benefice
M. Robert Cammell [as **1041–2**]
Thomas Wodyngton [as **1052**]
M. Walter Dobber, dioc. Salisbury, title of master and fellows of hospital of St. John the Baptist outside the East Gate, Oxford, dioc. Lincoln

Richard Faw and John Bedell, monks of Abbotsbury (*Abbodesbury*)
John Peryn, dioc. Bath and Wells, lett. dim., title of prior and conv. of Montacute (*de Monte Acuto*)
John Berwe, dioc. Salisbury, title of prior or master of hospital of Lechlade (*Lychelade*)
Richard Bryton, canon of Bradenstoke
William Hauke [as Hawke, **1044**, **1052**]
Robert Wawayne, dioc. Salisbury, title of house of St. John, Lechlade
John Chiddele, dioc. Bath and Wells, lett. dim.

Priests
Thomas Hungerford, friar of Marlborough
James Blacdon, friar preacher of Salisbury
John Haselbere [as **1043**, **1046**]
John Shirbourne [as Shirborne, **1043**, **1046**]
Thomas Philippe [as **1052**, variant *Bremer*]
Richard Marchall, canon of Keynsham (*Keynsam*), dioc. Bath and Wells
Gregory Fruyse and Richard Wichill, canons of Bruton, dioc. Bath and Wells
Richard Wichwode, vicar choral of Wells cath., lett. dim., title of abbot of Keynsham
William Asscheley, dioc. Bath and Wells, lett. dim., title of Thomas Rigge, esquire, same dioc.
John Dralans [as **1048**]
Edward Watton [as **1046–7**]

1054 [Fo. 170v] Orders celebrated by Richard, bp. of Achonry (*Caten'*), by authority of Robert, bp. of Salisbury, then abroad, in the conventual church of the friars preacher at Fisherton (*Fyssherton*) by Salisbury, 14 March 1416.

Acolytes
Walter Lugardyn, Walter Tresour, William Goldeworth, Walter Bayly, John Wynhyngham, Simon Frankleyn and William Otewell, dioc. Salisbury
John Trevisa and John Perkyn, dioc. Exeter
John Dyrneforde, John Carpenter, John Palmer, John Buk and Walter Couper, dioc. Salisbury
Philip Lange, dioc. Bath and Wells, lett. dim.
John Joce, dioc. Salisbury
Richard May, vicar choral of Salisbury cath.
John Goldryn, dioc. Salisbury
William Lane, dioc. Bath and Wells, lett. dim.
Robert Gawnt, John Wagger, William Ponde, William Crede, Thomas Reynolde, William Passenger, Walter Davy, Robert Taylor, Robert Swanhangre and Edward Rous, dioc. Salisbury
Thomas Rodeley, dioc. [Coventry and] Lichfield

Subdeacons

John Fovent [as **1053**], rector of Caundle Purse (*Candel Purse*)

Richard May [as above], dioc. Bath and Wells, lett. dim., title of benefice

Richard Thomma, dioc. Exeter, lett. dim., title of priory of Bodmin, same dioc.

Walter Luggardyne [as above, Lugardyn], title of Merton Hall, Oxford

Christopher Sourby, dioc. Carlisle, title of prioress of Goring

John Harry, dioc. Exeter, lett. dim., title of priory of Bodmin, same dioc.

John Plowden and John Barbour, vicars choral of Salisbury cath., title of benefice

Nicholas Bradestoke [as **1053**], title of priory of Poulton (*Pulton*)

John Carpenter [as above], title of prior of hospital of St. John, Wilton

Thomas Salter [as **1048**], title of monastery of Cerne

Thomas[1] Rodeley [as above], rector of Winterbourne Whitchurch (*albi monasterii*), dioc. Salisbury, title of benefice

Deacons

John Henley [as Henle, Henlegh, **1051–2**]

John Clere and John [Cholsey] [as **1051–2**]

John Stanlynche, dioc. Salisbury, title of New College, Oxford

John Canonby, dioc. Carlisle, lett. dim., title of Queen's Hall (*aula Regine*), Oxford

John Gofits [as Gofys, **1049**]

William Thomer, dioc. Bath and Wells, lett. dim., title of prior and conv. of Montacute (*Montis Acuti*), same dioc.

Robert Bolt [as Bolte, **1053**, variant *Bradley*]

Thomas Lambarde and Philip Schirbourne [as Lambard, Shirbourne, **1052**]

Robert Radyng, canon of St. Frideswide

John Effart of Guernsey (*insula de Gernesey*), lett. dim.

John Fleccher [as Flecchere, **1053**], title of abbot of Malmesbury (*Malmesbi'*)

Roger Frye, dioc. Bath and Wells, lett. dim.

John Davy, dioc. Salisbury, title of abbess and conv. of Tarrant (*Tarent*)

Philip Gooff [as Goffe, **1053**], title of monastery of Ivychurch (*de Ederose*)

[Fo. 171] *Priests*

John Fynchamsted [as Fynchamstede, **1037–8**, **1043**]

John de Trenley [as Trendle, Trenle, **1045**, **1050**]

William Lyme, monk of Reading

Peter Massy [as **1040**]

William Oxenforde [as Oxonford, **1045**]

John Goldemore

John Duke [cf. **1053**]

Adam Colyns

[1. *Sic*. Cf. **481**.]

1055 Orders celebrated by Richard, bp. of Achonry (*Caten'*), by authority of Robert, bp. of Salisbury, then abroad, in the conventual church of the friars preacher at Fisherton (*Fyssherton*) by Salisbury, 13 June 1416.

Subdeacons

Richard Bayly, dioc. Salisbury, title of the house of St. John, Lechlade (*Lychelade*), dioc. Worcester

Thomas Trybon, dioc. Salisbury, rector of Speckington (*Spekyngton*), dioc. Bath and Wells, title of benefice

John Houlyn [as Holyn, **1052**], title of abbot and conv. of Bindon (*Byndon*)

John Haye [as Hay, **1052**]

Thomas Stumpe, dioc. Salisbury, title of abbot and conv. of Abbotsbury (*Abbodesbury*)

Deacons

William Weston, dioc. Bath [and Wells], lett. dim., title of monastery of Stanley

John Carpenter [as **1054**]

William Ewen [as Eweyn, **1052**], title of abbot and conv. of Bindon

Andrew Forde [as **1053**], title of prior and conv. of Longleat (*Langlete*)

John Broune, dioc. Bath and Wells, lett. dim., title of prior and conv. of Montacute (*Montis Acuty*), same dioc.

Edmund Hende [as **1053**]

William Passenger [as **1054**], title of prior and conv. of Ivychurch (*de Ederose*)

Priests

Robert Bayly, dioc. Bath and Wells, lett. dim., title of abbot and conv. of Athelney

William Muntagew [as Montagu, **1047**]

John Spernnyn [as Spernyn, **1053**], dioc. Bath and Wells

John Davy [as **1054**]

John Burgh, dioc. Bath and Wells, lett. dim., title of prior and conv. of Montacute

1056 [Fo. 171v] Orders celebrated by Richard, bp. of Achonry (*Caten'*), by authority of Robert, bp. of Salisbury, then abroad, in the conventual church of the friars preacher at Fisherton (*Fyssherton*) by Salisbury, 19 Sept. 1416.

Acolytes

M. William Felter, dioc. Worcester, rector of St. Werburgh, [Bristol], same dioc.

M. William Hyke, dioc. Bath [and Wells], rector of West Coker (*Westkocer*), same dioc.

Ralph Carpenter and John Wylton, dioc. Salisbury

Robert Boton, dioc. Chichester, lett. dim.

John Norton, monk of Abingdon (*Abendon*)

John Martyn, John Vady, William Oliver, John Pycet, Thomas Derby and William Eweyn, dioc. Salisbury

Subdeacons

John Brygge, dioc. York, lett. dim., title of monastery of Sawley (*Psalley*), same dioc.

John Symmys, dioc. Salisbury, title of prior and conv. of Lechlade (*Lychelade*)

William Clegh, dioc. Exeter, lett. dim., title of monastery of Launceston, same dioc.

M. William Hyke [as above]

M. William Felter [as above]

David Maynell, dioc. St. Davids, vicar choral of Salisbury cath., title of benefice

John Barde, dioc. Bath and Wells, lett. dim., title of monastery of Athelney (*Athelneye*), same dioc.

Walter Gayde of Tilshead (*Tydelleshyde*), title of monastery of Ivychurch (*de Ederose*)

Bartholomew Shirburne

John Lyne, dioc. Exeter, lett. dim., title of monastery of Buckfast (*Bucfestrie*)

Thomas Dancastre and John Spaldynge, monks of Abingdon

John Norton [as above]

Henry Hamen, dioc. Salisbury, title of priory of Sandleford (*Sandelforde*)

Robert Boton, dioc. Salisbury [cf. above]

William Ponde [as **1054**], title of hospital of St. John, Wilton (*Wylton*)

John Bryge, dioc. York, lett. dim., title of monastery of Stanley [cf. above]

Robert Helton, dioc. Carlisle, lett. dim., title of monastery of Bruern (*Bruera*), dioc. Lincoln

John Grene, friar minor

M. John Morton, dioc. Salisbury, rector of Hinton Martell (*Henton Martyll*), title of benefice

Robert Gaunte [as Gawnt, **1054**], title of hermitage

Richard Shirborne, canon of Ivychurch

Deacons

John Graunson, dioc. Salisbury, title of priory of Montacute (*Montis Acuti*), dioc. Bath [and Wells]

Thomas Paye, dioc. Exeter, lett. dim., title of priory of St. Nicholas, Oxford (*Oxon'*) [*rectius* Exeter]

[Fo. 172] Baldwin Tybot, dioc. Exeter, lett. dim., title of abbot and conv. of Hartland (*Hertelond*), same dioc.

John Houlyn [as Holyn, **1052**, **1055**]

John Rowe and John Ryppeleygh, dioc. Exeter, lett. dim., title of monastery of Buckfast

William Curteys, Joyce Pyken, John Tyrell and John Camyll, dioc. Exeter, lett. dim., title of priory of Bodmin (*Bodmynie*), same dioc.

John Hay [as Haye, **1052**, **1054**]

Ralph Brouwon, dioc. Exeter, lett. dim., title of prior of Launceston, same dioc.

John Harry [as **1054**, variant *Bodmynie*]

John Papeiay, dioc. Exeter, lett. dim., title of monastery of Torre, same dioc.

Hugh Rede, dioc. [Coventry and] Lichfield [as **1034**]

Stephen Camell, canon of Montacute (*Montagu*)

John Scoche, dioc. Exeter, lett. dim., title of monastery of Tavistock (*Tavystoke*), same dioc.

Thomas Taylor, dioc. Exeter, lett. dim., title of monastery of Buckfast, same dioc.

John Payne, dioc. Exeter, lett. dim., title of monastery of Tavistock, same dioc.

Stephen Gylle, dioc. Exeter, lett. dim., title of priory of Frithelstock (*Frethelestoke*)

Thomas Salter [as **1048**, **1054**]

John Fovent [as **1053–4**, variant *Caundell Purse*]

John Roger, friar preacher

Priests

John Coarbura, rector of Didcot (*Dudecot*), title of benefice

John Wagger [as **1054**], title of house of St. John, outside Wilton (*Wylton*)

William Kynge, dioc. Exeter, lett. dim., title of monastery of Dunkeswell, same dioc.

William Monder, dioc. Exeter, lett. dim., title of abbess and conv. of St. Mary and St. John the Evangelist [Canonsleigh]

John Broune [as **1055**, variant *Montis Acuti*]

John Langer, dioc. Bath and Wells, lett. dim., title of prior and conv. of Taunton, same dioc.

John Walyssh, dioc. Exeter, lett. dim., title of prior of St. Nicholas, [Exeter], same dioc.

Thomas Gybbe, dioc. Exeter, lett. dim., title of priory of Tywardreath (*Trewardrayth*), same dioc.

John Milwarde, dioc. Exeter, lett. dim., title of abbot and conv. of St. Mary, Buckfast, same dioc.

Joyce Trebyda, dioc. Exeter, lett. dim., title of monastery of Bodmin, same dioc.

Ralph Stoute, dioc. Exeter, lett. dim., title of monastery of Buckfast, same dioc.

Brother Richard Estrop

John Perkyn [as **1054**], lett. dim., title of monastery of Bodmin, same dioc.

John Roser, dioc. Exeter, lett. dim., title of monastery of Rewley (*de Regali loco*) by Oxford

William Weston [as **1055**, variant *Stanleygh*]

Andrew Forde [as **1053**, **1055**, variant *Longlete*]

William Grynham, dioc. Bath [and Wells], lett. dim., title of priory of Montacute, same dioc.

John Brystow and Henry Kyngth, canons of Bruton
John Skewys, dioc. Exeter, lett. dim., title of monastery of Bodmin, same dioc.
John More, dioc. Exeter, lett. dim., title of priory of St. Nicholas, Exeter
John Carpenter [as **1054**, **1055**]
Robert Pulham, friar minor
Roger Frye [as **1054**, variant *Bustellysham*]
John Davy, dioc. Exeter, lett. dim., title of monastery of Neath (*Neethe*), dioc. Llandaff
William Eweyne [as Eweyn, Ewen, **1052**, **1055**]
Walter Wysbeche, dioc. Winchester, lett. dim., title of monastery of Malmesbury
Edmund Hynde [as Hende, **1053**, **1055**]

1057 [Fo. 172v] Orders celebrated by Richard, bp. of Achonry (*Caten'*), by the authority of Robert, bp. of Salisbury, then abroad, in the conventual church of Sherborne (*Shirburn*), 27 March 1417.

Acolytes
Richard Bullok, Stephen Baker, Thomas Wodelond, Thomas Yarty and John Southmede, first tonsure, dioc. Salisbury
John Kelly and Michael Lonytop, dioc. Exeter, first tonsure, lett. dim.
John Stanton, dioc. Bath and Wells, first tonsure, lett. dim.

Subdeacons
John Pennans, dioc. Exeter, lett. dim., title of priory of Bodmin (*Bodminie*)
Thomas Cook, dioc. Exeter, lett. dim., title of priory of Frithelstock (*Frydelstoke*)
Thomas Bowryng, dioc. Bath and Wells, lett. dim., title of monastery of Abbotsbury (*Abbotesbury*)
Henry Nycoll, dioc. Exeter, lett. dim., title of priory of Cold Norton (*Coldenorton*)
Henry Penbirthy, dioc. Exeter, lett. dim., title of priory of St. Nicholas, Exeter
M. Hervey Willyam, dioc. Exeter, lett. dim., title of priory of Llangennith (*Langenyth*)
John Oppy, dioc. Exeter, lett. dim., title of priory of St. Nicholas, Exeter
Walter Baker, dioc. Bath and Wells, lett. dim., title of hospital of St. John, Wells (*Wellie*)
John Brun, dioc. Exeter, lett. dim., title of monastery of Tavistock (*Tavystochie*)
Thomas Jannys, dioc. Salisbury, title of [hospital of] St. John, Lechlade (*Lechelade*)
John Nanslowen, dioc. Exeter, lett. dim., title of priory of Bodmin
John Kelly, dioc. Exeter, lett. dim., title of prior and conv. of Launceston

Deacons
Thomas Artour, dioc. Exeter, lett. dim., title of priory of Bodmin

William Bynham, dioc. Bath and Wells, lett. dim., title of priory of Montacute (*Montis Acuti*)
Walter Couper [as **1054**], title of monastery of Abbotsbury
Richard Skylour [as **1052**], title of monastery of Milton (*Myddilton*)
Walter Umfray, dioc. Bath and Wells, lett. dim., title of monastery of Romsey (*Romesey*)
John Davy [as **1052**], title of priory of Llanthony (*Lantony*)
Walter Tresur [as Tresour, **1054**], title of monastery of Tarrant (*Tarent*)
John Lane, dioc. Bath and Wells, rector of St. Mary within the North Gate, Bath, lett. dim., title of benefice
William Sampford and William Haselgrove, dioc. Bath and Wells, lett. dim., title of monastery of Sherborne
Thomas Hore, dioc. St. Davids, lett. dim., title of priory of Bruton
John Strotton [as Struton, **1052**], title of house of St. Margaret, Marlborough (*Marleburgh*)
Thomas Stepsoft, dioc. Salisbury, title of monastery of Milton (*Middelton*)
John Pretor, dioc. Exeter, lett. dim., title of priory of Bodmin
John Drake, dioc. Exeter, lett. dim., title of monastery of Newenham (*Nywham*)
John Paslew, dioc. Exeter, lett. dim., title of monastery of Cerne
John Hyre, dioc. Exeter, lett. dim., title of priory of Tywardreath (*Tywardynth*)
William Bate, dioc. Exeter, lett. dim., title of house of St. Nicholas, Exeter
John Mayow, dioc. Exeter, lett. dim., title of monastery of Forde
Thomas Felpys, dioc. Bath and Wells, brother of the hospital of St. John, Wells, lett. dim.
John Penpaly, dioc. Exeter, lett. dim., title of house of St. Nicholas, Exeter
John Ros, dioc. Exeter, lett. dim., title of prior of Launceston (*Lanceston*)

[Fo. 173] *Priests*
William Barton, dioc. Lincoln, archdeacon of Totnes (*Totton*) and master of the hospital of St. John [the Baptist], Wallingford (*Wallyngford*)
M. Stephen German, dioc. Bath and Wells, lett. dim., title of house of Chetwode (*Chetewode*)
M. John Morton [as **1056**, variant *Hynton Martell*]
M. William Hycke, dioc. Exeter, rector of West Coker (*Westcok'*), dioc. Bath and Wells, lett. dim. [cf. Hyke, **1056**]
John Monke, dioc. Exeter, lett. dim., title of monastery of Buckfast (*Bucfestrie*)
Thomas Forde *alias* Rowe, dioc. Exeter, lett. dim., title of prior of St. Stephen, Launceston (*Launcestr'*)
Thomas Uda, dioc. Exeter, lett. dim., title of prior of Bodmin
Thomas Strumpe [as Stumpe, **1055**, variant *Abbotysbury*]
Thomas Bulke, dioc. Bath and Wells, lett. dim., title of hospital of St. John, Bridgwater (*pontis Walteri*)
John Fowey, dioc. Salisbury, title of house of St. John, Lechlade (*Lechelade*)
Richard Opus, dioc. Exeter, lett. dim., title of prior of Bodmin

William Passenger [as **1054–5**]
John Cooksone, dioc. Exeter, lett. dim., title of prior of St. Nicholas, Exeter

1058 Orders celebrated by Richard, bp. of Achonry (*Caten'*), by authority of Robert, bp. of Salisbury, then abroad, in the conventual church of the friars preacher by Salisbury, 5 June 1417.

Acolytes

William Yerul, dioc. Exeter, first tonsure, lett. dim.
John Fyssheborn, dioc. Durham, first tonsure, lett. dim.
Robert Helyer, dioc. Salisbury, first tonsure
John Elleswyke, rector of Castle Rising (*Castel Rysyng*), dioc. Norwich, first tonsure, lett. dim.
Philip Raulyn, dioc. Exeter, first tonsure, lett. dim.
Hugh Trowne, friar preacher of Salisbury
William Botrygan, dioc. Exeter, first tonsure, lett. dim.
Roger Hylle, dioc. Salisbury, first tonsure
John ap John, dioc. St. Davids, first tonsure, lett. dim.
John Ellewell, John Rypon, John Anteage and Richard Wyot, dioc. Salisbury, first tonsure

Subdeacons

John Arthur, dioc. Exeter, lett. dim., title of priory of Bodmin (*Bodminie*)
Walter Bailif, dioc. Salisbury, title of monastery of Cerne
Robert Philp, dioc. Exeter, lett. dim., title of priory of Bodmin
John Stevenes and John Hoore, dioc. Salisbury, title of abbot and conv. of Eynsham (*Eynesham*)
Roger Hunte, dioc. Exeter, lett. dim., title of priory of St. Stephen, Launceston
John Elleswyke [as above], title of benefice
William Soper, dioc. Salisbury, title of priory of Sele (*Sela*), dioc. Chichester
Nicholas Abel, dioc. Bath and Wells, lett. dim., title of monastery of Athelney (*Athelneye*)
Hugh Hacke [as Hakker, **1040**], title of monastery of Tarrant (*Tarent*)
William Crede [as **1054**], title of hospital of St. John the Baptist by Wilton
Thomas Wodelonde [as Wodelond, **1057**], title of priory of Bradenstoke
John Boner, dioc. Salisbury, title of monastery of Cerne
John Ylond, dioc. Exeter, lett. dim., title of monastery of Tavistock (*Tavystochie*)
John Cowbrigge, dioc. Lincoln, lett. dim., title of monastery of Bruern (*Bruera*)
[Fo. 173v] John Fyssheborn [as above], lett. dim., title of monastery of Rewley (*Regalis loci*)
Thomas Fawkener, dioc. Exeter, lett. dim., title of priory of St. Nicholas, Exeter
William Thomas, dioc. Lincoln, lett. dim., title of monastery of Cold Norton (*Coldnorthon*)
John Wylton [as **1056**], title of prior and conv. of Ivychurch (*de Ederose*)

Deacons

John Cobethorn, dioc. Exeter, lett. dim., title of prior of Launceston

Henry Hucun, dioc. Exeter, lett. dim., title of prioress and conv. of Littlemore (*Litelmore*)

M. Hervey Willyam, dioc. Exeter, title of priory of Bodmin [cf. **1057**]

Thomas Cooke [as Cook, **1057**, variant *Frythelestoke*]

John Hele, dioc. Salisbury, title of prior and conv. of Bradenstoke

Henry Penbirthy [as **1057**]

John Brun [as **1057**]

John Pennante [as Pennans, **1057**]

John Everarde, dioc. Bath and Wells, lett. dim., title of [blank in MS.]

Thomas Jannys, dioc. Exeter, lett. dim., title of house of St. John, Lechlade (*Lechelade*) [cf. **1057**]

John Oppy [as **1057**]

Henry Kenegy, dioc. Exeter, lett. dim., title of priory of Bodmin

John Cowlyng and John Ellecombe, dioc. Exeter, lett. dim., title of priory of St. Nicholas, Exeter

Henry Nicoll [as Nycoll, **1057**]

William Michell, dioc. Bath and Wells, lett. dim., title of monastery of Muchelney (*Michelnye*)

John Nanslowen [as **1057**]

John Brydde, dioc. Bath and Wells, lett. dim., title of monastery of Athelney (*Athelnye*)

John Gyles [as **1044**], title of monastery of Montacute (*Montis Acuti*)

Nicholas Philp, dioc. Exeter, lett. dim., title of priory of Bodmin

Thomas Frye, dioc. Bath and Wells, lett. dim., title of monastery of Muchelney (*Muchelnye*)

William atte Nasshe, dioc. Salisbury, title of priory of Maiden Bradley (*Maydenbradele*)

John Netham, dioc. Coventry and Lichfield, lett. dim., title of Rewley

William Ponde [as **1054**, **1056**]

William Berebryt [as Berbryt, **1035**], title of priory of Bradenstoke

John Wynnygham, dioc. Bath and Wells, lett. dim., title of monastery of Abbotsbury (*Abbodesbury*)

Thomas Bowryng [as **1057**, variant *Abbodesbury*]

John Crefe, dioc. Exeter, lett. dim., title of priory of St. Mary, Clerkenwell

John Kelly [as **1057**]

M. Thomas Enkeston, rector of Loughborough (*Loughteborgh*), dioc. Lincoln, lett. dim., title of benefice

Priests

M. Walter Lugardyn [as Luggardyne, **1054**]

Thomas of St. Eugenia, monk of priory of Cowick (*Cowyke*), dioc. Exeter, lett. dim.

William Hendre, dioc. Exeter, lett. dim., title of prioress and conv. of Studley (*Stodeley*)

John Pretor [as **1057**]

John Purs, dioc. Exeter, lett. dim., title of monastery of Newenham (*Nywham*)
Walter Tresur [as **1054**, **1057**]
John Mayow [as **1057**]

[Fo. 174] Reynold (*Rinuoldus*) de Malendonkis, friar minor of Salisbury
John Columpton, dioc. Exeter, lett. dim., title of priory of St. Germans in Cornwall
David Maynell, dioc. Bangor, vicar choral of Salisbury cath., title of benefice [cf. **1056**]
John Hire [as Hyre, **1057**, variant *Tywardrath*]
John Drake [as **1057**]
Thomas Hoore [as Hore, **1057**]
Henry Hamme [as Hamen, **1056**]
William Bate [as **1057**]
John Stratton, dioc. Salisbury, title of house of St. Margaret, Marlborough (*Marleburgh*)
John Roos [as Ros, **1057**, variant St. Stephen, Launceston]
John Morton *alias* Bovye, dioc. Exeter, lett. dim., title of monastery of West Dereham (*Westderham*)
Walter Umfray [as **1057**]
John Houlyn [as Holyn, **1052**, **1055–6**]
Richard Skylour [as **1052**, **1057**]
William Bynham [as **1057**]
John Perrok, dioc. Salisbury, title of monastery of Newenham (*Nywenham*)
Richard Holewale, canon of Ivychurch
John Penpaly, dioc. Exeter, lett. dim., title of priory of Bodmin [cf. **1057**]
John Clyfton, dioc. Durham, lett. dim., title of monastery of Rewley

[The rest of fo. 174 r-v is blank. Three folios, which were presumably empty at the end of the episcopate, have been cut out of the gathering.]

Royal Writs and their Execution*

1059 [Fo. 175/1] Exchequer mandate to appoint collectors of the second and third moieties of a tax of one tenth and a half granted, on condition of no further taxation for two years from the feast of the Annunciation of the B.V.M. [25 March], by the convocation of Canterbury province meeting in St. Frideswide's conventual church, Oxford, 28 Nov.–10 Dec. 1407, for the defence of the realm and church, and whose terms were Easter [15 Apr. 1408], All Saints [1 Nov. 1408] and the following Easter [7 Apr. 1409]. Exempted are the benefices of poor nuns and hospitallers, concerning which the certificates of the ordinaries will be accepted, and those in the Marches of Wales and elsewhere which have been destroyed by wars and floods. Nicholas, bp. of Bath and Wells, then bp. of Salisbury, the present bishop's predecessor, was ordered to appoint collectors and to certify their names by the quindene of Hilary [27 Jan. 1408].[1] He notified the exchequer of the appointment of collectors of the first moiety; the present bp. is to appoint collectors of the second and third moieties, and to certify the collectors' names to the exchequer by the quindene of Trinity [24 June 1408]. *Teste* J. Cokayn. Westminster, 5 May 9 Hen. IV [1408]. By memoranda roll of the 9th year in Hilary *Recorda* Thresk.[2]

[1. Cf. *CFR 1405–13*, p. 94, 20 Dec. 1407.
2. The names notified by both Bishop Nicholas and Bishop Robert are listed in P.R.O., Exchequer K.R. Memoranda, E 159/184.]

1060 [EXECUTION] Commission to the abbot and conv. of Stanley to act as collectors of the second moiety in the archdeaconries of Salisbury and Wiltshire. The benefices of the poor nuns and hospitallers of these archdeaconries are exempted. The collectors are to make payment at the specified date and by sequestration of goods and other ecclesiastical censures to control any who refuse to pay. Culham, 16 June 1408.

Similar mandates to the rector and conv. of Edington (*Edyndon*) for the third moiety in the archdeaconry of Salisbury; to the prior and conv. of Bradenstoke (*Bradenestoke*) for the same in the archdeaconry of Wiltshire; to the abbot and conv. of Cerne for the second and third moieties in the archdeaconry of Dorset; to the prior and conv. of Bisham (*Brytlesham*) for the second moiety in the archdeaconry of Berkshire; to the abbot and conv. of Reading (*Redyng*) for the third moiety in the archdeaconry of Berkshire.

1061 [RETURN] [Fo. 175v/1v] Certification of the names of the collectors appointed [as in **1060**]. The benefices of the following are exempted: the poor nuns of Lacock (*Lacok*) and Kington St. Michael (*Estkyngton*) in Wiltshire archdeaconry; the poor nuns of Bromhall in Berkshire archdeaconry;

*For identification and description of the various types of writ see *Registers of Roger Martival, Bishop of Salisbury, 1315–30*, iii: *Royal Writs*, ed. S. Reynolds (Canterbury and York Soc., lix, 1965), pp. xii–xxxiii.

the poor hospitals of St. Nicholas, city of Salisbury, and of St. John, Wilton, in Salisbury archdeaconry; and the poor nuns of Tarrant (*Tarent*) in Dorset archdeaconry. Culham, 18 June 1408.

1062 Common pleas *admittatis* concerning the church of Castle Combe (*Castlecombe*), because Stephen Lescrop, knight, and Millicent his wife have recovered the presentation against Walter Medeford and Adam Uske, clerks, by default. *Teste* W. Thirnyng. Westminster, 2 May 9 Hen IV [1408]. Rotulet Cxxii Heuster.
[Enrolled P.R.O., CP 40/589.]

1063 [Fo. 176/2] Chancery mandate to give a pension to John Prentys, king's clerk, until he can be provided with a suitable benefice, on account of the new creation of Hallum as bp. of Salisbury, and to certify without delay of the action taken. *Teste me ipso.* Westminster, 1 Dec. 9 Hen. IV [1407]. By writ of privy seal. Waker[ing].[1]
[1. MS.: *Woker'*. Cf. chancery warrant, P.R.O., C 81/637/5446.]

1064 [EXECUTION] General notification by the bp. that at the king's command he has granted a pension of 100 shillings a year to John Prentys, clerk, to be paid in equal portions at Easter and Michaelmas [29 Sept.]. Sealed with the bishop's seal, [No place,] 1 Dec. 1407.

1065 Common pleas *inquiratis de bastardia,* received at London, 6 Nov. 1408, returnable on the octave of Hilary [20 Jan.], concerning Joan, wife of William Moyne, whom Walter Beauchamp, esquire, and Elizabeth his wife have asserted to be the illegitimate child of Margaret, wife of Gilbert de Roches, and therefore unable to inherit the manor of Whaddon from the latter.[1] *Teste* W. Thirnyng. Westminster, 18 Oct. 10 Hen. IV [1408].
[1. Elizabeth Beauchamp claimed the manor as daughter and heiress of Sir John de Roches. Gilbert de Roches was probably John's younger brother (*CCR 1396–9*, p. 500; *VCH Wilts.*, vii. 172, 181).]

1066 [EXECUTION] Commission to the archd. of Wiltshire or his official to hold an inquiry into the birth of Joan, wife of William Moyne, and to certify his findings, by letters patent and close, by Christmas. London, bishop's inn, 6 Nov. 1408.

1067 [Fo. $176^v/2^v$] Chancery *ne admittatis* concerning the chancellorship of Salisbury cath., the advowson of which is disputed among the king, the bp. of Salisbury, and Henry, bp. of St. Davids. *Teste me ipso.* Westminster, 14 Oct. 10 Hen. IV [1408].
[See *Fasti 1300–1541*, iii. 17–18.]

1068 [RETURN TO **1065**] Notification and report that an inquiry has been held to which were summoned William Moyne and Joan his wife, and Walter Beauchamp, esquire, and Elizabeth his wife. This revealed that the

Margaret mentioned in the writ was married when she was less than seven years old to Gilbert de Roches, who then spent the next fourteen years abroad. Meanwhile Margaret had two sons and a daughter, the said Joan, by one Thomas Gore, who publicly nurtured and recognized Joan. On the return to England of Gilbert, Joan was more than two years old, and on this account, Gilbert abstained thenceforth from the company of Margaret. Joan was thus found to be illegitimate. Sealed with the bishop's seal. Sonning (*Sunnyng*), bishop's manor, 14 Jan. 1409.

[The original return is P.R.O., Exchequer K.R., E 135/7/19, written in the same hand as entered it in the register. Thomas Gore was in possession of the manor of Whaddon in 1388 (Reg. Waltham fos. 87, 92^{v}; cf. *VCH Wilts.*, vii. 172).]

1069 Signification of the bp. to the Crown that Richard atte Beche and Alice Barefot of Wokingham (*Wokyngham*), excommunicated for contumacy when summoned to appear before the bp. for the correction of their souls, have remained obdurate for forty days and more, with a request for their capture by the secular authority. London, bishop's inn, 20 Jan. 1409.

[The original signification of excommunication is P.R.O., C 85/148/19. It is written in the same hand as entered it in the register, and was originally sealed on a tongue and folded into four. It is endorsed *Berk'*.]

1070 [Fo. 177/3] The like concerning John Elys *alias* Elyot of Aldbourne (*Aldeborne*), excommunicated for contumacy when summoned to appear before the bp. to answer charges of breach of faith and perjury at the instance of Hugh Vicary of Aldbourne. London, bishop's inn, 22 Jan. 1409.

[The original signification of excommunication is P.R.O., C 85/148/20. It is written in the same hand as entered it in the register, and was originally sealed on a tongue and folded into four.]

1071 Commission to the archd. of Salisbury or his official to inquire into the request of Walter Hungerford, knight, patron of the church of Rushall (*Rusteshall*, *Rustheshall*), that the church be appropriated, annexed and united to the priory of Longleat (*Langeleth*), in order to augment divine worship there. The annual value of the church is said to be not more than ten pounds, according to the taxation of the tenth, and a suitable portion is to be reserved for the support of a vicar to be instituted there. The archd. is to go in person to the church, having summoned the rector and others, and to make a full inquiry by trustworthy clergy and laymen of the deanery into the proposed union, ascertaining the value of the church and of the priory of Longleat, and the right of patronage, so that the bp. may be informed whether the union should be approved or not. He is to certify the bp. of the action taken. Potterne (*Poterne*), bishop's manor, 7 Oct. 1408.[1]

[1. Margin, later 15th-century hand: *Nunquam fuit ad plenum istud negocium executum ut credo. Videatur*. The advowson remained with the lords of the manor (Wiltshire Record Office, Reg. Aiscough, pt. i fo. 9).]

1072 Commission to Masters John Chaundeler, dean of Salisbury cath., and Simon Sydenham, archd. of Salisbury, at the request of Walter

Hungerford, knight, patron of the church of Rushall, to appropriate, annex and unite the church to the priory of Longleat, in order to augment divine worship there [as above, **1071**]. As the bp. is very occupied in business concerning the union of the universal Church,[1] the commissaries have full power to carry out the appropriation. London, bishop's inn, 12 Feb. 1409.

[1. Hallum left for the council of Pisa at the beginning of March 1409.]

1073 [Fo. 177ᵛ/3ᵛ] Commission to Richard [Clifford], bp. of London, to receive the resignation of Laurence Portyngale,[1] canon of Salisbury cath. and prebendary of Yetminster Prima (*Yatmynstre*) in the same, of his benefices and to collate them to Richard Clyfford [junior], priest,[2] and to notify the action taken. London, bishop's inn, 12 Feb. 1409.

[1. Otherwise known as Laurence Gomez (*CPR 1405–8*, p. 348).
2. Apparently ineffective (Wiltshire Record Office, Reg. Neville, pt.i fo. 11/17).]

1074 Common pleas *fieri faciatis de bonis ecclesiasticis* returnable on the octave of Michaelmas [6 Oct.], against John [Kyltale], parson of Padworth (*Padeworth*), for twenty-one marks [£14] being arrears of an annual pension of two marks [£1 6*s* 8*d*] payable in equal portions at the feasts of the Annunciation of the B.V.M. [25 March] and Michaelmas [29 Sept.], which the prior of Monk Sherborne (*Shirbourne*), Hants. (*in comitatu Suth't'*), recovered before William Thirnyng and his fellow-justices on the octave of Trinity 17 Ric. II [21 June 1394], and for five marks [£3 6*s* 8*d*] which were adjudged him for damages. Note of return of no lay fee by the sheriff of Berkshire on the quindene of St. John the Baptist [8 July]. *Teste* W. Thirnyng. Westminster, 13 July 10 Hen. IV [1409]. Rotulet CCCCxl Wawan'.

[Enrolled P.R.O., CP 40/594.]

1075 [EXECUTION] Mandate of Adam de Mottrum, precentor of Salisbury cath. and vicar general of the bp., to the archd. of Berkshire or his official to raise the money specified in the writ and to send it by the octave of the exaltation of the Cross [21 Sept.] by a trustworthy messenger. He is to inhibit the said John from impeding him on pain of excommunication and is to certify the vicar general by letters patent and close of the action taken. Sealed with the precentor's seal. Salisbury, 22 Aug. 1409.

1076 [WRIT AND EXECUTION] Mandate of the bp. to Geoffrey Crukadan, his official and canon of Salisbury cath., citing a summons (dated Westminster, 26 Oct. 11 Hen. IV [1409]) to a parliament to be held on the advice of the king's council at Bristol (*Bristoll*) on the quindene of Hilary [27 Jan.] for certain urgent matters touching the state and defence of the realm and church. The bp. is to attend in person, and is to warn the dean of Salisbury cath. and the archdeacons to attend in person also, the chapter by one proctor and the clergy of the dioc. by two proctors.[1] The bp. orders his official to execute the writ and to certify him by 1 Jan. 1410 of the action taken by letters patent sealed with his seal of office. Ramsbury (*Remmesbury*) park, 10 Dec. 1409.

[1. Printed in *Dignity of a Peer*, iv. 804–5.]

1077 [Fo. 178/4] Chancery mandate to receive the oath of William Cheyne, knight, as sheriff of Wiltshire, according to the enclosed form (*iuxta formam cuiusdam cedule presentibus annexe*), to give him the royal letters patent of his office which are sent by the same bearer and to notify the king's chancery without delay, in letters under seal, returning this writ. *Teste me ipso.* Westminster, 5 Nov. 11 Hen. IV [1409].
The like to receive the oath of Thomas Calston, king's escheator in Hampshire and Wiltshire. Westminster, 8 Nov. 11 Hen. IV [1409].

1078 [RETURN] Notification of the execution of the writ. London, bishop's inn, 14 Feb. 1410.

[The original returns are P.R.O., Ancient Correspondence, SC 1/43/120, 121. They are written in the same hand as entered them in the register and the wording is identical except that they are dated Sonning, bishop's manor, 17 March 1410. They were originally sealed on a tongue.]

1079 [EXECUTION] The oaths of Cheyne and Calston.[1]
Vous iurrez que bien et loialment servirez le roy en loffice del eschetour en lez countes de Suth't et Wiltes' et le prou le roy frez en toutz chostes que a vous appendent a faire solonc vostre sen et vostre poair et ses droitours quantque a la corone appent loialment garderez ne nassenterez a descres ne a concelement des droitz ne des fraunchises le roy et par la ou vous saveres les droitz le roy ou de sa corone soit en terres soit en rentes ou en fraunchises ou en suites concelez ou sustretz vostre loial peine metterez de ceo repeller, et si vous ne le poez faire vous le dirrez au roy ou a ceux de soun conseill' de queux vous soies certein qils le dirront au roy, et que loialment et a droiture tretrez le poeple de vostre ballie et a chescun frez droit auxi bien as pouvres come as riches en ceo que a vous appent affare, et pur doun ne pur promesse ne pur favour ne pur haiour tort ne frez a nully ne autry droit ne distourberez, et que rien ne prenderez par quoy le roy perde ou par quoy le droiture soit distourbe ou delaye, et que loialment frez retourner et loialment servir les briefs le roy, et que en propre persone les extentez des terres solonc lour verray value et enquestes frez, retournerez a vostre sen et a vostre poair si tost qils soient pris et ceo deinz en moys, et que vous ne prenderez null' baillif en vostre service pur qui vois ne vuillez respondre et que vous frez voz baillifs faire autiel serement come a eux appent, et que loial accompt rendrez al Eschequer le roy des issues de vostre dit baille, et que prenderez voz enquestes en lieux appiertz et ceo par endenture solonc le purport de les statutes ent faitz, si Dieux vous eide at ses seintz.

[1. In fact, just the escheator's oath, of Calston, is given.]

1080 [Fo. 178^{v}/4^{v}] Chancery *certiorari*, returnable without delay, whether Agnes de la Ryver, sister of Thomas de la Ryver, deceased, had taken vows as a nun in Shaftesbury abbey, and if so, when. *Teste me ipso*. Westminster, 20 Jan. 11 Hen. IV [1410]. Haseley.

1081 [RETURN] She took vows 48 Edw. III [1374], as stated in letters in the register of his predecessor Richard [Medford]. Sealed with the bishop's seal. London, bishop's inn, 7 Feb. 1410.

[The original return is P.R.O., Ancient Correspondence, SC 1/43/119. It is in the same hand as entered it in the register, and the wording is identical except that the date is 8 Feb. It is not clear how it was sealed.
The matter of Agnes de la Ryver had been raised in Medford's episcopate when a writ of 15 Feb. 1407 directed the bp. to certify whether Agnes, wife of Richard Clyveden, had taken vows in Shaftesbury abbey. He replied 4 Apr. that she had taken the veil when aged seven, and after nine years or more, in 1374, had made her vows as a regular and remained all her life in her vows (Reg. Medford fo. 122). The information was needed in a case in the court of common pleas in which Thomas Fouler accused William Sydecombe of stealing a horse on land in the manor of Westrop near Highworth, which land, Sydecombe asserted, belonged to him, inherited from his kinswoman, Agnes, wife of Richard Clyveden and daughter of Richard de la Ryver (P.R.O., E 135/6/76).]

1082 Common pleas *levari faciatis de bonis ecclesiasticis* returnable on the octave of Michaelmas [6 Oct.], against Walter Aymere, clerk, rector of Heddington (*Hedyngton*), for forty marks [£26 13*s* 4*d*], which Henry Colbache, clerk, recovered against him by judgment of the court, and for twenty marks [£13 6*s* 8*d*] which were adjudged him for damages, on the octave of Trinity 9 Hen. IV [17 June 1408]. Note of return of no ecclesiastical benefice by N[icholas], bp. of Bath and Wells,[1] a month after Easter [23 Apr.]. *Teste* W. Thirnyng. Westminster, 24 Apr. 11 Hen. IV [1410].

[1. See **110**.]

1083 [EXECUTION] Mandate of the bp. to the archd. of Wiltshire or his official to raise the money specified in the writ and to send it by the octave of the exaltation of the Cross [21 Sept.] by a trustworthy messenger. He is to inhibit Aymere from impeding him on pain of excommunication and is to certify the bp. by letters patent and close of the action taken. Sherborne (*Shirborn*) castle, 28 May 1410.

1084 [RETURN] £4 6*s* 8*d* raised from the ecclesiastical goods of Aymere and sent with this return. More cannot be raised on this occasion without harm to the church.

1085 Notification to the bp. received at Chardstock (*Cherdestok*), 10 July 1410, from the dean of St. Mary Arches, London, commissary general of the official of the court of Canterbury in his absence, that the tuitorial appeal of Richard Wade against sentence of excommunication, which he alleged was unjustly pronounced by the pb., has been dismissed. Wade failed to prosecute his case against John Dunnyng, chaplain, and Dunnyng was therefore dismissed from examination by the court. The bp., Dunnyng and any others with an interest in the matter are free to do what is their right, notwithstanding an inhibition obtained from the court in London, 16 May

1410 and directed to M. Richard Peryn, notary public, William Wasyn, John Pychard, Robert Down, James Aldrych, Richard Caldecot and Nicholas Taylor. London, 14 June 1410.

The bp. sent letters of signification to the Crown for the capture of Wade in the customary form, 10 July 1410.

[Wade was excommunicated 8 May 1410, **959**. The original signification of excommunication is P.R.O., C 85/148/23. It is written in the same hand as entered it in the register and was originally sealed on a tongue and folded into four. It is endorsed *Wiltes.*]

1086 [Fo. 179/5] Exchequer mandate, received at Sherborne (*Shirborn*), 7 Oct. 1410, to appoint collectors of a tax of one tenth and a half, to be paid in three moieties, granted by the convocation of Canterbury province meeting in St. Paul's, London,[1] for the defence of the realm, on condition of no further taxation before the feast of the Purification of the B.V.M. [2 Feb.] 1412. Exempted are the benefices of poor nuns and hospitallers and of others in the parts of Wales, the Marches and elsewhere which have been destroyed, concerning which the letters of the ordinaries will be accepted, and also the monastery of Barlings (*Berlyng*). The terms are the quindene of Michaelmas [13 Oct. 1410], the feast of the nativity of St. John the Baptist [24 June 1411] and the feast of the Purification of the B.V.M. [2 Feb. 1412]. The bp. is to appoint collectors and to certify their names to the exchequer by the octave of Michaelmas [6 Oct.]. *Teste* J. Cokayn. Westminster, 1 Oct. 12 Hen. IV [1410].

[Printed in *Reg. Bubwith*, i. 88.
1. It met 17 Feb. 1410 (cf. **822**).]

1087 [EXECUTION] Commission to the abbot and conv. of Cirencester, dioc. Worcester, to act as collectors of the tenth and a half in the archdeaconries of Wiltshire and Berkshire. The benefices of the following are exempted: the poor nuns of Lacock (*Lacok*) and Kington St. Michael (*Estkyngton*) in Wiltshire archdeaconry, and of Bromhall in Berkshire archdeaconry. The collectors are to make payment at the specified terms, and by sequestration of goods and other ecclesiastical censures to control any who refuse to pay. Sherborne, 8 Oct. 1410.

[Fo. 179ᵛ/5ᵛ] Similar commissions to the abbot and conv. of Glastonbury (*Glaston*) in the archdeaconries of Salisbury and Dorset. The benefices of the following are exempted: the poor hospital of St. Nicholas, city of Salisbury, and the poor hospital of St. John, Wilton, in Salisbury archdeaconry, and the poor nuns of Tarrant (*Tarent*) in Dorset archdeaconry. Sherborne, 8 Oct. 1410.

1088 [RETURN] Certification of the names of the collectors appointed and of the exempted benefices [as in **1087**]. Sherborne, 9 Oct. 1410.

1089 Chancery mandate to receive the oath of Humphrey Stafford, senior, knight, as sheriff of Somerset and Dorset, to give him the royal letters patent of his office which are sent by the same bearer and to notify the chancery, without delay, returning this writ. *Teste me ipso*. Westminster, 29 Nov. 12 Hen. IV [1410].

1090 [RETURN] Notification of the execution of the writ. Sonning (*Sonnyng*), 8 Feb. 1411.

1091 [EXECUTION] The oath of Humphrey Stafford. [As the escheator's oath, **1080**, with some slight differences of spelling and the following additions.] . . . qils le dirront au roy, et les debites le roy pur doun ne pur favour respiterez per la ou le prirez saunz tresgrande grevance des dettours lever, et que loialment . . . [as in **1080** to] ne autry droit ne distourberez, et que loialment acquiterez al Eschequere les gentez de queux vous avez rien resceu des debtes le roy, et que rien ne prenderez . . . [as in **1080** to] a vostre poair, et que vous remuerez les south viscontes qui feuront lan darrein passe, et que vous ne prenderez . . . [as in **1080** to] come a eux appent, et que nul brief resceiverez par vous ne par les vos nient enseale ne soutz seal de justices forsque en eir ou autres justices assignez en mesmes les countees ou justices de Neugate, et que vous metterez voz baillyfs de plus loialx de pais. Si Dieu vous eide et ses seintz.

1092 [Fo. 180/6] Chancery *mittimus* received at Potterne, 23 Apr. 1411, of a copy of the chancery enrolment of 6 Edw. I [1278] of certain letters patent relating to the prosecution of John Robtot, rector of East Hendred (*Esthenreth*). Westminster, 20 Apr. 12 Hen. IV [1411].
Mandate of Edward I to William de Spersholt to do his homage to Roger de Insula, son and heir of William de Insula, as his lord for the manor of West Hendred (*Westhanred*) and certain lands in East Hendred (*Esthanred*). William de Insula held these lands of the king in chief by serjeanty, and granted them by charter to William de Spersholt in fee simple at a rent of one penny *per annum* for all service as mesne-lord between the king and himself, but the king caused them to be taken into his hands until a fine of ninety marks [£60] had been paid by Spersholt for having entered the king's fee and for de Insula having alienated it without licence. Roger de Insula in the parliament held at Westminster on the quindene of Easter last past [2 May 1278], showed before the king and council that the king had been circumvented in the receipt of the homage of Spersholt, especially as Roger did his homage to the king therefor, and because his father died in the homage of Henry III and the king, and Roger holds of the king in chief nothing but the said manor and lands. Therefore the king grants that Spersholt do his homage to Roger on condition that Roger hold by serjeanty in chief, as his predecessors did. Gloucester (*Glouc'*), 7 Aug. 6 Edw. I [1278].
[The summary of Edward I's mandate is in *CPR 1272–81*, p. 275.]

1093 Notification to the bp. by John Gryffith, rector of Rushall (*Rusteshale*) and vicar of Enford that he has received the bishop's commission dated Potterne manor 23 Apr. 1411, addressed to him and John Barnarde *domicellus*. In the bishop's general visitation it was found that the occupiers of the fruits and revenues of Upavon (*Uphaven*) prebendal church had allowed the chancels of Upavon church and of Charlton (*Charleton*) chapel, dependent on it, to become ruinous, without necessary repairs to the walls, glass windows and roofs. Snow and rain fell on the high altars so that the sacrament of the mass had not been decently offered for a long time on behalf of the living and the dead, especially since even in fine weather the chancels were wide open to owls, pigeons and other harmful birds, by whose droppings the altars and chancels were most vilely fouled, and lights lit there were immediately blown out by gusts of wind. The principal manse of the church of Upavon, which was formerly a refuge for the poor, a lodging for travellers and a solace to other parishioners, had been allowed to be disfigured into a manifest ruin. The bp. therefore sequestrated the fruits, revenues and income of the church, saving the portions of the vicars of Upavon and Charlton chapel. The commissaries are to publish this sentence, warning people not to violate the sequestration, and they are to keep the sequestrated portion until the dilapidations are suitably repaired and until further notice. They, or one of them, are to notify the bp. at an opportune time of the action taken. John Gryffith, rector of Rushall, reports that he has published the sequestration, but that a certain Philip Walsteman, bailiff of Thomas Tyrwyn in the priorate of Upavon, and Peter at the Orchard in Charlton have violated and continue to violate the sequestration, so that he has been unable to take the fruits and revenues of the church into his custody. He has executed the bishop's commission to the best of his ability. The seal of the deanery of Marlborough (*Marleburg*) has been procured for application to the outside of these letters. Rushall, 14 June 1411.

1094 [Fo. 180v/6v] Exchequer *sequestrum relaxetis sicut pluries*, received at Potterne manor, 5 July 1411, concerning the revenues of Upavon church, as the king's clerk, Robert Malton, engrosser of the exchequer (whose constant residence is required there), and M. Thomas Malton, clerk, Robert Malton's farmer of the revenues of the alien priory of Upavon, which have been taken into the king's hands on account of the war with France, have reported that they were attending to the repair of various buildings of the priory (which were recently accidentally damaged by a fire) and also of various dilapidations of the buildings and chancels of the priory's churches. *Teste* J. Cokayn. Westminster, 18 June 12 Hen. IV [1411]. By red book of the exchequer and by the barons. Thresk.

1095 [Fo. 181/7] [RETURN] It is the responsibility of bishops to care for churches and their buildings. Therefore since in the bishop's recent visitation he discovered, at the complaint of the parishioners, that there were many notable dilapidations in the chancel of the church of Upavon and in its principal manse and in the chapels dependent on it, whose repair belonged to the rector of the church from the tithes and revenues, he ordered their sequestration until the dilapidations and ruins should be suitably repaired. However, certain persons have violated this sequestration, thus incurring sentence of excommunication. The Crown is begged to approve the bishop's action. Sherborne (*Shirborn*) castle, 15 July 1411.

1096 [Fo. 181v/7v] Exchequer *sequestrum relaxetis sicut pluries*, returnable on the morrow of Michaelmas [30 Sept.], concerning the revenues of Upavon church [see **1094**], or to appear in person before the treasurer and barons of the exchequer on that day. *Teste* J. Cokayn. Westminster, 11 July 12 Hen. IV [1411]. By red book of the exchequer and by the barons.
The aforesaid Robert Malton and M. Thomas Malton submitted to the bp., London, bishop's inn, 7 Dec. 1411. Having received security from them that they would repair the chancel suitably within a year, the bp. relaxed the sequestration.[1]

[1. The submission of the two Maltons is recorded at the bottom of fo. 181v with a marginal mark beside it corresponding to one by the writ of 11 July.]

1097 Common pleas *levari faciatis de bonis ecclesiasticis sicut pluries*, returnable on the octave of Michaelmas [6 Oct.], against Walter Aymere, clerk, for 33¼ marks [£22 3*s* 4*d*] owed to Henry Colbache, clerk, and for twenty marks [£13 6*s* 8*d*] which were adjudged him for damages [as in **1082**]. *Teste* W. Thirnyng. Westminster, 18 Oct. 13 Hen. IV [1411].
[EXECUTION] The bp. ordered the archd. of Wiltshire or his official to execute this writ, as he did the writ entered four folios earlier [**1082**].

1098 Common pleas *venire faciatis*, returnable on the octave of Trinity [5 June], against William Buttys, vicar of Preshute (*Presshute*), to answer John Osborn, warden of the free chapel in Marlborough (*Marleburgh*) castle, in a plea of six marks [£4] which are in arrears from an annual payment of forty shillings. Note of return of no lay fee by the sheriff of Wiltshire on the quindene of Easter [17 Apr.]. *Teste* W. Thyrnyng. Westminster, 21 Apr. 13 Hen. IV [1412]. Rotulet CCxiij J. Chosell.[1]

[Enrolled P.R.O., CP 40/605.
1. MS.: *J. Choc'*.]

1099 [Fo. 182/8] Chancery mandate, received 18 June 1412, to appoint collectors of a tax of one moiety granted, on condition that it is not raised before Michaelmas [29 Sept.],[1] by the convocation of Canterbury province meeting in St. Paul's, London, 1–19 Dec. 1411, and whose term is the feast of St. Martin in the winter [11 Nov.]. Exempted are the benefices of poor nuns and hospitallers and those destroyed or excessively reduced by wars or floods, concerning which the certificates of the ordinaries will be accepted; and in particular the monastery of Swineshead (*Swyneshed*), dioc. Lincoln; the monastery of Stanley, dioc. Salisbury; the poor nuns of St. Sepulchre, Canterbury, of Davington (*Davyngton*), the sisters of St. James, outside Canterbury, and the parish church of Stonar (*Stonore*), all of dioc. Canterbury; and the priory of the nuns of Malling (*Mallyng*), dioc. Rochester, which are excessively impoverished. The bp. is to appoint collectors and to certify their names to the exchequer by 1 Aug. at the latest. *Teste me ipso*. Westminster, 2 June 13 Hen. IV [1412].

[Cf. *CFR 1405–13*, p. 243. Printed in *Reg. Bubwith*, i. 124–5.
1. One moiety still remained due in Feb. 1412 from the grant made in the convocation of Feb. 1410, **1086**.]

1100 [RETURN] Certification of the names of the collectors appointed, namely, for the whole diocese, John Chitterne, archd. of Wiltshire, M. Geoffrey Crukadan, canon of Salisbury, and M. John Hurle, warden of the hospital of St. Nicholas by Salisbury. The benefices of the following are exempted: the poor nuns of Lacock (*Lacok*) and Kington St. Michael (*Estkyngton*), and the poor monastery of Stanley (*Stanle*) in Wiltshire archdeaconry; the poor nuns of Bromhall (*Bromehale*) in Berkshire archdeaconry; the poor hospitals of St. Nicholas, city of Salisbury, and of St. John, Wilton, in Salisbury archdeaconry; and the poor nuns of Tarrant (*Tarent*) in Dorset archdeaconry. Sonning (*Sonnyng*) manor, 20 June 1412.

1101 [EXECUTION] Commission to John Chitterne, archd. of Wiltshire, M. Geoffrey Crukadan, canon of Salisbury, and M. John Hurle, warden of the hospital of St. Nicholas by Salisbury, to act as collectors of the moiety throughout dioc. Salisbury. Sonning manor, 1 July 1412.

1102 [Fo. 182^{v}/8^{v}] Summons to a parliament to be held on the advice of the king's council at Westminster on the morrow of the Purification of the B.V.M. [3 Feb.] [as in **1076**]. *Teste me ipso*. Westminster, 1 Dec. 14 Hen. IV [1412]. Herland.
[Printed in *Dignity of a Peer*, iv. 813.]

1103 Common pleas *levari faciatis de bonis ecclesiasticis sicut pluries*, returnable on the octave of the Purification of the B.V.M. [9 Feb.], against Walter Aymere, clerk, for 33¼ marks [£22 3*s* 4*d*] owed to Henry Colbache, clerk, of the forty marks [£26 13*s* 4*d*] which Colbache recovered against him by judgment of the court, and for twenty marks [£13 6*s* 8*d*] which were adjudged him for damages [as in **1082**]. *Teste* W. Thirnyng. Westminster, 12 Oct. 14 Hen. IV [1412].

1104 Exchequer *fieri faciatis de bonis ecclesiasticis* returnable on the octave of Hilary [20 Jan.] for fifty shillings from the revenues of West Kington (*Westkyngton*) church, being arrears of an annual pension of 100 shillings granted by the king to John Werlowe and Nicholas Moryn 22 Dec. 3 Hen. IV [1401], which the church of West Kington formerly paid to the abbot of Fougères (*Figer*) in France, and which was now to be paid to Werlowe and Moryn or the one of them who lived longer, for the duration of the war with France, as is more fully contained in the royal letters patent concerning the grant.[1] The king has learnt from Werlowe that Moryn has died and that fifty shillings for the term of last Michaelmas [29 Sept.] have not been paid. Unless the parson of the church can prove to the bp. that the money has already been paid to Werlowe, the bp. is to raise it and pay it without delay to Werlowe or his attorney. If the parson shows the bp. tallies or acquittances concerning the debt, then he is to order him to be before the king's barons of the exchequer on the octave of Hilary [20 Jan.]. *Teste* J. Cokayn. Westminster, 12 Nov. 14 Hen. IV [1412], by letters patent to the court.
[1. *CPR 1401–5*, p. 33.]

1105 [Fo. 183/9] Summons to a parliament to be held on the advice of the king's council at Westminster three weeks after Easter [14 May 1413] [as in **1076**]. *Teste me ipso*. Westminster, 22 March 1 Hen. V [1413].
[Printed in *Dignity of a Peer*, iv. 816.]

1106 Chancery mandate, received by the bp. at Ramsbury (*Remmesbury*) 11 Oct. 1413, to appoint collectors of a tax of one tenth granted on condition that it is not raised before the feast of St. Martin in the winter [11 Nov.] by the convocation of Canterbury province meeting in St. Paul's, London, 6 March–8 May 1413, and whose term is the said feast. Exempted are the benefices of poor nuns and hospitallers and those in Wales, its Marches and elsewhere which have been destroyed or excessively reduced by the sea or war, concerning which the certificates of the ordinaries will be believed; and in addition the monasteries of Boxley (*Boxle*), dioc. Canterbury; of Elstow (*Elnestowe*), dioc. Lincoln; of Stanley, dioc. Salisbury; and of the nuns of Malling (*Mallyng*), dioc. Rochester; and the four parish churches of the city of Norwich recently accidentally burnt. The king's ministers are not to enter houses, granges or other places of ecclesiastical persons, to take things against the lords' will. The bp. is to appoint collectors and to certify their names to the exchequer by the quindene of Michaelmas [13 Oct.] at the latest. *Teste me ipso*. Westminster, 27 Sept. 1 Hen. V [1413].
[Cf. *CFR 1413–22*, p. 31]

1107 [EXECUTION] The bp. appointed the following collectors: the abbot and conv. of Forde, dioc. Exeter, who have various ecclesiastical goods in dioc. Salisbury, in the archdeaconries of Dorset and Salisbury; the abbot and conv. of Hailes (*Heyles*), dioc. Worcester, in Berkshire archdeaconry; and the rector and conv. of Edington (*Edyngton*), dioc. Salisbury, in Wiltshire archdeaconry. Ramsbury, 14 Oct. 1413.

1108 [Fo. 183v/9v] Summons, received at Sherborne (*Schirborn*) 29 Dec. 1413, to a parliament to be held on the advice of the king's council at Leicester (*Leycestr'*) 29 Jan. [1414] [as in **1076**]. *Teste me ipso*. Westminster, 1 Dec. 1 Hen. V [1413].
[Printed in *Dignity of a Peer*, iv. 818–19.]

1109 Chancery *ne admittatis*, received at Potterne (*Poterne*) 2 Aug. 1414, concerning the church of Barford St. Martin (*Berford sancti Martini*), whose advowson is disputed between John Cornewaill, knight, and Elizabeth his wife; and Elizabeth, widow of John de Clynton, knight, and John Taillour, clerk. *Teste me ipso*. Westminster, 26 June 2 Hen. V [1414].

1110 Exchequer *certiorari*, received at Blandford Forum (*Blaneford*), 3 Sept. 1414, returnable on the morrow of Michaelmas [30 Sept.], to search the bishop's register to discover whether the abbess and nuns of Tarrant (*Tarent*) held the church of Hanford (*Hamford*) throughout the reign of

Henry IV. *Teste* W. Lasyngby. Westminster, 8 July 2 Hen. V [1414] by the barons.

[There are no institutions to Hanford church in Reg. Medford or Reg. Hallum.]

1111 Chancery mandate, received 20 [*sic*] Nov. 1414, to appoint collectors of a tax of two tenths granted on condition of no further taxation for two years by the convocation of Canterbury province meeting in St. Paul's, London, 1–20 Oct. 1414, for the defence of the realm and church, and whose terms are the feast of the Purification of the B.V.M. [2 Feb.], and the same feast the following year [2 Feb. 1416]. Exempted are the benefices of poor nuns and hospitallers, the monastery of Stanley, dioc. Salisbury, and those in Wales, its Marches and elsewhere which have been destroyed by wars and the sea, concerning which the certificates of the ordinaries will be believed. The bp. or his vicar general is to appoint collectors and to certify their names to the exchequer by Christmas at the latest. *Teste me ipso.* Westminster, 24 Nov. 2 Hen. V [1414].

[Cf. *CFR 1413–22*, p. 90.]

1112 [Fo. 184/10] [RETURN] Notification by Geoffrey Crukadan, vicar general, of the names of the collectors appointed, namely the abbot and conv. of Bindon (*Byndon*) in the archdeaconries of Salisbury and Dorset, and the abbot and conv. of Malmesbury in the archdeaconries of Berkshire and Wiltshire, and of the exempted benefices [as in **1100**]. Salisbury, 1 Dec. 1414.

1113 Summons, addressed to the bp. or his vicar general, to a parliament to be held on the advice of the king's council at Westminster on the Monday after the feast of St. Luke the evangelist [21 Oct. 1415] [as in **1076**]. *Teste* John, duke of Bedford (*Bedeford*), warden of England. Westminster, 12 Aug. 3 Hen. V [1415].

[Printed in *Dignity of a Peer*, iv. 827.]

1114 [Fo. 184v/10v] On 26 Sept. 1411 in the parish church of Sonning (*Sonnyng*), John Wynterbourn, monk of Cerne abbey (order of St. Benedict) and proctor of the subprior and conv., appeared before the bp. and produced, exhibited and delivered the decree and process of the election by way of compromise held in the monastery of John Wede, formerly prior, as abbot, asking the bp. to approve and confirm it. After mature deliberation with the legal experts assisting him, and after a thorough examination of the process of the election, the bp. approved and confirmed it. His letter to John Wede declares that he has found the election to have been lawfully and canonically held, and that he is a suitable person, and he therefore confirms it with his pontifical authority, committing to Wede the care, rule and administration of the monastery, both spiritual and temporal. Sonning manor, 26 Sept. 1411.

1115 Mandate of the bp. to the conv. of Cerne, ordering the monks to obey John Wede, whose election as abbot the bp. has confirmed. Sonning manor, 26 Sept. 1411.

1116 Mandate of the bp. to the archd. of Dorset or his official, ordering him to do without delay what pertains to his office concerning the installation of John Wede, whose election as abbot of Cerne the bp. has confirmed. Sonning manor, 26 Sept. 1411.

1117 Letter of the bp. to the king notifying him that the office of abbot of Cerne was vac. by the death of Robert Simondesburgh and the conv. duly obtained the king's licence to elect a successor. John Wede, prior, was elected abbot, and the bp. has confirmed his election and blessed him by the laying on of hands. The bp. asks the king to extend his favour to Wede and to grant him the temporalities belonging to the monastery, according to the custom of England. [Undated.]

[The original letter to the king is P.R.O., Ecclesiastical petitions, C 84/40/16A. It was folded into two. The same clerk wrote it as entered it in the register, and the wording is identical, except that the date is given as 27 Sept. 1411. The temporalities were released to Wede 29 Sept. (*CPR 1408–13*, p. 299).]

1118 Commission to the archd. of Dorset or his official, following the election of Prior John Wede as abbot of Cerne which the proctors of the subprior and conv. have asked the bp. to confirm, to summon by name Wede and any co-elect and anyone in the monastery who wishes to oppose the election or the elect to appear before the bp. or his commissaries 26 Sept. in the parish church of Sonning. The archd. is to certify the bp. on that day by letters patent of the action taken and of the name and forename of any co-elect. [Undated.]

1119 [Fo. 185/11] On Sunday 27 Sept. 1411 in the parish church of Sonning, between masses, the bp. blessed John Wede, elected and confirmed as abbot of Cerne, according to custom, and the abbot received letters concerning this. General notification to this effect. Sonning manor, 27 Sept. 1411.

1120 [RETURN OF UNENTERED WRIT] Notification by Geoffrey Crukadan, vicar general, to the exchequer, citing a writ received 26 Aug. 1415,[1] of the names of the collectors of a tax of one tenth whom he has appointed, namely the abbot and conv. of Cerne in the archdeaconries of Salisbury and Dorset, the abbot and conv. of Abingdon (*Abyndon*) in the archdeaconry of Berkshire, and the prior and conv. of Bradenstoke in the archdeaconry of Wiltshire, and of the exempted benefices [as in **1100**]. Salisbury, 9 Sept. 1415.

[1. This unentered writ refers to the second of the two tenths granted by the convocation held 1–20 Oct. 1414 (cf. **1111**, *CFR 1413–22*, p. 90; *Reg. Bubwith*, i. 189).]

[Fo. 185ᵛ/11ᵛ and the top quarter of fo. 186/12 are blank.]

1121 [Fo. 186/12] Chancery mandate, received 11 Dec. 1416, to appoint collectors of a tax of two tenths granted by the convocation of Canterbury province meeting in St. Paul's, London, 9–23 Nov. 1416, and whose terms were the feast of the Purification of the B.V.M. [2 Feb. 1417] for one tenth and a moiety, and the octave of Easter [18 Apr. 1417] for the other moiety. Exempted are the benefices of poor nuns and hospitallers, and those in Wales and elsewhere destroyed or excessively reduced by enemy incursions or floods; the goods and benefices of the colleges of St. Mary of Winchester in Oxford and of St. Mary by Winchester (of the bp. of Winchester's foundation), and the church of Portland (*Portlond*), dioc. Salisbury, which was burnt, robbed and reduced by enemy incursions. The grant is made on condition that the payment of one of the tenths granted by the convocation meeting in St. Paul's, London, 18 Nov.–2 Dec. 1415, which was to have been paid at Martinmas [11 Nov. 1417], should be put off until the feast of the nativity of St. John the Baptist [24 June 1418]. And further that no one should be excused from the collection of these tenths by royal licence and that the assessment figures acted upon by the ordinaries shall be accepted without question by the exchequer. The vicar general is to appoint collectors and to certify their names to the exchequer by Christmas at the latest. *Teste me ipso*. Westminster, 28 Nov. 4 Hen. V [1416].

[Printed in *Reg. Chichele*, iii. 26–7; cf. *CFR 1413–22*, pp. 186–7.]

1122 [Fo. 186v/12v] [RETURN] Notification by Geoffrey Crukadan, vicar general, of the names of the collectors appointed, namely the abbot and conv. of Sherborne (*Shirbourne*) in the archdeaconries of Salisbury and Dorset, the abbot of Stanley (*Stanle*) in Wiltshire archdeaconry and the prior and conv. of Bisham (*Bustelsham*) in Berkshire archdeaconry, and of the exempted benefices [as in **1100**].

[The remaining three quarters of fo. 186v/12v are blank.]

1123 [Fo. 187/13] Notification of the abbot of Malmesbury to the bp. that he has held an inquiry in accordance with the bishop's commission into the proposed lease by the prioress of Kington St. Michael (*Kynton*) of certain lands and tenements to Robert Russell of Bristol (*Bristoll*) for the term of three lives. A majority asserted that the lease would be useful and necessary to the prioress and conv. William Westbury, the bishop's servant, was present at the inquiry, and the abbot has asked him to inform the bp. more fully in his letters which the bearer of the present letter has also. In addition, he will tell the bp. what amends Edward Cerne has promised for certain unlawful acts perpetrated against the liberty of the church. Malmesbury, feast of the decollation of St. John the Baptist [29 Aug.].[1]

[1. No year given. The clerk who made this entry was active in Hallum's chancery, 1409–13.]

1124 Letter of William Westbury, the bishop's servant, giving details of the inquiry [cf. **1123**]. The abbot of Malmesbury, having been required by the bp. to ascertain whether it would be prejudicial to the prioress and conv. of Kington St. Michael if they leased certain of their lands[1] to Robert Russell of Bristol, his wife and one of his children for their lives at an annual rent, asked Westbury to carry out the inquiry. He has discovered that the said lands are not worth more than forty shillings annually at most to the conv. The lessees will pay this amount, besides a fine of five marks [£3 6*s*8*d*]. Moreover, Russell will in a short time rebuild certain ruined houses on the lands at his own cost. Russell is a rich man and give many alms all round, and if the lease is effected Westbury expect that he will be the convent's best friend. He has heard this said by others, especially since Russell was born in the town where the said lands are. Thus, to his knowledge, the lease would be to the convent's benefit. Feast of the decollation of St. John the Baptist [29 Aug.].

[1. Possibly in Bristol, where the convent owned a messuage (*VCH Wilts.*, iii. 260; *Valor Ecclesiasticus temp. Henr. VIII* (6 vols., 1810–25), ii. 113–14).]

1125 Letter of the cardinal bishops, priests and deacons of the Roman Church to Robert, bp. of Salisbury, announcing that the pope [John XXIII] has created him a cardinal priest, and summoning him to the Roman curia as soon as possible to undertake with them the administration of the Church. Rome, 5 June, 4th indiction [1411].

[Cf. *Hierarchia Catholica*, i. 33. The king refused to sanction this creation or that of Thomas Langley, bp. of Durham, and it remained inoperative. The reason given in the king's letter to the pope was the impossibility of dispensing with their services in the government of England (British Library, Harley MS. 431 fo. 1).]

1126 [Fo. 187v/13v] General notification by Thomas Prestbury, abbot of Shrewsbury, chancellor of Oxford university, that M. Peter Clerk, scholar of the university, has been examined, in relation to various articles of faith contrary to the decree of the holy Roman Church, by the chancellor and twelve venerable men appointed by the university to reprove newly-introduced errors and heresies and certain books written by John Wycliffe. Clerk was brought to them as suspected of dissenting from the Catholic faith and was questioned many times. Finally he was examined concerning the sacrament of the altar, as to whether he believed as the Church has decreed. Clerk read the paragraph 'Una est vero fidelium universalis ecclesia', in the chapter 'Firmiter credimus', out of 'De summa trinitate et fide catholica',[1] and he declared publicly before them that this text was Catholic doctrine and that he believed firmly in it. Therefore since no one convicted Clerk of non-Catholic views on any article of faith, they have dismissed him and consider him Catholic. These letters patent, sealed with the chancellor's seal of office have been drawn up as a testimony. Oxford, 6 Nov. 1410.

Clerk exhibited these letters to the bp. of Salisbury at Potterne manor, 26 Feb. 1412.

[Cf. constitutions against Lollards of Dec. 1407, **955**, VI, XI.

1. *Corpus Iuris Canonici*, ii, col. 5, *Decretal. Greg. IX* 1, 1, c. 1, § 3.]

1127 Exchequer *certiorari* to the bp. of Salisbury or his vicar general, returnable on the morrow of the close of Easter [12 Apr. 1416], in relation to the collection of the tax of two tenths granted by the convocation of Canterbury province meeting in St. Paul's, London, 18 Nov.–2 Dec. [1415]. Exempted are the benefices of poor nuns and hospitallers, and those in parts of Wales and elsewhere which have been destroyed or excessively reduced by hostile invasions, floods and in other ways. As the barons of the exchequer have inadequate records of these exceptions in the exchequer rolls, [Fo. 188/14] the vicar general is to examine the registers and other records as to which churches in his dioc. are appropriated to nuns, hospitallers or other religious houses and from what date; whether there are vicarages in the appropriated churches and at what sum they are taxed and assessed; what sums the religious houses paid in the past towards a whole tenth from their portions; what churches are destroyed or excessively reduced by wars and floods and from what date; and in which archdeaconries and deaneries such appropriated churches and vicarages or destroyed and diminished goods and benefices are situated. *Teste* W. Lasyngby. Westminster, 12 Feb. 4 Hen. V [1417] by the said concession and by the barons.

[An earlier writ to the same effect is in P.R.O., K.R. Memoranda, E 159/193, dated 13 Nov. 4 Hen. V [1416], returnable by the quindene of Hilary [27 Jan. 1417]. As no return was made, a second writ was sent, which is that here included in the register.]

[The rest of fo. 188/14 and fo. 188^{v}/14^{v} are blank.]

Judicial Acta*

[Fo. 189/15. A space of 6.5 cm. has been left at the top of this folio, presumably for a heading to this quire.†]

1128 [*Matrimonial case between William and Agnes Roper of Hungerford*] On 28 May 1408 in Welford parish church, before M. John Haget, treasurer of Lincoln cath., bishop's commissary with sufficient authority to deal with this matter sitting in judgment, there appeared a certain William Roper of Hungerford who had been summoned to appear by William Broun, chaplain,[1] mandatory, at the instance of Agnes Roper of Hungerford, whose case begun before the bp. was still undecided, to answer concerning certain violent attacks and injuries. When asked whether Agnes was his wife, he replied no, because of a pre-contract made with one Alice Sawser. Also he alleged that on account of this pre-contract, a divorce had been pronounced between him and Agnes by William,[2] rector of Ham, by virtue of a commission addressed to the rector by the official of the dean of Salisbury cath. Agnes sought that William Sawser and his sister Alice of Hidden (*Hyddene*) should be cited, and the said bishop's commissary decreed that they should appear before the bp. or his commissary on 30 May in the same place.

On this day William Sawser and his sister Alice appeared before the bp., having been summoned to appear by William Broun, chaplain, and together with the defendant, William Roper, they swore on the gospels to speak the truth. Then, when William Roper was asked whether Agnes was his wife, or whether he had lawfully contracted marriage with her, he replied yes. Also whether he was known as her consort, he replied yes. Asked whether he was known as consort to Alice Sawser, he replied yes. Asked whether he had made a pre-contract with her before his marriage with Agnes, he replied no. Asked why he formerly went through a divorce from Agnes, whether he consented willingly to this or not, he replied that it had never been his will, but he had done it through fear, at the advice of certain people. Alice Sawser, asked whether William Roper had contracted marriage with her and was her husband, replied yes. Asked in what words he contracted marriage with her, she replied, 'I William take you as my wife, on account of the scandal which you have endured, being pregnant by me', and she had said, 'I take you as my husband'. Asked who had been present, she said three people, of whom two had died, but one was still living. Asked whether she knew that William Roper was married to Agnes or whether she had heard the customary proclamation in the church, she

*The calendar of the Judicial Acta amounts in many items to a verbatim translation. Entries are given a title to indicate the contents.

† This quire consists of single folios stitched inside the simple bifolium of fos. 189 and 193.

replied that she had heard from others but had not heard it herself in church, and what he did not deny nor contradict she forthwith dismissed because of the force of the same William. William Sawser, asked whether he had been present at the marriage of William and Alice, replied that he believed that a marriage had been contracted but he had not been present, although he had heard from his brother and Alice, and from the two others who had died, and that he had never heard that William had been married to Agnes, although he had heard the banns for contracting marriage, and that he knew nothing of a pre-contract between William and Alice. The bp. assigned the parties Monday 18 June to produce before him or his commissary the alleged process of divorce and any other evidence, in the church of St. Nicholas, Abingdon (*Abyndon*), or wherever else he should happen to be in his city and diocese.

On that day there appeared before the commissary Agnes and William, but Alice Sawser did not appear and was accused of contumacy. William Roper did not produce the process of divorce, wherefore the commissary decreed that he should be punished according to the form of law. Agnes demanded that Alice should be excommunicated on account of her contumacy and be summoned to explain why she ought not to be removed from the company and cohabitation of her husband William Roper, and why the lawful wife ought not to be restored to him. This the commissary decreed at the instance of Agnes, and appointed the Monday after the feast of St. John the Baptist [Monday, 25 June] for them to appear in the same place before the bp. or his commissary.

On that day there appeared the said parties and with them John Netterlanus, who had been summoned by the rector of St. John, Devizes (*Devysis*), mandatory, to give evidence in the case. He swore in the legal way to speak the truth, and said that he had known William Roper for about twenty years. He was not present when William contracted marriage with Agnes, although he had been present at the solemnization because he was then in William's service, and Agnes had been continually in William's house for two years. He was not present at the alleged pre-contract between William and Alice, although once in Lent when William could not for conscience's sake have carnal relations with Alice, he heard him say, 'Do not worry, Alice. I will always love you and never send you away'; however, he did not promise this with an oath.[3] Because the commissary did not receive a certificate of the denunciation of Alice as excommunicate, he ordered the vicar of Hungerford, mandatory, to be summoned for contempt and disobedience, and he ordered the sentence against Alice to be increased. He decreed that letters should be drawn up concerning these matters for the bishop's good pleasure.

[1. Of Holy Trinity chantry in Hungerford church, **246**.
2. Probably William Hildeslee (Reg. Waltham fo. 182v).
3. MS.: *manualiter*]

1129 [Fo. $189^{v}/15^{v}$] [*Proceedings against Robert Napper, vicar of Hungerford, for neglecting to make a citation ordered by the bp.*] On 30 Sept. 1408 in the prebendal church of Potterne (*Poterne*), before M. John Haget, bishop's commissary, specially appointed to deal with this matter sitting in judgment, certificates were received from William Broun, chaplain, mandatory, concerning the summons made against Robert Napper, the alleged vicar of Hungerford, that he failed to make the summons ordered by the bp. of William Roper and Alice Sawser of Hungerford to appear before the bp. in the unfinished case begun at the instance of Agnes Roper. Robert, however, did not appear, so the commissary excommunicated him, and decreed letters concerning this. When this came to the notice of the vicar, he appealed for protection to the archbishop's court of audience, where the case between Robert and the bp. of Salisbury proceeded to several legal actions. But because Robert did not prove his case the bp. was acquitted and the inhibition on him was relaxed. The bp. received letters to this effect 23 Nov. at Sonning (*Sonnyng*) manor, and he then excommunicated Robert and ordered him to be denounced as excommunicate. On 7 Dec. Robert appeared before the bp. at Salisbury, sought pardon and submitted to the bishop's mercy. At the instance of M. John Chaundeler, dean of Salisbury cath.,[1] the bp. absolved Robert from excommunication after he had first sworn to obey the laws of the church.

[1. The church of Hungerford formed part of the endowment of the prebend of Ogbourne in Salisbury cath. (*VCH Berks.*, iv. 198).]

1130 [*Proceedings against William Holtham, vicar of Ramsbury*] On 26 Nov. 1409 in the prebendal church of Ramsbury (*Remmesbury*), William Holtham, vicar of Ramsbury, who had been summoned to appear before the bp. or his commissary to reply to certain charges to be brought by the bp. concerning his soul's correction, made his appearance, and M. William Lyndewode D.Cn. & C.L., appointed by the bp. to this matter, adjourned the case to 6 Dec. On 6 Dec. William appeared again, swore to speak the truth and heard the charges brought against him by the commissary. To the first he alleged his purgation attested by a letter sealed by the dean of Salisbury; the second charge he admitted, submitting himself to the bishop's mercy; the other charges he repeatedly denied. Finally, on 23 Dec. he abjured etc., and also the suspect places, under pain of deprivation of his benefice.[1] Penance was enjoined on him that once before Whitsun [11 May 1410] he should go as a pilgrim to Salisbury and there in the cath. should offer before the image of the Virgin one candle of one pound's weight of wax, and that within that time he should distribute two marks [£1 6*s* 8*d*] of the country's money among his poor parishioners. He swore publicly that he would faithfully perform this penance unless he received another pardon from the bp. etc.

[1. This was probably a case of fornication (cf. similar wording in **1140**).]

1131 [Fo. 190/16] [*Proceedings against M. Thomas Turk, vicar of Bere Regis, for heresy*] Letter of the official of the dean of Salisbury cath. to the bp. or his commissaries, stating that he recently received the bishop's mandate (dated Potterne manor, 2 May 1411) addressed to the dean or his official, ordering him to summon M. Thomas Turk, vicar of Bere Regis (*Byre*) prebendal church, to appear before the bp. or his commissaries in Potterne prebendal church on 11 May to answer in person concerning certain charges of heresy, and further to do and receive as justice persuades. The official certifies that he apprehended Thomas in person in the city of Salisbury on 6 May, and summoned him. Sealed with the seal of his office, etc.

M. Thomas Turk appeared and lawfully excused himself on the articles brought before him by the bp., and was dismissed.

[Cf. Constitutions against Lollardy of Dec. 1407, **955**, XIII.]

1132 [*Proceedings against Walter Burgh, chaplain, and John Jordan of Netherbury, for maladministration of the will of Stephen Stanlak, formerly vicar of Sonning*] Letter of the official of the dean of Salisbury cath. to the bp. or his commissaries, stating that he recently received the bishop's mandate (dated Potterne manor, 3 Feb. 1412) addressed to him. The bp. had received the serious complaint of Robert Wysbeche and Philip Pounsard, proctors of the parish church of St. Andrew, Sonning (*Sonnyng*), alleging that Walter Burgh, chaplain, and John Jordan of Netherbury parish, the executors of the will of Stephen Stanlak, late vicar of Sonning,[1] long retained and still retain one missal and 13*s* 3*d* [*sic*] bequeathed to the said church. He therefore ordered the official to summon the executors to appear before him or his commissaries in Potterne prebendal church on the morrow of St. Valentine the martyr [15 Feb.] to reply to these charges, and to do and receive as the quality of the business requires. The official certifies that he has diligently sought Walter and John and made inquiries, but has not been able to find them, because Walter went away from Netherbury several years ago and lives elsewhere, and John died about three years ago. Sealed with his seal of office. Salisbury, 12 Feb. 1412.

When this letter was read before the bishop's commissaries, they decreed that Walter should be cited by ways and means. Letters will be sent out to this effect at the bishop's pleasure.

[1. He resigned 11 Aug. 1393 (Reg. Waltham fo. 153).]

1133 [*Purgation of Thomas Punche of Reading from charges of heresy or Lollardy*] General notification that on 2 May 1412 Thomas Punche of the parish of St. Giles, Reading (*Radyng*) appeared before the bishop's commissaries lawfully appointed to deal with this matter in Sonning (*Sonnyng*) church, and purged himself with a praiseworthy number of compurgators from the alleged crime of heresy or Lollardy, in writing or having written books in English containing doctrines and opinions contrary to the orthodox faith and the determination of the holy Roman Church, and of holding and observing these opinions in the town of Reading and neighbouring places. Sonning, 2 May 1412.

[Cf. Constitutions against Lollardy of Dec. 1407, **955**, XIII.]

1134 [*Suspension of Charminster prebendal church*] On 9 Aug. 1412 the bp. imposed a suspension on the prebendal church of Charminster (*Chermyn-str'*) because the clergy and people there did not show reverence and honour to the bp. as their ordinary, by ringing the bells, when he came to the church to confirm children (*crismandi pueros*) and exercise his pastoral office in other respects.

On 11 Aug. 1412 in his castle of Sherborne (*Shirborn*) he relaxed this, at the instance of the parishioners and other trustworthy men.

1135 [Fo. 190ᵛ/16ᵛ] [*Absolution of John Sterney from excommunication for violence to Nicholas Sterr, rector of Stanton St. Quintin*] On the Monday after the feast of St. Thomas the apostle 1409 [23 Dec.] in Ramsbury (*Remmesbury*) prebendal church, before the bishop's commissary sitting in judgment there appeared Nicolas Sterr, rector of Stanton St. Quintin (*Staunton*), who had been summoned by John Monketon, apparitor, to witness the absolution to be given to John Sterney of Clack (*Clak*), or to give reasonable cause why John should not be absolved from sentence of excommunication imposed because John laid violent hands on Nicholas. Because Nicholas did not oppose the absolution but entirely consented, the commissary absolved John after he had sworn to obey the mandates of the church. Penance was enjoined on him the same day.

1136 [*Proceedings against Nicholas Sterr, rector of Stanton St. Quintin, on charges of non-residence and immorality*] On 16 Jan. 1410 in Ramsbury prebendal church, Nicholas Sterr, rector of Stanton St. Quintin, appeared before the bishop's commissary to reply to certain articles concerning the correction of his soul. To the first article, namely that he was absent from the church of Stanton St. Quintin, serving the church of Somerford,[1] without having obtained a licence or dispensation of his superior, he alleged that the commissary's correction had been carried out. He was assigned the first juridical day after the Sunday when 'Quasimodo geniti' is sung [Sunday, 30 March 1410] to appear before the bp. or his commissary, wherever he might then be in the city or diocese of Salisbury, to hear the bishop's decree concerning this and to do what justice persuades. To the second article, namely that he had committed adultery for more than two years with Maud, wife of John Draper of Clack, he denied the charge and sought to purge himself in the legal way. He was assigned the next Saturday [18 Jan.] to purge himself of the said crime before the commissary and the prior of Bradenstoke (*Bradenestoke*), with five other men of his rank in the conventual church of Bradenstoke. On 18 Jan. he and his compurgators took an oath and he purged himself from the alleged crime in the legal way, with no one contradicting. The commissaries pronounced him well purged and wrongly defamed and decreed letters to this effect against his defamers. With regard to the article that he was a common frequenter of taverns and a contentious person, he was assigned the first juridical day after Sunday, 30 March, to hear the bishop's decree. Likewise concerning the article that when there was a case between him and John Sterney which was known to pertain to the church court he dragged John to the secular court, he was assigned the same day to hear the bishop's decree.[2]

[1. He was not the incumbent of Great Somerford or Little Somerford, but probably served as a chaplain in one of these.
2. Sterr exchanged the church of Stanton St. Quintin for a benefice in dioc. Bath and Wells 10 March 1410, **143**.]

1137 [*Purgation of John Melton, rector of Nettleton, from charges of immorality*] On Saturday 18 Jan. 1410 in the conventual church of Bradenstoke, before the prior of Bradenstoke and the bishop's commissary, both with sufficient authority for this, there appeared John Melton, rector of Nettleton (*Netelton*). He had been summoned for his soul's correction, because he was said to have carnally known Margaret his servant, but he denied this and sought to purge himself in the legal way. He and his five compurgators took an oath, and he purged himself from the alleged crime in the legal way, with no one contradicting. The commissaries pronounced him well purged and wrongly defamed and decreed letters to this effect.

1138 [*Purgation of John Donnynk, vicar of Chitterne, from charges of adultery*] On 5 May 1410 in the parish church of Chitterne, before the bishop's commissary lawfully appointed to deal with this matter, there appeared John Donnynk, vicar of Chitterne, who had been summoned. He purged himself in the legal way of the alleged crime of adultery committed with Joan, wife of Richard Wade, having sworn according to the form specified to him. The commissary pronounced him well purged and wrongly defamed, restored him by decree to his former status and reputation, and decreed letters of excommunication against his defamers in the legal way.

1139 [*Purgation of Richard Fyssher, rector of Stock Gaylard, from charges of adultery*] On 19 Aug. 1410 in the chapel of St. Mary Magdalen by Sherborne (*Shirborn*) castle, before the bishop's commissaries lawfully appointed to deal with this matter, there appeared Richard Fyssher, rector of Stock Gaylard (*Stoke Colard*), who had been summoned on charges of adultery with Christine, wife of Thomas Hykys of the same parish. He denied this and purged himself in the legal way with seven compurgators of his rank, according to the form specified to him. The commissaries decreed that he had been wrongly defamed and was well purged, and restored him to his former status.

[Fyssher nevertheless exchanged his benefice 6 Nov. 1410, Appendix A VII.]

1140 [Fo. 191/17] [*Proceedings against John Rook, vicar of Stinsford, on charges of fornication*] On 11 Aug. 1410 in the chapel of St. Mary Magdalen by Sherborne castle, before the bishop's commissaries, there appeared John Rook, vicar of Stinsford (*Stantisford*) and confessed that he had committed the crime of fornication with Felicity atte Persons, a woman of Alton Pancras (*Alton*) parish, and had continued with her for twelve years. He abjured her and the suspect places on pain of deprivation of his benefice. Penance was enjoined on him that before Christmas he should distribute 6*s* 8*d* among the poor and needy of his parish; also he should abstain entirely from eating fish on Friday until then; and that on seven Sundays he should openly and publicly genuflect at the font in his church and say one nocturn of his psalter. The right was reserved to impose a public penance if it was found that his crime was generally known.

1141 [*Purgation of John Cook, vicar of Thatcham, from charges of adultery*] On 22 Dec. 1410 at Sonning (*Sonnyng*), before the bishop's commissaries lawfully appointed to deal with this matter, there appeared John Cook, vicar of Thatcham (*Thacham*), accused of the serious crime of adultery with Alice, wife of Thomas Torner of Thatcham, and he purged himself in the legal way according to the form specified to him with a praiseworthy number of priests as compurgators, with the necessary people having been summoned and with no one objecting. The commissaries pronounced him well purged and wrongly defamed, and restored him by decree to his former status. He obtained a letter of his purgation in the customary form.

[Cook nevertheless exchanged his benefice 20 Apr. 1411 for one in dioc. Winchester, **244**.]

1142 [*Proceedings against William Mundy of Wokingham, on charges of heresy*] On 15 Feb. 1412 in Potterne prebendal church, before the bishop's commissaries sufficiently appointed for the following matter, there appeared William Mundy, chapman of Wokingham (*Wokyngham*), summoned concerning heretical wickedness and other charges concerning his soul's correction and well-being. When he had sworn in the legal way to speak the truth, the commissaries laid the following charges against him, to which he replied as follows. First, that he publicly held and affirmed that all those adoring or giving any reverence to images of the holy cross or of any saint, are cursed: he denied the statement. That all who confer anything on brothers of any order, or maintain them, are cursed, because they are enemies of God as voluntary mendicants: he replied that it is not alms to give anything to mendicant brothers inasmuch as their order is not founded on the law of God but expressly contrary, since they have chosen voluntary mendicancy, whereas the proverb says 'I give riches or poverty' etc.[1] That all who go on pilgrimage to St. Thomas of Canterbury or to the cross of Boxley (*Boxle*) or to the priory of Bridlington (*Bridelyngton*)[2] or other such places are cursed, because he did not believe, nor could he believe, that Thomas, archbishop of Canterbury, was a saint in heaven, even though he was called such on earth: he replied that he did not know whether it was permissible to make pilgrimages or not. That any married person who well and truly observes his married state is as high in dignity as the highest priest, namely the pope: he denied the statement. That God lied and made lies: he denied the statement. That the body of Christ consecrated on the altar by the priest is blessed bread and nothing more: he denied the statement.

Then the commissaries, having first considered William's replies given on each statement, deferred the case to the next day. And on the next day,

William appeared before them and humbly submitted himself to God and the Church, and he renounced all opinions held or preached against the holy Church or its decree. Having touched the holy gospels, he abjured all heresy and Lollardy and promised that he would firmly observe whatever the holy mother Church, that is the Roman Church, namely the pope and cardinals etc. had decreed or would decree in the future. He vowed and swore that he would condemn all that the Church had condemned or would condemn in the future.

All this the said William did again on 18 Feb. before the bp. sitting in judgment in his chapel of Potterne. And it was enjoined upon him, as part of his penance, that on the second Sunday in Lent [28 Feb. 1412], in the parish church of Wokingham, where he had been defamed concerning the said crime, between masses, in the presence of all the people, he should openly and clearly, in a loud and intelligible voice, say and confess that he had erred and had wrongly obtained false opinions contrary to the Church's decree, but now being better informed by the bp. of Salisbury and his advice, he had renounced them all and any others contrary to the Church's decree.

[Cf. Constitutions against Lollardy of Dec. 1407, **955**, XIII.
1. Proverbs 30:8.
2. John de Thweng, former prior of Bridlington, was canonized 24 Sept. 1401 (*CPL 1396–1404*, p. 458).]

1143 [Fo. 191v/17v] [*Proceedings against John Elys, rector of Donnington, on charges of fornication*] On 20 Feb. 1412 in the chapel of Potterne manor, before the bp. sitting in judgment, there appeared John Elys, rector of Donnington (*Donynton*),[1] who had been summoned in relation to certain matters concerning his soul's correction and well-being. He was charged with having for a long time committed fornication with a certain Isabel, his servant, begetting children by her, and he admitted the charge. Then the bp. made John abjure the said Isabel on pain, as follows:[2]

'Before you, reverend father in Christ, Robert by God's grace bishop of Salisbury, I, John Elys, rector of Donnington, Salisbury diocese, defamed by many on account of the serious crime of incontinence committed with a certain Isabel, my servant, having judicially confessed before you, reverend father, that I committed this crime with her, and wishing, with God's help, to avoid this sin and its occasions hereafter, do hereby promise that I will not in future keep the said woman or any other in my house or in any other, nor will have any carnal dealings with her or any other, nor will I communicate in any unlawful way with her or any other. And if I should happen to be convicted in any way concerning these matters, which God forbid, then I will resign my said church and anything I have in it into your hands or those of your successor, simply and without any difficulty. I am willing and concede that you or your successor shall compel me in this event by ecclesiastical censure summarily and without judicial formality to make this resignation. I bind myself by this faithfully to observe all and every one of these terms, and I swear by the holy gospels that I will faithfully keep and obey everything in it, expressly renouncing all contradiction and appeal and any remedy of defence which might suit me against the foregoing terms or any one of them.'

Finally the bp. reserved to himself the power of enjoining penance for the crime committed, at his own pleasure, and when it pleased him, etc.[3]

[Cf. *Corpus Iuris Canonici*, ii. col. 454, *Decretal. Greg. IX* 3, 2, c. 3, and note 3 below.
1. Margin, 15th-century hand: *Nota bene contra Johannem Elys capellanum*
2. Margin, in another 15th-century hand: *Forma abiuracionis consorcii concubine per rectorem factae*
3. Margin, 15th-century hand: *Hec forma non est observanda quia est expresse contra textum decretalis 'Clericos, de cohabitacione clericorum et mulierum'*]

1144 [*Proceedings against John Dyer of Hungerford on charges of violence to John Trumpelyn, chaplain*] Commission of the bp. of Salisbury to the official of the prebendal jurisdiction of Ogbourne (*Okebourne*) and the vicar of Hungerford, stating that he has received the plea of John Trumpelyn, chaplain, that although all who lay violent hands on a clergyman, and especially on a priest, are automatically excommunicated, in accordance with the canon, 'Si quis suadente diabolo',[1] nevertheless one John Dyer of Hungerford, a son of iniquity who does not have God before his eyes, boldly laid violent hands on John Trumpelyn knowing him to be a priest and a clergyman, bearing clerical dress and tonsure, in an unlawful case, to the grave danger of his soul, and the considerable detriment of the plaintiff, for which he begged the bp. to provide a suitable remedy. The commissaries are to cite John Dyer to appear before the bp. or his commissaries in Sonning (*Sonnyng*) parish church on the Friday after the feast of St. George [28 Apr.] to reply to the plaintiff and to do or receive as justice persuades. They are to notify the bp. as to the action taken. Sonning manor, 14 Apr. 1412.

On 28 Apr. the said parties appeared in person before the bishop's commissaries. John Dyer admitted his sin and submitted himself, and with the consent of the plaintiff was absolved from sentence of excommunication, after he had sworn to obey the mandates of the church and to perform the penance that should be enjoined.

[1. *Corpus Iuris Canonici*, i, col. 822, *Decreti Secunda Pars*, 17, 4, c. 29.]

1145 [*Interdict imposed on Heytesbury prebendal church for disrespect to the bp.*] Commission and mandate of the bp. to all the abbots and priors etc.[1] of the city and diocese of Salisbury, stating that when the bp. recently visited the prebendal church of Heytesbury (*Heyghtesbury*) to confirm children (*crismandi pueros*) and exercise his pastoral office in other respects as is fitting, the clergy and people did not wish to obey his lawful and canonical mandates, neither showed due reverence and honour to his episcopal dignity, but rather publicly refused this, on account of their rebellion, contumacy and even manifest contempt towards the bp. as their diocesan. The bp. therefore decreed and canonically warned under pain of interdict that no masses or other divine offices should be celebrated in the church by any chaplains or clergy, but that the church should be closed and suspended as far as entry for such purposes was concerned, until the chaplains and parishioners deserved pardon. However it has been established before the bp. that several people, both clergy and lay, have violently broken down the doors of the church and have contemptuously celebrated masses and other divine offices there, to the offence of God, the contempt of the bishop's monition and suspension and manifest injury to his pastoral dignity. The bp. therefore, invoking the name of Christ, lays the church under an ecclesiastical interdict, and orders the clergy to publish this sentence at appropriate times and in appropriate places, and to observe it and see that others observe it, until further notice. Ramsbury (*Remmesbury*) manor, 26 Aug. 1412.

[1. Presumably all the ranks of clergy are intended.]

1146 [Fo. 192/18] [*Submission of the chaplain of Heytesbury church*] On 28 Aug. 1412 in Sonning (*Sonnyng*) manor, before the bp., there appeared John Wad, chaplain of Heytesbury prebendal church, although he had been summoned for another day, to reply concerning his knowing and malicious disobedience to the bishop's inhibition and warning, and concerning charges of heretical wickedness. He excused himself on all these and was dismissed.

Afterwards, on 2 Sept. in Sonning parish church, before the bishop's commissaries lawfully appointed to deal with this matter, there appeared Richard Edward, another chaplain of the said church, and concerning the aforementioned charges he submitted himself to God and the Church, and he promised and swore that he would perform the penance that was enjoined and that would be enjoined on him. He was enjoined that on the first day after the relaxation of the interdict, when the greatest number of people were in the church of Heytesbury, and when he was about to approach the mass, he should take off his priestly vestments, except his chasuble, and in the presence of the people should genuflect to the font and say the seven penitential psalms with the litany; then he should rise and say in a loud and intelligible voice that he had erred and acted wrongly in not obeying the bp. in the aforesaid matters, but that now that he was better informed he wished and intended to obey. The bp. reserved to himself the rest of the penance, to be enjoined when he pleased.

1147 [*Relaxation of the interdict imposed on Heytesbury church*] Thereupon [see **1146**], a humble petition was made on behalf of the dean of Salisbury cath., prebendary of Heytesbury, that the bp. should relax the interdict. The bp., considering that the interdict did not proceed from the will, agreement or approval of the dean or of the majority of the parishioners, relaxed it as follows:

Notification by the bp. to the abbots and priors etc. that since Richard Edward, chaplain of Heytesbury, and others who were the cause of the interdict, have submitted themselves to the bishop's correction and ordering, at the petition of the dean of Salisbury cath., the bp., not wishing the majority of the parishioners to be punished any longer and having enjoined penance on the chaplain and others, relaxes the interdict and mercifully restores the clergy and people to their former state, reserving to himself the right to impose penance on Robert Leverych, parishioner[1] of the church, who was the principal cause of the sentence. Sonning manor, 2 Sept. 1412.

[1. MS: *parrochiali*. This could alternatively be parish chaplain, if *capellano* has been omitted.]

[Fos. 192^{v}/18^{v} and 193 are blank. Fos. 193^{v} and 194 contain business belonging to John Chandeler's episcopate, given below, **1150–6**. Fos. 194^{v}–196^{v} contain contemporary indexes. Fo. 197 has a memorandum, given below, **1159**.]

Entries in the Register not belonging to Hallum's Episcopate

1148 [Fo. 100] Will of Walter Dauntesey, knight, dated 26 Aug. 1420. To be buried in the parish church of Dauntsey (*Daunteseye*) before the altar of the Virgin Mary. Bequeathes 40*s* to the fabric of Salisbury cath.; to Dauntsey church, 1 pair of vestments with 2 tunicles and 3 copes, worth £10, 1 missal, 1 gradual and 1 chalice; to all the poor tenants of Dauntsey, Smithcot (*Smythcote*),[1] Marden (*Merdene*), Wilsford (*Wyllesford*) and Winterbourne Dauntsey (*Wynterbourne Dauntesey*), 10 marks [£6 13*s* 4*d*] at his executors' discretion; to a priest who shall celebrate for his soul and the souls of all the faithful for 1 whole year after his death, 106*s* 8*d*; for 100 masses to be celebrated with all speed on one day at his executors' discretion, 8*s* 4*d*. The executors are to conduct his burial according to their discretion. Bequeathes 40*s* to John Frye, his squire; 20*s* each to Richard Coke, his cook, William Pruet, Nicholas Baillif, John Botillier, Walter Botillier; 13*s* 4*d* to Wayte Fauconer; 6*s* 8*d* each to William Frye and William Hogges; 3*s* 4*d* to Arde Fauconer; 6*s* 8*d* to Catherine Partrych; 10*s* to John Bradford; 6*s* 8*d* to David Marchaunt; 3*s* 4*d* to Thomas Oxenherde; 20*d* to Richard Belamy; 20*d* to Henry Coponer; 20*s* to Thomas Trapper. He wishes there to be five poor men or women in the almshouse of Dauntsey who will pray for his soul and those of his ancestors; each is to receive 6*d* a week, and they are to be in the almshouse by next Michaelmas [29 Sept.]. His feoffees are to give to Thomasia his wife £10 of annual revenue for the term of her life, above that which was formerly ordained by the feoffees, on condition that they fulfil all his will. Bequeathes all his hawks and falcons to Edmund Daunteseye, his uncle; 40*s* to William Gore, his seneschal. His household is to be fully maintained for his family until next Michaelmas. He appoints as executors William Hankeford, knight, Thomasia, his wife, Edmund Dauntesey, Thomas Dru, William Gore and Thomas Felix, parson of Little Somerford (*Litelsomerford*) church. Any residue is to be disposed by his executors for the benefit of his soul.

[Sir Walter apparently had no issue and his sister Joan inherited his lands (*Collections of John Aubrey*, pp. 217–18). He was aged about 29 at his death (cf. **300**, **389**).
1. For Smithcot in Dauntsey, see *Wilts. Place-names*, p. 69.]

[Fo. 100^{v} is blank, except for *presentacio abbatisse* in the top left-hand corner, which has been struck out.]

1149 [Fo. 123] Mandate of Pope Alexander [IV] to the bp. of Salisbury, at the petition of John de Turbelvyle, lord of Hendred (*Henreth*).[1] The latter is so far from the mother church that particularly in winter he cannot conveniently attend it to hear the divine offices and receive the sacraments. The pope has therefore granted him a licence to build a private chapel on his own land and have his own chaplain to whom he is prepared to assign a sufficient income. He orders the bp. as diocesan to allow Turbelvyle to do this if it seems good to him. Lateran, 11 March 2 Alexander [IV] [1255]. Note by Thomas Candell,[2] notary public, that he copied this bull from a transcribed public instrument signed by one Thomas Hopkyns, which mentions the original papal bull made with hemp strings and with the *bulla* attached in the fashion of the Roman curia.

[Cf. **880**, **918**. This letter is written sideways in the margin of the folio in a 16th-century hand.
1. Cf. *VCH Berks.*, iv. 297.
2. Vice-registrar to the bp. of Salisbury *c.* 1538 (*ibid.*, iii. 19).]

1150 [Fo. 193v] Licence granted by the bp. of Salisbury [John Chandeler], to William Broghton, rector of Boxford (*Boxore*), to be absent from his benefice for one year. He is to study, and to pay one noble [6*s* 8*d*] at next Christmas. London, bishop's inn, 1 Nov. 1419.

[Neither this nor any of the four following licences is in Reg. Chandeler, but it seems that the quire of licences is missing from the bound register.]

1151 The like to T. Hanecok, chaplain, vicar of Winterbourne Whitchurch (*Whitchurch*). London, bishop's inn, . . . Oct. . . . [1] He has not yet paid the fee, but he will pay . . .[2]

[The folio is badly faded and no other details are legible.
1. About six illegible words.
2. Three illegible words.]

1152 The like to John Lange, rector of Chilcombe (*Childecombe*), for which the bp. received 6*s* 8*d*. 7 Nov. [1419].

1153 The like to the rector of Tockenham (*Tokenham*)[1] until next Michaelmas [29 Sept.], for which the bp. received 3*s* 4*d*. 7 Feb. [1420].

[1. Roger Celiworth (Reg. Chandeler, pt. i fos. 22v, 68).]

1154 The like to John FitzRanulph, rector of moiety of Child Okeford (*Childeokford*), for one year in the service of Joan Broke.[1] 8 July 1420.

[1. She had presented FitzRanulph to the church 28 July 1419 (Reg. Chandeler, pt. i fo. 23v).]

1155 Commission of the bp. of Salisbury to M. Alexander Sparew, official of Salisbury, to effect the exchange of benefices between M. J[ohn] Stafford, chancellor of Salisbury cath., and prebendary of Odiham (*Odiam*), and J[ohn] Fyton, canon and prebendary of Highworth (*Hyworth*) in the same. Chardstock (*Cherdstoke*), 6 March 1422.

[Exchange recorded in Reg. Chandeler, pt. i fo. 51, 7 March.]

1156 [Fo. 194] A record of the custom concerning the revenues of vacant benefices followed from time immemorial in dioc. Salisbury, and especially in the archdeaconry of Dorset. Whatever time of year a simple benefice under the archdeacon's jurisdiction shall fall vacant, all its fruits, revenues and proceeds for the whole period of the vacancy shall belong to the bp. and archd., together with the custody and support of the cure and all other duties, as they have belonged by ancient custom. If the benefice shall be vacant in the hands of the bp. and archd. on the feast of the Annunciation of the B.V.M. [25 March], in such a way that no predecessor or successor is alive or entitled in any part of that day, then all the greater fruits of the benefice belong and shall belong to the bp. and archd. for their disposal until next Michaelmas [29 Sept.]. If within three days of the feast of the Annunciation someone is instituted and inducted in the benefice by the bp. and archd., he shall have the lesser fruits with support of the duties from the day of taking possession. But if the benefice-holder should die on the feast of the Annunciation or afterwards, before Michaelmas, then all the greater fruits of the benefice until Michaelmas belong and shall belong to the deceased and his executors. And if within three days of the death a successor is peacefully instituted and inducted, he shall have the lesser fruits with support of the duties from the day of taking possession, as above, saving always the custom of the bp. and archd. for the whole time of the vacancy, and provided that due moderation without excessive extravagance is observed by the bp., archd. and deceased.[1]

This declaration was executed in the favour of the bp. and the archd. of Wiltshire, in respect of the greater fruits of the church of Christian Malford (*Cristenmalford*). The church was vacant for twelve weeks and three days, from the nativity of St. John the Baptist [24 June] to the eve of the Nativity of the B.V.M. [7 Sept.] 1424. John Pounteney, notary of John Chaundeler, bp. of Salisbury, drew up a public instrument concerning this which is written in the bishop's register in the seventh year of his episcopate.

[Cf. institution, 5 Sept. 1424, of M. William Spaldyngton B.Cn.L. to church vacant by death of M. Henry Mory (Reg. Chandeler, pt. i fo. 74). The public instrument mentioned is dated 8 Jan. 1425, and although Mory died between the Annunciation and Michaelmas, the bp. claimed and obtained the greater fruits of the benefice from the exector of Mory's will, and the public instrument testified to the full payment (*ibid.*, pt. ii fo. 45). The statement of custom shows that it was normally considered just that the executors should have the fruits of the spring sowing done by the late incumbent. Similar arrangements were apparently generally observed in the province of Canterbury (cf. *Registrum Roberti Winchelsey, Cantuariensis archiepiscopi, 1294–1313*, ed. R. Graham (Canterbury and York Soc., li, lii, 1952–6), ii. 1168–9, 1291), but exceptions were made.

1. A later hand has written at the top and bottom of the statement of custom *Anno Domini 1408°*]

The End Pages

Fo. 1 has a heading *Registrum Roberti Halam* in a nineteenth-century hand in the top right-hand corner. The rest of the folio is discoloured and has several apparently unrelated notes and figures. In very small fifteenth-century writing on the right-hand half of the folio is a dispensation, but part is missing at the edge of the folio, and the rest is barely legible:

1157 Dispensation granted by the bp. to John [illegible] and Constance Lane of Brightwell (*Bryghwelle*) who married in ignorance that they were related in the third or fourth degrees, and obtained a dispensation from Pope Alexander [V], allowing them to remain together. Ramsbury (*Remmesbury*) park, 24 Nov. 1409.

Fo. 1^{v} is blank.

Fo. 2 has *In the name of God the xxth of November in the yeare*, written in what is probably a sixteenth-century hand. There is a line of illegible writing below this written sideways on the folio.

Fo. 2^{v} has notes by three different fifteenth-century hands:

Requir[atur] calendare in fine libri

1158 Memorandum that on 9 May 1353 Robert Wryfeld,[1] bp. of Salisbury, dedicated the chapel of 'Upfont'[2] with three altars in honour of the Nativity of the B.V.M.

[1. Robert Wyville, 1330–75.
2. Possibly Fonthill Gifford or Upper Fonthill (*Wilts. Place-names*, p. 190), or more probably Urchfont, where a light of 'our blessed lady of the South Ile' was mentioned in a will of 1502 (*Wilts. Notes and Queries*, v. 157; cf. *VCH Wilts.*, x. 187).]

Registrum Roberti Halam. Req[uiratur] kalendare in alia fine libri.

Fo. 197 has an entry in a fifteenth-century hand:

1159 Thees be thos thynges that been necessary for the halowyng of a chyrche.
In primis ij laarge fattes full of water oon within the churche dore and an other with owte, and iiij laarge treyn bolles or basyns and a small ladyl of treen.
Item xiiij wex candelles everych of a foote long or more.
Item a dyssh full of salt and a dyssh full of aysshes fayre syfte.
Item a quarte of rede wyne and an handfull of ysope.

Item small wex roll candelles to make v crosses upon the awter yf the awter be to halowyng, and half a pound of incense.
Item oon lynnen clothe fayre wasshyn to make clene the awters which clothe after shall be brent, and a clene treyn cop or dysshe.
Item the church and the chauncell flore most be clene voyded from dextes and segees[1] and fayre swoped with a besom, in which flore fro the northe corner of the chauncell to the southe corner of the churche ende throw all the churche, and fro the este corner of the chauncell down to the west corner of the churche, ther most be made in the flore or pament an Andrewes crosse of small sonde of a foote of brede and an ynche thyck atte leest.
Item j senser withe colys.
Item ij elnes of new lynnen clothe for an apron for the Busshop and for brachyales. And also lynnen clothe suffycyent for aprons for his mynysters.
Item j short fourme with a tapete and quysshynes to knele at, and a tent withowte the west ende of the church yerd made of clothe, in whiche the Busshop and his mynysters shall be rayed. All thees thinges above saide except sond been necessary and requysyte as wel in the halowyng of a churche yerd by hym self as in the halowyng of a churche and awter, savyng over this in the halowyng of a churche yerd ther most be ordyned iiij laarge crosses of tree of iij feet of jeyght, whiche most stond fastened in the erthe at iiij corners of the churche yerd. And xij wex tapers to be set[2] upon every crosse iij.
Item at every corner of the churche yerd a fatt with fayre water.

[1. Possibly desks and seats (sieges) or sedges.
2. MS.: *at* struck out.]

In small, fifteenth-century writing, at the bottom of the folio is written *Nota pro libera capella infra castrum de Marleburgh fo. 51* [522].

APPENDIX A

Institutions and Exchanges of Benefices which appear to have taken place, but of which there is not record in the Register.

I Presentation by the king of John Burnham, vicar of Wantage (*Wantynge*), to church of Rowley (*Roule*), dioc. York, on an exchange with John Walkyngton. 7 Nov. 1408 (*CPR 1408–13*, p. 21).

II Presentation by the king of John Scot, vicar of Compton Chamberlayne (*Compton Chaumberlayne*), to church of Hardenhuish (*Hardynghuwyssh*), in the king's gift by virtue of the minority of William, son and heir of William Botreaux, knight, tenant-in-chief, on an exchange with Robert Bochard. 23 Jan. 1410 (*ibid.*, p. 161).

III Ratification by the king of Thomas Wysebech as prebendary of Netherbury in Terra in Salisbury cath. 13 Apr. 1410 (*ibid.*, p. 118).
[Cf. Vyring, pp. 46, 47.]

IV Presentation by the king of Simon Kynot, rector of Brixton Deverill (*Brighston Deverell*), to vicarage of Lewisham (*Leuesham*), dioc. Rochester, on an exchange with Thomas Oky. 30 June 1410 (*ibid.*, p. 207).
[Cf. p. 23. This exchange was probably on the missing folio of June 1410.]

V Gilbert Hallum admitted by proxy to prebend of Netherbury (*Nitherbury*) in Terra in Salisbury cath., vac. by death of Thomas Wisbech. 21 Aug. 1410 (Vyring, pp. 46, 47). Admitted in person 18 Oct. (*ibid.*, p. 53).

VI John Fyton M.A. admitted by proxy to prebend of Ruscombe Southbury (*Rottescombe*) in Salisbury cath., vac. by death of William Spaldwick. 13 Sept. 1410 (Vyring, pp. 49, 50). Admitted in person 18 Oct. (*ibid.*, p. 53).

VII Presentation by the king of John Hereward, rector of Winterbourne Farringdon (*Wynterborne Germayn*), to church of Stock Gaylard (*Stok Coilard*), by virtue of the custody of the lands and heir of John Walsh, tenant-in-chief of Richard II, on an exchange with Richard Fissher. 6 Nov. 1410 (*CPR 1408–13*, p. 244).
[For Winterbourne Farringdon, see **461**n.]

VIII Presentation by the king of William Cave, king's clerk, to church of Pimperne (*Pymperne*). 20 June 1411 (*ibid.*, p. 294).

IX Presentation by the king of John Juyll, chaplain, to church of Milston (*Mildeston*). 22 Jan. 1412 (*ibid.*, p. 360).

X Presentation by the king of Walter Shirington to church of Holy Trinity, Dorchester (*Dorchestre*). 15 March 1414 (*CPR 1413–16*, p. 156).

XI Mandate of Geoffrey Crukadan, vicar general, for admission of John Brunyng, abbot of Sherborne (*Shirborne*), to prebend of Sherborne in Salisbury cath. 12 March 1415 (Pountney, p. 14).

XII Commission of Robert, bp. of Hereford, to the bp. of Salisbury, to effect an exchange between William Rocbury, rector of Upton Cressett (*Upton by Morville*), dioc. Hereford, and William Lawley, vicar of Seagry. 15 March 1415 (*Registrum Roberti Mascall, episcopi Herefordensis, 1404–16*, ed. J. H. Parry (Canterbury and York Soc., xxi, 1917), p. 187).

XIII John Luke admitted by proxy, on vicar general's collation, to prebend of Hurstbourne (*Husbourne*) and Burbage (*Burbache*) in Salisbury cath., vac. by death of Adam Mottrum. 11 Aug. 1415 (Pountney, p. 19).

XIV Arnold de Monte S. Silvestri admitted, on vicar general's collation, to precentorship of Salisbury cath., vac. by death of Adam Mottrum. 11 Aug. 1415 (*ibid.*, p. 19).

XV Thomas Faukys admitted by proxy, on vicar general's collation, to precentorship of Salisbury cath. 2 Oct. 1415 (*ibid.*, p. 23).

XVI Exchange effected by Geoffrey Crukadan, vicar general, by authority of John Roland, vicar general of Nicholas, bp. of Bath and Wells, between William Moore, perpetual chaplain of Holy Cross chantry in Charlton Adam (*Cherlton Adam*) manor, dioc. Bath and Wells, and John Codewell, rector of Swyre. 20 Oct. 1415 (*Reg. Bubwith*, i. 225).

XVII Edmund Dutton admitted by proxy, on vicar general's collation, to prebend of Torleton in Salisbury cath., vac. by death of William Loryng. 15 Jan. 1416 (Pountney, p. 29).

XVIII Presentation by the king of John Skeffyngton, rector of Whaddon (*Waddon*), to church of Padworth (*Padeworth*), on an exchange with William Coudray. 1 March 1416 (*CPR 1413–16*, p 402).

XIX Richard Ullerston admitted by proxy, on vicar general's collation, to prebend of Axford in Salisbury cath., vac. by death of Edmund Bekenham. 25 March 1416 (Pountney, p. 33).

XX Presentation by the king of John Merston to church or free chapel of Wanborough (*Wambroke*). 19 May 1416 (*CPR 1416–22*, p. 12).

XXI William [*rectius* John][1] de Longville admitted by proxy, on vicar general's collation, to prebend of Fordington (*Fordyngton*) and Writhlington (*Wryklyngton*) in Salisbury cath. 10 June 1416 (Pountney, p. 37). Mandate for induction into *corpus* of the prebend, in dioc. Bath and Wells, same day. (*Reg. Bubwith*, i. 238).

[1. Cf. Reg. Chandeler, pt. i fo. 88.]

XXII Thomas Burton admitted by proxy, on vicar general's collation, to prebend of Torleton in Salisbury cath., vac. by death of William Loryng. 5 Aug. 1416 (Pountney, p. 41).

XXIII Hugh Holbache D.Cn.L. admitted by proxy, on mandate of Robert, bp. of Salisbury, issued at Constance, to prebend of Wilsford (*Wyvelesforde*) and Woodford (*Wodeford*) in Salisbury cath., vac. by death of Ralph Repyngton. 5 Aug. 1416 (*ibid.*, p. 40).

[Cf. *CPR 1416–22*, p. 123.]

XXIV Exchange effected by Geoffrey Crukadan, vicar general, by authority of John Roland, vicar general of Nicholas, bp. of Bath and Wells, between Thomas Galon, vicar of Kingston (*Kynggeston*) by Taunton, dioc. Bath and Wells, and John Hele, chaplain of Holy Trinity chantry in church of St. Laurence, Hungerford (*Hongerford*). 29 Aug. 1416 (*Reg. Bubwith*, i. 243).

XXV Presentation by the king of William Barton, chaplain, to church of Bridport. 1 Sept. 1416 (*CPR 1416–22*, p. 45).

XXVI Admission, by Philip, bp. of Lincoln, of Thomas Enkeston into *corpus* of prebend of Grantham Australis in Salisbury cath., being in dioc. Lincoln, vac. by death of Richard Prentys. 10 Oct. 1416 (Lincolnshire Archives Office, Reg. XIV (Repingdon) fo. 83v).

XXVII Exchange, effected by Henry, abp. of Canterbury, on certificate of Geoffrey Crukadan, vicar general, between Richard Bucke, rector of Etchingham (*Ecchyngham*), dioc. Chichester, *sede vacante*, and John Monke, vicar of Sherston (*Shirston*). 11 Dec. 1416 (*Reg. Chichele*, i. 141).

XXVIII Exchange, effected by Henry, abp. of Canterbury, on certificate of Geoffrey Crukadan, vicar general, between Robert Benet, perpetual chaplain of Arundell's chantry (*Arundellys chaunterye*) in Canterbury cath., and John Scut, rector of Woodborough (*Wodbergh*). 19 Feb. 1417 (*ibid.*, i. 157).

APPENDIX B

Original Documents of Hallum's Chancery not entered in the Register

I Letters testimonial certifying that John Sherman, acolyte, of dioc. Lincoln, was ordained subdeacon by Robert, bp. of Salisbury, 21 Dec. 1409, in the chapel of Ramsbury (*Remmesbury*) manor, by letters dimissory of his diocesan, and at the title of the prior and conv. of Poughley (*Pogheley*). Ramsbury, 21 Dec. 1409 (P.R.O., Exchequer K.R. Ecclesiastical, E 135/6/80).

[This was originally sealed on a tongue and folded into four. It is endorsed *Johannes Sherman.*]

II Licence to Henry Talbote and Agnes his wife and any others dwelling in the new inn in London Road, Reading (*Rading*), to have divine service celebrated in the oratory there, if it is decent, by suitable chaplains. Sonning (*Sonnyng*) manor, 10 Jan. 1411 (British Library, Additional Charter 19648).

[The seal, in red wax, is attached on a tongue, and there are the remains of a wrapping tie. The document was folded into four and has a filing hole. It is endorsed in a later hand, *Licencia concessa per episcopum ad celebrandum divina in hospicio novo.* In another, larger hand is written *Littera episcopi pro licencia celebrat' in oratorio etc.*
This licence is reproduced in *Palaeographical Soc. Facsimiles* (1st ser., 3 vols., 1873–83), iii, no. 258.]

III Signification to the Crown that John Bullok, lately of the city of Salisbury, excommunicated for contumacy when summoned to appear before the bp. to answer charges of breach of faith and perjury at the instance of John Hampton, brewer, of Salisbury, has remained obdurate for a year and more, with a request for his capture by the secular authority. Sonning (*Sonnyng*) manor, 27 Jan. 1411 (P.R.O., Chancery significations of excommunication, C 85/148/24).

[Probably originally sealed on a tongue, and folded into four. It is endorsed *Midd'.*]

IV The like concerning John Knyght of Upavon (*Uphavene*), excommunicated for contumacy when summoned to appear before the bp. for the correction of his soul. London, bishop's inn, 20 Nov. 1411 (P.R.O., C 85/148/25).

[Originally sealed on a tongue and folded into four. It is endorsed *Wiltes.*]

V The like concerning John Tylfote, senior, of Todber (*Todbury*), excommunicated for contumacy in relation to certain lawful and canonical monitions, who has remained obdurate for forty days and more. Potterne manor, 22 March 1412 (P.R.O., C 85/148/26).

[Originally sealed on a tongue and folded into four. It is endorsed *Dors.*]

VI The like concerning Richard Warde, millward, of dioc. Salisbury, excommunicated for contumacy when summoned to appear before the bp. to answer charges of withdrawal of tithes at the instance of William Coche, vicar of Laverstock (*Laverkestoke*), who has remained obdurate for forty days and more. Ramsbury (*Remmesbury*) manor, 12 Jan. 1413 (P.R.O., C 85/148/27).

[Originally sealed on a tongue and folded into four. It is endorsed *Wiltes.*]

VII The like concerning Thomas Helyere, clerk, of Bower Chalk (*Burchalk*), excommunicated for contumacy when summoned to appear before the bp., who has remained obdurate for forty days and more. Potterne (*Poterne*) manor, 22 June 1414 (P.R.O., C 85/148/28).

[Originally sealed on a tongue and folded into four. It is endorsed *Wiltes.*]

VIII Letter of Geoffrey Crukadan Inc.Cn. & C.L., canon of Salisbury and vicar general of Robert, bp. of Salisbury, then abroad, to the king, notifying him that he has examined the election held in the monastery of Sherborne (*Shirburn*), order of St. Benedict, of John Brunyng, monk of Sherborne, as abbot, and having ascertained that Brunyng is a suitable person and that the king's licence and consent had been previously obtained,[1] he has confirmed the election. Sealed with the seal of the official of Salisbury, which is to hand. Wilton, 12 March 1415 (P.R.O., Ecclesiastical petitions, C 84/40/50).

[Originally sealed on a tongue and folded into four.
1. Cf. *CPR 1413–16*, p. 289.]

IX The like concerning the election of John Dorset, monk of Abingdon (*Abendon*), order of St. Benedict, as abbot.[1] Sealed with the same seal. Abingdon, 16 March 1417 (P.R.O., C 84/41/26).

[Originally sealed on a tongue and folded into four. There is one filing hole.
1. Cf. *CPR 1416–22*, p. 62.]

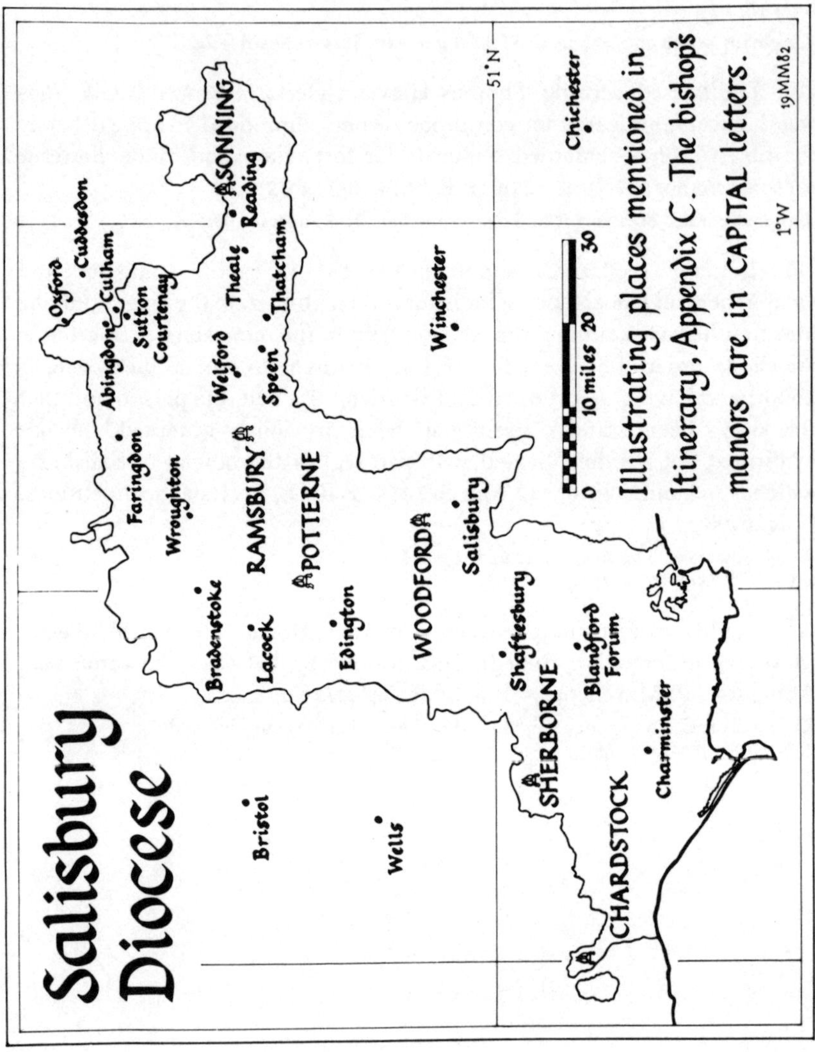

Salisbury Diocese

Illustrating places mentioned in Itinerary, Appendix C. The bishop's manors are in CAPITAL letters.

APPENDIX C

Itinerary of Bishop Hallum

1408

2 March	London[1]	*Proc. Privy Council*, i. 308 (council meeting)
28 March	Maidstone	Reg. Arundell (Cant.), i fo. 41
31 March	London	**928**
6–20 Apr.	Abingdon	**1, 43, 707, 1028**
23 Apr.	Cuddesdon	**2**
24–5 Apr.	Abingdon	**3–4**
6 May–1 June	Welford	**5–8, 708–12, 714, 929, 933, 1128**
2–4 June	Culham	**9, 713**
9 June	Sutton Courtenay	**10, 1029**
12 June–17 July	Culham	**11–16, 19–20, 43–4, 715–22, 931, 934–5, 937, 939, 1060–1**
20 July	Sonning	**21–2, 723**
22 July–3 Aug.	London	**23–6, 724–6, 729, 932, 936, 938** (convocation met 23 July)
5–6 Aug.	Sonning	Vyring, p. 15
10–29 Aug.	Culham	**27–8, 727–8, 943**
1 Sept.	Ramsbury	**29–30**
10–11 Sept.	Salisbury	**31–2, 730–1, 940**; Vyring, pp. 18, 20; Decanal Reg. Chandeler, pt. i fo. 118^v
14–16 Sept.	Woodford	**33, 732–3, 941**
20 Sept.–8 Oct.	Potterne	**34–6, 734–5, 945, 1030, 1071**
9–10 Oct.	Ramsbury	**38**
12 Oct.	Sonning	**39**
18 Oct.–16 Nov.	London	**40–2, 44–6, 736–42, 946, 1065–6**
22–3 Nov.	Sonning	**47, 741, 1129**
27 Nov.	Ramsbury	**48**
30 Nov.	Potterne	**49**
7 Dec.	Woodford or Salisbury	**50, 1129**
9–12 Dec.	Salisbury	**17–18, 743**
13–14 Dec.	Potterne	**744, 754**
22 Dec.	Sherborne	**745, 1031**

1. When in London, the bishop normally stayed at his inn in the parish of St. Bride, Fleet Street, **1026**, on the site of the present Salisbury Square and Salisbury Court, London E.C.4.

	1409	
9 Jan.	Salisbury	**54**, **746**, **755**; Vyring, p. 28
12–14 Jan.	Sonning	**944**, **1068**
15 Jan.–14 Feb.	London	**55–9**, **747–53**, **756**, **942**, **947–8**, **1069–70**, **1072–3** (convocation met 14 Jan.)
27 Feb.	Canterbury	**60–60A, 949**
[March–Sept.]	Council of Pisa	
15–26 Oct.	London	**112–15**
13–24 Nov.	Ramsbury	**116–18**, **798**, **1157**
30 Nov.–4 Dec.	Salisbury	**119–21**, **799–802**
7–31 Dec.	Ramsbury	**122–8**, **805–9**, **1033**, **1076**, **1135**, App. B I
	1410	
1–20 Jan.	Ramsbury	**129–32**, **810–15**, **1136**
27 Jan.–10 March	London	**133–43**, **816–21**, **826–33**, **1078**, **1081** (parliament met 27 Jan.; convocation met 17 Feb.)
17 March	Sonning	**834**
19–22 March	Salisbury	**144**, **1034**; Vyring, p. 43
29 March–1 Apr.	Woodford	**145–7**, **836–7**
4 Apr.–20 May	Potterne	**148–58**, **838–43**, **858**, **888**, **956–61**, **1035**
28 May–28 June	Sherborne	**159–69**, **698**, **844–7**, **962–4**, **1083**
10 July–10 Aug.	Chardstock	**170**n, **171–6**, **848–9**, **965**, **1084**
14 Aug.–11 Oct.	Sherborne[2]	**178–91**, **697**, **850–5**, **857**, **862**, **966–73**, **1036**, **1085–8**
20–6 Oct.	Salisbury	**192–6**; Vyring, pp. 51, 55
28 Oct.–?3 Nov.	Woodford	**197–200**, **859** and n, **975**
?3–5 Nov.	Shaftesbury	**860** and n, **976–7**
7 Nov.	Edington	**978**
11 Nov.	Lacock	**201**
17 Nov.	Wroughton	**202**
22 Nov.	Ramsbury	**861**
3 Dec.	Speen	**203**
7–31 Dec.	Sonning	**204–7**, **979**, **1037**
	1411	
5–10 Jan.	Sonning	**208**, App. B II
14–15 Jan.	Abingdon	**980–1**

2. He carried out a visitation of the archdeaconry of Dorset while based here, cf. **862**.

18 Jan.–6 March	Sonning[3]	**209–25**, **699**, **863–4**, **866**, **982–3**, **1090**, App. B III
8–20 March	London	**226–32**, **865**, **984–7**; *Proc. Privy Council,* ii. 7 (council met at Lambeth 19 March)
28 March–18 Apr.	Sonning	**233–42**, **867**, **1038–9**
20 Apr.	Thatcham	**244**
21 Apr.	Ramsbury	**245**
22 Apr.–6 July	Potterne[4]	**246–62**, **871–6**, **881**, **885**, **988–96**, **1040**, **1092–3**, **1095**, **1131**
10 July–23 Aug.	Sherborne	**263–74**, **700**, **1095**
1–4 Sept.	Chardstock	**275**, **878**
13 Sept.	Sonning	**276**
16–25 Sept.	London	**277–9**, **997–1001**
26–7 Sept.	Sonning[5]	**280**, **879**, **1114–16**, **1119**
15 Oct.	Potterne	**282**
21–4 Oct.	Salisbury[6]	**281**, **283–7**; Vyring, p. 61
30 Oct.–2 Nov.	Potterne	**288–90**, **1004**; Vyring, p. 69
4 Nov.	Sonning	**884**
7 Nov.	Colebrook (Islington)	**291**
10 Nov.–14 Dec.	London	**292–302**, **882–3**, App. B IV (parliament met 3 Nov.; convocation met 1 Dec.)
24–31 Dec.	Potterne	**303–4**, **1005**
	1412	
1 Jan.–9 March	Potterne	**305–16**, **702**, **1006**, **1008**, **1041**, **1126**
12 March	Abingdon	**703**
18–21 March	Potterne	**317**, **319**, App. B V
30 March–4 Apr.	Salisbury	**318**, **1042**; Vyring, p. 76
12 Apr.	Woodford	**320**
14–24 Apr.	Sonning	**321**, **1144**
6–20 May	London	**322–6**, **886**
21 May–26 July	Sonning	**327–42**, **918**, **1009–10**, **1043**, **1100–1**
31 July–6 Aug.	Ramsbury	**343–6**, **348**
9 Aug.	Charminster	**1134**
11–19 Aug.	Sherborne	**347**, **705**, **1134**

3. He carried out a visitation of the archdeaconry of Berkshire while based here, cf. **867**, **875–6**, **881**.
4. He carried out a visitation of the archdeaconry of Wiltshire while based here, cf. **1093**.
5. Visitation of Abingdon abbey, 27 Sept., while based here, **879**.
6. He carried out a visitation of the cathedral while here, cf. **886**.

26 Aug.	Ramsbury	**1145**
28 Aug.–19 Sept.	Sonning	**350–3, 889, 1012–13, 1146–7**
27 Sept.–12 Oct.	London	**354–9, 891**
15 Oct.	Sonning	**360**
20 Oct.–2 Dec.	Ramsbury	**361–77, 892**
9–21 Dec.	Potterne	**378–82, 890, 1044, 1102**
23–31 Dec.	Ramsbury	**383–4, 927**

1413

1–30 Jan.	Ramsbury	**385–91, 1017**, App. B VI
4 Feb.	Sonning	**927**
13 Feb.–24 March	London	**392–401, 824–5, 899–902;** Vyring, p. 98 (parliament met 3 Feb.; convocation met 6 March)
5 Apr.	? Sonning	**402** and n
6–11 Apr.	London	**403–5, 904**
14 Apr.–6 May	Sonning	**406–11, 1045;** Vyring, p. 103
16 May–8 June	London	**412–18** (parliament met 14 May)
19 June	Canterbury	**419;** Vyring, p. 107
22 June	Horton Kirby, Kent[7]	**420**
2 July	Sonning	**421**
4–6 July	Potterne	**911–12**
10–29 July	Sonning	**422–4**
30 July	Bradenstoke	**425**
2–26 Aug.	Ramsbury	**426–32, 908**
31 Aug.–2 Sept.	Woodford	**433, 909**
6 Sept.–5 Nov.	Ramsbury	**434–42, 951–2, 1046, 1106–7;** Vyring, pp. 113, 115
17 Nov.	Theale	**443**
19 Nov.–16 Dec.	London	**445–50, 1021** (convocation met 27 Sept.–20 Nov.)
17 Dec.	Potterne	**451**
23–31 Dec.	Sherborne	**452–7, 1047, 1108**

1414

1 Jan.–13 March	Sherborne	**458–73, 1048**
26 March	Sonning	**475**
5–7 Apr.	Salisbury	**476, 1049**
14–20 Apr.	Woodford	**477–83**
22–8 Apr.	Potterne	**484**

7. Hallum held this manor (*CCR 1419–22*, pp. 47, 62, 64).

11–22 May	Leicester	**485–91** (parliament met 30 Apr.)
28 May	Faringdon	**492** and n
2 June	Abingdon	**1050**
4 June–8 Aug.	Potterne[8]	**493–508**, **911–12**, **1109**, App. B VII
26–31 Aug.	Sherborne	**509–10**
3 Sept.	Blandford Forum	**1110**
26 Sept.–12 Nov.	London	**511–23**, **1026;** Pountney, p. 10
19 Nov.	Dover	**524–5**
[Dec.–4 Sept. 1417]	Council of Constance	

8. He carried out a visitation of the archdeaconry of Salisbury while based here, **913**.

APPENDIX D

Examples in the Register of Hallum's Literary Style

837 [*Commission to the subdean of Salisbury cath. and all parish curates and chaplains of the city of Salisbury to order the proper observance of Sundays and feast days.*]

Licet ab exordio condicionis humane die dumtaxat septimo ebdomade statuit omnium conditor ab operibus abstinendum, succedente tamen tempore gracie militans adiecit ecclesia dies plurimos ab omnibus catholicis feriandos et quosdam in diversis catholicorum partibus festivos superaddidit localiter observandos, hiis ergo diebus tanto devocius cunctos Christicolas pro ipsorum ceterorumque fidelium salute Deum sinceris mentibus oraturos ecclesiarum parrochialium limina frequenciori congressu calcare convenit quanto temporibus aliis variis sollicitudinum generibus occupati laudes ipsi Deo omnium largitori congruas cum sacrificio contriti cordis reddere non valebant. Sane frequens ad nos deduxit querimonia plurimorum quod nonnulli ecclesiarum civitatis nostre predicte parrochiani dies dominicos aliasque sanctorum festivitates prout Christi fidelibus convenit non observant, sed humana in deteriora labente natura quod in Dei electorumque eius honorem est preceptum id in abhominacionem et blasphemiam convertitur, dum videlicet conventicule negociaciones et alia exercicia illicita diebus huiusmodi potissime ingeruntur, pergule namque sive shoppe[1] vulgariter appellate diebus predictis cuilibet emere volenti sunt aperte et dum lucra capi sperantur indifferentes se ingerunt, discrecione non habita temporis aut diei. Sicque quod devocionis esset compendium in dissolucionis exigitur tumulum dum in ipsis festis colitur taberna pocius quam ecclesia, commessaciones habundant et ebrietates uberius quam lacrime et oraciones, lasciviis insistitur et contumeliis pocius quam cum Maria ad pedes Domini ocio contemplacionis, et breviter quod erat ad graciam ordinatum in noxiam tendere verisimiliter comprobatur.

[1. MS.: from *pergule* interlined.]

893 [*Indulgence of forty days granted by the bp. to those visiting and venerating the shrine of King Edward the Martyr in the monastery of Shaftesbury.*]

Gloriosus in sanctis suis et mirabilis in maiestate sua Dominus supernus in celestis curie concivibus et collegis qui dum in carne vixerant tanquam clara in mundo luminaria lucuerunt, fueruntque eorum corpora non solum suorum organa meritorum per que regni celestis invenerunt introitum, verum eciam spiritus sancti templa et scrinia donorum sacramenti septenarii ab eodem spiritu sancto celitus largitorum, a suis fidelibus per cunctas orbe dispersas ecclesias eo fervencius devociusque laudandus, ac sanctos ipsos in locis ubi ipsorum corpora sive reliquie quiescunt frequenciori visitacione venerandos ostendit quo ipsos mortales e terris assumptos in locis predictis assidue signorum et miraculorum operacione decorat, precesque ab eis pro suis supplicibus porrectas libenter acceptat ad quorum siquidem gloriam pertinet, ut pro interventu egentibus auxilium conferat ad salutem.

895 [*Mandate to the abbess and conv. of Shaftesbury forbidding the nuns to leave their house except for good cause.*]

Ad nostrum nuper, qui desideranter in votis gerimus quod vestra religio prosperetur ac in ea splendor honestatis preluceat quod in sui nitore delectetur altissimus, ex insinuacione famosa pervenit auditum quod nonnulle domus vestre moniales et sorores ipsam de sue superioris permissu aliquociens exeuntes in locis diversis extra eam fucatis et exquisitis coloribus perhendinant sepius et morantur, et modestie laxatis habenis se ab eadem diucius quam deceat absentando nimium seculariter evagantur, in illius cui suam integritatem voluntate spontanea devoverunt offensam, cultus divini diminucionem et scandalum plurimorum. Unde cum hiis que regularis decoris gloriam maculare seu divinam possent offendere maiestatem ex paterni et pastoralis officii debito celeriter occurrere teneamur, vobis omnibus et singulis dicti monasterii monialibus in virtute sancte obediencie sub pena districcionis canonice firmiter iniungendo precipimus et mandamus quatinus a presumpcionibus huiusmodi, si que per vos vel vestrum aliquas fuerint hactenus attemptate, penitus desistatis, ac talia illicita inposterum nullatenus committatis, sed cum vobis vel vestrum alicui propter causam necessariam probabilem sive iustam per superiorem cuius interest approbatam ex qua dumtaxat hec fieri licere decernimus egrediendi monasterio decetero licencia sit concessa, nunquam sole nisi tali moniali fueritis sociate que sic in monasterio probata fuerit quod de ipsa nichil valeat suspicari sinistrum ire esse vel morari extra monasterium presumatis, ac quam cito causa cessaverit huiusmodi seu aliunde vobis facultas affuerit, ad dictam domum vestram, frivolis excusacionibus omnino remotis, absque more diffugio protinus redeatis, et vestrum quelibet revertatur, ut ibidem honestius devotum et debitum virtutum Domino famulatum impedere valeatis, aliisque splendore vite sitis speculum et exemplar, ac ex vestris gratiosis operibus odor suavitatis emanans multos ad vestra trahat imitanda vestigia et plurimos ad propositum alliciat sanctitatis. Ne alias quod absit per curiosam vagacionem et incautam ad instar Dyne filie Jacob et Lye que per suum voluptuosum egressum florem virginitatis violenter amisit, portis vestrorum sensuum reseratis, introitus pateat maligno spiritui, ex quo vobis vel aliis in pravorum desideriorum ardore vel saltem levi cogitacione detur occasio delinquendi, vobis dilectis filiabus abbatisse priorisse et ibidem presidenti cuicumque conformiter ut supra inhibemus ne ex causis aliis quam supradictis seu aliter quam prefertur monialibus ipsis exeundi licenciam ullatenus concedatis. Si que ergo in premissis seu aliquo premissorum per vos communiter vel divisim minus licite perantea facta sunt, ea per vos ipsas discrecione previa revocantes, sine difficultate qualibet emendetis, ita quod de hiis ad aures nostras ulterius queremonia non ascendat, nosque providere super hiis aliter ac rebelles seu culpabiles in hac parte punire severius non cogemur.

1017 [*General notification that the bp. has declared the feast of the translation of King Edward the Martyr, who is buried in Shaftesbury monastery, to be observed annually as a solemn feast throughout the archdeaconry of Dorset. An indulgence of forty days is granted to those observing the feast.*]

Universis sancte matris ecclesie filiis presentes litteras visuris vel audituris Robertus permissione divina ecclesie Sar' servus humilis et minister salutem in eo qui de orto militantis ecclesie tam rosas in bello quam in pace lilia colligit suisque aspectibus representat. Assumptos de terra sanctos in dominice participium hereditatis, recepta de manu Domini superne benediccionis laurea, in perhennitate laudis et glorie consistentes studiis honorare solicitis, sonoris efferre preconiis, ac devotis obsequiorum cultibus venerare[1] tenentur qui terrenas incolunt naciones. Illos namque humana labia digne glorificant merito laudibus efferent et ad eos votiva iubilacione proclamant, hii namque benignas aures clamancium vocibus exhibent nec denegant suis inquilinis auxilium impartiri, devotorum incliti defensores, hii seduli consistentes ad superni patris dexteram in excelsis veniam peccatoribus impetrant ut ipsi horum intercessionis gracia de tenebris egredi et ad vere lucis introduci gloriam mereantur.

Inter illos autem gloriosus martir Edwardus athleta Dei electus quondam Anglorum[2] rex illustris tanto dignius et presertim a populo Anglicano precipuis meruit honoribus venerari et honorificencie attolli impendiis pocioris, quanto in choro beatorum maiori claritate choruscat, quantoque regnum Anglie tam in vita quam in morte excellencius pre ceteris illustravit, ut ubi ipsius glorificatus est exitus ibi in die festivitatis eiusdem sit leticie principatus. Iste siquidem est qui de regali[3] ortus prosapia et successione paterna in regni solio sublimatus, a regum rege Domino in omnia veritatis et iusticie dirigebatur, cuius et auxilio fretus magno cum ingenio, excellenti mansuetudinis dono, et summe humilitatis gracia indies crescendo resplenduit, dum a primis sue iuventutis auspiciis per viam veritatis incedens, cesis virtutum falce fallacis mundi blandiciis quibus frequenter fragilitatis humane condicio fallitur, se cunctis exhibuit effabilitate placidum, placiditate benignum, benignitate devotum, castitate laudabilem, morum venustate decorum, misericordia benivolum, pietate misericordem, et in rigore iusticie non severum. Iste est qui cor sursum habens ad Dominum et sua in ipsum vita prospiciens eum querere ac mente tenere non desiit, mandatorum suorum pervigil et intentus ac solicitus operator, dum tam in militari virtute quam in ecclesiasticis negociis disponendis strenuus et devotus contra hostes et male agentes quadam crudelitate utebatur, pie viventes et precipue in sacris constitutos ordinibus solerti cura veluti a patre piissimo didicerat, ab infestacione qualibet protegebat. Iste est per quem tunc in Anglorum populo magna extitit iocunditas, magna pacis constancia et magna rerum opulencia confluebat, qui eciam uberalitate fecundus quendam cotidie ritum consuetudinis agebat, inopes videlicet alere, pauperes recreare, nudis vestimenta largiri, pro magno itaque lucro computans ea que in tali opere consumpsisset. Iste namque quem fides firmum, spes erectum, Dei et proximi caritas fecit latum, circumspectum prudencia, temperancia in omnibus ordinatum, innoxium cunctis iusticia, audacem et strenuum fortitudo, virtutum omnium aromatibus redolebat velut plena divinorum omnium carismatum apotheca. Iste est qui consilio et prudencia probatissimus, facie decorus et hilaris, iuvenum et minus sapientum concilia postponere, Dunstani tunc archipresulis mentem salubriter intendere, ac secundum eius consilium et aliorum religiosorum spectabiliumque virorum sua iudicia curavit in omnibus exercere, qui tandem gloriosum subiens Dei pro amore martirium pro terrenis celestia, pro temporali regno commutavit eternum, et pro corona caduca et momentanea felicitatis eterne percipere meruit imarcessibile diadema.

Attendentes igitur piam devocionem quam clerus et populus archidiaconatus Dors' nostre diocesis penes predictum sanctissimum et gloriosissimum martirem, cuius corporis preciose reliquie in monasterio Shafton' archidiaconatus predicti in quadam capsa lignea auro et lapidibus preciosis mirifice cooperta celebriter requiescunt, magis peculiariter pre ceteris gerere dinoscuntur, cum ipsius et credimus speciali patrocinio in ipso archidiaconatu degentes, ac quicumque alii iuste precantes, in prosperis et votivis precipue confoventur, ad divini nominis dictique martiris laudem gloriam et honorem, diem translacionis eiusdem tanquam festum celebrem et solempnem per totum archidiaconatum predictum volumus decernimus pronunciamus et declaramus ac firmiter iniungendo precipimus, xx° die mensis Junii annis singulis perpetuis futurus temporibus celebrari, ut in ipsa die devote turbe fidelium ad ecclesias ibidem affectuose concurrant, et tam cleri quam populi gaudentes in cantica laudum surgant, tunc omnium corda vota ora et labia ympnos persolvant leticie spiritualis, tunc singuli alacri animo prona voluntate convenientes studia sua laudabiliter exequendo missarum et aliorum divinorum officiorum complementum expectent, pro ipsorum ceterorumque fidelium vivorum et defunctorum salute Deum devote et sinceris mentibus oraturi, sic festi ipsius decurrendo solempnia ut ipsi et alii catholici pro quibus oraverint prefatum gloriossimum martirem de Anglicis inter angelos constitutum cuius festum celebraverint intercessorem mereantur habere assiduum apud Deum.

Ut autem clerus et populus archidiaconatus predicti ad colendum prefatum festum eo libencius invitentur quo se illius consideracione prospexerint maioris ubertate gracie fecundari, nos de Dei omnipotentis inmensa misericordia, ac gloriosissime virginis Marie patrone nostre necnon beatorum apostolorum Petri et Pauli omnisque celestis exercitus meritis et suffragiis confidentes, cunctis parrochianis nostris vere penitentibus et confessis et aliis quorum diocesani hanc nostram indulgenciam ratam habuerint pariter et acceptam, qui in festo beatissimi martiris supradicti in aliqua ecclesia archidiaconatus sepedicti divinis officiis interfuerint, ac idem festum devote celebraverint, ut prefertur, xl dies indulgencie de penitenciis eis iniunctis misericorditer indulgemus preter perhenne retribucionis stipendium quod bene merentur non debebunt aliquatenus desperare. In cuius rei testimonium etc. Dat' in manerio de Remmesbur' xxij° die mensis Januarii anno Domini millesimo CCCC° xij°.

[1. MS.: *venerari*
2. MS.: *Angloorum*
3. MS.: *ragali*]

APPENDIX E

Calendar of Items concerning Hallum's Will
(I–IV from *Reg. Chichele*, ii. 126–30, 162–3; V from P.R.O., E 154/1/32)

I Will of Robert Hallum servant of the church of Salisbury, dated Gottlieben (*Godelf'*) castle, by Constance, 23 Aug. 1417.

If he dies here, he wishes to be buried in the greater church of the city of Constance, near the high altar, in front of the image of the Virgin, his protector. He bequeathes to the cath. church of Salisbury the better of his two sets of copes, of red and white, according to the choice of the rulers of that cath., a book of Decreta and a book called a Rosarium,[1] to celebrate for his soul and those of his parents and benefactors, namely William Courteney and Thomas Arundell, lately archbishops of Canterbury,[2] Nicholas Braybrok[3] and John Godewyk.[4] He bequeathes his second set of copes to the cath. church of Constance, in memory of his burial there.

After his debts have been paid, he makes the following bequests. He devises all his lands and tenements in England to Richard Hallum,[5] his brother, for the term of his life, on condition that he does not sell, alienate or diminish any part of them,[6] and also goods not specifically bequeathed, according to the executors' discretion. He devises the same lands and tenements to Thomas Hallum, if he should happen to survive Richard, under the same conditions, though Richard Dutton is to hold land to the annual value of ten marks [£6 13*s* 4*d*] for the term of his life. He wishes Thomas Hallum to have the wardship and marriage of William Lewyston, until he comes of age. After the deaths of Richard and Thomas Hallum and Richard Dutton, he wishes that the lands etc. should be sold, according to his executors' discretion, or incorporated as a chantry college (*collegio sive collegiis cantarie seu cantariis*) by which support should be given to priests or scholars going to the schools who should be obliged to pray for his soul and those of his parents and benefactors.[7]

He bequethes 100 marks [£66 13*s* 4*d*] to Thomas Hallum; £100, or 200 marks [£133 6*s* 8*d*] if possible, to Richard Dutton; 20 marks [£13 6*s* 8*d*] to Thomas Helde; £20 to Thomas Karenton; £40 to Robert Hynnerford, if he should happen to marry the testator's cousin, the sister of Thomas Mundeforde); 100 marks [£66 13*s* 4*d*] to William Hansham; 20 marks [£13 6*s* 8*d*] to Thomas Rodeley; 10 marks [£6 13*s* 4*d*] to Nicholas Sexpen'; 100*s* to Thomas Massy; 20 marks [£13 6*s* 8*d*] to John Merbury; £20 to Simon Merbury; 10 marks [£6 13*s* 4*d*] to Robert Punsard; 40 marks [£26 13*s* 4*d*] to Robert Werberton; 20 marks [£13 6*s* 8*d*] to John de Camera; £20 or 40 marks [£26 13*s* 4*d*] if possible, and one horse, to Thomas Grimesdych; £20 to William Barbour; 20 marks [£13 6*s* 8*d*] to Peter Astley.

All the members of his household are to be paid when they return to

England from the goods not bequeathed, according to the executors' discretion. He wishes that his inn (*hospicium*) and household should be kept together until his burial, at his expense, and should be brought honourably back to England.

The residue of his goods, after the funeral expenses have been deducted, is left for his executors to dispose in works of piety for the good of his soul and those of his parents and benefactors and all the faithful dead. He appoints as executors Richard Hallum, his brother, M. William Clynt, M. John Fyton, M. John Luk, Thomas Hallum, Thomas Faukys and Humphrey Rodeley, clerks. He appoints as supervisors, to advise and help the executors, Richard [Clifford], bp. of London, and John [Catryk], bp. of [Coventry and] Lichfield.[8] No acquittance is to be made without the agreement of Richard, bp. of London, and the majority of the executors.

[1. By Guy de Baysio: a collection of glosses on the Decreta of Gratian (*Dictionnaire de Droit Canonique*, ed. R. Naz (7 vols., Paris, 1935–65), vii. 731).
2. See Introduction for offices held by Hallum under these archbishops.
3. Braybrok left legacies to Hallum in his will, 1399 (Reg. Arundell (Cant.), i fo. 165^{v}).
4. Godewyk was Hallum's immediate predecessor as prebendary of Bitton in Salisbury cath., which he resigned by 26 Jan. 1395 (Reg. Waltham fo. 181^{v}), and Hallum was one of his executors in 1397 (Reg. Arundell (Cant.), i fos. 156^{v}–157).
5. Richard Hallum of Lancashire was living in London in 1407 (*CCR 1404–9*, p. 242).
6. Some of these were at Horton Kirby and Cliffe, Kent (*CCR 1419–22*, pp. 47, 62, 64; cf. E. Hasted, *History of Kent* (12 vols., Canterbury, 1797–1801), ii. 497–8, iii. 509).
7. Such a chantry does not seem to have been set up.
8. See Index of Persons and Places for offices and benefices held by many of the beneficiaries and executors. Bishops Clifford and Catryk were with Hallum at the council of Constance (*Foedera*, IV. ii. 91, 168).]

II Will proved before James de Camplo, bishop-elect of Penne (*Pennensi*),[1] auditor of causes in the papal chamber, and administration committed to M. William Clynt, M. John Fyton, M. John Luk, Thomas Faukys and Humphrey Rodeley, clerks, after they had given the customary oath, reserving the rights of Richard and Thomas Hallum, if they wish to come and claim it. Constance, the auditor's dwelling, 10 Sept. 1417, the papacy being vacant (*apostolica sede pastore carente*), in the presence of Thomas Priis, archd. of Bangor, Richard Dutton and Robert Hemerfordis, *domicelli* of dioc. Lichfield and Bath, and Conrad Ivede, clerk, of the city of Cologne.

[1. Cf. *Hierarchia Catholica*, i. 395.]

III Will approved by Henry, abp. of Canterbury, and administration committed to M. John Fyton B.Th., M. John Luke B.Th., Richard Hallum, brother of the deceased, Thomas Hallum, *domicellus*, and Thomas Faukys and Humphrey Rodeley, clerks. The executors took the customary oath to produce and exhibit an inventory of goods by the Purification of the B.V.M. [2 Feb. 1418], to administer the goods faithfully and to render an account when requested. The right of M. William Clynt[1] is reserved, should he wish to apply for the administration. Lambeth, archbishop's manor, 28 Oct. 1417.

[1. He had probably not returned from Constance.]

IV Archbishop's commission to M. William Lynwod, official, and M. John Estcourt, examiner general of the archbishop's court of Canterbury, to hear the account of the executors and to discharge them. Undated.[1]

[1. Between entries for 27 Aug. and 16 Nov. 1419.]

V Inventory of all the goods of Robert, bp. of Salisbury, according to the calculation of the executors, on the feast of St. Leonard, 5 Hen. V [6 Nov. 1419].[1]

Goods in inventory to be sold, by estimate	£226 18*s*
In the hands of the executors	£160
In the hands of Humphrey [Rodeley]	£22
In the hands of M. John Lucke	£45
In the hands of Thomas Stonor[2]	£91
In the hands of the farmer of Cliffe (*Cleve*)[3]	£28
Total	£572 18*s*

Sums owing to papal collector by estimate for Peter's pence and five years arrears for the bishopric of Salisbury	£85
To the bp. of Bath[4] by estimate	£50
To Thomas Stonor	£24
To the dean and chapter of Salisbury	£6 13*s* 4*d*
To John Langdon for one horse	£5
To the executors of Robert Rycroffte	£3 6*s* 8*d*
To William Gasberth	£1 6*s* 8*d*
To M. H[enry] Harborth	£2
To Thomas Faukys for his expenses from the testator's death to this day, which appear in his account	£5 10*s* 6*d*
To Thomas Hallum for the same, above what appears in his account	1*s* 6*d*
Total	£182 18*s* 8*d*

Names of the servants:[5]

M. Gilbert Hallum[6]	at least	£33 6*s* 8*d*
M. John Hurlegh		£26 13*s* 4*d*
M. Peter Partrich one book costing		£1
M. William Felter may have the books which are still in his hands		
M. John Appulton (apart from £6 13*s* 4*d*)		£3 6*s* 8*d*
M. Wynceslas Swesico		£2
John Kyrkeby		£20
Peter Croffte		£10
Laurence Sutton		£5
William Carentham		£10
Robert Hemerford		£2 13*s* 4*d*
John Roche		£2
Gerard Suche		£1
William Boydell		£6 13*s* 4*d*

John Smyth	£2		
John Hallum	£6		
The sister of William Boydell	£2		
The daughters of the same woman *lund'*[7]	£2	13*s*	4*d*
Thomas Monford, brother of the same[8]	£2		
To the bishop's suffragans	£2		
To Merton College, Oxford	£2		
M. Adam Oxon[9]	£2		
The bishop's kinsman in 'Chepe'	£5		
The bishop's kinsman with Ralph Shokelache in London	£2		
To the church of Warrington (*Werynton*), Lancs., one vestment with the arms of England in gold, costing	£5		
To the same church for its building and for one priest for one year	£10		
In the church of Daresbury (*Dersbury*)[10] for one priest for one year	£5		
Thomas Berdisley	£3	6*s*	8*d*
William Kegworth	£1		
Nicholas Eye (apart from £1)		6*s*	8*d*
John Cruche	£1	6*s*	8*d*
John Forde	£2		
Gilbert Marchall	£1		
George Athirton	£1		
John Wotton		13*s*	4*d*
Walter Fottman		13*s*	4*d*
Sum of all payments	£122	13*s*	4*d*[11]
Remainder	£267	7*s*	6*d*[12]
Paid to T. Helde for a debt	£1	6*s*	8*d*

[1. I am indebted to Professor R. B. Pugh, who called my attention to this. In this calendar, sums of money in marks or shillings have all been converted into pounds, shillings and pence to facilitate addition.

2. Husband of the bishop's cousin Alice (*CCR 1419–22*, pp. 47, 62, 64).

3. In Kent (cf. *ibid.*).

4. Nicholas Bubwith, a friend of Hallum, who was with him at Constance (*Foedera*, IV. ii. 91).

5. See Index of Persons and Places for offices and benefices held by these members of Hallum's household.

6. Called Hallum's heir in 1420 (*CCR 1419–22*, pp. 47, 62, 64).

7. Meaning not clear.

8. Cf. 'the sister of Thomas Mundeforde' in will, App. E I.

9. Or 'at Oxford'. MS.: *Oxon'*.

10. Daresbury, Ches., 3 miles south-west of Warrington.

11. This sum omits the payments of £33 6*s* 8*d* and £26 13*s* 4*d* made to Gilbert Hallum and John Hurlegh.

12. The debts and payments subtracted from the assets would seem to leave £267 6*s*.]

INDEX OF PERSONS AND PLACES

Abbreviations used:

abp.	archbishop	cl.	clerk
app.	appendix	conv.	convent
archd.	archdeacon	d.	died
Aug.	Augustinian	dau.	daughter
Ben.	Benedictine	dioc.	diocese
bp.	bishop	fl.	floret
can.	canon	preb.	prebend, prebendary
cath.	cathedral	r.	rector
ch.	church	v.	vicar
Cist.	Cistercian	vic.	vicarage

References are to the numbers of entries not pages.
In the interests of economy cross references are not given from benefices to holders, except in the case of bishops and heads of religious houses whose Christian names only are given in the register.

INDEX OF SUBJECTS